Tanzania under Colonial Rule

Jonathan Glassman

London, 2/85

Tanzania under Colonial Rule

edited by M.H.Y. Kaniki

for the Historical Association of Tanzania

Longman

LONGMAN GROUP LIMITED
LONDON

Associated companies, branches and representatives throughout the world

First published 1980

ISBN 0 582 64649.9

Printed in Singapore by
Singapore Offset Printing Pte Ltd

Typeset by Quality Typesetting (Pte) Ltd
in Monophoto Times New Roman

British Library Cataloguing in Publication Data

Tanzania under colonial rule.
1. Tanzania—Economic conditions
2. Tanzania—Politics and government
I. Kaniki, M.H.Y.
II. Historical Association of Tanzania
330.9'678 HC557.T3

Contents

Preface

Since the mid-1960s the History Department at the University of Dar es Salaam has acted in collaboration with the Ministry of National Education, the Historical Association of Tanzania and the Institute of Education in the preparation of relevant literature to be used in secondary schools and institutions of higher learning. Each of these institutions contributed in its own way in different undertakings. In its early stages, the material contained in this book was in the form of conference papers which were discussed by history teachers at Morogoro in June 1974. Different institutions and individuals contributed to the success of that conference. The Ministry of National Education released history teachers and tutors to attend the conference and paid for their travel and board and lodging. The Department of History co-ordinated the whole project and paid for the production of the papers and the travel, board and lodging of the authors. The Historical Association, in collaboration with the two above-mentioned institutions, sponsored the conference. To all these institutions go our gratitude and appreciation. I should also like to thank all those who participated in the discussions where the contents of this book were critically scrutinised. Finally, I should like to thank the secretary of the History Department, University of Dar es Salaam, Mrs F. Maghimbi, for typing the manuscript.

M.H.Y. Kaniki
Dar es Salaam
September, 1977

Notes on Contributors

David Arnold, Ph.D. (Sussex), was formerly a Lecturer in History at the University of Dar es Salaam, Tanzania. His main area of interest is the history of the Indian sub-continent.

Brian D. Bowles, Ph.D. (East Africa), is Head of History at the College of St Mark and St John, Plymouth, United Kingdom. He taught History at Dar es Salaam University from 1970 to 1976. He has written a number of articles on economic aspects of colonial East Africa.

Douglas E. Ferguson, Ph.D. (California), is Associate Professor of History at the University of California (UCLA). He taught History at the University of Dar es Salaam from 1973 to 1977. With M.A. Sheriff he is editing a book, *Zanzibar under Colonial Rule*.

K.F. Hirji, M.Sc. (London), is Lecturer in Transport Statistics at the National Institute of Transport, Dar es Salaam, and formerly taught Mathematics at the University of Dar es Salaam. He has written a number of papers on mathematics and education.

John Iliffe, Ph.D. (Cambridge), is Assistant Director of Research in History at the University of Cambridge. He taught History at the University of Dar es Salaam from 1964 to 1971. Author of *Tanganyika under German Rule, 1905–12*, he has also edited *Modern Tanzanians* and (with G.C.K. Gwassa) *Records of the Maji Maji Rising*.

Martin H.Y. Kaniki, Ph.D. (Birmingham), is Associate Professor in History at the University of Dar es Salaam. His main area of interest is the economic history of West Africa. He has published (with I.M. Omari) *Guidelines for Writers* (1975) as well as many articles in learned journals.

Marjorie Mbilinyi, Ph.D. (Dar es Salaam), is Associate Professor in Education at the University of Dar es Salaam. Author of *Education of Girls in Tanzania* (1969), she has also edited *Who Goes to School in East Africa?* and (with C.K. Omari) *Peasant Production in Tanzania*.

Walter Rodney, PhD. (London), was formerly Associate Professor of History at the University of Dar es Salaam. His publications include *A History of the Upper Guinea Coast, 1545–1800, How Europe Underdeveloped Africa* and *The Groundings with my Brothers*.

M.A. Sheriff, Ph.D. (London), is Associate Professor and Head of the History Department at the University of Dar es Salaam. His main area of interest is Tanzanian economic history. He has contributed a number of chapters to books and (with D.E. Ferguson) is editing *Zanzibar Under Colonial Rule*.

A.J. Temu, Ph.D. (Alberta), is Professor of History at the Ahmadu Bello University, Zaria, and former Professor of History at the University of Dar es Salaam. Author of *British Protestant Missions*, he has also edited (with I.N. Kimambo) *A History of Tanzania* (1969).

Introduction

M.H.Y. Kaniki

This book basically emerges from papers presented to the History Teachers' Conference held at Morogoro, Tanzania, in June 1974. The Department of History at the University of Dar es Salaam has, on a number of occasions, used such conferences as a forum for testing teaching materials before they were used in schools and other institutions of learning. In this way it has been possible to modify presentations for more effective communication. With the exception of chapters 6, 8 and 9, the material in this book was presented to and discussed by teachers of history in secondary schools, teachers' colleges and at university level. The earlier versions of chapters 6 and 9 were discussed at the History Staff Seminar at the University of Dar es Salaam. The authors of each chapter benefited a good deal from the comments and observations made in the course of the discussion. Only chapter 8, which was written much later at a short request, has been included without being discussed. With the exception of this chapter, therefore, what is contained in the following pages represents revised versions of original papers.

The present work makes an important shift in the historiography of Tanzania and Africa as a whole by applying political economy as a methodology of analysing colonial relations. Since the late 1950s, especially during the first decade of Independence, many historians and others were preoccupied with the important task of destroying the colonial interpretation of history. Indeed, much was achieved in decolonising Tanzanian history and rehabilitating the Tanzanian (and African) to his proper place in the past of mankind. It was out of this endeavour that there emerged what came to be called the Dar es Salaam School of History. But with the exception of John

Iliffe's *Agricultural Change in Modern Tanganyika* (1971), these previous works dealt essentially with political issues, leaving aside socio-economic relations, or, at best, making incidental reference to them. This was a serious omission, especially as regards the colonial period. It has become increasingly clear that colonial relations are basically economic relations, and any examination of colonial relations which does not make a critical analysis of the political economy of colonialism leaves a substantial gap. It is in this respect that the present work is especially important. Most chapters explicitly or implicitly show the significance of the economic base at different phases of colonialism. In this way most of the important realities of the colonial period have been brought to light, thereby filling in a major gap which had existed in the historiography of Tanzania and East Africa.

One basic theme which previous works greatly neglected is that of productive relations among Tanzanian societies. There has been a tendency, for example, to praise societies which achieved a substantial level of political centralisation during the pre-colonial period in an effort to prove that Tanzanians of the past, like people elsewhere, were advanced enough to establish and manage political entities of substantial size and appreciable complexity. But little effort, if any at all, was made to detect and identify the advantages and disadvantages of these large-scale political organisations. The relationship between those who appropriated the surplus and those who maintained the systems was either neglected completely or treated as a peripheral issue.

Evidently the methodology applied in this case failed to expose important realities of the country's past. Matters were worsened when the same methodology was applied to the colonial period, when the level of economic exploitation and social differentiation and the contradictions within society became more glaring. Unless the relationship between those who had economic power and those who had political power is analysed it would be impossible to identify the real forces behind the colonisation process. It would be impossible, for instance, to assess accurately the role of German industrialists in the colonisation of East Africa. Nor would the real dimensions of colonial exploitation and oppression be exposed without such analysis.

Most aspects of human activity during the colonial period have been considered in some detail to cater for a wide readership, but this book is especially meant to help teachers in secondary schools and teacher training colleges. The material dealt with and the level of analysis and discussion should also benefit university students and teachers and other interested readers. Despite this wide coverage, this book is in many ways complementary to *A History of Tanzania* (1969), edited by Kimambo and Temu.

In chapter 1, Dr Sheriff considers the nature and major characteristics of Tanzanian societies at the time of the imposition of colonial rule. He rejects the diffusionist theory of political institutions and emphasises the material base of societies, and peoples' ability to manipulate their environment. In this chapter Tanzania is divided into three major ecological regions, a semi-arid centre, and the two highland areas to the north and south where precipitation was adequate and reliable. The semi-arid centre, at least until the beginning of the nineteenth century, experienced no agricultural prosperity, and because surpluses were both small and unpredictable, there was little to support non-producers. It was mainly for this reason that societies remained essentially fragmented and classless. In the north-eastern highlands and north-western Tanzania on the other hand, appreciable surpluses were realised. Thus centralised political institutions emerged and class formation occurred. Iron-working groups dominated the political scene and thrived on the surplus they appropriated, but their technology could not raise the general standard of living. The states were generally small but the trend was towards larger ones. Dr Sheriff notes that favourable environment does not necessarily lead to the rise of large and centralised political institutions. Despite a more favourable environment in the southern highlands, for instance, there were no large kingdoms before the Ngoni invasions during the middle of the nineteenth century.

The integration of Tanzania into the international (capitalist) economic system took place through trade. At all stages the Indian Ocean played an important role. The variety of commodities and the complexity of the operations increased tremendously during the nineteenth century. Although it was the headquarters of the commercial empire, Zanzibar did not control the interior politically. Zanzibar, however, exercised substantial political influence. Apart from the Omani rulers, Arab traders, Indian merchants, and some chiefs and kings, who formed a tiny minority, the local population gained almost nothing from the trading activities of the region. If anything, they lost substantially, in both human and material resources.

Dr Arnold, in chapter 2, examines the external factors which contributed to the partition of East Africa during the last quarter of the nineteenth century. He argues that the main motivation to partition that part of the continent came from the economic circumstances of Western Europe at that particular time. Having reached its highest form, capitalism needed markets abroad for both manufactured goods and capital. Industrialists and other big capitalists had by then become very influential in national politics, especially in Britain and Germany. They pressurised their governments to acquire spheres of influence abroad for the benefit of their capital. The governments responded positively, partly in order to solve their own political problems. Chamberlain, for example, supported and advocated overseas expansion in order to provide employment in Britain, thereby minimising class antagonism at home. Bismarck assisted German industrialists against British competition and supported the cause of colonisation in order to win popular support at home. In these endeavours both Britain and Germany took advantage of the political and economic climate in East Africa. Trading relations between East Africa and Western Europe had existed for over a century, and British involvement in the affairs of Zanzibar from the early nineteenth century strengthened British motivation to establish a colonial empire in East Africa. By the last quarter of the nineteenth century all Britain and Germany had to do was to consolidate their presence and expand the scope of their operations by controlling the sources of raw materials.

In chapter 3, Professor Temu discusses the responses of Tanzanian societies to the imposition of colonial rule. He presents the invasion as the last of the external factors which affected Tanzanian societies during the nineteenth century. The response to the invasion was determined by the structure of each society at the time. Though all societies were determined to preserve their sovereignty, the reaction to invasion was not uniform. In a number of cases rulers of weak states or dissatisfied individuals allied themselves with the German invaders. It did not take long, however, before such leaders and societies discovered the futility of their strategy; they too lost sovereignty. In the coastal areas there was no active resistance until the pinch of the German presence was deeply felt and the African labouring class was united. The Germans employed both diplomacy and military force depending on the circumstances. Diplomacy paid off especially in dealings with the Arab ruling class on the coast. Military confrontation was especially intense against the Hehe under Mkwawa and the Kibosho Chagga under Sina. Two factors appear to have been decisive in determining German success. The first was lack of unity among Tanzanian societies; and the second, probably more important, was the superiority of German weaponry.

The Maji Maji war occurred in areas which had not initially resisted German invasion. But unbearable exploitation by the colonial system led to a mass attack of the different agents of imperialism. Here, as in the primary resistance, the maxim gun finally settled the issues at stake.

Dr Rodney critically examines the political economy of colonialism in chapter 4. He argues that in establishing the colonial state the Germans, under the influence of monopoly capitalists, were guided by a belief in the superiority of plantation agriculture over peasant production. For the same reason, the economy was export-oriented. Though some allowance was made for peasant production, the Germans essentially regarded peasants as potential labourers. When peasants showed reluctance or opposition to join wage labour forces many were compelled to work for the Germans either directly or indirectly through the imposition of taxation. It was partly in response to this coercion that the Maji Maji war broke out. Coercion was somewhat reduced after Maji Maji, especially as the Germans realised that in many cases peasants were more efficient producers than the European planters. This awareness explains the dual reliance upon peasant and plantation agriculture—a reliance which has remained a striking feature of the Tanzanian economy ever since. In either case, however, the African was a loser in colonial economic relations. He was paid disproportionately little for both his products and his labour.

The burdensome war of 1914–18 brought no improvements, as the differences between German and British colonialism were superficial. When the international economic crisis came in 1929–34 Tanganyika had to suffer with other dependencies. By the 1930s the real foundations of underdevelopment were well established.

Dr Bowles continues the examination of the political economy in chapter 5. He shows how the concept of comparative advantages was used to justify the process of underdevelopment through concentration on export production. In order to meet the demands of the Second World War, government interference in the peasant sector was greatly increased. European producers, on the other hand, were encouraged to grow more through guaranteed prices and subsidies. Guaranteed prices were also applied to the peasant sector after the futility of compulsion was proved, but in this case the guaranteed prices themselves were exploitatively low.

During the post-war years, especially until the early 1950s, the intensive drive for increased agricultural production met with remarkable success. But the motivating force was not a desire to develop the local population; Britain was all out to overcome her dollar and food shortage. Impatience with peasant methods led to the extension of European plantation and farming. None of these schemes succeeded. On the other hand peasant production expanded, partly in response to increased prices. Ironically, it was government profits realised in this sector which were invested in Britain in the effort to solve Britain's financial problems.

The period shortly before independence witnessed a relaxation of government control in the peasant sector, in response to the realities of the day. Peasant protest became disruptive and, where nationalist sentiments were effectively articulated, became out of control.

The significance of colonial education under the Germans is examined by Mr Hirji in chapter 6. Colonial education, carrying with it Christian and bourgeois values, was effectively used as an ideological apparatus in the establishment of an intellectual climate conducive to the exploitation of the material and human resources of the country. Christian missionaries played an important role in this, and were successful within a relatively short period. By the outbreak of the Maji Maji war the areas with effective missionary activities had been neutralised to the extent of presenting no military opposition against colonial exploitation. The skills and values acquired through the education system acted as a base on which a petty bourgeoisie was created. Education also encouraged the rise of a dependent peasantry which worked as an appendage of the metropole.

Dr Mbilinyi continues with the examination of colonial education in chapter 7. She notes the way colonial education departed from the ideals of the traditional education which had been offered for generations before the colonial era. Based on nineteenth-century British and American educational systems, colonial education under the British was geared towards two major objectives. First, it was meant to produce a differentiated society in which the privileged elements of the pre-colonial period would be strengthened and consolidated. Such elements would be the chief agents of change under colonialism. The second objective was to produce people who would be educated enough to carry out specific duties in the colonial state and economy without feeling too independent to receive orders from their colonial oppressors. In short, colonial education was used to produce the kind of person likely to promote the interests of imperialism.

Dr Iliffe examines wage labour and urbanisation in chapter 8. He sets out with the thesis that under normal circumstances people do not work for others unless they are under some compulsion. Until the mid-1940s compulsion was mainly political and social, but after this date it took a more economic turn. People had been working for others before the colonial era, he argues, but the wage labour force as it existed from the 1920s to 1961 was a creation of colonialism. The expansion of wage labour was accompanied by urbanisation and the organisation of labour. But before the mid-1950s the labour movement had achieved little, due to two major factors. First, the labour movement was weak organisationally and financially. Second, the employers, like the colonial administration, opposed and stopped attempts to establish an effective labour organisation.

In chapter 9, Dr Ferguson considers the attitudes and practices of the colonial administration in dealing with disease and health problems. He argues that the impact of colonialism in Africa reduced the level of health of the population. Famines were caused by the wars of conquest, new diseases were introduced, and malnutrition lowered the general resistance of the people to disease. European medicine was introduced into the country, but medical facilities were provided along capitalist and racial lines. Access to medical facilities, as would be expected in an unequal society like colonial Tanganyika, was the prerogative of the privileged classes. Facilities for the African population were both inferior and inadequate. Only the European areas were provided with adequate facilities. These areas also had good sanitation but elsewhere such preventive measures were greatly neglected. Nor were local personnel trained. Tanganyikan doctors were not registered before 1953 and only fourteen were in government service after more than seventy years of colonial rule. The study brings to light colonial biases against the local population, and illustrates the way the colonised were forced to pay for the health of their oppressors.

In the last chapter, Dr Kaniki examines the process of decolonisation, concentrating on the period between the mid-1950s and the early 1960s. He builds on some of the conclusions reached in the previous chapters, thereby amplifying the fact that colonialism, like capitalism, produced its own grave-diggers. The struggle for independence gained its potency from two major sources—the political consciousness of the frustrated educated elite and the discontent and radicalism in the rural areas. The political climate during the early 1960s was no longer conducive to the maximum exploitation of resources in Tanganyika. The British had to change their strategy.

The nationalist movement in Tanganyika demonstrated and enjoyed great unity, partly as a response to government opposition. In Zanzibar, on the other hand, there was great disunity along racial, class, and ethnic lines. This disunity benefited the Arab privileged minority to whom the British were determined to hand over political power. After observing the sheer defiance of democratic principles by both the British and the Arab minority on more than one occasion, African nationalist leaders were left with only one alternative—armed struggle. Thus, shortly after the departure of the British they took over political power in a bloody revolution.

Leaders played an important part in the decolonisation struggles, but they did not create the grievances. All they had to do was to take advantage of the contradictions of the colonial situation by articulating grievances and giving direction in protest activities. Neither on the mainland nor on the islands was there a clear idealogy during the struggle period. Independence was won within the capitalist framework established by colonialism. A social revolution had to wait until the political kingdom was won.

Although every effort was made to cover all aspects of both the mainland and the islands, it was unfortunately not possible to include a chapter on 'the political economy of Zanzibar to 1957'. It was finally decided to publish this book in the present form and devote a whole volume at a later date to the history of Zanzibar under colonial rule.

1. Tanzanian Societies at the Time of the Partition

Abdul M.H. Sheriff

Tanzania has had a very long history of man on her soil, stretching back over two million years, though in this volume we are concerned largely with the later, colonial phase.[1] Here we are using the term history in its broad sense to mean the study of the interaction between man and his environment, and between man and man, whatever the source or technique used to uncover the evidence. In this chapter we shall attempt to delineate in broad outlines the pattern of development of Tanzanian societies in the pre-colonial period, the impact of the Ngoni invasion, and the development of long-distance trade by which much of Tanzania was more or less incorporated into the international capitalist economy.

Development of societies in the pre-colonial period

Many of the existing histories of the pre-colonial period in East Africa have concentrated rather narrowly on political history, and have often been diffusionist in their interpretation. The colonial school traced all significant achievements in East Africa, be they remarkable administrative systems or impressive material cultures, to some northern invaders, undoubtedly as a justification for the European colonial invasion of the late nineteenth century. Over the past fifteen years there have been repeated attempts to refute this obviously racist interpretation, but what is striking is the fact that many of these apparently alternative explanations turn out to be variants of the same diffusionist theory. Murdock, who played so seminal a role in stimulating a re-examination of the various aspects of African history, argued that the highly centralised kingdoms of the interlacustrine region owe their origin to some Ethiopian invaders from whom the Bantu-speakers inherited many of their ideas of political organisation.[2] Oliver's argument, though more complex, still argues in favour of the northern invaders' 'superiority in the scale of their social and political organisation, and . . . their sense of moral destiny to dominate', a distinct echo and justification for European domination. From the interlacustrine hotbed these ideas of political and social organisation, and of chieftainship (*ntemiship*), spread southwards into western Tanzania, the southern highlands and the north-eastern highlands, in what one comrade described as a '*ntemi*-bug epidemic'.[3]

Oliver's broad diffusionist argument has now been shown to have many gaps and discrepancies, and Kimambo has posed a powerful rebuttal. From an examination of the various regions of Tanzania he has concluded that 'there was no single group responsible for transmitting the ideas of change . . . to all parts of Tanzania. Secondly, even where ideas diffused from one area to another, local initiative transformed these ideas and adapted them to the needs of that particular society. Thirdly, changes were introduced in society . . . as a means of solving problems of communities which were becoming more complex . . . In some cases the people themselves found solutions within their own societies.'[4] Kimambo thus suggests an evolutionary argument for the development of societies as a possible alternative. Many of the existing interpretations err in putting the cart before the horse, in dealing with *ideas*, especially of political organisation, which relate to the superstructure, before they have dealt with the *material* basis of societies. Thus Oliver sees no contradiction between advanced political and social organisations and the low level of material achievement of the northern invaders. By focusing their attention on the diffusion of ideas these writers have often overlooked the fundamental, generally indigenous, factors which bring about development in most societies.

The first factor that obviously influences the development of societies is the environment. In general terms it sets limits to human endeavours in the utilisation of natural resources to satisfy needs, but these limits are highly elastic, determined by the level of technology attained by a given people. With a low level of technology man largely *adapts* to the environment, *extracting* wild foods by hunting and gathering. As the technology develops man can *manipulate* the environment to *produce* food through pastoralism or agriculture. What are the most significant features of the Tanzanian environment? Tanzania can be visualised as a bowl of a fairly harsh environment at the centre, surrounded by a series of better-watered and relatively more fertile areas along the broken rim. Only twenty per cent of the land area along this rim receives more than thirty inches of reliable rainfall capable of supporting dependable agriculture and some of the highland areas yield fertile volcanic soils. These are areas of high potential which can support a heavier density of population once the appropriate technology has been developed to clear the forest and till the soil. The rest of Tanzania can expect less than thirty inches of reliable rainfall, mostly concentrated during the short rainy season. The soil is generally poor and deteriorates rapidly when utilised. The usual vegetation is grassland or the *miombo* woodland which at the present time is heavily infested by tsetse fly. This area thus has a much lower potential where hunting and gathering, pastoralism or extensive shifting cultivation can be expected to support a lower density of population. Man, however, has not always merely adapted to these environmental limitations, but has often actively developed technology to stretch the limits. The question which arises then is: what determines technological change?

Another important factor is the growth of population which forces people to shift from a more extensive system of land use which can support a low density of population, to a high density intensive system. But this shift is possible only with the development of tools and techniques of food porduction, from the hoe to the plough, from shifting to permanent cultivation, accompanied by artificial fertilisation, crop rotation, terracing and irrigation. These changes naturally bring about changes in property rights to land, from communal ownership with individual rights to use land under shifting cultivation to individual ownership under permanent cultivation.[5] Ukara Island in Lake Victoria is a good example of these changes. Under the pressure of increasing population the Kara evolved perhaps the most intensive system of land use in sub-Saharan Africa, involving stall-feeding of cattle, application of massive amounts of animal manure, crop rotation, terracing, etc. By these means the Kara were able to increase productivity of the land threefold compared to the mainland opposite, and the island supports a population density of over 500 persons per square mile.[6]

However, such growth under population pressure means that changes occur when the carrying capacity of the land is reached and the people, therefore, constantly live at subsistence level. They do not produce a surplus adequate to support substantial division of labour and specialisation, both of which are necessary for further increase in productivity and genuine development. These specialisations may occur as a result of the uneven distribution of certain essential natural resources such as iron, salt, clay suitable for pottery, or rich grassland to support pastoralism. Some specialists who control certain strategic economic functions may use their position to extract a larger return for their services, that is to appropriate part of the surplus produced by the rest of the community. In many pre-colonial African societies control over iron-working, so essential in the production of agricultural implements and tools of warfare, enabled iron-smithing clans to establish a dominant political role over the rest of the society. Elsewhere, control over cattle, which is a more convenient form of storing wealth than vegetable foodstuffs, and whose manure is so important for agricultural intensification, may have provided the basis for the establishment of a differentiated and stratified society. In such a society, the cattlemen were the rulers who extracted tributes in kind and in labour. Surplus appropriating classes have an active interest in pushing through technical changes to increase agricultural productivity, to increase the size of the surplus, long before the carrying capacity of the land has been reached. The size and reliability of the surplus, which is determined by the type of environment, the total size of the population, and the level of technology attained in combination, determine the level of social and political organisation of the society. Thus, while the Kara, who produce little surplus to support any specialist classes, have an egalitarian and only rudimentary political organisation, the Pare and the Haya, whose population densities probably never attained the level of Ukara, developed stratified societies and complex political organisations. Until the late Stone Age Tanzania was for the most part inhabited by bands of hunters and gatherers. Some of these communities have survived almost up to the present, though now confined to the most isolated and unfavourable environment. The Hadza or Tindiga occupy one of the most isolated areas around Lake Eyasi, receiving less than twenty inches of rainfall a year. They practise a hunting/gathering type of economy, subsisting primarily on wild roots and fruits, wild animals being systematically hunted during the dry season when vegetable foods are scarce. Though they acquired an expert knowledge of their environment, the level of their technology is very low, their tools consisting of digging sticks and bows and arrows. With such a technology the environment can support only a very sparse population, the average being about two square miles per person. It does not allow aggregation of many people, and Hadza bands consisted of between twenty and fifty persons, often constantly on the move. Their economy consumed most of their time in the acquisition of food, and there was very little permanent surplus to permit them to diversify their activities, even between the sexes. Territory was owned by the tribe as a whole. The Hadza were therefore a truly classless society at a very low level of development, and they had no chiefs or headmen and paid no taxes to anybody.[7]

The Sandawe of Kondoa district practised a similar economy and occupied a larger area until about a century or so ago, when they came under increasing pressure from the expanding Nilotic Tatoga from the north and the Bantu-speaking Turu and Gogo from the west and south. Forced to subsist on an area too small for a hunting and gathering type of economy, the Sandawe began to make a transition to a food-producing economy, adopting the pastoral and agricultural activities of their neighbours. Sandawe traditions attribute these changes to the Barabaig (Tatoga) clan of Alagwa whose ownership of cattle and reputed powers as rainmakers (which becomes increasingly important in a food-producing economy) enabled them to occupy a dominant ritual and political position in Usandawe. The introduction of food-producing techniques increased the capacity of the land to support a heavier density of population, and brought about social differentiation, although distinct and antagonistic classes may not have emerged.[8]

The grasslands of north-central Tanzania can support about thirty animals per square mile, which can in turn provide adequate subsistence for two persons subsisting largely on pastoral products. Any increase in the total population can be accommodated either by intensifying production or by out-migration. The Masai have practised burning of bush to permit extension of the grassland, and the annual burning of grass to stimulate growth of more nutritious grass, but the pastoral system soon reaches the limit of its productive capacity. The history of Masailand is thus dominated by periodic struggles for the control of the grassland, the vanquished being edged out to the peripheries to subsist on a more mixed type of economy. In the early decades of the nineteenth century the struggle began between the pastoral Masai and their cousins, the Iloikop (Kwavi) who were eventually pushed out of the grasslands to establish more agriculture-based economies, such as that of the Arusha on Mount Meru.[9]

The environment limits not only the number of people that the grassland can support but also the amount of surplus that they can produce and store. Milk is highly perishable, and human capacity to consume milk is limited by the bellysize. Thus, though there was some differentiation within the Masai society in terms of the number of cattle owned by individual families, the richer families, at most, had a more abundant supply of milk during the normal dry season, and might survive better through a drought. The low level of regular surplus production meant that the economy could not support a high degree of economic specialisation and social differentiation. There was some amount of exchange with neighbouring agricultural people, conducted primarily by women. There was also an iron-smith caste, which does not appear to have occupied an influential political position, probably because of their precarious dependence for food on the pastoralists, especially during the critical dry season, but there were few other specialists.

The Masai were, therefore, a classless society. Property rights were fairly diffused and probably contributed to the lack of sharp social differentiation. While the grasslands were owned by the tribe as a whole, water rights were held by the clan; the cattle, apparently originally owned by the clan, are at present owned by individual families. The low level of material production of their economy is accordingly reflected in their social and political organisation. The dominant principle governing their social relations was equality, and the only significant differentiation in the society was according to age and sex. Lacking a centralised state structure, the Masai evolved, in common with several other pastoral people of East Africa, a political structure based on age-sets. The males were divided into a number of age-sets with recognised economic functions and social status: the uncircumcised boys who looked after the cattle; the warriors who lived in separate camps and guarded the country; and the married men arranged into various grades of elders, who managed their livestock economy and exercised greater political influence over the whole community. The elders held disproportionate economic and matrimonial privileges through their control of the cattle, but their declining virility with age probably limited the abuse of these privileges. Moreover, the fact that the warriors themselves aspired to, and had every expectation of attaining, elderhood meant that the relations between age-sets were not fundamentally antagonistic. In this society political, military and judicial powers were widely distributed, all the major decisions being taken by the age-set as a whole, while the 'leaders' were empowered merely to execute them. Even the *laibon*, often wrongly described as a paramount chief, was only the chief ritual expert with no political or judicial powers, though as an intermediary between this world and the unknown there was enough mysification of the institution to enable him to exercise a great deal of influence and to extract a 'fee' for his ritual duties.

The moister parts of central Tanzania receive about thirty inches of rainfall, but it is concentrated in a single short rainy season and is not very reliable. The soils moreover are generally poor, and the area on the whole can support a precarious agriculture, subject to frequent famines. Subsistence farming was thus often inadequate and had to be supplemented during the dry season by hunting, honey collecting and trade. The carrying capacity of the land was therefore rather low, the average density being about twenty persons per square mile. The uniformity of the environment meant that the occupants were predominantly subsistence farmers though in Usukuma at the present time cattle play an important complementary role in the economy. The unequal distribution of certain essential commodities such as iron and salt led to the growth of regional trade and the development of some specialist groups, such as Rongo iron workers, but they do not seem to have been able to use their position to obtain a powerful political voice in the state, as in Upare, for example, No full-time specialists emerged in the salt industry, salt-working such as that around Lake Eyasi being a dry season activity in which a fairly large section of the community participated.

The dominant sector of the economy was agriculture which had a great influence on the social and political life of the people. Since the environment can support a fairly sparse population, as the population grew it was easier to colonise new areas than to cluster in large communities. As the areas of a 'tribe' grew too large to be governed from one centre it was more convenient to split it up under sons of chiefs who recognised the seniority of the original chiefdom. The dominant tendency was thus political fragmentation despite cultural homogenity over a large area. The chiefs were originally essentially influential leaders who led groups of people in clearing and colonising new areas of bush, as their title, *Ntemi*, implies (*Kutema* = to cut and slash). The *Watemi* were earthly leaders who were not isolated from their subjects, like other divine kings, but shared even their meals with them. By the nineteenth century their position had been institutionalised to personify the state. They were said to 'own' all the land in the chiefdom, but there was nothing to prevent any subject from cultivating a piece of land not being used by another. The chiefs and headmen were entitled to tribute in grain and livestock, and in labour from their subjects who had to till their ruler's fields for two days every year. However, this surplus wealth was not allowed to accumulate in the hands of the rulers, for there was great social pressure to redistribute it, great emphasis being placed upon the virtues of generosity by which to attract more subjects. Thus, though there was some degree of social differentiation in the Nyamwezi and Sukuma societies before long distance trade, antagonistic social classes had not emerged among them.[10]

The environment appears to have played an important role in determining the level of social development in all these examples. By restricting the amount of surplus that could be produced at a certain level of technological development, it tended to hinder the division of labour, the development of non-agricultural specialisations, and the evolution of highly stratified societies and centralised political organisations. However, as mentioned above, geographical limitations are always elastic, and Engaruka yields an intriguing example of how human ingenuity could stretch these limitations in the pre-colonial period. Situated in the Rift Valley in north-central Tanzania, Engaruka receives only about fifteen inches of rainfall which is also unreliable. Yet, the area was inhabited, between the fourteenth and eighteenth centuries, by people who exploited the several streams flowing down the side of the Rift Valley to irrigate about eight square miles by an elaborate system of stone-built furrows. The area supported a population density of perhaps over five hundred per square mile. Unfortunately the population was dispersed, probably by pastoral invaders, and from archaeological evidence alone we are at present unable to determine the level of their social and political development.[11]

The southern highlands

The southern highlands are an enigma in that despite an apparently favourable environment, population density remained low and no large centralised kingdom arose before the era of the Ngoni invasion and long-distance trade.[12] The area receives more than forty inches of reliable rainfall, rising to more than one hundred inches in the Rungwe mountains where there is hardly a dry season. The soils are not particularly fertile except in the numerous volcanic craters sprinkled across the terrain in the north, and in the alluvial plains at the head of Lake Nyasa. Nevertheless, the Nyakyusa developed a system of intensive cultivation and stock-breeding, contour ridging to prevent soil erosion, and crop and land rotation by which crops were planted in a rational succession followed by varying periods of rest and grazing to enable the land to recover its fertility. Moreover, cattle dung and green manure were used regularly to fertilise the land. The main staple crop of the area was the banana, supported by millet, beans and groundnuts, while maize and rice are said to have been introduced towards the end of the nineteenth century. As a result the Nyakyusa lived a fairly comfortable life. The people were exceptionally well-fed, and though shortages and famines did occasionally occur, they did not know regular 'hunger-months' as is common in other parts of Tanzania.

However, the region as a whole was apparently relatively sparsely populated during the pre-colonial period, with many belts of unoccupied land separating Nyakyusa communities, belts which were still apparent as late as the mid-1930s. It is difficult to explain this apparent contradiction, but one possible technological bottle-neck was the shortage of essential minerals. The Nyakyusa obtained their iron goods from the Kinga and salt came from Ubena through Ukinga as well, but both commodities were extremely scarce. Thus they continued to use wooden hoes, and they may well have been hindered in clearing the thick natural vegetation for agricultural purposes. This may partly explain the relative intensity of cultivation despite abundance of land.

As the population density was low and land fairly abundant during the pre-colonial period, land was not owned by individuals but by the village community as a whole. The individuals had only use rights, except in the case of the valuable soils in the volcanic crater which were owned by certain old families. The relative abundance of land was the underlying factor which seems to have governed the pattern of social and political organisation of the Nyakyusa. It shifted the emphasis from land to labour which was the scarce resource, for, as the Nyakyusa say, 'a village consists in men, not in land'. In view of this, and lacking a strategic industry within the community, there was little basis for economic specialisation and social differentiation in the society. The Nyakyusa therefore evolved a unique social organisation which was egalitarian, much to the consternation of the colonialists who found them 'lacking in all subservient virtues'. Every aspect of the economic and social life of the Nyakyusa discouraged any conspicuous differentiation in the society, forcing rich men to distribute their cattle widely among relatives and friends to avoid witchcraft. The most characteristic aspect of their social organisation was the age-village in which people of the same age lived together as equals for all their adult lives. As their sons began to marry they established their own villages which were formally inaugurated every thirty or thirty-five years. There are similarities with the age-set system of the Masai discussed above, though in the case of the Masai and other people in the north, it was a temporary phase of residence in the cycle of their lives. Obviously this system could work only so long as there was abundant land to be colonised, and it began to break down when land shortage reared its head among the Nyakyusa.

These age-villages were presided over by the *amafumu*, the head-men who were elected from among the villagers. They were the guardians of the villagers' land-rights, the arbiters in land problems and disputes, and the political and ritual leaders of the villages. But they were servants rather than rulers, for their powers were restricted to the execution of communal will and consensus democratically arrived at by the whole village. This was probably the pre-existing pattern of social organisation which was democratic and truly classless. However, we should always recognise the rather low level of material achievement that the society represented, lacking marked division of labour and economic specialisation. The Nyakyusa were largely self-sufficient peasants who did not seem to excel in any of the crafts except house-building, buying much of what they needed from their neighbours in exchange for pots from the Kisi, barkcloth from the Ndali, and iron and salt from the Kinga.

A new pattern of political organisation was superimposed over the area by the invasion, some time in the sixteenth century, of cattlemen who controlled a larger supply of iron resources from

Ukinga. These two resources were essential for the further development of the economy, for iron permitted more efficient clearing and cultivation, and cattle provided supplementary food as well as manure for a more intensive cultivation of the soil. Control over these two resources enabled the invaders to obtain a more dominant political influence. However, their powers and privileges should not be exaggerated, for what is significant is the balance of power which was established between the chiefs and the commoners. Although theoretically the chief had a right to evict somebody if he wished to occupy the land himself (giving him another plot elsewhere), or to take food or milk if he needed it to entertain people at the capital, there were two effective checks against the abuse of their privileges: witchcraft of which the *amafumu* were the prime source, and migration, a powerful weapon in a region of scarce labour. Although a substantial proportion of the cows captured in raids went to swell the chief's herds, he was also expected to show a great deal of generosity to retain his subjects. Unlike many other chiefs in Tanzania he had no claim to one of the tusks of a fallen elephant. By all these means the chiefs were prevented from expropriating too large a surplus and accumulating too large a proportion of the wealth of the country to live entirely as a leisured class. They continued to hoe their own fields. In terms of the exercise of political power their authority was severely restricted by the *amafumu*, who kept the chief informed of all important matters but remained the real land authority: even when the *amafumu* failed to resolve a dispute and took it to the chief, the chief relied heavily on his headmen to secure a settlement and might not push a settlement for fear of witchcraft. Finally, it was the commoner priests who chose the chiefs, and put them to death ritually when it was expedient for the good of the people.

Among the Nyakyusa, therefore, the invasion by the cattle-owning and iron-welding people did not lead to the establishment of a rigidly stratified society with antagonistic classes. The chiefs freely intermarried with the subjects to produce a more egalitarian society which did not permit the expropriation by the chiefs of too large a surplus from the subjects. Thus no large, centralised kingdom emerged. In its place there were numerous small chiefdoms which split at every generation and in which there was a very limited degree of class differentiation. This has led one scholar to question whether these were not princedoms in an amorphous, highly decentralised Nyakyusa society.[13] This was to some extent true of the other-societies in the southern highlands before the Ngoni invasions.[14]

The north-eastern highlands

The north-eastern highlands, stretching from Usambara through Upare and Kilimanjaro, to Mount Meru, form one of the high potential areas encircling the semi-arid centre. They receive more than thirty inches of reliable rainfall. Moreover, Kilimanjaro and Meru are volcanic mountains which yield fairly fertile soils. These areas can therefore support a higher density of population and with a suitable technology and crops, can produce a more regular surplus which can stimulate the development of the economy and society.

These mountain areas were originally thickly forested, and required two essential things for effective occupation—adequate tools to clear the forest, and suitable crops to grow in the area. From archaeological evidence it appears that the areas were settled by iron-using people, probably Bantu-speaking, from the middle of the first millennium A.D. It is also likely that they cultivated bananas, said to have been introduced from south-east Asia. Bananas yield a regular and dependable crop with little effort after the initial clearing, and by reducing the threat of famine, they encouraged the growth of population. Moreover, by requiring a limited amount of labour for pure subsistence, they enabled the people to enjoy a greater amount of leisure or to produce a larger surplus to support non-agricultural specialisations. In these areas iron-working appears to have played a crucial role in the development of societies. According to existing traditions iron-working clans initially exercised a dominant political influence over the rest of the society. The Shana blacksmith clan ruled over Ugwono in Upare before about the sixteenth century. In the Vugha section of Usambara, according to *Habari za Wakilindi*, Turi's clan

> holds the country because god
> gave them the gift of working
> iron and skill in war, that is
> how he got the country.[15]

Increased food production as a result of these innovations appears to have permitted the growth of population which in turn called for adjustments in the social and political organisations to cope with the increasing complexity of the societies. So long as land was abundant the normal response was territorial expansion or dispersion to clear new forest lands, and an extensive shifting cultivation system, but fertile areas even on these highlands are limited. The need therefore arose for a more intensive cultivation of the land for longer and longer periods by the use of crop rotation and fertilisers. This brought about a gradual change in the ownership of land, from the communal to more individual ownership. There is a shift in emphasis from control of the production of iron tools, which remains significant, to control of land and labour, an increasing amount of the latter being needed to produce the necessary foodstuffs under the more intensive system. There is thus a need for a fundamental reorganisation of the society and reallocation of resources by a centrally organised authority. It is very significant that in the revolutionary reorganisation of Ugweno society under the Suya clan in the sixteenth century, a special ministerial post was created to supervise agriculture and to encourage people to cultivate in season.[16] The purpose undoubtedly was not only to produce enough subsistence for the whole population, but also to produce enough surplus to feed the increasing number of 'bureaucrats'. In their efforts to establish a centralised state the Suya created a hierarchy of councils, some for the districts and some for the kingdom as a whole. They also centralised the system of initiation to serve as an educational and political institution. Both these reforms required a large amount of tribute in the hands of the king and his chiefs, generally members of his family, to disburse to the people. The Pare under the rule of the Suya thus achieved a marked economic development of the available natural and human resources to produce enough surplus to support a class society organised in a highly centralised state.

On Kilimanjaro the precise role of iron-smithing clans in the evolution of the numerous small Chagga chiefdoms is not clear since a good pre-colonial history of the Chagga is still lacking. The proliferation of chiefdoms, estimated at over a hundred at the beginning of the nineteenth century, may partly be explained by the geography of this volcanic cone which is deeply dissected by the streams flowing down the mountain. People who lived on individual ridges developed largely self-sufficient agricultural and political systems to suit their needs, though they also co-operated over large areas for defence, trade and marriage. As population increased on the mountain, and so long as the Chagga were prevented from expanding into the plains by the pastoral Masai, they were forced to intensity their agriculture with crop rotation and fertilisation of the land with ashes and cattle manure. But in a situation of land scarcity cattle could hardly be allowed to graze freely. They were therefore either driven down to the plains to graze when possible or stall-fed in their own huts with grass carried the whole distance from the plains by women. The Chagga also had to extend the growing season by irrigating their land with a remarkable system of irrigation networks. These networks were generally controlled by the local water users' associations, but some particularly large canals, constructed by communal effort, were claimed by the chiefs who also claimed those canals whose owners migrated or died without heirs. The chiefs were therefore in a position to demand a tribute or customary 'gifts' from the cultivators, especially in the form of finger millet, often used to make beer. Whether they based their demands also on their claims to 'own' all the land in the chiefdom as well is not clear.[17]

Neither is it clear what activated a series of centralising and unifying movements which began with Orombo's expansion from Keri in the east from the end of the eighteenth century, and continued under Sina of Kibosho, so that by the end of the nineteenth century there were only thirty-seven chiefdoms in place of the original hundred.[18] Though guns imported from the coast featured among the Chagga arms, it is not at all certain whether long-distance trade itself, in providing a new source of wealth from ivory, especially to certain chiefdoms more easily accessible to the coast, stimulated this movement of unification. The results of this process of centralisation, however, were apparent by the last quarter of the nineteenth century with the greater amount of wealth and autocratic behaviour displayed by the ruling classes among the Chagga.

In Usambara[19] the need for the enlargement of scale in social and political organisations arose out of the infiltration by the Cushitic-speaking Mbugu and Nango people some time during the eighteenth century. Culturally distinct and economically more dependent on pastoralism, they shattered the cultural unity of the Shambaa. There may also have been competition for land. The leadership provided by the blacksmith clan was no longer adequate for a society which was becoming both economically and culturally more complex. It is at this juncture that Mbegha appeared, a migrant from the Nguu mountains to the south, most vividly remembered as a hunter of pigs. The significance of this is uncertain, but it is possible that in the conflict between the Shambaa agriculturists and the pastoral invaders, land may have suffered from neglect, leading to the encroachment of the destructive pigs. By offering protection from the pigs Mbegha was able, in the confused state of Usambara, to establish a rival centre of power which grew under his son into a full-fledged centralised state. In this state the Kilindi dynasty, now growing into a large privileged class, ruled over the rest of the society. The state was well established through a compromise with the Nango, who were fully assimilated into the society but at a price of a more favourable position—the king had to marry a Nango girl, and the offspring was to be heir apparent. A section of the Kilindi reacted violently against this compromise and seceded to establish a rival state in Mshiwi. By this act they weakened the Kilindi kingdom centered on Vugha which always feared to impose its rule too firmly on the Shambaa provinces lest they shift their allegiance to its rival. And yet the capital was in great need of a large tribute to feed the large bureaucracy and the army. The Kilindi rulers therefore turned to foreign conquests, of the Zigua and the Bondei who were ruthlessly exploited. This inevitably led to a violent revolution by the Bondei after the death of Kimweri in 1869, which all but wiped out the hated Kilindi, though the state survived in some form in Usambara.

The north-eastern highlands thus saw a series of successful attempts at economic development and political centralisation in the pre-colonial period, as a result of which stratified societies and elaborate state structures were established. These attempts in most cases arose out of the internal dynamics of African societies attempting to cope with the development of their economies and the increasing complexity of the societies concerned.

North-western Tanzania

North-western Tanzania forms part of the interlacustrine region which, on the whole, is a favourable environment for human occupation. It was one of the earliest areas to be settled by iron-using, presumably Bantu-speaking, agriculturists. The climate is influenced by the 'maritime' conditions created by the large water body, Lake Victoria, which ensures a heavier and more reliable rainfall, especially near the shores of the lake. Thus Bukoba receives an average of eighty inches of rainfall annually, which decreases to about thirty-five inches as we move inland into Karagwe. This gives rise to two belts of country relevant to our discussion. The first is the grassland belt that extends from Karagwe to the highland areas of Kigoma region. Before the rinderpest of the late nineteenth century, this belt supported large herds of cattle, but the economy was mixed, with a large variety of grain and root crops and some plantains playing an important role in the subsistence of the inhabitants. The second belt lies within fifteen miles of the shore of Lake Victoria where the rainfall is both more abundant and more reliable, with hardly a dry month. However, the soil is not too rich, and continuous cropping is possible in limited favourable patches only with heavy fertilisation of the land with plant and animal manure. In both these belts, therefore, it is the combination of a tree crop and cattle that is distinctive about their economy.

The area appears to have had a long history of state formation, which, as mentioned in the introduction, has generally been attributed to the diffusion of political ideas by the pastoral invaders from the north. Traditions certainly speak of a distinct ethnic group of pastoralists who established states in which they occupied the dominant position. Wrigley has persuasively argued that pastoralists could afford to carry only a limited amount of 'cultural luggage' during their wanderings, and as people who normally did not require a highly centralised state for their own governance, they could hardly be credited with the diffusion of these ideas to others.[20] The diffusionists certainly erred in accepting the traditions at their face value, rather than as ideologies to justify social relations which developed over the centuries. It is possible that states may have emerged as a result of the coming together of distinct agricultural and pastoral communities both of which may formerly have lived under less sophisticated forms of government. To deal with the now more complex plural society they may have been forced to evolve a state system in which one of the communities may emerge politically dominant. The more purely evolutionary thesis would seek to trace the development of states as a result of social differentiation within the same society which is most likely to occur among settled agriculturists. Since cattle are one of the few forms available to these societies to store wealth, differentiation may occur in terms of ownership of cattle. This may eventually give rise to occupational difference between the social classes which may harden through the imposition of caste restrictions against inter-marriage. Under these conditions the ruling class may seek to justify their dominance by claiming distinct origin from a 'superior race'. And yet the ruling classes in the interlacustrine region invariably speak the language of their subjects, and some recent studies have shown that they share many common clans with their subjects, which belie their claim to distinct origin.

The region, as mentioned earlier, was probably settled by iron-using agriculturists from some time during the first millennium A.D. When the area was sparsely populated the dominant form of agriculture was shifting cultivation involving the cultivation of millet, sorghum, and perhaps some root crops and bananas. Land under these conditions was probably communally owned, and the unit of political organisation was the clan though social interaction, in terms of exchange and marriage, probably extended beyond the clan. However, *good* land was in short supply, and as the population increased land began to acquire value. The increase in population may have been caused partly by natural increase, but in the case of both Karagwe and Buha there was also apparently immigration of people from neighbouring countries. In the case of Karagwe, Katoke argues that Bantu-speaking people who had earlier migrated through Karagwe into Bunyoro were pushed back into Karagwe by other invaders from the north. For reasons which are not very clear, some of these returning Bantu-speaking clans, especially the Sita, emerged as more prestigious and powerful, and able to assert their dominance over their cousins who had remained behind in Karagwe.[21] In Buha the immigrants were from the densely populated neighbouring kingdom of Burundi, but they came to occupy a more subordinate position since they could obtain land only by entering into special relations with the host clans which claimed ownership of the land. The *Bateko*, who were initially heads of the village founders' clans, began to assume the increasingly important role of allocating land in return for a certain fee, and eventually the role of a landlord demanding tribute in kind and in labour to work on his own plots. The exploitation of the immigrant cultivators enabled the Bateko to enjoy a higher standard of living and relatively greater security during famines. However, their exploitation was limited by the need to keep the clients working on their land since not only the amount of tribute but also power and prestige depended on the number of clients a *Muteko* had. Thus social differentiation had begun to occur within the society based on control over the distribution of land and, therefore, over the clients. Though the ruling group had emerged from within the society, the wealthy members of the community in Buha 'began to look for a new identity that would distinguish them from the common folk. It became fashionable to trace their origin from outside the community.'[22] One wonders if the claim to Bunyoro origin of the dominant clans in Karagwe in the pre-Hinda period does not arise in the same way.

According to existing traditions this initial phase of the history of north-western Tanzania was followed by the invasion of the northern Hima pastoralists under the central figure of Ruhinda. He is alleged to have been a descendant of the Bachwezi whose rule in Bunyoro was overthrown by the new Bito dynasty. From his headquarters in Karagwe, Ruhinda is said to have built up a vast empire which included Karagwe and the coastal Haya states, Buzinza and Buha. The empire, however, was short-lived, and it split up into the constituent states on the death of Ruhinda. While these events are not intrinsically impossible they have not been subjected to critical study. There are major discrepancies in the dating of the alleged invasion, ranging from the fifteenth century to Karagwe to the late eighteenth century in Buha. It is at least arguable that the Ruhinda episode represents a tremendous telescoping of historical events which occurred over a long period. At the same time there is very little independent proof that the Hima were indeed a distinct ethnic group which came from the north, rather than merely a wealthy group which emerged from within the society but which claimed an external origin to reinforce its social superiority and justify its rule, in the same way as the Bateko had earlier done in Buha. It has been noted, for example, that the ruling Hima/Hinda/Tutsi speak the same language as the subordinate Iru, and many of the lcan names and totems are shared by the two classes in society, which would be difficult to understand if they had different origins. The apparent physical differences between them can easily be explained in terms of the different diets on which they have been living over the centuries.

Whatever the precise origin of the ruling classes in these kingdoms, what is of greater significance to the history of north-western Tanzania is the social and political systems that were established. The single most important institution which characterised these systems was the patron-client relationship which had already begun to emerge, previously based on control over land. Mbwiliza argues that in Buha there was a change in the basis of social relations to one based on control of cattle, called *Ubugabire*. Under this system a client obtained 'protection' and the custodianship of one or more heads of cattle from his patron in return for recognition of the patron's superior status and menial services, such as collecting firewood, building houses or fences and working in the patron's gardens. While land probably continued to be important, the increasing emphasis on cattle suggests that there was an increasing need not only for dairy products, but also for animal manure to sustain the increasingly intensive cultivation, especially in the highlands. This situation gave the owners of cattle a dominant social and political position in the society. In Karagwe, Katoke argues, there was no total integration of cattle into the agricultural system since the Hima pastoralists occupied the open grasslands while the Banyambo agriculturists settled on the plateau or on the slopes of the ridges. There was, however, an exchange between the two communities for each other's products and as the dominant class, the Hima retained the right to demand grains or beer as their tribute. In Buha, where the ruling Tutsi and the subject Iru were more directly integrated in the economic system, the patron-client relationship extended from the *Mwami* at the head of pyramid of society to the Hutu at the base. The system was mediated by a series of administrators, *Batware*, who governed various regions and districts. They were, therefore, simultaneously clients of the Mwami or superior grades of Batware above them, as well as patrons of inferior grades of Batware or the Hutu below them. This patron-client relationship thus defined fairly precisely the class distinctions in the society, and to maintain those distinctions and the social distance to justify the rule by one over the other, a host of social barriers were erected. Thus the Hima and the Hutu/Iru were not supposed to eat together, except on certain festive occasions, and they were not supposed to intermarry, though there have been cases of the Hima taking Hutu/Iru girls as concubines or wives.

Unlike Karagwe and Buha, the coastal Haya zone[23] along the western shores of Lake Victoria, which receives up to eighty inches of rainfall, is not very suitable for pastoralism. The pastoral Hima, therefore, did not extend much into the area though the ruling classes still claimed Hima origin. The economy here was based on intensive cultivation of the small patches of fertile land to produce bananas and other crops. Intensive agriculture was made possible only partly by the use of animal manure but more generally by returning all parts of the banana plant into the soil. In a situation of scarcity of good land such as that in coastal Buhaya where only a fifth of the land is good enough for cultivation, social relations were based on control over land. At the same time, the banana culture, once established, required only a limited amount of labour, only two to three hours a day throughout the year to feed the household. There was, thus, a large potential surplus of labour which permitted the development of a large variety of non-agricultural crafts practised by the cultivators in their spare time but very few full time specialists emerged. The potential surplus of labour, however, also permitted the development of social differentiation in the society between the Iru cultivators and the *Nfura*, who could assert control over scarce good land, and who, therefore, could demand a tribute from the cultivators. Thus the *Nyarubanja* system developed. The Nyarubanja were 'estates' which grouped together a number of agricultural plots, one of which was occupied by the patron (*mutuazi*) while the rest were given to the clients (*batuarua*). In the social relationship thus created the patron provided 'protection', the use of the plot, and occasionally some heads of cattle, in return for recognition of his social superiority and tribute both in kind (bananas, beer, barkcloth and coffee for chewing purposes), and in labour (*nsika*, working for a month each year clearing the patron's plantation, building, cutting fire-wood and herding cattle). These estates were created by the *mukama* in favour of the chiefs or the *mulangira*, princes of the royal house, some of whom may have been chiefs as well. Thus the Nyarubanja system established not only the patron-client relationship between the cultivators and the ruling class, but also a hierarchical administrative system in which the cultivators were integrated into a state system consisting of a series of regional administrators rising to the mukama at the top of the pyramid.

The societies of north-western Tanzania had thus developed complex social and political systems in the era before the advent of long-distance trade. This development was given a further impetus by a development of regional and long-distance trade to the extent that they had stimulated local production and trade. In Buha the development of trade brought wealth to the Hutu clans which had specialised in such crafts as pottery and iron-smithing, and especially to the Chunyunyu salt traders who brought salt from Uvinza. With this wealth, converted into cattle, they themselves were able to enter into patron-client relationship with other people. Their success gave them social prestige and power which began to rival that of the Tutsi overlords and led to some rebellions. Similar development may have occurred in Karagwe and the Buhaya states. These developments, however, were cut short by the terrible rinderpest epidemic of 1889 which wiped out most of the cattle population, and by the imposition of colonial rule which prevented the system from regenerating itself.

In this section we have attempted to delineate in broad outlines the pattern of automonous development of Tanzanian societies. It is apparent from the discussion that the environment played an important role in the economy that the people could practise in the pre-industrial period, though the environment can at the same time be manipulated with adequate technology to do man's bidding to some extent. What is important for the development of societies is the amount and distribution of the surplus that the economy can produce. In the more unfavourable environment, such as central Tanzania, the surplus was both small and precarious, and it was therefore difficult to sustain non-agricultural activities and elaborate social and political systems. Where the surplus was both abundant and reliable, it was capable of supporting not only the development of useful crafts which can in turn help increase productivity, but also social differentiation and political centralisation. Tanzanian societies in the pre-colonial period were thus on a viable path of sustained development according to their own pattern. In the nineteenth century, however, they were confronted firstly by the Ngoni invasion which they were capable of absorbing, but more importantly by long-distance trade which in the long run absorbed them into the international capitalist economy.

The Ngoni invasion[24]

Some of the political developments traced in the previous section may have been induced by the invasion of some external force, though we also attempted to explain the internal dynamic of change in pre-colonial societies. The Ngoni invasion of the nineteenth century provides an important case to test some of the theories of state formation, since it led not only to the establishment of a number of Ngoni kingdoms in Tanzania but it is also credited with introducing military techniques and inducing political centralisation among other Tanzanian societies in self-defence.

The Ngoni were part of the 'Zulu aftermath', refugees fleeing from Shaka's conquests in South Africa in the 1820s. Starting as small bands of several hundreds of peoples, they snowballed into a vast armed nation on the march, numbering more than a hundred thousand by the time they entered Tanzania in the 1840s. The question of great historical interest are, firstly, how this spectacular growth of the Ngoni nation was accomplished, and secondly, what were the consequences for the population that lay across its path?

The Ngoni came out of a highly dynamic situation in Zululand where in the early decades of the nineteenth century a highly centralised military estate arose under Shaka. The king occupied a central position personifying the nation and controlling many of the resources. He claimed ownership of all the cattle, and he received all the cattle and captives captured in war, though both of these resources were distributed among his subjects. The population was organised according to overlapping principles. They were organised along lineage lines, each segment consisting of the different wives of the king and their children and dependents. As these segments grew they would split and multiply in each generation. At the same time the youth of the nation were organised in age-regiments which cut across territorial and lineage lines and were directly under the control of the king, which served to integrate the nation and centralise the authority of the king. Changes were also introduced in military techniques especially in the use of the short stabbing spear, which made the age-regiments highly efficient fighting units.

The Ngoni, refugees though they were, shared in this common heritage of social change as they embarked on their long, arduous march to the north. They faced two inter-related problems of how to subsist and how to survive in the hostile environment they had been pushed into in view of their small numbers. During the migratory phase of their history there was perhaps little alternative to a predatory life of raiding for cattle and food, but at several places they settled for several years exploiting in a more orderly fashion the agricultural resources using the conquered people as agricultural labourers, such as the Nsenga in Zambia. The area, nevertheless, was rapidly depleted and this pattern of economy thus required constant movement for survival. At the same time the small band of conquerors had an active interest in augmenting their numbers for greater security. However, with the constant need to move and the lack of an elaborate administrative structure to rule, the Ngoni needed not 'subjects' who would have been an encumbrance to be dragged along, but compatriots who had been assimilated enough to share in the interests and ideals of the Ngoni. Thus, while the act of conquest may have been brutal, the Ngoni opened their society to rapid assimilation of the captives. The captives were initially allocated as individuals to different segments of the society as 'children', but they were also rapidly inducted into the age-regiments where social distinction between the 'true Ngoni' and the captives was kept to the minimum. The captive, by the adoption of the Ngoni way of life, and especially by valour in the battlefield, could raise his status. Moreover, protection offered by the Ngoni state was an additional inducement to the conquered to accept assimilation into the Ngoni nation. Very little social distinction was maintained between the original Ngoni and the many ethnic groups assimilated during the march through Zimbabwe, Zambia and Malawi.

By this process the Ngoni under Zwangendaba grew prodigiously, multiplying more than a hundred times over within a generation by the time they reached Ufipa. The 'snowball' had grown not only administratively in terms of sheer size, but perhaps also unsupportable by the environment which was by no means the most fertile. When the strains began to appear in the Ngoni society they followed cleavages along segmentary lines. In 1845 Zwangendaba died at Mapupo and the kingdom split into at least five groups led by his sons or other close relatives, three of which migrated southwards again into Zambia and Malawi. The fourth known as the Tuta, migrated north into central Tanzania where they remained migrant raiders. They became the model for the *ruga-ruga* bands of professional mercenary warriors who terrorised the region. One of their captives was Mirambo who learnt their fighting techniques and language, employing the former in his attempt to establish a vast empire. This was one of the ways by which Ngoni military techniques were diffused in large parts of Tanzania. The Tuta themselves finally settled in Kahama, gradually being absorbed in Unyamwezi as they continued to assimilate the Nyamwezi into their society.

The last group was called the Gwangwara, who, under Zulu-Gama, moved to the south-west, to the Songea area. Here they met the Maseko Ngoni who had migrated independently, passing to the east of Lake Nyasa and across the Ruvuma. The latter had settled in Songea in the 1840s, establishing their hegemony over indigenous people such as the Ndendeuli. The Maseko were far stronger and their leader Maputo was accepted as the overlord. Maputo, however, hoped to fully integrate the two Ngoni groups by eliminating the Gwangwara leaders. The plot backfired and the Gwangwara defeated and drove the Maseko to the south of the Ruvuma. Their Ndendeuli subjects, who had adopted Ngoni military and political ideas, apparently tried to establish a successor state, and when defeated by the Gwangwara, moved to the Kilombero valley to establish their Mbunga kingdom in the 1860s.

The Gwangwara had consisted of two segments of Zwangendaba's kingdom which had co-operated during their march though they had retained their separate leaderships. With the Songea area now firmly under their control the two segments began to drift apart geographically and politically. The Njelu shifted south and settled around Mbinga under a more decentralised political system compared to the Mshope who settled around Mtakano under Chipeta and Chabruma.

With more or less permanent settlement in the Songea area there was bound to be a change in the economy and society of the Ngoni from the pattern which characterised their migratory period. Most of the previous authors have assumed that the migratory pattern of raiding and assimilating characterised Ngoni history until they were 'pacified' by the Germans. However, it would appear that if the Ngoni had continued to lead a predatory life 'like a swarm of locusts forced to continue advancing as it destroys its own livelihood', they would not have been able to settle down. It is therefore very likely that once they settled in the Songea area, the pattern of their economy must have changed to a more orderly exploitation of the local agricultural resources, using the indigenous people more effectively as cultivators, while the Ngoni cared for their huge herds of cattle. With the allocation of agricultural activities to the conquered people on a more permanent basis, the latter's social status was bound to be affected, assimilated into the Ngoni society but not to the same extent as the captives had been during the migration. Raiding continued at the periphery of the Ngoni state but to a more limited extent, which would have provided much less opportunity to the subjects to show their valour and to capture their own captives with which to build up their social status. Thus a more statified society emerged, with greater distinction being maintained between the 'true Ngoni' (consisting of the original Nguni-speaking people, the

Tonga, Kalanga and Sanga who had been assimilated in Mozambique, Zimbabwe and Zambia), who constituted less than twenty per cent of the total population, and the 'new Ngoni', more recently assimilated Ndendeuli, Ngindo and Pangwa.

What was the legacy of the Ngoni invasion to the pre-colonial history of Tanzania? One very obvious legacy was the creation of the 'Ngoni' nation on Tanzanian soil which consisted predominantly of indigenous people of southern Tanzania. This belies the colonial image of widespread massacre of people by the Ngoni, though destruction undoubtedly occurred during the conquest phase of their history. At the same time it should be noted that the decrease in the amount of destruction as the Ngoni settled down was accompanied by a greater degree of degradation of the conquered people in the Ngoni society. The Ngoni invasion also led to the introduction of Ngoni military techniques which were adopted by various Tanzanian societies either in self-defence against the Ngoni themselves, or to enable political reorganisation and empire-building as in the case of Mirambo and the Sangu. However, the older hypothesis that it was the need to defend themselves against the Ngoni that induced political centralisation among the Sangu, the Hehe and other societies in southern Tanzania has not been sustained by recent research. The Hehe,[25] in particular, had embarked upon political centralisation under Munyigumba in the 1860s, apparently in response to internal social pressures, and before Ngoni pressures became significant for them. They were later to adopt Ngoni military techniques through the Sangu and by the late 1870s were strong enough to deal a devastating blow to the Ngoni. The consequence of the Ngoni invasion were thus varied and can shed light on other such invasions which might have occurred in north-western Tanzania and elsewhere. What is historically significant is that, as in the case of these earlier invasions, Tanzanian societies, after the initial shock, were able to absorb the Ngoni into the local context. No continent-wide Zulu state was established which expropriated the life-giving surplus for the support of a ruling class outside Tanzania. This is the important contrast from the effects of long-distance trade and the incorporation of Tanzania into the world-wide economic system.

Integration of Tanzania into the international economic system[26]

Until the end of the eighteenth century, most of Tanzanian societies in the interior were developing independently of the external global forces. This means not only that they were politically independent but also that their economic and social development was closely in tune with their political development. Their economy was symmetrical and internally integrated, by which we mean that they produced what they consumed and the surplus was retained within the community to support the development of non-agricultural crafts and social differentiation. The coast, on the other hand, had commercial contact with the outside world for more than two thousand years, largely as a supplier of certain staples like mangrove poles and grains, luxuries like ivory and gold, and at various times, slaves. In return, the coast generally received manufactured commodities like iron tools and arms, cloth and beads. As a result of this trade numerous city-states grew up along the coast inhabited by a mixed coastal population which prospered by international trade and which evolved its own distinctive Swahili culture.

These city-states were utterly dependent on international trade, and when the Portuguese sought to replace the old Indian Ocean commercial network by their own system, many of the city-states crumbled. In this new system the role of the eastern coast of Africa was to supply essential provisions to Portuguese vessels, and ivory and gold to pay for Asian spices since Portugal produced little that Asia needed. Though Portuguese control over the East African coast was not absolute, the disruption of the Indian Ocean economic system and the ruthless exploitation of eastern Africa to which Portugal could contribute little in return gradually sapped the prosperity of the city-states.

Portugal, however, was just emerging out of feudalism, and was not able to channel the wealth looted from the East into productive development of its economy. Its frail economy was thus unable to sustain extensive conquest of the major centres of population (as opposed to points along the coastal fringes), and effective exploitation of the vast natural and human resources of the East. It was left to other nations of Western Europe, particularly Britain, to divert that wealth into the development of industrial capitalism.[27] This was probably the most significant development of the history of Tanzania since the agricultural revolution, and the discovery of iron nearly two millennia previously, since from that event followed European economic expansion and colonialism. The scientific revolution which accompanied the industrial revolution in Western

Europe meant that the technological gap between Tanzania and her external trading partners, which was relatively small in the pre-capitalist period, began to widen tremendously and at an accelerating rate. Such was the dynamism of this development that one area after another of what became the Third World, and not merely their coastal fringes, were incorporated into this gigantic economic system as satellites revolving around the Euro-American metropole. As Rodney has pointed out, the bigger the technological gap between the two interacting partners, the more detrimental were the consequences to the weaker party.[28] The satellites were therefore underdeveloped and exploited of their natural and human resources as never before, being converted into suppliers of raw materials to the metropolitan industries, and consumers of their manufactured goods.

The incorporation of Tanzania into this economic system went through several stages. At each stage it gave birth to a specific class of people, the *compradors* ('bepari') who served as the local commercial agents and who sought to perpetuate the international connection by which they prospered. We shall examine two aspects in the economic exploitation of Tanzania before colonialism: the export of labour (slaves) and the use of slave labour within Tanzania for the production of commodities for export (especially cloves); and the export of other raw materials such as ivory and gum copal in their raw form. In exchange Tanzania received manufactured goods in their final processed form, quite often luxuries to be consumed by the compradors. The massive imports of textiles, metal wires and guns may have hindered the development of existing comparable industries, though the high cost of transportation before the age of the railways probably postponed the wholesale destruction of these indigenous industries until the colonial period.

The external slave trade and the plantation economy

The incursion of the north-western Europeans into the Indian Ocean and the establishment of the Dutch and English East India Companies gradually weakened the Portuguese hold on the arteries of trade in the Indian Ocean. The Omanis took advantage of their weakness to throw the Portuguese out of Muscat in 1650, but they in turn succumbed to the temptations of oceanic raiding and commerce. Having built up a powerful navy they began to harass the Portuguese in East African waters and to explore the commercial possibilities there. Their anti-Portuguese offensive met an early response among the Swahili city-states, led by Pate, which were fretting under the heavy burden of Portuguese commercial monopoly. Together they drove the Portuguese from the East African coast north of Cape Delgado in 1698. Little did the Swahili realise that the logical outcome of Omani initiative in East Africa was their economic and political dominance.

Omani participation in maritime activities inevitably began to transform Omani society. Traditional Oman had been a continental theocracy with its capital in the interior and disdaining trade. Its maritime adventures began to bring wealth from booty and trade to the coastal ports, and to their mercantile inhabitants. The balance of economic and political power thus began to shift from the interior to the coast where Muscat became the new capital, from the feudal and tribal overlords to the merchants, and from the theocracy of the Yaarubi dynasty to a secular mercantile state of the Al Bu Said dynasty. There was an expanding market for Omani dates in British India, partly for re-export to Europe, and the wealth acquired by the coastal merchants in their raids and trade enabled them to invest in the establishment of a plantation economy using slave labour from East Africa in order to expand production. Despite traditional opposition, even the Yaarubi rulers actively participated in these activities although they had to justify it as part of the crusade against the Portuguese infidels. One of them, by the time he died in 1711, had acquired a third of all the date palms in Oman, 1 700 slaves and fifty-four vessels, the three elements in the new and dynamic sector in the Omani economy. By this process both East Africa and Oman were indirectly linked with the international economy, the former as the supplier of slave labour, and the latter as the supplier of slave-grown dates. This development, however, seems to have had a fairly limited potential, for the demand for slaves seems to have soon levelled off at about 1 000 per annum.

The export of slaves from East Africa, however, was given a boost in the later part of the eighteenth century by a French demand for labour in their Indian Ocean islands of Mauritius and Reunion where they had embarked upon the production of sugar. The major source initially was the Portuguese colony of Mozambique, but by the 1770s demand was exceeding supply. Moreover, in the 1780s as a result of the rising price of slaves on the west coast of Africa, there was an additional demand from the Americas to be met. This combined demand could be met only by an extension of the French slave trade to the coast of Tanzania where the French sought to obtain control either by treaty with the Swahili ruler of Kilwa or by establishing their own 'factories'. Neither of these attempts was particularly successful, but the high prices that they were prepared to offer for slaves stimulated the expansion of the hinterland behind Kilwa as far as the shores of Lake Nyasa to supply this enlarged demand. By the mid 1780s the French were taking away nearly 2 000 slaves per annum from the coast of Tanzania as well as over 6 500 who were being taken away from Mozambique. The extension of the French slave trade to the coast of Tanzania offered commercial advantage not only to the local Swahili rulers and traders but also to the expansionist Omanis who, having tasted the fruits of international trade, refused to be confined to the economic opportunities of their own desert homeland. Thus, when the French sought to bypass their commercial centre at Zanzibar and make a deal with the rebellious Swahili ruler, the Omanis struck hard and decisively to resubjugate Kilwa. However, they had no intention to disrupt the lucrative French slave trade.

It was the Anglo-French naval warfare from the last decade of the eighteenth century that was to deal a fatal blow to the French slave trade, culminating in the capture of Mauritius by the British in 1810. This was momentous because the British, entering the era of industrial capitalism, found slavery increasingly unprofitable, and in 1807 they had abolished the slave trade to their colonies. The fall of Mauritius to the British thus seemed to deprive the Omanis and the Swahili merchants of the larger market for their slaves while the slave trade to the Americans was made more hazardous by British anti-slavery patrols. The British followed this up in 1822 by forcing the Omani ruler to sign a treaty outlawing the export of slaves to the south of Cape Delgado.

The strangulation of the slave trade to the south was bound to threaten the prosperity of the merchants who had participated in it and who had become so dependent on it. They therefore desperately sought for an alternative use for the now redundant slaves. Some of the Arab traders who had been in intimate contact with the French at Mauritius introduced cloves into Zanzibar by about 1810. Seyyid Said, however, realised the potential of this commodity for his commercial empire, and he embarked upon a major expansion of the clove plantation economy both on his own numerous plantations and on those of his Arab subjects. In the 1840s the cultivation of cloves was extended to Pemba. Once established the plantation economy acquired its own momentum and exceeded the original purpose of absorbing the redundant slaves. By the 1860s the islands of Zanzibar and Pemba were absorbing about 10 000 slaves per annum. The development of the plantation economy created a new land-owning class. Some of them, who had accompanied the Omani ruler from Oman, owed their position as a privileged group to whom the Omani ruler granted land and provided clove seedlings. Others ascended to the position by diverting their commercial profit from the earlier French slave trade or from the long-distance ivory trade into the interior to invest in land and slave labour for the cultivation of cloves. Many of these landowners were Arabs, but by the 1860s they also included some indigenous Shirazi, and also a few Indians who had begun to acquire control over clove plantations mortgaged to them. After the abolition of the slave trade in 1873 a larger number of the Shirazi in Pemba were able to participate in the clove economy though generally as smaller landowners and probably not using much slave labour.

Zanzibar had thus acquired its own economic base instead of merely serving as an entrepot for slaves and ivory passing through to external markets. However, that base was almost entirely dependent on international trade since only a minute portion of the cloves could be consumed within Tanzania. The original attraction of cloves was the high price reigning at the beginning of the nineteenth century as a result of the Dutch monopoly over the commodity. The massive expansion in the production of cloves in Zanzibar effectively buried that monopoly, and the price therefore came crashing down. The price in 1870 was a tenth of that in 1830. The economy, moreover, suffered from many of the now familiar disadvantages of the tremendous fluctuation in the production of cloves. The dangers of this dependence became particularly apparent in 1872 when the hurricane wiped out more than four-fifths of the clove trees in Zanzibar.[29]

The commercial empire

The other major sector of the commercial economy was the export of raw materials such as ivory and gum copal, and such staples as food grains and mangrove poles, and the import of manufactured goods like cloth, metals and beads. The demand for East African ivory has a very long history as has been indicated above. By the eighteenth century India was the major market for the production of ivory bangles which were considered an essential part of bridal jewellery. The demand was kept up by the fact that these bangles were regularly destroyed when Hindu women were cremated together with their jewellery. This demand during the eighteenth century appears to have been met by the supply from the coastal belt of East Africa, but the existence of a belt of inhospitable *nyika* just behind the coast prevented an easy access to the ivory resources of the East African interior. Therefore, the major supplier of ivory at that time was Mozambique where long-distance trade had already been established into the far interior. Towards the end of the eighteenth century the Portuguese authorities attempted to squeeze the maximum amount of revenue from this trade by imposing heavy duties both on the export of ivory and on cloth and beads imported in exchange. The result of this greed was catastrophic. By 1801 the export of ivory from Mozambique had fallen to nearly a half.

The immediate consequence was a sharp increase in the price of ivory which made it worthwhile to penetrate the nyika to exploit the ivory resources of the interior. The centre of the supply of ivory thus began to shift from Mozambique to the East African coast. Indian demand, however, must have been limited at this time, and by the second decade of the nineteenth century the price of ivory had more or less reverted to late eighteenth-century levels. This suggests that the supply of ivory from East Africa had been expanded adequately to meet the Indian demand and the price, therefore, had stabilised.

However, from the second decade of the nineteenth century a new demand arose in the industrialised west which was to have a significant and long-term effect on the economy of East Africa. Europe had formerly obtained 'hard' ivory from West Africa. With the increasing affluence of the richer classes of Europe and the United States demand arose for 'soft' ivory, which was procured from the eastern half of Africa, for the manufacture of such luxuries as ivory combs, billiard balls and piano keys. To supply this demand Bombay emerged as the major port re-exporting the ivory from East Africa. All British efforts to establish a direct trade with East Africa failed apparently because of the entrenched position of the Indian merchants in the ivory trade of East Africa. American traders were able to establish themselves gradually as the most important western traders at Zanzibar though they remained heavily dependent on Indian traders who continued to dominate the local trade in ivory.

This new demand for ivory grew so rapidly that despite the rapid expansion in the supply, the price of ivory rose steeply from about $10 per *frasala* in 1825 to $90 in 1873, an increase of 350 per cent. At the same time, as a result of mechanisation, the price of manufactured imports, especially cloth, declined by about fifty per cent. The terms of trade were thus favourable to the development of the ivory trade. As a result long-distance trade routes developed linking the coast with the far interior across the nyika. By the 1870s most of Tanzania, Kenya and Uganda, eastern Zaire, northern Zambia, Malawi and northern Mozambique had become part of a vast hinterland, supplying ivory to Zanzibar and thus integrated to varying degrees into the international economy.

The integration of this vast region in middle Africa was not achieved merely by the extension of the trade routes from the coast into the interior, but also by the transformation and assimilation of pre-existing regional trading networks of the interior into the coast-bound long-distance trade route system. These regional trading networks had evolved among agriculturists to supply the essential commodities such as iron and salt. With the rise of the demand for ivory at the coast these regional trading networks were linked and extended to the coast to supply that demand. In the interior ivory previously probably had little demand, often used as door posts, etc. The external demand for this resource added value to it, and specialised elephant hunting groups emerged to hunt the elephants, and traders and porters to deliver the ivory to the coast. Initially these activities may have been confined to the idle dry season, thus utilising hitherto surplus labour, but the greater distances to be covered between the coast and Katanga—between which, for example, the Nyamwezi traded—and the lucrativeness of the ivory trade, meant that more and more people began to concentrate on the ivory trade as a full time activity. This implied a diversion of labour from essential economic activities such as agriculture, which was of great significance, especially in such areas as Unyamwezi where population density was probably low and where a high enough density to keep off the tsetse fly is required. At the same time, massive importation of manufactured cloth may have destroyed or hindered the development of indigenous textile industries, such as the barkcloth industry in the West Lake area or the hand-woven cloth industry of south-western Tanzania. It has been suggested that the existence of long-distance trade routes stimulated the expansion of the iron industry in certain areas since iron hoes were exchanged for ivory or food provisions by passing caravans. This may well have stimulated the diffusion of iron hoes into areas deficient in the metal, and stimulated production of agriculture. This may be one of the few positive contributions of long-distance trade, but it depended so much on the existence of long-distance trade, and the continued demand for ivory that any disruption of this trade, as a result of wars or exhaustion of the ivory resources, was bound to have a devastating effect on the local economy.

Long-distance trade was also bound to have an effect on the social and political systems of the societies of the interior which had an active role in it. As was mentioned in the first section the social function of the Nyamwezi chief was originally derived from his leadership in clearing the bush and establishing agriculture. Whatever ritual superstructure was subsequently built around him, he continued to practise farming and derived only a limited amount of tribute or gifts from his subjects and this was often quickly re-distributed since a chief was expected to show generosity. The demand for ivory created a new source of wealth over which chiefs were quick to assert their rights, demanding one of the tusks from every elephant hunted in their territory—fifty per cent tax. It appears that in the pre-existing political system in Unyamwezi it was the sub-chiefs or headmen who were normally responsible for administrative duties. It is they who now began to collect the ivory tax as well as the *hongo*, the toll which passing caravans had to pay. This new wealth appears to have enabled many of the headmen to usurp the chiefship themselves, as new trader chiefs, and to attempt to monopolise the trade in ivory. It has been argued that these chiefs were part of a larger class of merchants, *wandewa*, which emerged as a result of long-distance trade, and that they combined with the coastal traders who were trading or settling in Unyamwezi to play a prominent role in the politics of many of the Nyamwezi chiefdoms, allowing both groups of traders to share in the wealth accruing from long-distance trade.[30]

Close co-operation between these two groups was marked in some of the Nyamwezi chiefdoms, such as Unyanyembe. But they were also potential rivals. As the century wore on and the coastal caravans became larger, better organised and better financed, they began to supersede the Nyamwezi in the control of long-distance trade. Whereas Burton in 1858 suggests a predominance of Nyamwezi caravans, Stanley in 1871 speaks of the decline of Nyamwezi commercial activities in Unyamwezi, Nyamwezi adventurers being forced to seek new opportunities elsewhere, in Ukimbu under Nyungu ya Mawe, and in Katanga under Msiri. It is in this light that we should see repeated conflicts between Nyamwezi chiefs like Mnwa Sele, Mirambo and Nyungu ya Mawe, and the coastal traders. Each of them sought to restrict the activities of the coastal traders and the wealth they derived from trade in or through Unyamwezi. They realised that the fragmented political structure of Unyamwezi was giving opportunity to the coastal traders to play one Nyamwezi chiefdom against another and thus expand their trade. They therefore sought to unite the Nyamwezi in a large empire. However, the alliance between the coastal traders and the *wandewa*, especially in Unyanyembe, had become a powerful force. Mnwa Sele was defeated fairly rapidly. Mirambo and Nyungu ya Mawe carried on the struggle for a long period, each setting up an extensive empire, though trade, which was periodically disrupted, was not entirely stopped. These Nyamwezi rulers, in fact, did not wish to stop the trade by which they benefited. They merely wished for a larger share of the profit which was derived by the coastal traders who had penetrated the interior. They may also have wished to establish control over the sources of ivory in the interior in order to bargain from a position of strength with the Omani rulers of Zanzibar who controlled the coastal termini.

This vast commercial empire that extended nearly half-way across middle Africa was presided over by the Zanzibar sultanate which attempted to set up an administrative structure for the exploitation of this import/export trade. The control exercised by Zanzibar was based not on any political control over the whole region but rather on the control of its commercial outlet at the coast. The Omani rulers had embarked on a systematic conquest of the various city-states that studded the coast, subjugating especially Kilwa in 1785 and Mombasa in 1837. Though Omani control over the whole coast was not absolute—they had particular difficulty in controlling the Lamu archipelago—the control was sufficient enough to enable them to set up an administrative machinery to charge customs duties on trade passing through the various ports. By the mid-nineteenth century a distinct pattern of taxation had emerged. Zanzibar was most dependent on the Mrima coast from which came most of the ivory, gum copal and slaves. To maintain control over this strategic area Seyyid Said barred foreign traders from direct trade with the coastal ports between Tanga and Kilwa, and then imposed the heaviest duty on these commodities which amounted to about twenty-five per cent on ivory by the late 1840s. The coast to the north and to the south were strategically less important to the Zanzibar economy, had a greater potential for direct foreign trade, and were under weaker political control. To induce them to stay within the Zanzibari hegemony they were left open to direct foreign trade though few seem to have traded directly, and they were subject to much lower levels of taxation, amounting to a half or a quarter of what the Mrima coast paid. Apart from these internal duties on exports, customs duties were charged on manufactured imports which by the various commercial treaties with European and American powers was fixed at five per cent. Despite this heavy taxation the external trade of East Africa continued to expand throughout the first three-quarters of the century, yielding a handsome revenue to the Omani rulers which rose from about $40 000 in the first decade of the nineteenth century to over $300 000 in the late 1860s.

Who were the beneficiaries of this commercial system besides the Omani ruler? The first group consisted of the Arab traders who had expanded their commercial activities after expelling the Portuguese from East Africa, and had prospered with the French slave trade, perhaps for too long to take a more direct role in the rising ivory trade with India in the first quarter of the nineteenth century. They, however, continued to dominate, with the Swahili, the local entrepot trade between Zanzibar and the mainland ports. The decline in the French slave trade forced some of the Arabs, as we have seen, into the clove plantation economy on Zanzibar, but others diverted their attention to the long-distance trade into the interior which remained the preserve of the Arabs and the Swahili before the colonial period, gradually superseding the Africans during the second half of the nineteenth century. Several colonies of these coastal traders were established in the interior, such as at Tabora and Ujiji where some of them even began to branch out into agriculture to supply provisions to the passing caravans.

These coastal colonies by no means controlled the interior

politically, but in alliance with the class of African merchants such as the *wandewa* among the Nyamwezi, they were able to exercise an important political influence over large areas. The rise of the *wandewa* represents an important social revolution in the interior to the extent that economic and political power shifted from the traditional chief whose office had assumed a more ritual role, to the new trader chiefs who sought to build empires, with the help of the Ngoni-inspired *ruga-ruga*, in order to control the trade of their territories or that passing through them. But they were a declining class since their economic base was weakening with the exhaustion of ivory in large parts of their territories. Their wealth increasingly came to depend upon the tolls they charged on trade passing through their territories, hence the ferocity of their struggle with the Arab traders from the 1860s.

The final commercial group which benefited from the commercial empire were the Indian merchants. Most of them originated from the maritime states of Gujarat and Cutch, particularly the latter which was not only one of the poorest, subject to frequent famines, but also in the process of being underdeveloped as heavy importation of British cloth began to strangle the local textile industry. The expansion in the demand for ivory, especially for the European market, provided these merchants with a golden opportunity to improve their economic well-being by taking an active middleman's role. As people rising from an economic depression and therefore used to a meagre standard of living, the flourishing trade in East Africa enabled them to accumulate capital rapidly and begin to assert their economic power. At the beginning of the nineteenth century they could be treated as 'foreign' traders who were excluded from local entrepot trade between Zanzibar and the coast. Their rapidly increasing wealth forced the Omani ruler and the Arab/Swahili merchant class, which thus far had the monopoly over the entrepot trade, to admit the Indians into that monopoly. By about 1820 an Indian firm had acquired control of the customs of Zanzibar, paying an annual rent to the Sultan. This firm retained control of the customs for the next half-century, and by the 1870s it had over two million dollars invested in East Africa, with loans to Indian and Arab merchants and landowners, to the Sultan and even to European and American traders at Zanzibar. The growth of Indian economic power in East Africa kept pace with the growth of the Indian community from just over 200 in 1818 to nearly 4000 in

1870. They formed the nucleus of the present Indian communities in East Africa, for though some of them exported their capital to India to establish an economic base there, most of them used their capital within East Africa to expand their economic activities during the colonial period. It is this powerful economic group which the British sought to bring under their control as a means of acquiring a powerful influence in the affairs of East Africa on the eve of the partition.

International trade had thus given rise to a number of economic groups in East Africa who thrived on international trade and therefore had an active interest in its continuation. They differed in specific origin, ethnic composition or precise occupation: Arab and Swahili traders, Arab and Shirazi landowners, Indian traders and the Nyamwezi *wandewa*—but they were all part of the same economic system which evolved during the nineteenth century as an extension of the international capitalist economy based in Western Europe and North America. The role of Tanzania in this system was to produce the raw materials for which there was little local use: ivory collected from Eastern Zaire to the coast; gum copal from the coastal belt; slaves from southern Tanzania, Malawi and northern Mozambique, used on Zanzibar and Pemba to produce cloves for export to Europe, North America and India. In return Tanzania received large quantities of manufactured cloth from the United States and Britain which displaced Indian cloth and may have killed or hindered the development of textile industries in the interior. Tanzania also received glass beads, copper and brass wire for decoration and arms and gun powder for destruction.

The impact of the international economy on Tanzanian societies varied. In certain areas such as Usambara and Upare where the kingdoms had their economic base in the highlands, long-distance trade passing along the plains created a rival economic base and contributed to the disintegration of those kingdoms.[31] Elsewhere the wealth from long-distance trade may have allowed some states occupying strategic positions to expand and establish their hegemony over smaller states, which created not only large empires but also perhaps more marked social differentiation between the rulers and the ruled, such as on Kilimanjaro and in Unyamwezi.[32] Areas which had the misfortune of being assigned the role of producers of slaves such as southern Tanzania, went through a catastrophic period of social disruption and depopulation. Perhaps the most fundamental economic pattern that emerged in Tanzania during the nineteenth century was the creation of a proto-colonial economy which was dependent on the export of a few raw materials and the import of manufactured goods. The diversion of labour from essential economic activities, such as agriculture and industries, to hunting and transporting ivory and slaves to the coast transformed the economies of at least some of the societies in the interior, such as the Nyamwezi and the Yao, which were most dependent on long-distance trade. These economies became less self-reliant, lacking internal integration between production and consumption, and were thus under-developed. However, the lack of cheap and rapid transportation prevented a more widespread underdevelopment of Tanzania as whole until the colonial period.

Notes

1 For a more detailed treatment of the pre-colonial period see I.N. Kimambo and A.J. Temu, eds, *A History of Tanzania*, Nairobi, 1969, chs. 1–4.

2 G.P. Murdock, *Africa*, New York, 1959, pp. 196–200.

3 R. Oliver and G. Mathew, eds, *History of East Africa*, Vol. 1, Oxford, 1963, pp. 191–9.

4 *History of Tanzania*, p. 18.

5 E. Boserup, *The Conditions of Agricultural Growth*, London, 1965.

6 W. Allan, *The African Husbandmen*, Edinburgh, 1965, pp. 199–206.

7 J. Woodburn, 'The Future of the Tindiga', *Tanganyika Notes and Records* (*T.N.R.*) 58/59, 1962, p. 269.

8 J.L. Newman, *The Ecological Basis for Subsistence Change among the Sandawe of Tanzania*, Washington, 1970, chs. 2–3. E. Ten Raa, 'Sandawe Prehistory and the Vernacular Tradition', *Azania*, iv, 1969, pp. 91–103.

9 This is based on A.H. Jacobs, 'The Traditional Political System of the Pastoral Masai', D. Phil., Oxford, 1965; H.A. Forsbrooke, 'An Administrative Survey of the Masai Social

System', *T.N.R.*, 26, 1948, pp. 1–50.

10 A. Roberts, 'The Nyamwezi', in A. Roberts, ed, *Tanzania Before 1900*, Nairobi, 1968, pp. 117–22; 'Nyamwezi Trade', in R. Gray and D. Birmingham, eds, *Precolonial African Trade*, London, 1970, pp. 39–47; R.G. Abrahams, *The Political Organisation of Unyamwezi*, Cambridge, 1967, chs. 1–2.

11 J.E.S. Sutton, 'Engaruka and its waters: Ancient irrigated agriculture in Masailand', University of Dar es Salaam, History Seminar Paper, 1973.

12 This is based on M. Wilson, *Good Company*, Boston, 1963; *Communal Rituals of the Nyakyusa*, Oxford, 1959; *The Peoples of the Nyasa-Tanganyika Corridor*, Cape Town, 1958, pp. 10–21; G. Wilson, *The Land Rights of Individuals among the Nyakyusa*, Livingstone, 1938; P.H. Gulliver, *Land Tenure and Social Chance among the Nyakyusa*, Kampala, 1958, chs. 1–11.

13 S.R. Charsley, *The Princes of Nyakyusa*, Nairobi, 1969.

14 We have very limited information about the other societies in the southern highlands, but the general pattern of development was towards small chiefdoms. The Sangu, the Hehe and the Ngoni are dealt with in the second section.

15 Abdallah B. Hemedi L'Ajemy, *Habariza Wakilindi*, translated by J.W.T. Allen as *The Kilindi*, Nairobi, 1962, p. 36.

16 The discussion on the Pare is based on I.N. Kimambo *A Political History of the Pare in Tanzania, c. 1500–1900*, Nairobi, 1969.

17 Allan, pp. 162–6.

18 K.M. Stahl, 'Outline of Chagga History', *T.N.R.*, 64, 1965, pp. 35–42; *History of the Chagga People of Kilimanjaro*, The Hague, 1964.

19 The discussion on the Shambaa is based on S. Feierman, *The Shamba Kingdom*, Madison, 1974.

20 C.C. Wrigley, 'Some Thoughts on the Bachwezi', *Uganda Journal*, 22, 1958, pp. 11–7.

21 The discussion on Karagwe is based on I.K. Katoke, *The Making of the Karagwe Kingdom*, Nairobi, 1970.

22 The discussion on Buha is based on J.F. Mpwiliza, 'The Origins and Development of Heru Kingdom from about 1750–1930', History B. A. Dissertation, University of Dar es Salaam, 1974.

23 The discussion on Coastal Buhaya is based on P.C. Reining, 'The Haya: The Agrarian System of a Sedentary People', Ph.D., University of Chicago, 1967.

24 This section is based on T.T. Spear, 'Zwangendaba's Ngoni, 1821–1890', M.A. thesis, University of Wisconsin, 1969; J.A. Barnes, *Politics in a Changing Society*, Manchester, 1967; J.D. Omer-Cooper, *The Zulu Aftermath*, Evanston, 1969; P.H. Gulliver, 'A History of the Songea Ngoni', *T.N.R.*, 41, 1955, pp. 16–30.

25 A. Redmayne, 'Mkwawa and the Hehe Wars', *Journal of African History*, ix, 3, 1968, p. 425; 'The Hehe', in Roberts, ed, pp. 37–58.

26 This section is based largely on A.M.H. Sheriff, 'The Rise of a Commercial Empire: An Aspect of the Economic History of Zanzibar, 1770–1873', Ph.D., University of London, 1971; C.S. Nicholls, *The Swahili Coast*, London, 1971; Roberts, 'The Nyamwezi' and 'Nyamwezi Trade'.

27 See E.J. Hobsbawn, *Industry to Empire*, London, 1969.

28 W. Rodney, *How Europe Underdeveloped Africa*, London and Dar es Salaam, 1972, p. 18.

29 For a fuller account of the impact of the slave trade see E.A. Alpere, *The East African Slave Trade*, Nairobi, 1967.

30 A.C. Unomah, 'Economic Expansion and Political Change in Unyanyembe, (ca. 1840–1900)', Ph.D., University of Ibadan, 1972.

31 See Kimabo, *Pare*, pp. 142–3, and Feierman, pp. 182–4.

32 N.R. Bennett, *Mirambo of Tanzania, ca. 1840–84*, New York, 1971; A. Shorter, *Nyungu ya Mawe*, Nairobi, 1969.

2. External Factors in the Partition of East Africa

David Arnold

For nearly four hundred years before the partition of the 1880s and 1890s there had been intermittent European contact with the coast of East Africa. In the sixteenth century the Portuguese had gained a foothold on the coast, but they had lacked the military and economic resources to penetrate inland and the fall of the garrison at Mombasa in 1698 marked the virtual end of Portugal's bid to establish control north of the Ruvuma River. For well over a century no other European power made a determined effort to succeed where the Portuguese had so clearly failed. 'Before 1856', wrote Coupland with pardonable exaggeration, 'there were not many parts of the world about which the western peoples knew less or cared less than they knew or cared about East Africa.'[1] And yet within the next forty years European aloofness rapidly gave way to penetration, partition and conquest. What had changed? Why was there such a momentous transformation in European attitudes to East Africa?

Explanations for this late nineteenth-century invasion of East Africa have not been lacking, but writers have tended either to focus too exclusively on the diplomatic manoeuvres of statesmen in Europe—the so-called 'official mind of imperialism'[2]—or, having nodded politely in the direction of changes in the western societies, proceed to omit them from further consideration.[3] The factors most frequently cited—the struggles between the nation states of Europe, Britain's hostility to the East African slave trade and its concern for the control of the routes to India—can all be seen as contributing to the partition, but they do not in themselves provide a complete explanation. It is necessary to look deeper, for the dynamics behind the penetration and annexation of East Africa are to be found not in the minds of the third Marquis of Salisbury and Prince Otto von Bismarck but in the changing character of the capitalist societies of Western Europe and the United States. The progress of industrialisation in these countries rapidly increased their capacity and incentive to penetrate and control the economy of East Africa; and, at the same time, the economic competition between the industrial states created a race hectic and hesitant by turns, for the markets of the world. East Africa was not the most valued of these markets, but potentially at least it was too important to be omitted. And its economic potential had been demonstrated in the half century before partition by the Zanzibar sultanate of the Omani Arabs.

The Zanzibar system

Seyyid Said's transfer of his capital from Muscat to Zanzibar, conventionally dated as 1840, is often seen as a turning point in the history of modern East Africa. Its primary significance is that by moving to the island Said was establishing himself as the essential middleman between the suppliers of tropical products on the mainland and the American and European traders visiting the coast. There was clearly scope for such an intermediary. By attempting to oust the Arab and Indian merchants of the coastal towns, without themselves becoming middlemen, the Portuguese in the sixteenth and seventeenth centuries had done more to disrupt trade from the interior than to capture it. Malaria, the absence of major navigable rivers and the difficulties of transportation on the mainland discouraged Europeans from venturing inland for trade; the profits appeared too small, the hazards too great. At the coast, however, the demand for the products of the interior was on the increase long before 1840. In the late eighteenth and early nineteenth centuries there had been a flourishing trade in slaves from Kilwa to the French islands in the Indian Ocean to provide labour for sugar cultivation. American merchants, initially attracted to Zanzibar as a source of fresh water and food for their ships, soon discovered that they could sell muskets and mill-cloth from Massachusetts and purchase gum copal and ivory in exchange. By the 1840s American cloth had supplanted Indian calico and was becoming a widespread item of trade in the interior; the products of western industries were finding a new market. Through the encouragement of Said himself, the island of Zanzibar also contributed to the growth of external trade. The clove plantations, the most successful of his projects to transform the island's agriculture, were from the beginning intended to boost the value of exports.

By asserting monopoly control over the whole coastline, Said channelled East African imports and exports through Zanzibar. In place of the policy previously followed at Zanzibar of exacting the highest possible duties on trade goods, he appreciated the opportunity for an expanded market (and the increase of his own revenue) that would result from low import duties and the abolition of export charges. His commercial treaties with the United States (1833), Britain (1839) and France (1844) paved the way for regular commercial relations and the integration of the Zanzibar-based economic system with that of the trading states of the North Atlantic.

To satisfy the enhanced demand for ivory and for slaves to work on the clove plantations, Said encouraged Arab and Swahili traders to advance inland along the trade routes previously used only by the Africans of the interior. By the 1840s Arab caravans had reached the Great Lakes and were beginning to penetrate beyond into the Congo basin using their settlements at Unyanyembe and Ujiji to maintain the long-distance trade. The extension and intensification of the interior trade required considerable financial backing from Zanzibar and Said sought this from Indian merchants. The Indian commercial connection with East Africa was an ancient one but it had been disrupted by the Portuguese and by European rivalries in the Indian Ocean in the eighteenth century. With the attainment of naval supremacy by Britain during the Napoleonic wars and with the abolition of the East India Company's monopoly of overseas trade in 1813, Indian commerce with East Africa revived. As ruler of Muscat from 1806 Said had welcomed Indians as merchants and financiers and, though in the early years of his reign they were subjected to heavy taxation and arbitrary exactions in Zanzibar, he soon saw that the success of his commercial system depended on increased Indian participation. He granted them religious toleration on the island and in 1833 appointed an Indian merchant to the influential and profitable post of customs collector at Zanzibar. Previously, Indians had only been temporary visitors to the East Africa coast, but under Said many became permanent residents; the Indian population of Zanzibar rose from about 200 in 1819 to an estimated 3 000 in 1860. Indian merchants purchased the cargoes from American and European ships at Zanzibar, supplied these imported goods and their own financial backing for the caravans to the interior, and acted as export agents for the western business houses. One of the reasons for the leading role of the Americans in Zanzibar trade by the mid-nineteenth century was their close commercial co-operation with the principal Indian merchants. By the 1870s Indians also had a tight hold on the revenues of the sultanate, and in addition to investing their profits in the clove plantations, they were extending loans to the European traders[4]. Since Indians rarely participated directly in the interior trade, they and the Arab-Swahili traders were complementary parts of Said's economic system.

For Seyyid Said the role of middleman brought wealth and prestige. His clove plantations and investments in caravans and slave trading made him the richest merchant in Zanzibar. An even larger part of his wealth came from the farming out of the customs collections for these duties were considered his personal income not that of his estate. In 1828 the total customs revenues from Zanzibar were estimated at about £10 000, by 1834 they had doubled, and in 1859, three years after Said's death, they reached about £50 000. In the latter year exports from Zanzibar were calculated to be worth £755 000, of which ivory (£146 666), cloves (£55 666) and gum copal (£37 166) were the major items; imports, mainly of cloth, fire-arms, beads and wire, were estimated to be worth £908 911[5].

Although certainly very profitable, Said's position as middleman was neither easy nor secure. The Omani Arabs had succeeded in breaking Portugal's weak grasp on the East African coast by the end of the seventeenth century but they had not replaced it by a strong, centralised empire of their own. The Omani domain was a loose confederation of Arab traders, occasionally bound by common interest, more often riven by internal rivalry and factionalism. On his accession Said's authority over the coast was far from strong as the protracted struggle with the Mazrui clan of Mombasa demonstrated. The very geography of Said's domain, scattered along nearly three thousand miles of coastline from the Persian Gulf to Cape Delgado, and the absence of a fixed law of succession emphasised the internal weakness of the sultanate.

Externally, the position was even more precarious. Said's small navy was barely adequate to patrol and pacify his far-flung empire; it was quite incapable of fending off a determined European attempt to dismember his domain. This vulnerability was made apparent by the unofficial British 'protectorate' over Mombasa from 1824 to 1826 and in the early 1840s by the French annexation of Nossi Be and Mayotte, islands over which Said had shadowy claims. At Muscat during the Napoleonic Wars, Said had been able to exploit Anglo-French rivalries in the Persian Gulf and the Indian Ocean to preserve his independence and profit from their conflicting ambitions. By his commercial treaties and diplomacy at Zanzibar he tried to do the same, juggling with the political and commercial rivalries of Britain, France and the United States. But by 1840 it had become difficult for Said to control the game; he was losing his room to manoeuvre. The dominance of British naval power (and the distressing French appetite for his possessions) made Said more and more dependent on British support during the last sixteen years of his reign.

The British had their own reason for wishing to nudge Said into acknowledging their supremacy. Not the least of these was the British concern to protect the routes to their Indian treasure house. Although the British, acting through their East India Company, had thwarted the French bid for military and economic pre-eminence in southern India during the Seven Years War of 1756–63 and had limited their opponents to a few tiny enclaves, they continued to suspect French ambitions in India. Napoleon's invasion of Egypt in 1798 and his intrigues with rulers in the Persian Gulf and southern India caused a new wave of British annexations in India and ripples of diplomatic and naval activity in the gulf. The final defeat of Napoleon in 1815 did not end British fears for the safety of their Indian empire. The expansionism of Muhammad Ali's Egypt in the 1830s was, for example, seen as a French-inspired attempt to control the route to India.

India was a prize too valuable to lose. In addition to the readily accessible wealth that was plundered from India in the early period of British rule, the country provided the cotton textiles that were a principal item of British trade with Europe, America and West Africa in the seventeenth and eighteenth centuries. Indian cotton and later opium were essential commodities in British trade with China. With the onset of the Industrial Revolution in Britain in the late eighteenth century, cotton textiles from the mills of Lancashire rapidly displaced Indian hand-made cloth in foreign trade and, more gradually, within India itself. India became one of the principal markets for British cloth and its economy was distorted to provide agricultural raw materials—cotton, oilseeds, and jute among them—for Britain's industries and international trade.

It was, therefore, as ruler of Muscat, of a town poised so strategically on the route from the Middle East to India, that Said first attracted the attention of the British. He was cajoled and coerced into siding with them during the French Revolutionary and Napoleonic Wars, and as an ally he was encouraged to consolidate his hold on the Persian Gulf.[6] It was also in Britain's interest to maintain, even strengthen, his position on the East African coast as a check to any possible revival of French naval power in the Indian Ocean. The Indian merchants in Zanzibar constituted a further link between Britain's empire in India and the sultanate. In the fifty years between the outbreak of war with France in 1793 and the occupation of Sindh in 1843 the British gained control of western India either by outright annexation or by overawing the local princely states. Since this was the area from which most of the Indians at Zanzibar originated, the British claimed that they were British subjects and hence under British jurisdiction. The increasing number of Indian traders on the island and their crucial part in the Zanzibar system thus provided an important pretext for British intervention in the internal affairs of the sultanate. It was because of this connection that the British (like the Portuguese before them) regarded their relations with East Africa as primarily an aspect of their Indian Empire.

The East African slave trade was a second major reason for the assertion of British influence over Seyyid Said. Although the West African slave trade and the plantations in the Americas that it supplied played a considerable part in the development of British overseas commerce, with the advent of the Industrial Revolution the British bourgeoisie favoured a free labour economy in which the workers would compete to sell their labour for wages. The British revulsion against slavery became a crusade, endowed with all the moral fervour and assertiveness of a nation confident of the material strength of its civilisation. Had a minor European power declared itself against the slave trade, it might have been of little consequence. But Britain in the first half of the nineteenth century was sustained by the world's first industrial economy and armed with its most powerful navy. Britain, therefore, followed up the abolition of its own slave trade in 1807 with attempts to persuade and coerce other slave-trading states to follow suit. In 1822 Said signed the

Moresy Treaty with Britain banning the export of slaves from his domain to the territories of any Christian power. The treaty became the basis for subsequent British intervention in the external trade and entitled British naval vessels to seize Arab dhows alleged to be carrying slaves. In the decades that followed, dhow-chasing in Zanzibar waters was a constant reminder to the sultan of British naval power; neither France nor the United States could offer a rival show of strength. With the internal traffic in slaves, however, the British did not at this stage interfere. Since the economic and political power of the Arab-Swahili ruling class rested largely upon the internal trade and slave labour on the Zanzibar plantations, a premature move by the British to outlaw slavery would undermine the sultanate and hence the system of indirect control that they wished to preserve.[7]

But if India and the slave trade were Britain's primary concerns at Zanzibar, a direct commercial interest was not absent. Unlike their American counterparts, the British consuls were not themselves traders, but they nonetheless felt an obligation to encourage British commerce. The replacing of slaving by 'legitimate' (in effect meaning European) trade could be invoked to justify this though it was a paradox that the growth of Zanzibar's export trade, especially of cloves, had stimulated slavery. Britain's treaty with Said in 1839 was partly motivated by jealousy of the Americans with whom Said had signed a commercial agreement six years earlier. Although Britain had now entered the era of Free Trade, the British Consuls, beginning with Hamerton in 1840, sought to break the dominance of the American traders. In fact, their success was very limited and it was the disruption caused by the Civil War in the United States in 1861–5 and the subsequent decline in American shipping which gave Britain the upper hand in Zanzibar's foreign trade.

The British did not need to annex Zanzibar. They could achieve most of their ambitions through informal rule without the expense, the responsibility for administration, and, doubtless, the opposition that annexation would entail. It was, from the British viewpoint, unfortunate that American cloth sold infinitely better than British cloth, but beyond a degree of pressure from the consuls, British merchants could expect little direct assistance from their government in that respect. Moreover, the possibilities of suppressing the external slave trade and of guarding the route to India were far greater if the British could work through one dependent ruler than if they had to negotiate with several of conflicting loyalties.

With the death of Said in 1856 this indirect rule over Zanzibar was strengthened, Britain's consuls and navy dictated the succession to the sultanate and in 1861 it was the arbitration of the British Governor-General of India which brought about the separation of Zanzibar from Muscat. In 1862 the British persuaded the French to sign a joint declaration guaranteeing the independence of the sultan's domain. To judge by his earlier hostility to the British, Seyyid Barghash seemed likely to challenge British supremacy on his accession in 1870, but he was soon forced to see that if he wished to remain sultain he had to accept British direction and (under the threat of a naval blockade) a further restriction on the export of slaves as integral parts of the middleman's role that he had inherited from Said. The close relationship which grew up between Barghash and John Kirk, the British Consul-General at Zanzibar from 1873 to 1886 who became 'a sort of unofficial prime minister of Zanzibar'[8] was merely a logical outcome of the pattern of dominance established in Said's day.

The Zanzibar system was profitable for the sultans, but it rested on British domination and protection. For how long would it be before the middleman at Zanzibar was pushed aside and replaced by direct European exploitation and control of the mainland? In the early years of Barghash's reign the signs of impending change were already apparent.

The impact of industrial change

Before the second half of the nineteenth century the Europeans who visited coastal East Africa had lacked either the capacity or the inclination to penetrate and dominate the interior. But by the 1870s there were Europeans—explorers, missionaries and businessmen prominent among them—who believed that the region could and should be opened up for direct exploitation. This belief reflected confidence in the rapidly growing technical skills and economic power of their industrial societies. At the same time Britain, for so long the pioneer of industrialisation, was losing its position as the 'workshop of the world' in the face of competition from Germany, the United States, Belgium and other newly industrialised countries. In consequence, the pressures on East Africa to provide a market for European manufactured goods and to supply raw materials were greatly increased at precisely the time when Europe had acquired the capacity to draw the regions more closely into its economic system.

The initial stages of the Industrial Revolution in Britain were characterised by factory production of cotton cloth and by small-scale manufacture of textile machinery, cutlery, glassware and pottery. But by the 1830s British capital was urgently in need of new fields for investment and new areas of industrial expansion. Railways provided the breakthrough and enabled British industry to escape from the threat of stagnation. Between 1830 and 1870 extensive rail networks had been completed in Western Europe and the Eastern United States, and between 1840 and 1870 the world's railway mileage shot up from less than 5 000 miles to 130 000. During the second half of the century railways, generally employing British capital and construction firms, spanned North and South America, Eastern Europe, India and Australia. Initially many of the lines in Britain were built for passenger traffic, but it was soon apparent that the major economic contributions of the railway lay in the bulk transportation of freight and in stimulating heavy industrial production, especially iron, coal and machinery. In Britain, Germany, Belgium, and France railways hastened the integration of the national economies and fostered regional specialisation. On a world-wide scale, railways produced a similar re-orientation. The manufactured goods from industrial centres in Western Europe and north-eastern United States could be carried far into the continents of the globe undermining local economies which had previously been largely isolated. In return the railways drew from these areas the primary products in demand in the industrial regions. Around the industrial zones of Western Europe and the American north-east there was now a ring of satellite economies—Russia, India, China, Australia, New Zealand, Canada, the south and west of the United States, and Argentina.

The railway was not the sole contributor to the rapid expansion of the international economy in the second half of the nineteenth century. Bulk transportation by rail was complemented by improvements in the capacity and speed of long-distance shipping. Sailing vessels reached a peak of performance in the third quarter of the century, but of greater long-term significance was the triumph of steam navigation by the 1880s, despite earlier problems of construction and propulsion, and the introduction of refrigerated holds for the shipping of perishable foodstuffs. These developments enabled the haulage of bulk cargoes over vast distances at relatively low costs. As a result, between 1850 and 1890 the world's mercantile fleets increased from nine million to twenty million tons. British shipyards and shipowners were responsible for a large percentage of this growth and the building and running of steamships provided, like the railwavs, a major stimulus to the iron, coal and engineering industries.

Railways and steamships themselves made possible regular international communications, but the mid-century also witnessed the beginning of telegraph services. The first telegraph line was opened in the United States in 1844 and though Americans and Germans pioneered the development of overland and submarine telegraphic communications, the British quickly utilised their discoveries. In 1865, Britain was linked by cable to Calcutta and later lines were laid westward across the Atlantic and eastward to Australia, thereby drawing closer together the net of British imperial control.[9]

The opening of the Suez Canal in 1869 marked the beginning of the impact of the revolution in transport and communications on East Africa. Itself an achievement of modern engineering, the canal lopped two thousand miles off the sea journey from Western Europe to India, and since the canal could not be used by sailing ships, it hastened the development of steam navigation. The canal was constructed by French engineers and largely with French capital, but it was Britain which reaped the benefit. The Suez Canal rapidly became the main route for British imports of raw materials and food from Asia, Australia and New Zealand and for the export of British manufactures to the East. Already in the first years after its opening three-quarters of the shipping through the canal was British and by the 1890s sixteen per cent of British imports and twenty-one per cent of British exports passed through it. Since the canal was the quickest route by which troops could be sent to the East from Europe, it was of enormous economic and military importance to Britain.

The canal brought East Africa closer to the principal highways of expanding international trade. Direct British trade with Zanzibar had been growing during the 1860s, but between 1871 and 1879 the tonnage of British shipping at the harbour increased sevenfold. The value of all trade passing through Zanzibar had averaged £1 million a year between 1862 and 1872; by 1879 it had more than doubled to £2.2 million.[10]

Steam navigation strengthened the links between Zanzibar, India and Europe and made shipping independent of the monsoon winds which had previously dictated the flow of trade in the western Indian Ocean. At the time of Said's death in 1856, there had been no scheduled steamer calls at Zanzibar; but in 1871 a mail service began to link Zanzibar with the main British postal services in the Indian Ocean via the Seychelles. By the late 1870s three international steamship lines, one French and two British-owned, were running regular mail and passenger services to East Africa. The most important of these connections was the British India Steam Navigation Company headed by William Mackinnon, who was later to become the chairman of the Imperial British East African Company. Mackinnon's steamers plied between Zanzibar and Bombay and were subsidised by the British Government to carry mails to Aden. Zanzibar's communications were also supplemented in the late 1870s by submarine cables to Aden and Natal.

In 1860 Rigby, the British consul at Zanzibar, had complained that the absence of regular communication services with the island had been a severe hindrance to the growth of British trade in East Africa. Within twenty years of his complaint, the capital of the sultanate had been tightly bound within the new network of trade and communications. It was, moreover, inevitable that attempts should be made to apply these innovations to the penetration of the East African mainland.

Through the investigations of Krapf and Livingstone, Burton, Speke and Baker, European ignorance of the East African interior was replaced between 1847 and 1873 by at least a sketchy knowledge of its principal geographical features. At times unwittingly, but more often deliberately, these missionaries and explorers acted as the vanguard of European intervention. Livingstone in particular by coupling Christianity with the spread of 'legitimate' trade and by his earnest desire to end the internal slave traffic, provided a moral and material rationale of the closer integration of the interior with the economies of industrial Europe. The evangelical missionary movement had in large part been a reaction against the social disruption caused by industrialisation in Britain. While Engels and Marx had seen in the conditions of the British workers the epitome of the class oppression and exploitation inherent in industrial capitalism, the British bourgeoisie saw only the need for the adoption by the proletariat of the ethics of the middle class: self-improvement and enlightenment through education, temperance, religion and thrift. The evangelicals had first directed their attention to the correction of what they saw as the evils within their own society, but their abundant faith in their religion and in the material superiority of their society soon led them to propagate their views overseas, especially in India, China and Africa. The European ignorance of most of tropical Africa and the existence of the slave trade made Africa a particularly alluring field for missionary endeavour; here was a vast continent simply waiting, so it seemed to them, to be 'saved' from an even worse plight than had afflicted the urban poor of industrial Britain. Through the press, through public lectures and the publication of their journals, the missionaries and explorers attracted the attention of Western Europe and North America; they held that attention with accounts of the horrors of the internal slave trade and made dramatic appeals for its substitution by trade in western manufactures and local raw materials. Industrial capitalism could not have wished for a better publicity campaign.

Livingstone, whose own early career was a case-study in the middle class virtue of self-help, approached missionary work in East and Central Africa in a way characteristic of his own industrial society. Not only did he believe in the moral and material progress that would result from the spread of 'legitimate' trade, but he also sought to implement his objectives through the use of steamers on the rivers and lakes of the interior. Between 1858 and 1861 he attempted to use steam launches on the Zambezi, Shire and Ruvuma Rivers and, though his efforts were almost entirely abortive, the notion that steamers were the key to open Eastern Africa to Christianity and European commerce was not readily abolished. In 1875 the Free Church of Scotland missionaries were financed to conduct religious propaganda and trade around Lake Nyasa; the African Lakes Trading Company later took up the commercial side of their venture, hoping by the use of steamers to capture the lucrative ivory trade from the Arabs. With a similar idea in mind, in 1877 a Leeds businessman offered the London Missionary society £5 000 to purchase a steamer to operate on Lake Tanganyika. But on neither lake did the steamers lend to the easy development of European commerce which their promoters had anticipated.[11]

Other schemes for transportation on the mainland were advanced. There were experiments with ox-carts and camels in the 1870s and King Leopold of Belgium imported Indian elephants in the hope that they would prove a suitable means of transport to the Congo Basin. Livingstone had discussed the possibility of building rough roads from the coast to tap the interior trade and in 1876 James Stevenson, a Glasgow manufacturer and missionary patron, proposed a road to link Lakes Nyasa and Tanganyika named 'Stevenson Road'. It was cleared for the Lakes Company in 1878 but construction of the Dar es Salaam to Nyasa road was abandoned in 1881 after only seventy-three miles had been covered. Neither proved to be a commercial success.[12] Tsetse flies, malaria (despite the increasing use of quinine) and the difficulties of under-cutting Arab and African traders demonstrated the problems that still faced European commercial intervention. While human porterage remained the most successful method of transportation to the coast few commodities other than ivory were sufficiently profitable to attract European traders into the interior.

It was, therefore, becoming clear that railways alone, not steamers or exotic animals, could undercut the Arab-Swahili caravans and prise open the economy of the mainland. By the late 1870s it was being appreciated that railway construction would have to be a necessary *preliminary* to European exploitation. When in 1877–8 Barghash considered granting a concession to Mackinnon and his business associates, the prospecting concessionaires included among their proposals the construction of railways as well as roads and telegraph lines. Barghash, however, fearing that the concession would entail virtual loss of his claims to sovereignty over the main-land, shied away from the scheme. A year later, in 1879, there was also a French request for a railway concession from Bagamoyo to Ujiji but, under pressure from Kirk, Barghash refused to grant it.[13]

The mid-1880s saw a revival of British interest in East African railway schemes. In 1884 Harry Johnston, the naturalist and self-appointed advocate of British imperialism in tropical Africa, proposed the creation of a British colony around Mount Kiliman-jaro. In order to encourage European settlement in the area and to promote trade to the coast he suggested the building of roads and a railway. Once they had been constructed, he argued, 'trade will flow entirely into English hands'.[14] In April of the following year Frederick Holmwood, Kirk's principal assistant at Zanzibar, tried to revive Mackinnon's interest in an East African concession and again railways figured large in the proposals. The area around Kilimanjaro was, Holmwood claimed, 'the richest and most healthy in Tropical Africa' and it needed only railways to make it prosperous for European commerce.[15] Without government backing, however, Mackinnon and his associates would not undertake a concession in East Africa, but it is significant that once the British East African Company was formed under Mackinnon in 1888 the building of a railway to Uganda was one of its major objectives.

Crucial though the railways were seen to be, their construction would demand considerably greater capital resources than a missionary society or a handful of merchants could muster. Moreover, to build, run and derive profits from a railway would also require inputs of a different kind. It would need troops or police to guard it, engineers and clerks to run it, and an administration that would preside over the production of cash crops, or minerals whose transportation to the coast would provide the railway company with its profits. These were inputs such as only a well-financed trading company or colonial administration could provide. In colonial India or in the former colonies of North and South America there was already in existence a political, economic and administrative environment conducive to railway construction. In East Africa such preconditions did not exist; they would have to be created. Railways would, therefore, have to await a political initiative and before the late 1880s the British Government saw no reason to take that initiative.

The British Government did not conceive its task as one of transforming the internal economies of non-colonial territories for the benefit of businessmen. That is not to say that commercial expansion was of no significance to nineteenth-century British ministires, but they would not (with their attachment to laissez-faire) do the merchants' work for them. As the fate of China in the 1840s demonstrated, they were prepared to coerce foreign states into opening their ports to western trade and, once this had been achieved, keeping them open for British enterprise. But Zanzibar was already open to foreign trade and followed a system of virtual free trade. As British Foreign Office spokesmen repeatedly stressed, Zanzibar offered 'a very easy commercial system', it was up to the merchants to seize the opportunity.[16]

Nevertheless, in the face of growing external pressures on Zanzibar, British Governments had to amend their attitude. With

Egypt pressing southward down the Nile into Uganda and King Leopold's International African Association active in the Congo, the British favoured the expansion of Barghash's authority in the interior to pre-empt any claims from rival powers. In 1877 Kirk suggested to the Sultan the formation of a military force at Zanzibar for this purpose. It was set up under a British naval officer, Mathews, and from an initial corps of five hundred it was soon increased to over a thousand, equipped by the British with modern rifles. Although Barghash's navy had been destroyed by a hurricane in 1872, the sultanate was supplied with steamers (of which there were six by the time of Barghash's death in 1888) which were used by Mathews to suppress disturbances at Kilwa and Mombasa in the late 1870s and in 1880 his force established an advance base at Momboya, about 120 miles inland from Bagamoyo. In May 1885 a detachment under Mathews was sent to Kilimanjaro to forestall the anticipated German annexation of the region by persuading the local chiefs to declare themselves under the Sultan's protection.[17] Alarmed, too, at the activities of Leopold's agents in the Lake Tanganyika area, Barghash tried from 1882 to use the trader Tippu Tib to extend his authority into the Congo basin. However, by the time Tippu returned to Zanzibar in 1886 events in Europe had already precluded the Sultan's expansion inland. The Zanzibar system had been built upon commerce and control of the coast; it did not possess the administrative structure that the British now wished upon it. Even if the sultanate had made greater advances in that direction, the fate of Tunisia and Egypt in 1881–2 suggest that it would not have survived the onslaught of European economic and political intervention for very long.

Zanzibar and the East African mainland were of growing economic interest to Western Europe in the 1870s and early 1880s. Zanzibar remained the world's major supplier of ivory, a commodity which had risen rapidly in value since Said's death through the increasing demand in Europe and America. Ivory was, however, no longer the principal export. In 1879 it ranked third in value to rubber (£250 000) and cloves (£170 000).[18] The sudden emergence of rubber as the principal export item since the early 1870s reflected not only the changeover from slave trading at Kilwa, but also the demands of the industrial states which now needed rubber as an insulating material for the new electrical industry. Before rubber plantations were established at the end of the nineteenth century, wild rubber from South America and Tropical Africa was the only source of supply.

The import of Zanzibar was also reflecting changes in the western economies. In addition to the continuing market for cotton textiles, in the 1870s a demand emerged for American kerosene, itself a by-product of the new petroleum industry in the United States. In 1872, 2 000 cases of kerosene were imported into Zanzibar; by 1879 the figure had risen to 25 000 cases and kerosene was displacing local vegetable oils for lighting on the island and in some coastal areas.[19] A further indication of the impact of changing western technology on the East African economy was the massive import of firearms. In the first half of the century, European and American muskets had been purchased as trade goods for the interior, but from about 1860 there was a rapid increase in the volume of arms imports into Zanzibar. In part this may be attributed to an increasing demand in the interior associated with the intensification of the slave trade; but it was also a consequence of the large supply of obsolete arms and ammunition created by the transition from muzzle-loading muskets to breech-loading rifles and again to repeater guns which characterised western arms production between the mid-1860s and the mid-1880s. Europe's surplus was off-loaded in the African market.[20]

But the economic attraction of East Africa lay less in the existing character and volume of trade than in its potential. Livingstone, Cameron and Stanley had depicted for the West an Africa rich in minerals and agricultural products. Cameron, in particular, emphasised that although ivory would soon be exhausted, there were 'other lucrative sources of trade' which could be readily tapped once the proper communication links had been established. His lengthy list of available products included cotton, sugarcane, palm oil, tobacco, coffee, grains, rubber, as well as hides and such minerals as coal, copper and gold. He further suggested the construction of a railway from Mombasa to Lakes Tanganyika and Victoria which, he claimed, would at once make a profit from the ivory trade and by attracting Indians into the interior, would open up the economy for other forms of trade. In return Tropical Africa would absorb Britain's 'overglut' of manufactured goods.[21] Johnston's Kilimanjaro colony was to produce coffee, sugarcane, wheat and citrus fruits as well as tapping the existing trade in ivory; hides, beeswax, and iron. Since it was anticipated that it would be a long time before the local Africans became fully integrated into the money economy, Johnston's European settlers would be initial producers of cash crops and at first the main consumers of British manufacturers. Consul Holmwood in 1885 also stressed the potential of the Kilimanjaro region as an area for European settlers and, since 'tropical Africa will never become a manufacturing country', as a valuable market for British goods.[22]

There were mounting economic pressures in the industrial countries to warrant careful consideration of the potential of East Africa as a source of raw materials and especially as an outlet for manufactured commodities. In the first half of the nineteenth century Britain's industrial pre-eminence had been virtually unchallenged, but by the late 1870s it was facing severe competition from other industrial or industrialising countries. Germany, in particular, had leapt ahead as an industrial economy since the 1850s and the political unification of the country in 1871 also marked the integration of a previously fragmented economy.

During the period from 1873 to 1896 the industrial states were sunk in what is generally known as the Great Depression. Although trade and industry were not crippled for the whole twenty-three years, prices and profits remained low and there was widespread pessimism throughout capitalist Europe and North America as to the prospects for further economic advance. A major crisis of capitalism had set in. It was partly a consequence of the success of the transport revolution: cheap foodstuffs were flooding into Western Europe and although this produced an improvement in the living standards of the urban workers, it undermined the economies of the remaining agricultural sectors in these countries. The depression was also caused by industrial over-production—too many manufacturers chasing too few markets. Improved methods and the enlarged scale of production in the several industrial states created a glut of manufactured goods.

In response to these depressed conditions, European industrialists and agricultural producers sought government intervention to protect their interests. They pressed for a reversal of the trend towards Free Trade which had been such a marked characteristic of economic relations in the middle decades of the century; instead they wanted tariffs to protect their home markets from foreign competition. And they got them. From the late 1870s most of the nations of Europe introduced protective tariffs, and the United States, which had built up its industries behind moderate tariffs from the beginning of the century, began to make them more positively protectionist after 1875. Britain alone of the industrial states did not budge from its adherence to Free Trade. As the first industrial economy in a still largely agricultural world, Britain had benefited most by Free Trade and the working of laissez-faire capitalism, and its agriculture had been virtually sacrificed by the 1870s in favour of cheap foodstuffs to feed the urban population. Despite mounting evidence of the disadvantages of clinging to Free Trade it had become such an item of faith among the British middle class and among the growing number of working class voters that it remained untouched until the First World War.

The British economy was far more oriented to external trade than were the economics of other industrial countries. By the 1880s eighty per cent of Britain's wheat consumption was imported and a large share of its major industries—textiles, iron and steel, coal—depended largely either on imported raw materials or on overseas markets. With the spread of industrialisation and the imposition of tariffs, Britain found it increasingly difficult to compete in European and North American markets during the last quarter of the century. In addition to this disadvantage, as the pioneer of industrialisation, Britain had become complacent about its lead: in consequence, British technology and industrial organisation was falling behind that of Germany and the United States. The advances in steel-making and in the new chemical and electrical industries were either initiated or most quickly utilised by German and American industrialists; whereas by the 1880s industrial enterprises in Europe and North America were being consolidated into trusts and cartels to restrain competition and to control prices and output. British industry in general resisted this trend and remained more attached to small-scale production units. The age of monopoly capitalism dawned in Germany and the USA in the 1880s; it was not to reach Britain in any strength before 1900.[23]

British industry had from the beginning been closely tied to trade with less advanced economies; from the 1870s this pattern became even more pronounced. India, in particular, was a major market for Britain's textiles and iron goods, and its exports of primary products helped to subsidise Britain's trading deficit elsewhere. British manufacturers and traders had long hoped that China would become another India, its enormous population a seemingly unfailing outlet for the products of industrial Britain. South America, too, assumed increased importance in British overseas trade from the 1870s. But in both these areas British commerce was feeling the pinch of competition from other industrial countries.

The 'New' or 'Economic' Imperialism that dominated international politics in the 1880s can, therefore, be seen primarily in terms of the intensification of competition between the principal industrial states for a share of the world's markets. It was indeed a 'scramble' to partition the non-industrial world into colonies or 'spheres of influence' where the interests of one industrial state would prevail, secure from the competition of its rivals. It was an almost hysterical reaction to the crisis in industrial capitalism, feeding on a fear that the economic and hence political future of an industrial country rested on the exclusive control of markets and raw materials.[24]

Although Britain clung to the principle of Free Trade, in reality it was hard to maintain. It was widely believed by British businessmen, politicans and officials that since France and Germany had shifted from Free Trade to Protectionism at home, any overseas territories that they annexed would be served for the sole exploitation of the colonising power and British trade would be severely hampered or excluded by tariffs and other forms of discrimination. This belief was, for example, among the arguments that Holmwood put forward in 1884 for greater British control of East Africa.[25] At the Berlin Conference of 1884–5 one of the principal British concerns was to preserve the Congo as an area for international Free Trade, and hence for British enterprise, at a time when other parts of Africa were rapidly passing into French and German hands. British diplomats were eager to keep such areas open where possible, but they were prepared to resort to annexation where there seemed a danger of British exclusion from a valuable trading area.

With an economy so dependent on overseas trade, Britain could not afford to be pushed out of actually or potentially rich markets. But it was not this factor alone which prompted British politicians to move towards a more agressive imperialism in the 1880s; there were also pressures within British society which contributed. Primarily, these pressures can be explained in terms of the rapidly increasing power and political consciousness of the British working class.

Since the collapse of the Chartist movement in 1848–9 — the time of revolutionary upheavals in continental Europe—the British workers had been largely quiescent and they had, to some extent at least, shared in the prosperity of the mid-century boom. Living standards for the worker had begun to improve; factory legislation, cheaper food and higher wages helped to blunt the antagonism of worker to employer in the industrial centres. But by the 1880s a revival of class conflict was apparent. The trade union movement was beginning to reach beyond the skilled to the unskilled workers; the extension of the franchise to urban workers in 1887 and to rural labourers in 1884 created a significant working class vote even though universal franchise was withheld. Although many trade union leaders were content to seek political gains and parliamentary representation through the Liberal Party, by the early 1880s the first moves were being made towards a working class party. In 1881 a Marxist Party was formed, soon to become known as the Social Democratic Federation, followed in 1884 by the short-lived Socialist League. Coupled with large-scale unemployment caused by the Great Depression, these developments induced fear of a working class revolution in the minds of the propertied classes. As if to confirm their fears, in February 1886 a mass meeting of the unemployed in London became a direct assault on the wealthy: clubs and carriages in London's West End were attacked and the police were unable to check the crowds of unemployed until they had caused considerable damage to property. The incident was, in itself, a small one and the socialist leaders were too cautious to take advantage of it, but it heightened the awareness of both Liberal and Conservative politicans, Joseph Chamberlain and Lord Salisbury among them, of the rising power of the workers.[26]

Chamberlain, who had been President of the Board of Trade in the Liberal Government of 1880–5, began to question the old liberalism of laissez-faire and to favour state intervention on behalf of the workers at home and to press for a more aggressive policy overseas. Colonies were to provide new markets to revive trade and curb unemployment. Imperialism, as Cecil Rhodes later observed, was a bread and butter question and might be necessary to prevent class warfare in British society. Britain could only retain her industrial supremacy if it was united internally (and thus class antagonism minimised) as well as strong externally. By 1895, when Chamberlain became Colonial Secretary in a Conservative Government under Salisbury he had made imperialism and social reform his twin objectives; subsequently with markedly less success, he was to add the abandonment of Free Trade for Tariff Reform. But already in 1885–6 he was an advocate within the Liberal Government for staking British claims in East Africa. As a Conservative aristocrat, Salisbury's move to imperialist expansion was less dramatic than that of Chamberlain, the Birmingham manufacturer and middle class radical. But, nonetheless, Salisbury too wished to relieve internal social tension by moderate social reform and his role in the partition of Africa reflects a concern similar to Chamberlain's for the protection and growth of British industry and commerce. His style was aristocratic but his actions mirrored the apprehensions and aspirations of the British bourgeoisie.

For Britain the Great Depression thus produced a struggle to adjust in the fact of growing competition from industrial rivals and of internal conflict; the adoption of imperialism was one way of meeting these challenges and of preserving Britain's industrial capitalism. For Germany the depression represented a crisis of rapid capitalist growth and, coming so soon after the unification of 1871 it threatened to undermine the conservative political system that Bismarck, the German Chancellor, had been striving to create.

In order to restrain the liberalism and nationalism of the emerging bourgeoisie which had been manifested by the revolutions of 1848 in Germany, Bismarck had yoked the cause of liberal nationalism to the traditionalism of the Prussian Junker aristocracy. To cement this alliance Bismarck had satisfied the demands of the National Liberals for political unification and, in the period 1867 to 1878, for moderate social and economic policies. The onset of the depression called for major readjustments in Bismarck's political system so as to maintain the conservative *Reich*. Rapid industrialisation had created an urban proletariat and with it came the formation of socialist organisations, the principal of which was the Social Democratic Party founded in 1875. At the same time the policy of Free Trade to which Prussia and Germany had been moving during the 1860s and early 1870s left German agriculture and industry vulnerable to outside competition: the Prussian landholders were being undercut by cheap wheat from Russia; the steel and cotton industrialists were faced with British and French competition. By 1878 these two classes had allied in their demand for protective tariffs.

Bismarck saw the need for the state to play a more positive economic and political role than had been customary under laissez-faire capitalism. Under his direction (and it was Bismarck that Chamberlain later sought to imitate in Britain) the capitalist state became committed, cautiously at first, to a policy of state intervention. In 1878 Bismarck used the opportunity created by attempts to assassinate the German Kaiser to outlaw the socialists and to clamp down on trade unions, but he linked this with the introduction of state-sponsored welfare schemes between 1883 and 1889 designed to wean the marketing class away from socialism and a class identity and to cultivate the workers' loyalty to the capitalist state. In 1879 he moved decisively away from his former allies, the middle class National Liberals, to co-operate with the industrialists and the Junkers. The protective tariffs introduced in 1879 thus marked the beginning of state protection for industry and agriculture in the new Germany and since the power of the Junkers was declining relative to that of the industrialists, Bismarck was, in effect, acknowledging the increasing importance of heavy industry in the German economy.[27]

The first wave of the depression between 1873 and 1879 had resulted in protectionism and, when three years of improved trade were followed by a further period of depressed conditions, apprehension in German business circles as to the future for industry and exports stimulated demands for a colonial programme. Intellectual support for the colonial movement came from two quarters. The first comprised explorers and geographers, four of whom had attended King Lepold's conference on the Congo in 1878 at Brussels and two years later set up a 'German African Society' to promote interest in the continent. The second quarter was constituted by German writers, politicians, and academics who felt that their nation needed colonies overseas in which to settle Germany's surplus population. Between 1860 and 1880 there had been a massive migration of Germans overseas, mainly to the United States but also in lesser numbers to southern Brazil and Chile. If, it was argued, Germany had its own colonies these emigrants would not be completely lost to Germany but would retain close political and cultural ties, as well as economic connections that would be beneficial to the parent country. Thus when the interest of the German colonial societies turned to East Africa they thought not only in terms of cash crop production by the indigenous population and the consumption of German manufacturers, but also of white settlers in the upland areas. East Africa was to be Germany's

Australia as well as its India. The *Kolonialverein* (Colonial Association) formed in 1882 was primarily the agency for industrialists and merchants concerned for the expansion of Germany's overseas trade, but the *Gesellschaft für Deutsche Kolonisation* (Society for German Colonisation) formed in 1884 by Carl Peters drew its support mainly from the petty and middle bourgeoisie and was primarily interested in the creation of settler colonies.[28]

Ironically, in view of Germany's own adoption of protectionism, it was fear of exclusion from African trade that seems to have prompted the first official moves towards German colonisation in Africa. A mistaken interpretation of an Anglo-French agreement regarding the Sierra Leone coast signed in 1882 led the German Government to believe that France and Britain intended to monopolise trade on the coast of West Africa, a move which would damage the position of German traders already there.[29] Bismarck had repeatedly expressed himself against the creation of German colonies, but his objection was mainly formal colonisation; he was less hostile to protectorates in which German chartered companies could operate like the English East India Company in India before 1858, and for which they, not the German Government, would have to bear the cost and burden of administration. He was, therefore, prepared to authorise protectorates ,in 1884–5 when German commercial interests overseas seemed to be in danger. With growing competition between the industrial states and with the rise of protectionism, Bismarck feared that the complete exclusion of Germany from African and Asian trade would be detrimental to his country's long-term economic progress. At it was a responsibility of the capitalist state, as he saw it, to offer positive assistance to that progress. Although German trade with Africa in the mid-1880s was small, it was again its potential value which was considered important. As Bismarck later remarked: '. . . in twenty or thirty years' time, people will accuse that faint-hearted Chancellor of not having sufficient courage to secure what later may turn out to be such valuable possessions'.[30]

A further consideration behind Bismarck's decision to support the colonial movement in the mid-1880s was the need to build up national unity in the newly-created Germany, to give the state a greater sense of legitimacy than had come about through military victories and political agreements. The drive for colonies was attracting the sympathies of both the industrialists and the petit-bourgeoisie. For a politician who wanted to win elections and domestic political struggles in order to preserve his own conservative leadership, Bismarck found the appeal of nationalism a useful one. It not only helped him win a favourable majority in the German parliament in 1884, but it also detracted from the class and sectional conflicts within Germany.

Although in the early 1880s German colonial ambitions were initially focussed on West and South-West Africa, the east coast had long been an area of German commercial interest. In the 1840s, Hamburg merchants had begun a profitable trade by shipping cowrie shells from Zanzibar to West Africa where they were used as currency. By 1859 there were four German firms operating at Zanzibar and in that year the Sultan signed a commercial treaty with a representative of the German ports of Lubeck, Bremen and Hamburg. By 1870 German trade with Zanzibar had risen to second place after that of British India and it amounted to twenty per cent of the island's total trade. Kirk commented that he would not be surprised to soon see a German colony on the coast.

Certainly such an idea was in the air. In 1864 the German explorer von der Decken, travelling on the East African coast, had written about the economic advantages that Germany would gain from a colony there; also in view of the construction of the Suez Canal, he saw the value to the rising German naval power of a base on the coast, suggesting the purchase of Mombasa as a suitable site. Ten years later Vice-Admiral Livonius recommended to the German Government a protectorate over Zanzibar itself, but his proposal was shelved and not published until 1885.[31] Only by that date had Germany's internal demand for colonies become sufficiently pressing for its Government to act.

The scramble and the partition

The opening moves in the scramble came, however, not from Britain and Germany, nor from that other industrial giant, the United States, preoccupied with its internal development and its economic and political expansion in the Americas and the Pacific. Instead they came from the monarch of a smaller industrial state, King Leopold of Belgium.

Belgium was among the first European states to follow Britain into intensive industrialisation and Leopold was himself deeply influenced by the new industrial age. It was not surprising, therefore, that he conceived for Belgium a future as an imperial power. In 1863, two years before his accession to the Belgian throne, Leopold wrote a book (which was never published) in which he rejected the then-prevalent theory of Free Trade. He wanted Belgium to assume 'a more important place in the world' by acquiring an overseas empire that would be an exclusive market for its manufactured goods, a source of raw materials and wealth for the parent country, and a home for Belgian emigrants; in general, colonies would provide Belgium with profit and prestige.[32] Since Belgium had only attained statehood in 1830 and the position of its German-born monarch was insecure, Leopold (like Bismarck) may well have hoped the colonial adventures would foster internal unity and play down class tensions within the industrial society.

In the thirteen years after writing his book, Leopold, without support from within Belgium itself, dabbled in various schemes for Belgian colonies in Asia and Africa, but by 1876 his ambitions seem to have finally fixed on Central Africa to which attention had been drawn by the explorations of Livingstone, Stanley and Cameron. His International African Association was rapidly transformed from what claimed to be a purely humanitarian and scientific society into the vehicle for Leopold's colonial plans. The speed and cynicism of this transformation triggered off a race for control of tropical Africa. His method and those of his agents represented a new departure in European penetration and exploitation. By the end of 1883, for example, Stanley had at his disposal in his treaty-making for Leopold a troop of one hundred European and six hundred Africans, armed with a thousand repeater rifles, twelve Krupp guns and four early machine guns[33]. Leopold was also eagerly seeking the support of British and Belgian bankers and manufacturers to finance and implement his schemes for exploiting the Congo basin. In 1885 Mackinnon and his Manchester associates formed a company to build a railway to tap the interior; the project was, however, later entrusted to a Belgian construction company. Leopold was rushing in where the businessmen and governments of other countries, especially Britain, had been hesitant to tread.

His scheme soon had repercussions among the other European powers interested in Africa. Prompted by the explorer de Brazza, the French were not loath to follow where Leopold was leading. Still smarting from its defeat by Germany in 1870–1 and bitterly aware of falling behind Britain and Germany in economic strength and military power, France was beginning to see compensation in aggrandisement overseas. The British decision to occupy Egypt in 1882, though not at first intended to be a permanent step, intensified this drive: France wanted an African empire of its own. The French sought to expand their earlier coastal possessions deeper into the interior of northern and western Africa; the east coast had no immediate interest for them. But in East Africa the activities of Leopold's agents in seeking access from Zanzibar to the Congo aroused the suspicions of Barghash and Kirk and prompted the setting up of Mathews' force in 1877 to strengthen the Sultan's control of the interior. In fact by 1883 Leopold had lost interest in the east coast route and in gaining control of the area immediately to the west of Lake Tanganyika. Nevertheless, in 1884 Johnston was still warning of the danger of Leopold snapping up the Kilimanjaro bargain[34]. The British Government was more concerned with protecting free trade on the Congo. It was with the intention of preventing the Congo being closed to British commerce by French (or perhaps Belgian) customs duties that the British Government signed a treaty with Portugal in February 1884 recognising that country's long-standing claim to the Congo mouth. The treaty, however, proved immensely unpopular with the British middle class press and public (because Portugal's complicity in the slave trade was notorious), and the government was forced to abandon this treaty. Egged on by an indignant Portugal and by the ambitious Leopold, Bismarck decided to hold an international conference to settle the issue of the Congo—the Berlin Conference of 1884–5.

Bismarck, too, was disturbed by the character and scale of Leopold's Congo enterprise. In August 1884 Leopold, seeking German recognition for the territorial claims of the International African Association, drew a map of the proposed boundaries of his Congo state. The area claimed was far larger than the few posts of the association could possibly justify: from 4° North, across to Lake Tanganyika and southward to 6° South. This alarmed Bismarck, but in October 1884 he agreed to recognise the Congo Free State. However, in January 1885 Leopold, not satisfied with even this vast area, extended his claim a further four degrees to the south to the watershed of the Congo and the Zambesi.[35]

Coupled with Bismarck's concern at the possible loss of German trade with West Africa discussed earlier, the ambitions of the Belgian king persuaded him of the need to act quickly for German commercial interests before the whole of Africa was gobbled up. Accordingly, in April 1884 Bismarck announced a German protectorate over Angra Pequena in South West Africa followed by the annexation of the Cameroons and Togoland between July and October 1884. In October, too, the German explorer Rohlfs was appointed Consul-General at Zanzibar and rumours abounded in the German press that his appointment would shortly be followed by a German protectorate over the sultanate. In November, when the Berlin Conference opened, Carl Peters of the *Gesellschaft für Deutsche Kolonisation* arrived in Zanzibar and shortly after began his treaty-making on the mainland west of Bagamoyo. Although the German Government frowned on Peters' activities at first, his treaties formed the basis for the declaration of a German protectorate in East Africa on 3 March 1885, a day after the Berlin Conference had closed. The allocation and division of East Africa had begun.

It progressed quickly. The initial British response to the rumours of German ambitions in East Africa had been to cling to the traditional policy of acting through the Sultan. In December 1884 Kirk persuaded Barghash to sign an agreement that he would not cede sovereign rights or territories to any association or power without prior British consent. Gladstone, the British Liberal Prime Minister from 1880 to 1885, rejected the proposals for a more 'forward' policy advanced by Chamberlain and other members of the Cabinet: informal influence, not the burden of colonial administration, was what Gladstone believed in.

But clearly the old system could not survive much longer. When Barghash protested at the German protectorate over territories that he claimed lay within his sultanate, the German Government responded by sending five warships to Zanzibar. This was the first time that a Sultan of Zanzibar had had to face an effective naval presence other than that of the British and it was an indication of the changing balance of power in East Africa. In consequence, Kirk persuaded the Sultan that he withdraw his protests against the German protectorate. The British, who had once warded off French attempts to snatch part of the sultanate, were now assisting in its dismemberment by Germany. And in the wake of Germany, Italy, imitating German tactics of threatening the Sultan with naval force, sought concessions for itself from Zanzibar; even Portugal moved troops up to the north of Mozambique to enforce a claim to Tungi

Bay. How the sultanate would be divided among the European powers was now a matter for arrangement among themselves; the Zanzibari middleman no longer had a role to play.

The geographical area of the German protectorate was at first extremely ill-defined, but Peters and his associates (now organised as the German East African Company—*Deutsche Öst-Afrika Gesellschaft*, or DOAG) with the support of Bismarck set about extending it with treaty-making expeditions southward across the Rufiji and northwards to Kilimanjaro. The protectorate urgently needed an outlet to the sea to be a viable proposition, and again Barghash was coerced into granting the DOAG the use of Dar es Salaam. These German moves brought into question the whole nature of the Sultan's authority over the coast. The 1862 Anglo-French declaration had guaranteed the independence and integrity of the Sultan's domains but had failed to define them. Mathews' force had made Zanzibar's control of the coast more effective than previously, but in the face of the German onslaught this was virtually ignored. In September 1885 a joint commission of Britain, Germany, and, because of the 1862 declaration, France, was appointed to define the limits of the Sultan's authority. After extensive investigations, during which the British representative, Kitchener, found considerable evidence of the Sultan's control over a broad coastal belt and inland around Tabora and Kilimanjaro, the views of the German commissioner were accepted: in addition to Zanzibar, Pemba and Mafia the sultanate retained a narrow strip of coast from Tungi Bay to Lamu and thence intermittently to Warsheik. On the coast Germany was granted rights to Witu as well as Dar es Salaam. The report of the commission produced in June 1886 soon became part of a broader agreement—again determined arbitrarily without consultation with the Sultan. In October and November 1886 the British and German Governments agreed that the Sultan's domains on the mainland would be confined to a strip ten miles in width along the entire coast with the exception of two German harbours, but they divided the interior between themselves; a German sphere of influence to the south, a British one to the north. The boundary between the two was drawn from the mouth of the River Umba to Lake Victoria skirting round the north of Mount Kilimanjaro. The French, who were given little say in the division, were consoled with the recognition of their protectorate over the Comoro Islands, where the Sultan also had claims. Barghash, denied a voice in either the commission or the Anglo-German settlement, had no alternative but to accept the decisions of the European powers in December 1886.[36]

During this first phase of the partition of East Africa the British Government had been conciliatory towards Germany. This was not because of British disinterest in the area but because in 1885–6 the British Government was faced with crises elsewhere which were reckoned of greater importance to imperial interests than East Africa. The British occupation of Egypt in 1882 had been intended to suppress the nationalist revolt of Arabi Pasha, to protect British investments in the country and to guard the route to India. But in the process of attempting to salvage a regime favourable to their interests, the British commander, General Gordon, at Khartoum in January 1885 plunged Gladstone's government deeper into Egyptian affairs.

On the borders of India, too, British interests were being challenged. Russian troops were moving into Afghanistan, which commanded the north-western approaches to the British empire in India. In the early months of 1885 there seemed a possibility of war between Britain and Russia for control of Afghanistan. Without an ally among the European powers, Britain was eager to cultivate German friendship so as to strengthen its international position. Conceding German demands in East Africa seemed a high but necessary price to pay for diplomatic support.

But the British were determined not to lose all the East African prizes. Although Kilimanjaro fell within the German sphere of influence in 1886, the area to the north was considered well worth retaining, especially as it could provide access to Uganda, the 'pearl of Africa', as Stanley described it. There had already been missionary activity at the court of Kabaka Mutesa of Buganda and commercial interest had been awakened by reports of the early explorers of the fertility of the land and its wealth of ivory. The importance of Uganda in the eyes of the British occupation there seemed to be the more vital since it appeared to British imperial strategy to dominate the course and headwaters of the Nile and to prevent their control by a possibly hostile European power. The Conservative government of Lord Salisbury, in office from July 1886 to August 1892, sought to exclude Germany in the south, and Italy moving in from the east through Ethiopia, from advancing into the upper Nile valley.[37] The ramifications of the British preoccupations with the Suez Canal and India were also affecting the Salisbury government's attitude to the East African coast. Although little heed had been paid to the suggestion of Kitchener in 1886 that the British should acquire Mombasa as a naval base to counterbalance the German naval presence at Dar es Salaam, it was appreciated that in the event of the closing of the Suez Canal during a major international conflict Zanzibar would command an important stretch of the Cape route to India. Moreover, the strategic importance of Zanzibar had been increased not only by the German protectorate on the mainland, but also by the French annexation of Madagascar. Again, commercial motives on the coast were not absent. Kirk and Holmwood emphasised that most of the trade of Zanzibar passed through the hands of British Indians and they therefore argued that the British Government should allow its subjects to pass under the rule of another European powers,[38] and Zanzibar, despite the German protectorate, remained and was likely to long remain the entrepot of East Africa.

Salisbury's government was prepared to take a more positive attitude towards East Africa and to provide the support for British commercial enterprise which had previously been lacking. On the initiative of Holmwood, Mackinnon made a second attempt to form a company to exploit East Africa. In May 1887 the British East Africa Association was set up, transformed a year later into the British East Africa Company with a capital of £250 000, subscribed by Mackinnon and his associates. Salisbury agreed in September 1888 to grant the company a charter which was tantamount to official approval and backing.

No small consideration in Salisbury's mind seems to have been the company's plan to build a railway from the coast to Uganda which would bring the latter firmly within British control. The 1886 agreement with Germany had not defined limits for the western boundaries of the British and German spheres of influence and Salisbury was eager for commercial and strategic reasons that the British company should stake out its claim there before the Germans. Once established, the company had its economic incentive to get to Uganda first: failure to do so would be a 'very serious blow' to its commercial future since Ugandan ivory was expected to provide the initial profits for the company until other forms of trade and exploitation could be developed.[39] It sent out its first expeditions from Mombasa at the end of 1889, but by the time the company's agent, Jackson, reached Buganda in April 1890 Carl Peters was also treaty-hunting in the area.

The Ugandan question was, however, settled without reference to the activities of Jackson and Peters. Bismarck had not favoured unlimited German expansion in eastern Africa: Peters, Bismarck notes as early as October 1886, 'has an appetite that is far greater than our requirements of our powers of digestion'.[40] Bismarck had been disillusioned, too, by the effects of the DOAG's administration in East Africa. The outbreak of organised resistance against German rule in 1888 had drawn the German Imperial Government into precisely the expense and responsibility that Bismarck had wished to avoid and in 1890 it had to take over direct control of the protectorate. With Bismarck's fall from power in March 1890, Caprivi, his successor as Chancellor, was eager to reach an agreement with Britain over East Africa and to stabilise the situation there. For their part the British were in a stronger position than in 1885–6. The Egyptian issue was less pressing; the Afghanistan crisis had passed; and British co-operation had been essential to the Germans in their suppression of the Abushiri rising. Indeed, it became clear during the rising that Britain would not allow Germany to intervene in Zanzibar itself and British participation in the Anglo-German naval blockade in 1888–9 was partly designed to restrain Germany from any aggressive designs against the Sultan. As Salisbury observed, 'the English and Indian interests are both too strong' to permit Germany to add Zanzibar to its East African empire.[41]

In 1890 Anglo-German agreement was, accordingly, far more a recognition of British interests than that of 1886. German East Africa was now contained, boxed in on the north, east and south-west by British possessions, and to the west along Lake Tanganyika by the Congo Free State. The north-western boundary of 1886 was extended across Lake Victoria to give Uganda to the British. In the south-west the British missionaries in the Lake Nyasa area and the 'Stevenson Road' provided a suitable pretext for fixing the boundary between Lakes Nyasa and Tanganyika. Even if Salisbury was himself willing to compromise with German claims to the 'hinterland' of German East Africa, evangelical public opinion in Britain created a powerful lobby for the exclusion of the Germans and the Portuguese from the shores of Lake Nyasa. Germany was also persuaded to abandon her claims to Witu which, it had been feared by Mackinnon and Salisbury, would be used as a base for a second German colony on the coast that would cut off British East Africa from the interior. Although the Sultan was allowed to keep a nominal sovereignty over the coast of British East Africa, his right to the southern coast was finally ceded to Germany for a payment of £200 000. Germany was obliged to recognise a British protectorate over Zanzibar, the final stage in the long process of reducing the sultans to mere puppets of the British. Germany was compensated for these concessions and compromises not in Africa but in the North Sea. The tiny island of Heligoland (from which the 1890 partition is often known as the Heligoland Agreement) was ceded to Germany. Although a barren rock, the island had been coveted by German naval enthusiasts because it commanded the approaches to Germany; it was a suitable sop to German nationalist sentiment.[42]

The Anglo-German agreement of 1886 had been the first sketch for the partition of East Africa; that of 1890 virtually completed the process. During the next year Britain signed treaties with Italy and Portugal to demarcate the remaining areas of British interest in eastern Africa. The actual partition of East Africa was, therefore, arranged in the course of five years, but it was the culmination of more than fifty years of increasing European involvement in the region. The sultanate of Zanzibar had served its purpose. By 1890 it was confined to the islands of Zanzibar and Pemba and was firmly under British control. Its role on the mainland was over, discarded in favour of direct European exploitation and rule.

In the long-term perspective the partition of Africa in the 1880s and 1890s may appear an historical anomaly, a curious interlude in which domination through informal control was superseded by colonial rule. The strength of American imperialism today suggests that indirect rule is the more 'natural' form of domination by advanced capitalist economics over their satellites. But in the late nineteenth century the partition of tropical Africa was an historical necessity for the capitalist industrial states. The pressures created by the Great Depression and by the intense competition between several industrial economies drove the politicans and rulers of Western Europe to seek formal and exclusive control of such areas as they could acquire. Moreover, by the 1870s and 1880s informal rule through the Zanzibar sultanate or other intermediate had too many limitations: they could not readily provide a suitable environment for European trade and investment in the interior. A period of direct European intervention was necessary to create an infrastructure—railways, a cash crop economy, a western-oriented business class and administrative elite—and only once it had been firmly established did formal colonial rule become obsolete. For by then the economic and social structure had become so moulded to suit the requirements of metropolitan capitalism that the colony could not easily escape from its grasp.

Notes

1 R. Coupland, *The Exploitation of East Africa, 1856–90*, London, 1939, p. 102.

2 R. Robinson and U. Gallagher, *Africa and the Victorians: The Official Mind of Imperialism*, London, 1961, A.J.P. Taylor, *Germany's First Bid for Colonies, 1884–5*, London, 1938.

3 In particular, J. Flint, 'The Wider Background to Partition and Colonial Occupation', in R. Oliver and G. Mathew, eds., *History of East Africa*, 1, London, 1963, pp. 352–90.

4 J.S. Mangat, *A History of the Asians in East Africa*, London, 1969, ch. 1.

5 C.E.B. Russell, *General Rigby, Zanzibar and the Slave Trade*, London, 1935, pp. 342–3; C.S. Nicholls, *The Swahili Coast*, London, 1971, pp. 202, 234–5, 373.

6 A detailed account of these developments can be found in Nicholls, *Swahili Coast*, ch. 4.

7 R.D. Wolff, 'British Imperialism and the East African Slave Trade', *Science and Society*, xxxvi, 4, 1972, pp. 450–1.

8 Coupland, *Exploitation*, p. 266.

9 E.J. Hobsbawn, *Industry and Empire*, London, 1968, pp. 109–91; W. Ashworth, *A Short History of the International Economy, 1850–1959*, London, 1952, pp. 62–75.

10 Coupland, *Exploitation*, pp. 77 8, 319.

11 R. Oliver, *The Missionary Factor in East Africa*, London, 1952, pp. 34–44.

12 J.B. Wolf, 'Commerce, Christianity, and the Creation of the

Stevenson Road', *African Historical Studies*, iv, 2, 1973, pp. 363–71.

13 Coupland, *Exploitation*, pp. 306–7, 343.

14 R. Oliver, *Sir Harry Johnston and the Scramble for Africa*, London, 1957, pp. 66–8.

15 M.E. Chamberlain, 'Clement Hill's Memoranda and the British Interest in East Africa', *English Historical Review*, lxxxvi, 344, 1972, p. 542.

16 Chamberlain, 'Hill's Memoranda', pp. 538, 539–40.

17 R.N. Lyne, *An Apostle of Empire: Being the Life of Sir Lloyd William Mathews*, London, 1936, pp. 45–7, 66–74, 92.

18 Coupland, *Exploitation*, p. 319.

19 N.R. Bennett, 'Americans in Zanzibar, 1865–1915', *Tanganyika Notes and Records*, 60, 1963, p. 8.

20 R.W. Beachey, 'The Arms Trade in East Africa in the Late Nineteenth Century', *Journal of African History*, iii, 3, 1962, p. 45.

21 V.L. Cameron, *Across Africa*, London, 1877, ii, pp. 324–34.

22 Oliver, *Johnston*, pp. 67–8; Chamberlain, 'Hill's Memoranda', p. 542. Not all the early explorers were optimistic about the possibility of trade and European exploitation in East and Central Africa; see J. Thomson, *To the Central African Lakes and Back*, London, 1881, ii, ch. 6.

23 D.S. Landes, *The Unbound Prometheus*, Cambridge, 1969, ch. 5.

24 For an interpretation of British imperialism see D.C.M. Plath 'Economic Factors in British Policy during the "New Imperialism"', *Past and Present*, 39, 1968, pp. 121–38.

25 Chamberlain, 'Hill's Memoranda', p. 540.

26 B.B. Gilbert, *The Evolution of National Insurance in Great Britain*, London, 1969, pp. 21–39.

27 H.U. Wehler, 'Bismarck's Imperialism, 1862–90', *Past and Present*, 48, 1970, pp. 139–42.

28 H.P. von Strandmann, 'Domestic Origins of Germany's Colonial Expansion under Bismarck', *Past and Present*, 42, 1969, p. 15.

29 H.A. Turner, 'Bismarck's Imperialist Ventures', in P. Gifford and W.R. Louis, eds., *Britain and Germany in Africa*, Newhaven, 1967, pp. 48–56.

30 Strandmann, 'Domestic Origins', p. 145.

31 R. Coupland, *East Africa and its Invaders*, London, 1938, pp. 316, 381–6; *Exploitation*, p. 81.

32 H. Brunschwig, *French Colonialism, 1871–1914*, London, 1966, pp. 31–2.

33 N. Ascherson, *The King Incorporated: Leopold II in the Age of Trusts*, London, 1963, p. 122.

34 Coupland, *Exploitation*, pp. 331–5, 346–50; Oliver, *Johnston*, p. 70

35 J. Stengers, 'The Congo Free State and the Belgian Congo before 1914', in L.H. Gann and P. Duigan, eds., *Colonialism in Africa, 1870–1900*, Cambridge, 1969, pp. 275–6.

36 Coupland, *Exploitation*, ch. 19.

37 Robinson and Gallagher, *Africa and the Victorians*, ch. 10.

38 Mangat, *Asians in East Africa*, pp. 25–6.

39 M. Perham, *Lugard: The Years of Adventure, 1858–98*, London, 1956, chs. 10 and 11.

40 C.J. Lowe, *The Reluctant Imperialists*, vol. I, London, 1967, p. 125.

41 *Ibid.*, p. 128.

42 A.C. McEwen, *International Boundaries of East Africa*, London, 1971, pp. 174–7; Lowe, *Reluctant Imperialists*, pp. 133–7.

3. Tanzanian Societies and Colonial Invasion 1875–1907

A.J. Temu

European influence before partition

During the last quarter of the nineteenth century Tanzanian societies, among others in East Africa, faced the last of the external factors which confronted them in the nineteenth century. In chapter 1 Dr Sheriff has discussed the economic, political and social set-up of these societies, and has analysed in detail the way the other factors—long distance trade and the Ngoni invasion—affected their political, economic and social institutions. One bold generalisation which can be made about the impact of these factors is that they made strong societies stronger and weak ones weaker. European imperialism was the last external factor affecting Tanzanian societies and indeed those of East Africa in the nineteenth century. It began to encroach on them during the last twenty years of the century, at a time when they had already taken initiatives and made major innovations to solve the problems brought mainly by the other two external factors.

On the eve of this invasion the societies of Zanzibar and Pemba and the coast opposite had many similar characteristics. Two main social classes could be identified: the Arab ruling and landed aristocracy and the African labouring class, a majority of whom were slaves.[1] Between the two was a small class of Indian financiers and money lenders. The ruling class had developed commercial contact with Europe and Asia for many centuries but this contact intensified when the Sultan, Seyyid Said, moved his headquarters to Zanzibar in 1840. The growing demand for ivory, cloves and rubber by industrial Europe and America gave a further incentive to the Sultan and the Arabs to develop and exploit the ivory trade with the deep interior of Tanzania which had been largely in the hands of the Africans themselves before the 1840s.

The same demand for cloves and rubber led to the development of large plantations of these crops on the islands and on the coast; cloves were developed on the islands while rubber was developed on the coast, particularly the southern coast. Land and labour were required for the development of these plantations; thus the Arabs acquired large areas of land and stepped up the importation of labour in the form of slaves from the mainland, to work mainly on the clove plantations. The impact of this commercial contact between the islands and Europe was that it drew the whole of today's Tanzania into the international capitalist trading network.

From the late 1830s onwards trading houses were established in Zanzibar from leading firms in Europe and America in order to tap this trade and consular missions from Britain, America, France and Germany were established in Zanzibar to develop and strengthen this association.[2]

If the amount of customs duties realised in Zanzibar can be taken as an indicator of the integration of East Africa into the capitalist world, this integration had by the second half of the century become spectacular. For between 1828 and 1859 the amount realised from exports of ivory, cloves, gum-copal, cowries and sesame seeds had multiplied fivefold, having been £10 000 in 1828. In 1867 Zanzibar earned £663 500 from exports of ivory, $321 000 from exports of cloves and $100 000 from exports of gum-copal, cowries and sesame seeds each. The tonnage of European and American shipping using Zanzibar harbour rose from 18 877 tons in 1859 to 27 626 tons in 1871, thus further demonstrating this integration.[3] The role of the Sultan as the initiator and director of this trade cannot be overemphasised. But it is significant to note that his was essentially the role of a middleman.[4]

Alongside this commercial penetration of East Africa went missionary penetration which, as it became intensive in the last quarter of the century, after 1873, served to further integrate Tanzania with the western world.[5] Missionaries of different societies from Europe came and used Zanzibar mainly as a base for stepping into the mainland which was the main target of their operations. For there were large societies of Africans to be converted to Christianity and to be 'civilised'.

The first missionaries to arrive in Zanzibar were those of the

Church Missionary Society in 1844. Their original intention had been to work among the Galla but having found Ethiopia hostile to the establishment of a base there, they decided to approach them from the East African coast. After obtaining permission from the Sultan of Zanzibar to establish their mission in his country, the CMS moved into the Kenya coast and established a mission station at Rabai, a few miles from the coast, where they immediately began to work among the freed slaves they had brought with them. Not before the abolition of the slave trade in 1873 did the CMS establish another station at Freretown in 1874. Using these two stations as their base they moved through the Mombasa-Taveta caravan route and established a mission station in Moshi on the slopes of Kilimanjaro in 1885. This was in response to the invitation extended to the CMS by Mandara, Chief of Moshi, to build a mission in his country. By the following year, when the first partition of East Africa was agreed upon by Britain, Germany and France, four other stations—Mamboia, Mpwapwa, Uyui and Masalala, in central and western mainland Tanzania — had been established.[6]

The Universities Mission to Central Africa arrived in Zanzibar and moved into the interior to establish their first station at Magila in the Usambara mountains in 1868 and at Masasi and Newala in southern Tanzania in 1876. In 1860 the missionaries of the order of Les Filles de Marie had arrived in Zanzibar from the Reunion and they were soon joined by two Fathers of the Holy Ghost Mission. The order of Les Filles de Marie decided to withdraw from Zanzibar due to lack of financial resources and manpower and left the ground to the Holy Ghost Fathers. In 1868 the Fathers established themselves at Bagamoyo where they bought land and worked mainly among the liberated slaves. From here they moved into the Uluguru mountains where they established a mission station at Monda, a few miles from Morogoro. Further inland, in Unyanyembe, the Fathers of the Société de Missionnaires d'Afrique (Pères Blancs) arrived and established a station at Tabora in 1881. Their number was increased by the arrival of Father Lourdel and a group of ex-slaves fleeing from Mwanga's purge of Christians in his court, in the kingdom of Buganda in 1886.

Missionary societies from Germany were as late in the field as the Germans were in the European race for colonies.[7] Indeed, German missionary societies followed in the footsteps of the German East Africa Company and the German Imperial Government.

First to arrive were the Benedictines who established a station at Pugu a few miles from Dar es Salaam in 1888, then the representatives of Berlin III established themselves in Dar es Salaam in 1890 and branched off to the neighbouring areas to establish a station at Kisarawe (1891) and Maneromango (1895). From 1891, Berlin I and the Moravians, who approached the southern province and highlands of Tanzania from South Africa, established mission stations in the area: the Moravians at Rungwe and Berlin I in Usangu. The Lutheran Society followed much later and began to work among the Chagga, taking over the CMS mission station at Moshi in 1893.

Up to 1900 these missionaries had made little if any impact among the African societies. Like the earlier societies which had preceded them, they worked among the freed slaves. Most of them, like the Berlin I and the Moravians, avoided the Muslim coast and the Muslim settlements, but even these did not have much success before 1900. The reason for this is not difficult to discover, for during this period Germany was in the process of conquering the interior, and the missionaries, like the imperial conquistadores, were resisted and attacked. The Berlin III had after all grown out of the German Colonisation Society and, viewed from that perspective, its operations and activities were the same as those of the imperial agents. Nevertheless, these had laid the foundation for the further integration of Tanzanian societies with the West. After 1900, with the help of imperial agents, missionaries began to expand their work among the peoples of mainland Tanzania.

One aspect of the missionaries' work which brought them into sharp conflict with the Arab landed aristocracy and ruling class was their opposition to the Arab social institution of slavery, the abolition of which the missionaries turned their attention to after the abolition of the slave trade in East Africa in 1873. Elsewhere I have discussed the conflict which occurred from 1880–90 between the Muslim society on the Mombasa coast and the Christian missionaries who had established mission stations in their midst.[8] Suffice it to mention here that the campaigns that the missionaries waged against the Arabs, and especially against their social institution of slavery, was one cause of the antagonism between the two. More important, perhaps, was the economic ruin of their plantations and estates brought about by the missionaries' action of harbouring runaway slaves between 1875–90, thus robbing them of the labour force required for the development of these estates. Open conflict erupted on the coast with the result that a lot of the property of the missions and houses were destroyed. The missionaries might have been driven out of the coast in the 1880s had it not been for the intervention of the British Consul General, who, working through the Sultan of Zanzibar, helped to ease the tension. The timely arrival of the British East African Company on the scene in 1888 saved the situation for, anxious to establish peaceful trade, the directors of the company were prepared to conciliate the Arab aristocracy as best they could. Consequently they entered into negotiations with them and agreed to pay them a compensation of £3 500 for the total of 1 400 slaves who were found in the mission stations.[9]

On the mainland coast no such conflict occurred because the UMCA established themselves further into the interior in a primarily non-Muslim area and did not, at least initially, pose such a serious economic threat to the local rulers of the area, Kimweri of Shambala in particular. But more importantly they had been welcomed by Kimweri himself who, during the period of his rule from the early nineteenth century to the 1860s, controlled them and their activities.

At Bagamoyo, forty miles north of Dar es Salaam where the Holy Ghost Fathers had settled and bought a large piece of land and worked among the liberated slaves, the Fathers adopted a conciliatory policy towards the Arabs and successfully avoided provoking them into attacking them as occurred with the CMS on the Mombasa coast. Being less arrogantly hostile to slavery, the Holy Ghost Fathers refrained from giving direct incentives to the slaves to run away from their masters to seek refuge in their stations. Consequently they were not drawn directly on to the politics of the coast and of the island as the CMS on the Kenya coast, for example, were, making the Arabs and Swahili less hostile to them. It is no wonder then that Abushiri and Bwana Heri, the two future leaders of the coastal resistance, never came to attack them. Rather they used them as intermediaries when seeking negotiations with the German aggressors, thus demonstrating the success of the Holy Ghost Fathers' cautious policy towards the Arab landed aristocracy on the Tanzania coast and islands.

The further into the interior of Tanzania one got, the more the power of the Sultan of Zanzibar diminished. African chiefs here did not recognise his political claim to their areas and they conducted their affairs with outsiders in the way they themselves thought best. For various reasons the missionaries posed a political and social threat to them and hence provoked them into reacting violently against them. As a result, from the beginning of their work till the 1890s the missionaries were not able to penetrate and to work among the African societies for they faced violent opposition from them. In most cases the opposition to their work was so strong that they were forced to abandon their stations. In 1883, for example, the Ngoni attacked and completely destroyed the UMCA station at Masasi. Indeed the Ngoni treated the white missionaries as enemy chiefs and once they had defeated them they extorted tribute from them as they had done from all tributary states of the area. The effect of their defeat on the tributary states of the Ngoni was shattering. For their hope of forming military alliances with the white missionaries against the Ngoni vanished when they discovered that they did not possess the power or the military potential they believed them to have had. It is no wonder then that when the missionaries approached them in their attempt to settle among them, they were lukewarm and refrained from welcoming them.[10]

At Moshi, the CMS faced the same sort of opposition and although they did not withdraw from there till the German authorities forced them to do so for their supposedly unfriendly attitude towards them against the recalcitrant Meli who had succeeded Mandara in 1892, they had not made any progress towards their work by the beginning of the 1890s.[11] Mandara had allowed them into his country with the hope that they would provide him with guns and arms to fight against Mangi Sina of Kibosho, the overlord on Kilimanjaro from the early 1870s to 1890s. But when they failed to give him the military support and the political power he wanted he was bitterly disappointed with them. In 1880 he closed the market to them and by the following year, three years after their arrival in Moshi, he had neither allowed them to preach among the people nor given them children for their school. When Meli took over upon his father's death in 1890 he became engaged in a bitter struggle against German imperialism.

The same was true of the White Fathers at Tabora. For from 1881 when they established themselves there to 1889, they encountered handicap after handicap in the hands of Isike, the Ntemi of Unyanyembe. Isike treated them like the commercial bourgeoisie and demanded very heavy tribute from them which he increased from time to time. Between 1885 and 1889 German imperialism in Tanzania was at its peak, as was European imperialism in the whole of East Africa. This made Isike all the more suspicious of the White Fathers' motives as Europeans. Besides, the whole coast was at war with the German intruders then and Abushiri, one of the leaders of the war, had written to Isike, asking him to slaughter all the Europeans in the interior. Isike did not, however, do so, but he summoned them to his court and made them pledge their loyalty to him. Upon receiving rumours from the Arabs that the White Fathers intended to attack him, he sent his *ruga ruga* to ransack their buildings only to disprove the rumours. But Isike's harassment of the White Fathers served to demonstrate the precarious position in which they had placed themselves in Isike's country. By 1889 their existence there had become so fragile that they fled the country to Uganda, only to return at the beginning of the new century when they were more sure of the protection of the imperial power.[12]

I have cited these examples to show that before the conquest of mainland Tanzania by Europeans in the 1880s, missionaries were operating there within the context of African political sovereignty and, in the case of the islands and the coast, that of the Arab ruling class. Clearly these examples demonstrate fully the power of African polities in the interior of Tanzania. For the missionaries could only survive and work successfully here with the willingness and support of the African rulers. In contrast, witness for example that the missionaries working in Buganda between 1887 and 1900 had achieved tremendous success mainly because the ruling class initiated their coming and accepted their culture and civilisation.

Conquest and resistance

In the mid-1880s came the partition of East Africa which was completed in 1890 with the cession of Zanzibar and Pemba to Britain; the mainland had been assigned to Germany in 1886. The first partition of East Africa was followed by the various forms of resistance by the Africans and the Arabs against the two major powers, Britain and Germany. Quite a lot of material has been produced on African resistance to the imposition of colonial rule. Many writers have identified two stages of the process, namely primary and secondary resistance or resistance and rebellion.[13] For Tanzania this covers roughly the period 1888 to 1907. The external factors motivating the conquest of Tanzania have been dealt with by Dr David Arnold in chapter 2. It will suffice to mention again that the commercial intercourse between Tanzania and Europe, particularly after 1840, laid the groundwork for the conquest, as did the missionary penetration, albeit peripherally. Certainly this is true of German missions in southern Tanzania which were established after 1880 and which the German Government aimed at using for the expansion of its power in that area.[14]

The German invasion of mainland Tanzania was the most disrupting military incursion the country had ever experienced, and the Africans reacted to it militarily just as they had done to other military attacks. This reaction certainly was not uniform for it varied, depending upon the social, political and military organisation of each society which was confronted by the German onslaught. In this context it is not difficult to see that weaker peoples like the Bena, the Yao, the Safwa in southern Tanzania and individual leaders like Merere of Usangu, Marealle and Mandara of Kilimanjaro and the *abamukama* of lesser Kiamutwara and Kianja sought military alliance with the Germans. These alliances were at best based on opportunistic calculations.

For those who welcomed the Germans were totally ignorant of the power and the motives of the German invaders. They welcomed them to form especially military alliances with them as two sovereign peoples (just as they had done with other African peoples before) and they little knew that this alliance would lead to the final dismantling of their sovereignties. As John Iliffe has observed, the way different societies reacted to this invasion was essentially determined by their desire to maintain their sovereignty and it was not that those who co-operated wanted to lose their sovereignty. 'Some African peoples co-operated with the Germans while others resisted. To understand this, one must realise that the objects of both were the same: to retain as much power and independence as possible.'[15]

Merere of Usangu, for example, welcomed the Germans in 1891 out of a desire to form a military alliance with them against the Hehe who, beginning with the period of Mwinyigumba, had seriously reduced his sovereignty and power in the southern highlands. Marcia Wright has told us that his request for the Germans to come to his aid was not without precedent, for in 1877 Frederick Elton with his party had, at Merere's request, provided him with military aid which helped disperse the Hehe who had laid siege to his fortifications. This helped to enhance his prestige among, for example, the Bena and the Ngoni whose alliances with him, which had been faltering, were assured with the establishment of his power.[16] Indeed the survival of Merere and his sovereignty prior to this depended upon alliances with the neighbouring peoples such as the Bena and Ngoni. Merere therefore formed an alliance with the Germans on the same understanding and belief.

On the lakeshore the abamukama of Kianja and Kiamutwara welcomed the Germans because they wanted moral and military help to establish their authority over Kayoza, the omukama of Bugabo, who dominated these states. To cite one other example, Mangi Mandara of the Kilimanjaro area did likewise because of his desperate search for outside alliances against Sina of Kibosho, the overlord on the mountain. The alliance he formed with Germans was the last of a series of alliances he had contracted with the other chiefs on the mountain and with other peoples — the Swahili and Europeans in particular — outside Kilimanjaro. Before this he had sought an alliance with the Waarusha, the internal enemy of Kibosho, encouraged Swahili teachers to establish themselves at his court, and invited Europeans including missionaries (CMS) to come to establish themselves there. All of these moves were intended to enhance his power and to help him conquer Mangi Sina of Kibosho, without which he could not hope to establish his authority over the other chiefs on the mountain. Hence his co-operation with the Germans is the final phase of his struggle over Sina, and it is no wonder therefore that Mandara signed a treaty with von Juhlke in 1885 accepting German protection.

We may now turn to the phase of German aggression and conquest of Tanzania which began in 1884 and lasted till 1900. German aggression, of course, began on the mainland coast in 1884, with Karl Peters' supposedly treaty-making activities with local chiefs of the immediate hinterland on behalf of the Society for German Colonisation, a highly imperialistic body. Equipped with the treaties he returned to Germany to have the society solicit the approval of the Kaiser to his activities. Bismarck, the German Chancellor, recognised the treaties and further gave imperial charter to the German East Africa Company which was formed the following year with authority to exploit the newly acquired areas. Between 1884 and 1887 treaties had been signed in Usangara, Uzigua, Rufiji Valley, Ukami and Kilimanjaro. By then the company had set up eight stations in the Uluguru Valley, one in Uzigua, on the Wami

River, two in Usagara, two in the Pangani Valley, one on the coast on the frontier with British territory and one at Bagamoyo. As Dr Arnold has noted, the Sultan of Zanzibar had protested vehemently against the incursions of the German treaty-makers into his dominions but this was to no avail.

On the Tanzania coast the company faced great competition from local traders whose commercial interests, dating back many centuries but particularly to the beginning of the nineteenth century, were highly sophisticated. To be sure, the company faced financial collapse after only three years of operation because it was inexperienced and undercapitalised. To save the situation they pressed the sultan for a lease for the collection of the customs on the coast which the 1886 delimitation treaty did not allow them. A treaty was signed in 1888 in which the Sultan agreed to hand over the collection of the customs revenue to the company. However, he little knew that the German company would take it to imply the administration of the coast which they immediately set about to conquer and to administer. For the agents of the company wanted not only the collection of the customs on the coast but its entire control and conquest in order to take over the economy of the coast from the Arab commercial and ruling class.

It should be noted that these coastal towns had developed into independent economic units owing varying degrees of allegiance to the Sultan. As thriving commercial cities, their main interest was the maintenance of their economic base which this relationship, however loose it might have appeared, had helped to ensure and promote.Immediately following upon the 1888 treaty the company's flag replaced that of the Sultan on the coast thus marking the beginning of the company's administration there and the severing of the relationship that had hitherto existed between the coastal ruling class and the Sultan. Moreover, it signalled the end of the domination of the coast by the Arab ruling class which only yielded to the change of flags with arrival of a warship and a demonstration of force in every city. Even then many of the ruling and commercial leaders chose to flee the towns rather than succumb to this humiliation.[17]

The intrusion of the company into the coast and especially the taking over of the administration of the coastal towns where the company stationed inexperienced and arrogant German officials, was a major threat to the economic base of the cities which the Arab ruling class had jealously protected. Economic activity was the main feature of life here which, as Brown has argued, was characterised by the politics of business rather than the business of politics.[18] The imposition of the company administrators on the coast by force brought this economic activity to a standstill for the leading ruling merchants fled the towns. The arrogance of the inexperienced administrators, and especially their disrespect for the Muslim culture and religious places, was another cause of bitterness against them while their cruelty to the African labouring class served to alienate them from a majority of the African population. Hemedi has rightly described the German incursion on the coastal towns as a 'plague of Europeans' thus dramatising sharply the attitude of the coastal peoples towards them.[19]

Upon taking over the administration of the coastal towns, the German officials brought in a number of regulations all intended to cement their power as well as to earn the company profits.[20] They imposed a number of tax measures in each town such as head tax, burial tax, inheritance tax and tolls. In the social sphere they declared that both sexes were equal, a decree that was a serious affront to Muslim traditions. What is worse, they themselves did not practise this. Of even more serious concern to the coastal peoples was another decree the company introduced the same year requiring the registration of land and property within a period of six months. This decree essentially amounted to a seizure of their land as the Germans fully knew that land here was held customarily and none of the owners could, therefore, produce written proof of ownership, without which such land, the decree stated, would be confiscated by the company. This, together with the company's attack on the economy of the Arab ruling and commercial class, constituted the main cause of their resistance, for, once effected, the measures would certainly have brought economic ruin to the Arab ruling and commercial class. The jumbes in the interior, upon being required to register their land and pay the numerous taxes, rallied their support and loyalty to the Sultan and proceeded to put up the Sultan's flag where none had existed before as a demonstration of their loyalty to him. It was also a symbol of their resistance to the German intruders. Yet a more serious evidence of their resistance was that they began to draft their warriors to the coast to help the Arabs to fight the Germans. As already mentioned, the Africans had been treated badly enough during this short period of German interlude on the mainland to have cause to rise against the Germans.

All they required was a strong leader to mobilise them.

Perhaps the uprising that broke out on the coast would have occurred earlier had the leadership emerged among the ruling class. For there had been intense feeling against the German intruders since the issuing of the charter in 1885. Indeed the Sultan had, between 1885 and 1886, sent agents into the interior instructing the people not to co-operate with the Germans. And in 1886 Bwana Heri, the Governor of Saadani, and Ismail, the Governor of Winde, both future leaders of the coastal resistance, held a meeting in Uzigua with chiefs and other local leaders to mobilise the people for action against the Germans.

Open fighting first occurred at Pangani and Saadani where the radical leaders Abushiri and Bwana Heri emerged to lead militant Arabs and Swahilis in open hostility against the Germans. About the same time militant African warriors who had been despatched from the interior by dfferent jumbes arrived at Pangani to join them. They arrested the Germans in the town and, when negotiations between them and the British for reconciliation did not lead to German withdrawal from there, Abushiri and his followers continued to fight insisting that he would raise all other coastal towns against the Germans. Elsewhere in the other towns, namely Tanga, Bagamoyo and Dar es Salaam, uprising broke out, and the Germans were driven out. In Kilwa, further south on the coast, fighting erupted. In Lindi, we are told, the Germans observed an ultimatum served on them by the local people to withdraw, with the result that there was no fighting there. By the end of August, the month during which the resistance on the coast broke out, the radical Arabs and the Africans had succeeded in driving the 'plague of Europeans'[21] from all the coastal towns.

From the beginning of the outbreak at Pangani and Saadani to the first few months of 1889, the resisters were on the offensive. In November 1888 Abushiri had established another area of fighting at Bagamoyo, where the Germans, ditched in a fortified house, continued to hold the city. After several engagements which failed to dislodge them from their house, he moved from the city and established his camp at Kaole five miles from there and attempted in vain to drive the Germans out of Bagamoyo. In December fighting broke out at Dar es Salaam and the Lutheran Mission was attacked and completely destroyed. In the following year they attacked the Benedictine mission at Pugu and a nun and two brothers were killed and freed slaves there were re-enslaved. The mission was attacked more for its association with the DOAG and with the German Colonisation Society than for the fact that it harboured runaway slaves.

During the first few months of the year (1889) the resistance movement began to weaken, mainly due to the divisions extant in the movement. From the beginning there were two divisions: one of the militants and the other of conservative Arabs both of whom had different objectives for resisting; the only common denominator was that both hated the German intruders. The conservative Arab ruling and commercial class had joined the movement primarily to safeguard their economic interests. They were not willing to embark on a prolonged war because it would ruin their trade which was the main basis of their economy. Once their position was insured, as it appeared to be in the initial period of the war, they were willing to compromise with the German company and to maintain their relationship with the Sultan after their quick success in driving out the Germans from the coast. But not so the common people and the Swahili and, in particular, the radical leaders of the movement, Abushiri of Pangani and the Bwana Heri of Saadani. For they wanted to assert the independence of the coast and totally rejected the domination of the Germans and of the Sultan.[22] These militants were not willing to compromise at the moment of their success despite the fact that by the beginning of the year the war and the blockade laid on the coast by Germany in collaboration with the British had brought trade to a standstill. Furthermore famine was striking the land and the moderate wing of the ruling class was pressing for moderation and compromise.

In April 1889 when there was a temporary lull in the hostilities, Abushiri was prepared to negotiate for peace on condition that the Germans would not be allowed on the coast. But this was also the time when the German Government was not prepared for the company's showdown on the coast. Indeed the German Government had voted money for the war effort. In addition von Wissmann had been appointed with commission to conquer the coast for which he recruited Sudanese and Zulu soldiers to form the main fighting force of the invading army. At the same time, Wissman took over the administration of the company and almost immediately despatched a force of seven hundred well armed and well drilled African levies to Bagamoyo ready to confront Abushiri and the

Arabs. In May 1889 a large force attacked Abushiri's fort at Kaole and succeeded in routing his equally large army. There were many casualties on both sides but Abushiri lost a lot more men among whom was Ismail, the Governor of Winde. This was a decisive war in which the superior firing-power of the Germans had been demonstrated in a pitched battle with the enemy. So decisive was it that it threw despair into the ranks of Abushiri's soldiers and warriors many of whom, accepting defeat, abandoned the movement. Despite renewed pressure for peace from many Arabs and Swahili, the radical forces still in power in the coastal towns remained steadfast. After the battle of Bagamoyo, Wissmann moved north and defeated Pangani, Saadani and Tanga, whereas in Bagamoyo he burnt villages, crops, houses and property.

By the time Wissmann attacked these towns, Abushiri had fled the coast for the interior and pitched camp at Kondoa on the Wami Valley from where he tried in vain to mobilise the people against the Germans. For example, Kingo Mkubwa, the leading chief of the area, refused him support. His attempt to win the support of the people of Usagara also ended in failure, despite the fact that when Abushiri was in the area, he attacked the German station at Mpwapwa killing one of the two Germans there. Even his approach to the Hehe and Mafiti who had expanded into the area for the alliance ended in disaster. Furthermore this approach served to cut off any support he might have had from the people of the area since they saw it as a further attempt to decimate them, for the Hehe and Mafiti soldiers with whom Abushiri sought an alliance had constantly attacked them. So rather than throw in their lot with Abushiri many of them sought the support of Wissmann who was trying to expand German influence and authority in the area. Indeed in September the same year Wissmann reached Morogoro with about six hundred Zulu, Sudanese and Nyamwezi soldiers. But this small number of soldiers made it necessary for him to adopt a policy of compromise with the inhabitants and to avoid that of repression and open fighting which had been adopted at the coast by the company. It was this policy which among other factors won him the support of Kingo Mkubwa.

Unsuccessful in rallying the support of the people of the Wami Valley and Usagara against the German aggressors, Abushiri moved to Saadani to join Bwani Heri there. Both fought guerilla warfare, but separately. However, Abushiri was finally captured and executed in December 1889, leaving Bwana Heri as leader of the resistance movement in Zigualand. So successful were his guerilla tactics that for the rest of the war period he was never defeated in battle. Zigualand was, however, devastated by German depredations. The resulting famine led to the starvation of both the general population and Bwana Heri's soldiers and this forced him to negiotiate for peace. Though not militarily defeated, on 7 April 1890 he formally surrendered, leaving the Germans to dictate terms of peace to him. As it happened the Germans became very conciliatory and not only spared his life but offered him the governorship of Saadani, acting as their agent.

After subjugating the northern part of the coast, the Germans turned to the conquest of the southern coast where the Yao put up strong resistance, especially in Kilwa. After three days of bombardment from the sea, the resistance was broken. The African leaders in the immediate hinterland remained passive, most probably because the presence of the Germans did not affect them directly. But when from 1894 German traders began to penetrate the interior and to interfere with the monopoly of the ivory trade held by the African leaders there, they rose against them to protect this monopoly. This affected the Yao in particular, and we are told that Macheba, one of the leading chiefs of the Yao, rose against the Germans in 1899 when German traders who had penetrated the interior threatened the monopoly of the ivory trade he held, despite the fact that he had remained neutral during the coastal resistance. He adopted the tactics of hit and run so successfully that the troops of the enemy were not able to come face to face with his warriors. However, the German-led forces, in their usual cruelty, destroyed villages, crops, houses and property and forced Macheba to cease hostilities and to enter into agreement for peace with them.

In 1891 Germany felt it necessary to replace the rule of the company by direct imperial rule because the company had failed to contain the coastal resistance. A civilian administrator, von Soden, was appointed Governor of German East Africa the same year. As a civilian he wanted to avoid a military conquest of the colony which was far too expensive for Germany. Therefore he chose to expand into, and to protect the already well-established long distance trading routes which would, once they were firmly held, promote the exploitation of the interior. So after the coastal resistance was suppressed German agents began to expand into the interior mainly along the Pangani valley and along the central caravan trading routes.

Along the Pangani valley the Germans first moved into Usambara where their first contact was with Semboja, then the most powerful of the Usambara chiefs. He resided at Mazinde, the capital of Southern Usambara lying along the caravan trade route. Semboja's power was based on his control of the trade with the coastal traders and the intrusion of the Germans into the country threatened not only this control but also the friendly relationship he had established with the coastal traders. That is why he opposed their intrusion when they first appeared in Mazinde in 1888. As Steven Feiermann has told us, Semboja demonstrated his opposition to German intrusion in October that year by imprisoning and seizing the property of two explorers, Hans Meyer and Oscar Baumann, then passing through Mazinde.[23] This, he points out, was only a peripheral contribution to the coastal resistance which was then raging. Elsewhere in Usambara only eastern Kilindi contributed more tangibly to the resistance for they despatched soldiers to the coast to fight alongside Abushiri soldiers. After the Germans had defeated the coastal resistance Semboja reconciled himself to their presence in his capital where they established a station in 1890. Indeed, he paid a heavy fine for the property of the explorers he had seized and for his acceptance of the Germans he was henceforth paid a monthly salary. About the same time Kibanga was named chief of all East Usambara and Bondei after a visit he had made to the Germans at Tanga to assure the Germans of his loyalty.[24] Now unopposed in their expansion across the Usambara country, German agents moved upon the valley to its uppermost reaches and left Semboja's kingdom pretty much to itself. But this was to be a short interlude in the history of Usambara as an independent kingdom. For in 1895, upon the death of Semboja, the Germans found an opportunity to interfere with its independence: they executed Mputa, the rightful successor, for the murder of a man who had committed adultery with one of his wives, an act which was justifiable in the traditions of the Shambala, and placed Kinyasi as chief, not as an independent sovereign but as a German agent especially for the recruitment of labour for German planters.

Coast men and later Europeans had reached the Kilimanjaro mountain, the upper reaches of the Pangani valley, through either the Mombasa-Taveta trade route or along the Pangani valley.[25]

European contacts with the mountain went back as far as 1848 with Krapf and Reubmann's first visit there. Mandara, the chief of Moshi, who was in search of alliances, wrote to the missionaries at Mombasa as early as 1875 inviting them to come and establish themselves in Moshi. It was not until 1885 that the first CMS station was established there, although Reubmann and other CMS missionaries after him made several visits in the intervening period. The explorers, von Decken and Johnson, visited Moshi in 1862 and 1884 respectively. Only the latter discovered that Mandara was not certainly the paramount chief of the mountain; rather, he discovered, it was Sina who controlled the mountain from the 1870s to 1891.

In a desperate search for alliances against Kibosho, Mandara signed a treaty with von Juhlke in 1885 ceding the mountain to the company.[26] Company agents were thereafter stationed at Moshi and the first representative of the Imperial Colonial Administration, von Eltz, was also stationed here in 1890. But because Mandara was not a representative of the chiefs of the mountain, he did not have the authority or the power to justify his entering into an agreement with outside powers on their behalf. If any chief had the claim to this it was Sina who had turned the others into tribute-paying chiefdoms. Sina did not, however, dismantle the hegemonies of the tribute-paying chiefdoms as the Germans later came to do because he was primarily interested in cattle, slaves and spears from them. As long as he could get these and he could conduct trade with the coast men without interruption, he left them alone.

The assumption of the role of paramountcy on Kilimanjaro by Mandara misled Europeans, particularly the German aggressors, into believing that once they entered into an agreement with him they would establish themselves on the mountain without much opposition. Certainly Mandara's warm welcome gave them this hope. But they soon discovered that Sina was the power to reckon with. Although Sina had known of the German treaties signed with Mandara between 1885 and 1889, he did not move to punish Mandara for collaborating with the Germans nor did he hasten to drive out the intruders. This was probably because the German intrusion had not by then affected his sovereignty, or his commercial activities. For it was not until 1890 when von Eltz, the imperial representative, encouraged two Roman Catholics to establish a mission station at Kibosho, that his sovereignty was threatened.[27] This was the first time that Europeans made any attempts to establish themselves there, and so hostile was Sina to them that they had to abandon their design.

The occasion for open hostilities between Sina and the Germans occurred when the latter forced their flag on him the same year. For to demonstrate his opposition in defence of his sovereignty, he hauled down the flag, replacing it with that of the Sultan. The Germans in their desperate search for local chiefs to ally with had further infuriated him when they placed him under the sovereignty of the chief of Uru, the same man that Sina had installed. Sina confronted Wissmann's strong force consisting of German officers, Zulu, Sudanese and Chagga soldiers provided by Mandara, and in a fierce battle lasting for two days, his warriors were finally defeated.

The fortification of Kibosho and the valour of Sina's warriors withstood German fire-power for two days. This was the first time that Sina's warriors had ever been defeated and the main factor contributing to his defeat was the new weapon, the Maxim gun, which was much superior to the guns and spears of Sina's warriors. There were also minor factors which contributed to the defeat of Sina in 1891: Kisarike, chief of Uru, led the Germans to Sina's fortress and Rindi provided them with soldiers. Sina's conquest ended the era of African sovereignty in Kilimanjaro, for almost all the other chiefs there began to accommodate themselves to German sovereignty as best as they could. Only Meli, who had inherited the chiefdom of Moshi upon the death of Mandara, rose against the Germans the following year but was defeated. The German conquerors, however, were conciliatory to Sina as they had been to Bwana Heri not because they were less cruel than before but because with so few men and resources they could not risk a prolonged war. So they tried to persuade as many people as possible to ally with them. Indeed they left Sina as chief of Kibosho, although two chiefdoms had been taken from it, until his death in 1897. However he was no longer an independent sovereign, for he was now dependent on the authority of the Germans.

The other route of expansion into the interior which the Germans followed was inevitably the central trade route along which lay Usagara, Ugogoland, and further to the west, Unyanyembe. To establish their control along the route the Germans set up forts along it; the first ones being at Mpwapwa and Kilosa. But the area was also one into which the Hehe had expanded and had established settlements, among them those of Wota near Mpwapwa and Ulaya near

Kilosa.[28] From these settlements Hehe warriors attacked the caravan route, Usagara and Ukami for ivory and slaves. Furthermore, they were expanding deep into the coast, and were bound to clash with the Germans who were expanding inland.

The expansion of the Hehe was especially threatened because the Germans' aims were essentially the same as theirs: to establish political control of the area and to develop trade. Hehe, Mbunga and Mafiti soldiers had campaigned in this area throughout the 1880s and the early 1890s. During the coastal resistance, Abushiri had sought their aid. The Mbunga, for example, came to Abushiri's aid and in 'October 1889 mounted a force of 4 000 warriors which engaged the Germans in several battles only to be repulsed after several casualties on both sides'.[27] Open confrontation between the Germans and the Hehe was inevitable. Fearful of the military power of the Hehe, the German aggressors were at first anxious to avoid open conflict and sought peace with them. The Hehe, however, stubbornly turned down their approaches for peace. Furthermore, they punished those Africans who accommodated the Germans, brandishing them as traitors.

The first military engagement between the Hehe and the Germans broke out in 1891, when a large military expedition under Zelewski which had been despatched to punish the Hehe was ambushed by Mkwawa's force at Lugalo and completely destroyed. So shattered was German prestige that, as Marcia Wright says, 'the question of what to do about the Hehe became an issue influencing all policy consideration in the central and southern region .[30]

Meanwhile the German aggressors had between 1891 and 1894 been making preparations for the complete conquest of the Hehe. First they established military garrisons in the north, especially at Kilosa and Kisaki, and secondly, they desperately looked for local alliances on their southern flank. Regarding the latter, they were successful in obtaining an alliance with Merere, the chief of Usangu, and Kisaki, chief of Bena, both of which had been reduced to tributary states by the Hehe. Once these objectives were achieved the Germans were ready to launch a severe military attack upon the Hehe. In 1894 Tom Prince, in the second command of a large army, stormed the Kalenga fort having approached it from the direction least expected by the Hehe. Although attacked by surprise the Hehe nevertheless held on and fighting raged on for the whole of the day. Not surprisingly there were heavy losses on the side of the defenders who surrendered the fort that evening. Mkawa however had succeeded in escaping from the fort unnoticed. From then until 1898 he fought a guerilla war in defence of Heheland and her sovereignty. In July that year he committed suicide rather than wait to be captured by the approaching 'barbarians'. His death marked the end of the Hehe and the beginning of German sovereignty in Uhehe.

Further west into Nyanyembe representatives of the Germans—Emin Pasha, Langheld, Bulow and Stuhlman—arrived in 1890 to make treaties there.[31] Isike was the overlord here during this time. Although he had become the Ntemi of Unyanyembre in 1876, it was not until 1884, following the deaths and the disintegration of the empires of his three rivals—Ivimba Kavbugando of Uluila, Nyungu ya Mawe of Kiwele, and Mirambo of Urambo in western Tanzania—between 1881 and 1884, that he became the unchallenged ruler of the area. Furthermore, the commercial bourgeoisie, the *Vbandevba*, who had hitherto held considerable economic, social and military power, had been ruined in the Mirambo wars of the previous decade already dealt with by Dr Sheriff in chapter 1. The Arabs of Tabora had also suffered the same fate and they were no longer the political power they had been before the wars. Isike's position and power thus assured, between 1884 and 1890, he introduced a number of reforms to improve the lot of the common people as well as to strengthen his own position economically and politically. Among these, two important ones need to be mentioned for they considerably reduced the power and position of the Vbandevba. First was the introduction of a variety of taxes payable by all traders in Nyanyembe and secondly, the introduction of measures forbidding the murder of servants, slaves and porters by the Vbandevba. While these measures alienated the Vbandevba, the Arabs and the missionaries alike, they strengthened Isike's economic and political position and improved the condition and status of the common people. Another result of this alienation of the Arabs and the Vbandevba was that they were ready to co-operate with outside forces against him to recover the power that they had lost. Thus when the Emin Pasha expedition arrived in 1890, the Arabs of Tabora readily signed a treaty of protection with him in August of the same year. As a reward for their co-operation, Emin Pasha appointed one of them, a certain Seif bin Saad, the Liwali of Tabora and mistakenly made him also Liwali of all Unyanyembe. Thereafter a German military station was established at Tabora.

The appointment of Seif bin Saad as the Liwali of all Unyanyembe was only in name for it could not become effective until Isike was out of the way. But it was an affront on Isike's sovereignty. Isike, however, did not challenge the establishment of the Germans in his country immediately, most probably because he wanted time to make preparations for war against intruders, but also because the establishment of the German military station did not immediately affect his sovereignty. Only when the Germans first attacked one of his villages in April 1892 did he mobilise for open war against them. The Arabs and the Vbandevba welcomed the German aggressors on Isike and the former in particular further told the Germans that Isike was attempting to rally all the Nyamwezi against them in an attempt to incite them and so hasten the attack on him. Consequently the Germans took the initiative and between July and September 1892 besieged his fort four times only to be repulsed each time. The Germans had to call for more reinforcements of guns and Sudanese soldiers without which the war might have taken a different turn. In the following months the Germans rebuilt their forces and with the arrival of Tom Prince with reinforcements of guns and Zulu soldiers, the Germans were ready for the conquest of Isike. Open war again broke out in January 1893. The German forces besieged the fort and fighting continued for three long days after which Isike's army fell. Isike slew himself rather than face capture. 'However the German soldiers rushed the mangled remains of the Nyanyembe despot to a nearby Mrumba tree', says Unomah, 'and hanged his body. So ended the career of one of Africa's great resisters of colonial domination'.[32]

Evidently, Isike would have been defeated because the German forces had much superior fire-power. But perhaps more significant in this confrontation were the elements in Unyanyembe society which co-operated with the Germans to hasten the fall of Isike and hence the dismantling of Unyanyembe hegemony. Unomah has argued that although by 1890 the Arabs of Tabora were inwardly against German imperialism, they seem to have reconciled themselves to it, probably believing that the Germans were a lesser evil than Isike, and hence they co-operated with them. The Vbandevba had been alienated from Isike since the beginning of his rule and in their attempt to recover the power they had lost under him, they were prepared to co-operate with a rival who held any promise of reconciling them. They found such a personality in Nyaso, a princess of Ifundikira family around whom in 1887 their movement against Isike began to crystallise. Then Isike had succeeded in warding off civil war between the supporters of Nyaso and Swetu when conflict between the two arose with Swetu's invasion of the kingdom of Uganda then under the Ntemiship of Ndisha, a close friend of Nyaso. To settle their dispute Isike arranged a duel for them from which Swetu withdrew because he and his supporters were weaker. Nyaso emerged from the crisis commanding great respect, and from then on many of the Vbandevba, anxious to look for an alternative to the oppressive rule of Isike, rallied round her against Swetu and indirectly against Isike because of his intimate relations with Swetu. When Isike laid a trap to eliminate her, the trap misfired only to enhance her popularity. So when the Germans arrived on the scene in 1890 they found Nyaso and the Vbandevba in a desperate search for support against Isike. In 1892 the Germans offered her the Ntemiship of Unyanyembre in return for a joint military force against Isike. It was this support for the Germans in Unyanyembe society which finally determined the fall of Isike in January 1893.

With the fall of Isike, the Germans made Nyaso Ntemi of Unyamyembe in exchange for an offer of protection from them for which she signed a treaty the following month. But, unlike Isike, Nyaso signed away the independence of Unyanyembe, she herself becoming the agent of German colonial rule. At first she retained much of the traditional role of Ntemiship, thus giving the illusion that the Germans were another external force just as the Arabs had been. But in time she was reduced to the role of recruiting porters and labourers for work on German plantations on the coast, thus contributing to the underdevelopment of the region. Even the Vbandevba, who had allied with Nyaso against Isike were soon to discover that the intrusion of the Germans into Unyanyembe delivered the blow which finally broke their hegemony and with it any hope of the recovery of their former political and economic power. For the German colonial administration introduced a host of regulations among which were those which required them to stop robbery, to act as recruiters of porters and labourers and to stop slave trading. These regulations shattered the very foundation of their economy and power.

If events in the kingdoms on the southern shores of Lake Victoria were less dramatic and bloody than those elsewhere in Tanzania, they were nevertheless to produce results which altered the history of the societies inhabiting the area, because their earlier satellite relationship with Buganda and Rwanda was to be severed with the partition of East Africa in 1890. But even more crucial was that these societies lost their independence and became colonial peoples. As a result of this the kingdoms in the south and south-west of the lake came under Germany.

It has been shown in chapter 1 that these societies, namely the Haya, differed from those of the north and Rwanda in that no strong centralised kingdoms developed here. Instead there had developed several small weak kingdoms which were often in rivalry with one another. From the 1870s to the 1880s Buganda (and to some extent Rwanda also) exploited this weakness, for by supporting one of the rivals they were able to dominate the area and turn these kingdoms into satellites. Kiziba became a satellite of Buganda in the 1870s and the 1880s. So did Karagwe about the same time although her satellite relationship alternated between Buganda and Rwanda.

During the beginning of the 1890s the Germans found the same sort of situation existing here and exploited it to penetrate the area, not to turn the kingdoms into satellites like Buganda had done, but to subject them to German rule. This they accomplished through conquest.[31] For example, by the end of the 1880s two of the three Kiamutwara 'successor states', Kianja and Lesser Kiamutwara, were dominated by Bugoba under omukama Kayoza. To redress this situation they sought alliance with the Germans who arrived on the scene in 1890. The omukama of Kiamutwara welcomed the Germans, with whose help he repelled Kayoza's attack upon his kingdom. The Germans on their part used Kiamutwara as a base and the people of Kiamutwara as allies to establish their influence and power over the Haya kingdoms. In 1891 Kiziba, the first of the Haya kingdoms to resist the Germans, having appealed to Baganda in vain for help, was defeated by German forces with the help of the omukama of Kiamutwara.

Mention has already been made of Haya resistance to missionaries during the pre-colonial period. This resistance was again dramatically demonstrated in 1892 when upon the flight of the White Fathers from Buganda after their defeat in the Protestant-Catholic war of the same year, the German military authorities in Bukoba sought to settle them permanently in Hayaland. Sensing that they would meet stronger resistance with most of the kingdoms, they decided to settle these missionaries in the kingdom of Kiamutwara which, having accommodated the German aggressors, the authorities believed would do likewise with the missionaries. But the omukama's accommodation of the German aggressors was based on the understanding that the Germans would leave his country once they had given him assistance against his rivals. Unfortunately this belief was based on his ignorance of the international scene. But to accept this is not to say that he would not resist German occupation of his kingdom. For once it became clear that the motives of the Germans were different from what he believed them to be, as is evidenced by their forceful imposition of the White Fathers on him, he rose in arms to resist this settlement of foreigners in his kingdom. Thus war, which ended with the defeat of the omukama of Kiamutwara, broke out between Kiamutwara and the Germans in 1892. Kiamutwara was resisting not only the settlement of missionaires in their kingdom but the imposition of German power and rule. Consequent upon its defeat Kiamutwara lost some of the land on which the White Fathers were settled to form the Kashozi mission. Bordering Kiamutwara-Bugabo the Kashozi mission land was placed under Bugabo as reward for the assistance it had given the Germans in the conquest of Kiamutwara. But it was also intended to serve as a buffer between the two rival kingdoms, particularly as it was to be an independent mission state.

A change of German military commanders at Bukoba brought new fortunes to Mukotani of Kiamtwara. For the new Commander, Langheld, adopted a conciliatory policy towards him. Thus compromised he moved ahead to consolidate his power and between 1893 and 1895 he built himself an independent source of power which he obtained by amassing guns in his court uninterrupted by the Commander. Furthermore, Langheld allowed him to employ two of his former Sudanese NCOs as his bodyguards; these factors enhanced his position in the area so much that confrontation between him and German power was bound to occur and in 1895 German forces attacked Mukotani after he had refused to hand over 'a cache of breech loading rifles'.[34] This attack was part of a German move to subjugate those abamukama who resisted German expansion into the area. For the German forces simultaneously also launched a heavy attack upon Mutatembwa of Kiziba who had once again risen to resist them. At the same time, Ukerewe island under Lugongo had also risen to oppose German intervention as had the Nera chiefdom of Usukumaland further south. These resistances were suppressed with German forces in alliance with African levies from collaborating kingdoms like that of Kianja under Kahigi whose collaboration began in 1890 and never wavered throughout the whole period. But the Germans did not have the resources to press their successes to the end as they did in Heheland and Kilimanjaro area. Perhaps because the nature of resistance here was less turbulent, they ignored these people with the hope that they would submit on their own. But this was not so because Kiziba again rose against German occupation in 1897. This time war occurred over the refusal of the Germans to accept the succession of Mutatembwa by Mutahangarwa, an arrangement that Austen says had the prior confirmation of the military commander at Bukoba.[33] War was sparked off by the new omukama's refusal to give up corpses of plague victims for autopsy, which the Germans wanted as part of their campaign to combat plague then raging in the area. Mutahangarwa, however, believed that the Germans wanted the corpses in order to make a meal out of them. But what made matters worse was that the military officer in the area had established his headquarters in the area dominated by Keshebula, demonstrating clearly German support of him for the Kiziba throne. This act appeared a betrayal of the earlier arrangement. Furthermore, both Mutatembwa and his son Mutahangarwa saw it as a result of Keshebula's intrigues and moved to punish him and his followers. Four months of fighting did not end with any success on either side; the Germans therefore divided Kiziba between the two with their candidate getting the lion's share. In 1899 the Germans transferred their support to Mutahangarwa, Keshebula having proved a bad collaborator. Land was also transferred from Keshebula who, as a result, was left with little more than a village. It was only after 1899 that Kiziba began to adapt to colonialism. But the events here show the complexity of affairs in Hayaland.

Mention must be made of Kianja under Kahigi which, like Lesser Kiamutwara, accommodated the German aggressors from the beginning.[34] From 1890, Kahigi never wavered in his support of the new intruders, and as a reward for his accommodation and support he was not therefore conquered. Indeed, he reaped some benefits from the newcomers for in 1895 three subchiefdoms were taken from Lesser Kiamutwara and added to Kianja and in 1899 part of Bukara kingdom was also added when Keshebule the omukama fled his kingdom to Uganda under threat of attack by German forces engineered by Kahigi. But compared with the loss of independence Kianja incurred, these benefits were only in its relationship with the rest of the colonial peoples: something Kahigi realised after Germany began the effective occupation of the area, particularly after 1900.

Regarding German penetration to the south-east of Tanzania mainland, we have already alluded to Machemba's resistance against German invasion. Two groups of people can be identified in this area.[37] First there were those like the Yao, the Makonde, the Makua, the Ngindo, the Mwera and the Nyasa who had been conquered by the Ngoni and forced into tribute paying states, and second were the Ngoni themselves who had built up a powerful military empire in the region. The former had not only been weakened and reduced by the raids of the latter but they were also small-scale societies.

When the Germans began to expand into the area after 1890 it is not surprising that the societies of the former group accommodated them primarily to form military power in this region. One would have expected the Ngoni, on the other hand, to offer the German intrusion the greatest military challenge, perhaps equal to that offered by the Hehe between 1891 and 1898. But as it happened the Ngoni offered them the least resistance and avoided any full-scale military confrontation with them, despite the fact that before the Hehe wars, the Ngoni believed the Germans to be weak. The Ngoni seem to have decided to remain neutral in any conflict resulting from German intrusion in the area, which would explain why they refused to join the Hehe who approached them for military alliance against the Germans. Indeed in 1894, prompted by a desire to retain a monopoly over the Rufiji and to ensure that his kingdom remained intact, Chabruma, the chief of Ngoni Mshope, sent a peace mission to Kilwa to enter into negotiation for a treaty with the Germans, a treaty in which he wanted the Germans to recognise the sovereignty of the Ngoni Mshope under him as an independent state. This was not likely to materialise as the Germans were not coming in as equals of the African sovereign rulers but as their superiors. Furthermore, when the peace mission was at Kilwa a group of Ngoni raided and plundered its hinterland without the knowledge of Chabruma, only to provoke an immediate military expedition against the Ngoni and to put an end to the negotiations. When the expedition marched on to Chabruma's capital, Chabruma did not resist and left the attackers to ravage the city where they looted cattle and foodstuffs.

Ngoni raiding activities into the area could not have stopped after the Germans had taken over the coast for this was the basis of the Ngoni economy. Although these activities could have been curtailed among the Mshope, as required by the Germans under the centralised authority of Chabruma, the same was not true of Njelu which, lacking centralised control, was by this time divided between two factions and the military *manduna* were acting independently[36]. Thus Njelu Ngoni, and particularly the young warriors, continued to raid the area, especially the Lindi hinterland, between 1894 and 1897. In 1896, for example, the Njelu made a massive attack along the Ruvuma River particularly in the hinterlands of Mikindani and Lindi where they burnt villages and turned the inhabitants into captives. The Germans answered this by mounting a large force for the conquest of Njelu Ngoni. In July that year the force marched on to Songea and the Ngoni gave up without any resistance. The entrance of the Germans in the capital was to be a permanent one for soon after they began to construct a military station there under the command of von Kleist and a small force. From this post von Kleist moved to secure his hold on the rest of Njelu and the submission of Chabruma, which he secured without resistance. One explanation for this surprising submission without resistance of any significant magnitude from so strong a military power is that the Ngoni realised that the power of the Germans had changed with the defeat of the Hehe in 1894 when they learned of the superior firearm power. Furthermore, their ancestors had warned them against military engagement with the Germans predicting that such a confrontation would result in their defeat, and their respected Arab trader, Rashid Masoud gave them a similar warning.

The establishment of the military post at Songea inevitably began German military rule in Ngoni and the integration of military Ngoni into a much larger military rule. But unlike the Hehe, the Ngoni military states remained intact for they were not militarily conquered. As such they were well placed to offer the Germans unequalled military challenge eight years later.

In this chapter I have attempted to deal with some of the major military confrontations between the German imperialists and the peoples of mainland Tanzania. Ernst Nigmann identified forty-eight confrontations before the Maji Maji war in his location sketches of 1911.[39] The significance of these military operations cannot be overemphasised, nor can the lessons that the Germans as well as the Tanzanians drew from them. Two points should be made here. Firstly, these wars were more destructive and claimed more lives of Africans than previous wars and famines had done. This invalidates, as Helge Kjekshus has argued, the oft repeated colonial belief that the inter-tribal wars and famines of pre-colonial Tanzania had depopulated much of the area. Rather, he has argued emphatically, it was the colonial wars which did so.[40] Secondly, armed struggle was not the only way by which the peoples of mainland Tanzania resisted German invasion. Indeed the military defeat of the African leaders did not mean acceptance of German rule by a majority of the African peoples of Tanzania for many of them continued to show their opposition to the German penetration in various other ways. In his preliminary investigation of African reaction to German rule in north-east Tanzania, G.O. Ekemode has suggested that the opposition of the Shambala to the work of the German Bethel Mission in the area in the 1890s, despite the fact that the Mission did so much relief work during this time when the area was suffering from famine, was more a demonstration of Shambala opposition to German rule than of their unwillingness to abandon their traditional religion. This, he has argued, is particularly because the UMCA in Bondei, which did likewise for the Bondei during the famine, saw an unprecedented rate of the expansion of their work among the Bondei about the same time. When, beginning in the late 1890s, the Germans introduced hut tax, began to demand both public and private work and required the chiefs to collect the tax and to recruit labour, the Shambala adopted the strategy of passive resistance rather than open violence as was the case in southern Tanzania.[41] This strategy as a form of resistance to German penetration and rule was more widely adopted by the African peoples, though with varying degrees of success, than had hitherto been realised. Again, Ekemode has somewhat exaggeratedly pointed out that among the Shambala it later expressed itself in their acceptance of Islam instead of Christianity.[42] Among the other peoples of Tanzania it expressed itself in other ways such as refusal to pay tax or even desertion.

By 1900 the Germans had succeeded in establishing their

sovereignty over mainland Tanzania through conquest or mere demonstration of military superiority. Their presence in the territory was characterised by the military posts commanded by military personnel, thus demonstrating the military nature of their penetration. More specifically, perhaps, it demonstrates the intense state of affairs in the country which could only be contained through military force and repression.

It is significant to note that in this repression African soldiers and *askaris* recruited by the Germans featured predominantly. Two types of these are immediately distinguishable. One, those who Wissmann first recruited in 1889 for the conquest of the coastal resistance, namely Sudanese and Zulu soldiers. Once they were introduced into the area, essentially as mercenaries, they proved crucial to the success of the Germans. Thus they were reinforced throughout the period of conquest and remained a permanent feature of the German invading forces. Second, soldiers or levies recruited from accommodating chiefs such as those provided by Merere and Kiwanga during the Hehe wars, by Rindi against Sina in 1891 as well as those which provided the main force of Nyaso in alliance with German forces against Isike in 1893. As Walter Rodney has recently remarked, evidence is mounting from various parts of the continent to show that the military conquest of colonial Africa was almost invariably achieved by European-led, but not European troops.[43] In connection with Ovimbundu resistance to the Portuguese, Rodney has shown that African forces constituted the main body of the Portuguese army, and they were instrumental in the crushing of Ovimbundu resistance to the imposition of Portuguese rule. This is certainly true of the conquest of Tanzania as the few examples cited above indicate. Not only did the Germans raise levies from those weaker societies who were anxious to co-operate with them but they required those whom they had conquered to provide them with soldiers. The class perspective of this is clear, namely that the Germans conquered and later built up her colonial forces and police from Africans, that is, from the oppressed class.

But what was even more crucial in the conflict was that the Germans equipped the African troops which they led with superior arms. One aspect of the technological revolution which took place in Europe during the nineteenth century was the advances made in weaponry and firearms. While African societies had made advances in the discovery of new types of spears, particularly the short stabbing spear, Germany, like the other industrial powers, had discovered the machine gun—the Maxim gun—which, together with improvements in organisation and logistics in warfare, was far superior to the short stabbing spear. True, in that conflict many of the Africans used guns which they had bought from the Arabs, but these were often old-fashioned. They supplemented the spear, rather than replaced it. For example, Sina's large forces were defeated by the Maxim gun as were those of Mkwawa and Isike, not to mention the coastal resistance. Looked at in this perspective, it becomes easier to understand why the large forces put up by Sina, Mkwawa, Isike and later on the Maji Maji fighters were defeated by relatively small forces of African troops led by German officers.

After 1900 with the German military suppression of the major resistance almost completed, the Germans could embark more firmly on the exploitation of the territory in spite of the fact that their occupation of mainland Tanzania was still a peripheral phenomenon. To effect this a transport system was required, and the Germans had begun the construction of railroads in the early 1890s; the first line, which was constructed to tap the fertile Pangani valley, reached its railhead at Moshi on the slopes of Kilimanjaro in 1911, while the second line, constructed along the central trade route, reached the western edge of the country, Ujiji, in 1914. Germans were settled on the coast after the coastal resistance, and, with the beginning of the railroad in the north, settlers were also settled all along the Pangani valley to engage as they were doing on the coast, in plantation agriculture, mainly for the metropolis.

Plantation agriculture required land and labour for which the colonial administration alienated African land and forced the African, through legislation and various administrative regulations, to work on them. Cash crops, mainly coffee and sisal, were grown on these plantations while on the southern coast and hinterland rubber was developed. Also in this area, in 1902, the Germans, anxious to get out of the depression, began communal farms on which cotton was grown as an experiment for it had failed to grow on the northern coast. Each headman in whose area these communal farms were established was charged with the responsibility of developing the farms with the labour force of the peasantry who were required to work on them on prescribed days. To raise revenue for the running of the territory the Germans introduced taxation which also served as an indirect incentive for labour since it forced the Africans to go out to earn the wage for which to pay tax.

The development of this colonial economic structure is dealt with in the next two chapters. What is of crucial importance in this chapter are the measures that the German colonial administration introduced during the early period to guarantee the exploitation of the colony. When these measures were applied to the masses of the population they brought home to them for the first time the reality of the colonial situation—its exploitative and oppressive nature *per se*—for they ran directly counter to the day-to-day activities of the masses in their painful search for a livelihood. As a result the masses rose against the colonial administration in what for mainland Tanzania was the Maji Maji war.

The Maji Maji war, which first broke out in the Matumbi Hills in July 1905 and spread all over the whole of south-eastern Tanzania to encompass most of the peoples south of a line from Dar es Salaam to Kilosa and thence to the northern tip of Lake Nyasa, can be seen in that perspective. This was the area that had offered almost no significant resistance during the period of conquest yet in 1905 the masses revolted. By then the peasantry was feeling the full impact of the oppressive measures: taxation, introduced in the colony in 1898, was now being forcibly demanded and defaulters were being jailed; the weight of forced labour on the communal farms was cutting deep into the peasants' day-to-day life in pursuit of a livelihood and together with increasing alienation of land for the purpose it threatened his very existence. Also, the *akidas* and jumbes who were brought in as low-grade administrators to breach the gap between the German officials and the peasantry had become excessively oppressive and corrupt, thus driving the masses into rebellion.

The Maji Maji war has recently been a subject of serious and scholarly studies. Beginning with John Iliffe's work, students of the University of Dar es Salaam branched off to investigate the movement in different districts of the Maji Maji area. More recent contributions include the serious study of the outbreak area by Dr Gwassa, a study of the Ngoni by Dr Redmond, and L.E. Larson has just completed a study of the Mbunga and part of the Ngindo.[44] So in addition to the work done before 1961, we now have a substantial body of material to draw conclusions from, thanks to the effort of the Department of History of the University of Dar es Salaam which initiated and supervised some of these investigations.

These studies have revealed to an extent not realised before that the Maji Maji movement was not only anti-European and anti-oppressive colonial administrative pressures. Far more than that it was a movement against economic imperialism. For the period between 1894 and the opening of hostilities saw the further integration of the southern interior into the capitalist economic system resulting from the great expansion and intensification of the trade in rubber, then in great demand in industrial Europe. The ensuing exploitation of rubber and the influx of coastal men into the interior was made possible with the establishment of German rule in the area. From 1894 coastal traders—Swahili, Arabs and Indians flocked into the interior and established trading networks around the military *bomas* while in the interior there developed petty African traders engaging in the supplying of rubber to the big traders centred near and around the bomas as well as in the export of foodstuffs.

Prior to this, trade between the coastal trader and the interior had been conducted with, and had affected largely, the political and military leaders of the region leaving the body of the masses largely untouched. Now, however, trade reached down to the villages, the massses serving as points of contact with the traders. Thus for the first time the African masses in the region were drawn into this system of ruthless economic exploitation with the resulting social disruption that the system itself engendered. The masses reacted very sharply against the exploitation of the traders who had established themselves there as shown by the fact that when rebellion broke out at Matumbi Hills the Maji Maji fighters moved on to wipe out the trading community—Indians, Swahili and Arab traders—from the hills and on the following day they destroyed the Indian coastal trading settlement at Samanga. It was the same at Mahenge where the trading community, a majority of whom were African traders, fell the first victims of the attack. The same pattern was repeated at Madaba where the Arab traders were the first victims of the Ngindo attackers. And when the Maji Maji war spread to Liwale, Redmond has told us that the trading community there was first attacked. It would appear therefore that the major factor precipitating the Maji Maji war in the whole region was the widespread economic exploitation resulting from German intrusion into the area. To say this is not to write off the other factors. Nor does this mean that colonial administrative pressures and oppression of other forms did not bring untold suffering to the Africans in this area. But these were universally applied to Africans throughout the country, though in some regions such as Kilimanjaro, with greater intensity. Economic imperialism seems to have been the peculiarity of the southern region and to explain the Maji Maji movement from that context helps us to understand more fully the way the rebellion broke out there, an area characterised by small-scale societies of diverse ethnicity.

Dr Gwassa has noted that in the outbreak area the maji played a crucial role in unifying the people for with the promise of invulnerability that it offered it gave them faith and hope. This is certainly true also of the Ngindo where the *hongo*, the distributors of the Maji, provided the leadership. Among the Matumbi people had arisen the prophetic leader Kinjikitile Ngwale, who offered them the sacred water, the *maji* which, once taken, would release them from the existing beliefs and superstitions by giving them a new and freer life. News of this medicine had been spreading since 1904, and by 1905 large numbers of people flocked to his home to partake of the maji. They were told to drink the water and to observe certain rituals and rules for which in turn they would receive certain benefits, the major one being immunity from bullets. Equipped with this belief, those who partook of the water could not wait any longer and they immediately moved to drive the Germans out of their country. And so began the Maji Maji war in the area.

In the stateless societies such as the Matumbi and the Ngindo where no strong political and military organisations had developed Kinjikitile and his agents, the hongo, provided the leadership. However, in areas where this vacuum did not exist such as among the Ngoni and the Mbunga, the hongo acted as messengers of the maji and therefore of the wider war leaving the leadership extant in those areas to use it for its own purpose. Thus although the Ngoni leaders had tried the maji and found it vulnerable, they used it not for the immunity it was supposed to give but to attract people to the cause. For it gave them faith in victory and those who took it did not question its supposed effectiveness, since they were reborn.

When the war broke out the Maji Maji fighters took the initiative. But this initiative soon passed from their hands as the maji failed to give them immunity and caused many of them to desert. More importantly the Germans moved in with full force, and again their Maxim gun was far superior to the fighters' spears and clubs. The cruelty with which they treated the leaders once captured is unmatched elsewhere and the massive execution of those they captured threw those remaining into despair. The fighters were finally defeated in 1907. Altogether the war claimed 75 000 Africans.

The suppression of this primarily peasant movement against colonial oppression and exploitation marked the end of African wars against Germany in Tanzania. It began the period during which the Germans could consolidate the creation of an economic infrastructure already begun, and begin the transformation of the pre-colonial economy into a colonial one, as will be shown in the next two chapters.

Zanzibar

Before bringing this discussion to a close we must turn our attention, even if only briefly, to Zanzibar, the island part of Tanzania. The British declared a protectorate over Zanzibar in 1890. This imposition of British rule was not followed by major resistance, as occurred, for example, against Germany on the mainland, or against Britain in the neighbouring territory of Kenya. Nor was it followed by the Maji Maji type of war. One possible explanation for this may well lie in the long and close relationship between Britain and the Sultanate of Zanzibar dating back to the 1840s. This relationship was not one between two equal powers, however, for from then till 1890 the position of the Sultan was dependent on the support of Britain, the major partner in this relationship. Thus as Dr Arnold has shown in chapter 2, in the 1840s and 1850s Sultan Seyyid Said accepted British influence for their support against his enemies in Mascut and East Africa as well as for their aid and support to further his territorial ambitions, particularly over Bahrain.[45] In 1861 the British forced the Sultan of Oman, Seyyid Thuwain, to recognise the independence of Zanzibar and the East African dominions. Although Majid, then the Sultan of Zanzibar, agreed to pay an annual subsidy of 40 000 crowns for this arrangement, the main significance of this settlement was that it tied the Sultan of Zanzibar even more to Britain than ever before, for having delivered the award they ensured that the independence of Zanzibar from Oman was maintained. In 1873 the British demonstrated their power over the sultanate even more sharply by forcing Seyyid Barghash, who became Sultan in 1870 upon the death of Seyyid Majid, to sign a treaty for the abolition of the slave trade from which Zanzibar derived its labour force so necessary for her economy. Faced with a choice of bombardment or of alienating the Arab slave-owning class which was bound to occur should he sign the treaty, Seyyid Barghash chose the latter and signed the treaty, thus demonstrating dramatically that it was the British who held power in Zanzibar.[46] From these examples it is evident that the position and power of the sultanate from then till 1890 became dependent on British goodwill and support. The degree of this dependence was indeed remarkable for the British determined who the Sultan would be whenever the sultanate fell vacant, a process that they formalised with the declaration of the Protectorate.

By the late 1880s, the occupation of Zanzibar by one of the major imperialist powers, Germany or Britain, was inevitable, however strong it might have been. The question at issue was which of the two would impose its rule on the islands. This question was outside the realm of the Sultan of Zanzibar for the decision was taken in Europe by the statesmen of the competing powers. As it happened, Britain traded Heligoland for Zanzibar, a decision which was more acceptable to the Sultanate of Zanzibar.

This declaration of British Protectorate over Zanzibar appears at least initially to have been no more than the formalisation of the relationship that had hitherto existed between Britain and Zanzibar. As such it is possible to argue, as Flint has done, that the Sultan, Seyyid Ali, and the Arab ruling class did not resist the imposition of British rule by force because it did not, at least in the eyes of the Sultan, appear to imply anything more than what had existed before.[47] Furthermore, and perhaps more fundamental, was that the weakness of the sultanate already evidenced by its dependence on Britain for more than fifty years, had to a very large extent predetermined the nature of the reaction of the Sultan and also of the Arab aristocracy to the imposition of the British protectorate. Looked at in this way it is little wonder that there was no resistance from the Sultan when the British took over the administration of Zanzibar, including the top echelons of the Sultan's advisers and administrators, with British civil servants responsible to the first minister, plus a newly-created post to be held by a Briton, to which Lloyd Mathews was appointed. Even when the British reduced his personal income to a third of the total Zanzibar revenue and declared the rest public revenue accountable only to the public treasury, the Sultan only protested by telegram to the Foreign Office. In addition to these measures, the Consul General, Sir Gerald

Portal, required the Sultan to dismiss his bodyguard; to avoid force, the Sultan reluctantly agreed to do so by phasing it out within three months.

Towards the end of 1892, Seyyid Ali took the opportunity of Sir Gerald Portal's transfer from Zanzibar to request the Uganda mission to press the new consul, Mr Rennell Rodd, for a reversal of these measures, apparently under the illusion that the so-called *coup d'état*[48] had been undertaken in the name of the Consul General. Were it not for the weakness of the sultanate, coupled with its understanding of the strength and power of the British for over fifty years, the Sultan would have pressed these demands with force of arms.

But as it happened the Sultan could only follow up the refusal of Mr Rodd to reverse these measures by another telegram to the Foreign Office which provoked them into instructing him that only communications which had been passed through the Consulate would be entertained, thus not only humiliating him further but also demonstrating to him very sharply the real meaning of the British Protectorate.

With the death of Seyyid Ali in March 1893 and the ensuing struggle by the heirs-apparent to the throne, so characteristic of Zanzibar succession politics, came the opportunity for the British to demonstrate by force that they were masters of Zanzibar by installing their own candidate as Sultan. Sensing that there might be trouble on Seyyid Ali's death which became imminent when his health deteriorated during the first two months of the year, the British had taken precautions to prevent civil chaos which if not contained might have led to an open resistance against them. Two warships were despatched into Zanzibar waters and the British Consulate and the Customs House were heavily guarded. So too were the local forces in Zanzibar town put on alert.

Upon the death of Seyyid Ali on 4 March, Rodd, escorted by marines, installed Seyyid Thuwain as Sultan, having driven out of the palace Seyyid Barghash who had secretly entered it and proclaimed himself Sultan. The Consul further followed this by making the installation of Thuwain as Sultan conditional on his taking an oath of allegiance to the Queen of England as sovereign of Zanzibar and her dominions, putting a seal on the administrative and financial arrangements that Sir Gerald Portal had carried out on the island, so signing away officially the independence of Zanzibar. Furthermore the Consul forced the Sultan to relinquish to the Zanzibar treasure the £200 000 invested in Britain which the Germans had paid him for the purchase of the mainland coastline and to accept henceforth a monthly salary of 18 000 rupees. Since Thuwain was anxious to become Sultan he accepted these conditions which reduced the sultanate, though placed in a more exalted position than other African rulers similarly subjected to British rule, to an agency of British rule in Zanzibar.

In other areas such as in the very sensitive issue of the abolition of slavery, an important social institution of Zanzibar, upon which rested the economy of the Islands to which the British were committed, they adopted a conciliatory policy. As this was a question which, if interfered with, would have united the Arabs against the British, the latter adopted a policy of gradual rather than immediate abolition. Because of this it is understandable that in 1890 the British allowed Seyyid Ali to nullify the Anti-Slavery Decree that he had signed by a proclamation eight days later and resisted the pressure the British Anti-Slavery movement brought to bear to abolish slavery immediately upon taking over Zanzibar. The British did so for economic reasons, maintaining that immediate abolition would ruin the economy of Zanzibar and infuriate the Arab aristocracy, for slave labour was the main basis of that economy. But this gradual approach to this very sensitive question came to erode the social and economic bond around which the Arabs would have found immediate cause to rally together and rise against the British.

Even when the decree for the emancipation of the slaves was finally brought about and signed by the Sultan in 1897 it was intended more to please the humanitarian and Anti-Slavery movement circles in Britain than to bring about a total emancipation of the slaves. For the decree was attached with such conditions as made it impossible for the slaves to obtain their freedom.[49] For example the decree stated that the exploitation of slave labour was not to be a criminal offence as was the case in other British colonies and the slaves claiming emancipation could only obtain it on application to the district courts in which sat Arab *walis* who belonged to the slave-owning class. Furthermore, emancipation was conditional on compensation. Another binding condition in the decree making it impossible for the slaves to obtain total manumission was the provision that freed slaves were subject to taxation. Those who could not produce proof of employment and domicile were to be declared vagrants, thus making them vulnerable to re-enslavement. Other problems such as the English language, in which the decree was written, the way in which the decree was treated by the authorities in Zanzibar since no attempt was made to publicise it, and the length of time it took for those who wished to claim their freedom to obtain it, added to the problem of obtaining emancipation under the decree. In such circumstances total abolition of slavery became, as the British officials wanted it, gradual indeed. After ten years only about eighty-five per cent of the slaves had obtained their freedom, the slavers having been fully compensated. By that time the question of slave labour was of very little economic importance for it had been replaced by tenancy and wage labour. As such its abolition was no longer of any serious economic consequences to the Arabs. In 1909 final abolition of slavery was enacted without arousing any resistance from those still owning slaves and no more compensation was payable after the end of 1911.[50]

The other major class in Zanzibar which was affected by the imposition of British rule in the Islands was of course the slaves themselves. These had every reason to welcome the British Protectorate for it signalled their emancipation, a process which had certainly begun with the abolition of the East African slave trade in 1873. Estimated at 60 000 in the 1850s, about two-thirds of the Islands' total population, the slave population as a class had failed to unite against their slavers because they lacked cohesion and political consciousness. Writing about them during the reign of Seyyid Said, Nicholls says, 'their interests were more personal than political: to obtain manumission, to escape or to better themselves and become absorbed in society'.[51] Their only salvation seemed to be the British and it is only natural that they should have welcomed the imposition of British rule. But to say that the slaves as a class had no reason to resist the British Protectorate is not to mean that once their emancipation had been effected, British rule was to be a panacea. Rather it came to involve ruthless exploitation of the former slaves' labour throughout the whole period, and their true emancipation came only with the Zanzibar revolution of 1964.

Notes

1 C.S. Nicholls, *The Swahili Coast: Politics, Diplomacy and Trade on the East African Littoral 1798–1856*, London, 1971, pp. 287–8.

2 *Ibid.*, pp. 156–62.

3 Roland Oliver and Gervase Mathew, *History of East Africa*, vol. I, Oxford, 1963, p. 236.

4 For a further discussion of this see Nicholls, especially chs. 6 and 7.

5 Roland Oliver, *The Missionary Factor in East Africa*, esp. chs. 3 and 4.

6 C.P. Groves, *The Planting of Christianity in Africa, vol. III, 1878–1919*, London, 1953, p. 80.

7 For details of this see Marcia Wright, *German Missions in Tanganyika, 1891–1914*, Oxford, 1971.

8 A.J. Temu, *The British Protestant Missions in Kenya 1873–1930*, Longman, 1972, pp. 20–28.

9 *Ibid.*, p. 29.

10 Patrick Redmond, 'A Political History of the Songea Ngoni from the 19th Century to the Rise of Tanganyika African National Union'. Draft of Ph.D. Thesis which was later presented to the University of London, 1972, ch. 3, p. 3.

11 A.J. Temu, pp. 39–40, pp. 48–51.

12 A.C. Unomah, 'The Economic Expansion and Political Change in Unyanyembe ca. 1840–1900', thesis submitted to the University of Ibadan for the Degree of Doctor of Philosophy, 1972, pp. 295–8.

13 For further discussion see T.O. Ranger, 'Connections between Primary Resistance movements and modern mass nationalism in East and Central Africa', Parts I and II in *Journal of African History*, ix, 3 and 4 respectively; A.R. Rotberg and Ali Mazrui, *Protest and Power in Black Africa*, New York, 1970, especially the introduction.

14 Marcia Wright, especially *German Missions in Tanganyika 1841–1914*, Oxford, 1971, pp. 6–8; also Groves, *Planting of Christianity in Africa*, vol. III, pp. 73–5.

15 John Iliffe, 'Tanzania Under German and British Rule' in B.A. Ogot and J.A. Kieran, eds., *Zamani*, Nairobi, 1968, p. 292.

16 Marcia Wright, 'Chief Merere and the Germans' in *Tanzania Notes and Records*, 69, Dar es Salaam, 1968, p. 42.

17 For further details see Robert D. Jackson, 'Resistance to the German invasion of the Tanganyika Coast, 1888–1891' in Rotberg and Mazrui, pp. 55–6.

18 Walter Brown, 'Bagamoyo, A Historical Introduction', *Tanzania Notes and Records*, 71, 1970, p. 73.

19 Rotberg and Mazrui, eds, *Protest and Power in Black Africa*, p. 51.

20 *Ibid.*, pp. 57–8.

21 *Ibid.*, pp. 57–8.

22 *Ibid.*

23 Steven Feierman, *The Shamba Kingdom, A History*, Madison, Wisconsin, pp. 194–203.

24 *Ibid.*

25 For details of this see Kathleen M. Stahl, *History of the Chagga People of Kilimanjaro*, London, 1964; also see G.O. Ekemodi, 'African Reaction to German rule in North East Tanzania 1885–1900'. Paper read at the School of Oriental and African Studies, University of London, 24 Nov., 1971.

26 Stahl, pp. 236 and 250–1.

27 *Ibid.*, pp. 178–9; also Ekemodi, p. 5.

28 Alison Redmayne, 'Mkwawa and the Hehe wars' in *Journal of African History*, ix, 3, p. 415.

29 This information was conveyed to me by Lorne Larson who was currently finishing his Ph.D. thesis on the 'History of Mahenge District'.

30 Wright, 'Chief Merere and the Germans', *TNR*, p. 44.

31 Unomah, pp. 308–12.

32 *Ibid.*, p. 319.

33 The pages that follow have been based on Ralph Austen, *Northwest Tanzania under German and British Rule*, Yale, 1968.

34 *Ibid.*, p. 35.

35 *Ibid.*, p. 40.

36 *Ibid.*, pp. 47–9.

37 Redmond, *A History of the Ngoni*, especially ch. 3.

38 *Ibid.*, pp. 9–17.

39 Ernst Nigman, in Helge Kjekshus, 'Ecology Control and Economic Development', p. 68 map therein, paper read at the History Departmental Seminar, 14 Feb. 1974, University of Dar es Salaam.

40 Helge Kjekshus, pp. 46–68. The author has argued impressively that the population of mainland Tanzania was stagnant or showed a slight tendency of expansion throughout the nineteenth century. Marshalling his evidence from written sources and travellers accounts, he has maintained, contrary to popular view, that there were no immediate growth signs in population after the establishment of foreign rule and the so-called pacification. Rather he sees the year 1890 as the turning point in population growth, for then began the downward dip in population. He explains this in terms of the breakdown of the man-controlled ecological system which characterised the 1890s, linking this directly to colonialists.

41 Ekemode, pp. 6–7.

42 *Ibid.*, p. 8.

43 Walter Rodney, 'Resistance and Accommodation in Ovimbundu/Portuguese Relations', paper read at History Departmental Seminar, 29 Aug. 1973, University of Dar es Salaam, p. 8.

44 Gilbert Gwassa 'The Outbreak and Development of the Maji Maji War 1905–07', Ph.D. thesis presented to the University of Dar es Salaam, 1973.

45 Nicholls, *The Swahili Coast*, p. 195.

46 J.M. Gray, 'Zanzibar and the Coastal Belt, 1840–84', in Roland Oliver and Gervase Mathews, eds., *History of East Africa*, vol. I, Oxford, 1963, p. 259.

47 J.E. Flint, 'Zanzibar 1890–1950' in Harlow, Vincent and others, eds., *History of East Africa*, vol. II, Oxford, 1965.

48 *Ibid.*, pp. 642–3.

49 L.H. Hollingsworth, *Zanzibar Under the Foreign Office*,

London, 1953, pp. 141–2.

50 *Ibid.*, p. 157.

51 Nicholls, *The Swahili Coast*, p. 289.

4. The Political Economy of Colonial Tanganyika 1890–1930

Walter Rodney

The creation of the colonial economy by violence, 1890–1900

The nineteenth century was a period of considerable change in East Africa. Means of maintaining a livelihood, socio-political structures and cultural values were all steadily transformed. Coming on the scene in the latter part of the century, the colonialists altered the pace and direction of change, and forcibly wrested from the colonised population the initiative for controlling their own evolution. This could not happen overnight. Rather, the institutionalisation of colonial structures of production and political control occupied a phase, which in Tanzania lasted for about twenty years, beginning in 1885 and intensifying during the 1890.[1]

In 1890, the Imperial German Government undertook direct political supervision of the colony of Germany East Africa. The DOAG, the chartered company which previously shouldered this responsibility, was unable to carry out the first task of colonisation: namely, conquest. From 1890 onwards, the German Government brought about subjugation and started to organise an economy geared towards exporting its surplus, particularly in the form of primary agricultural commodities. Annual reports for German East Africa during the 1890s and the first years of this century indicate a high level of investigation of the topography, geology, climate and the plant and animal species.[2] The building of roads, bridges and the Usambara Railway (Tanga Line) were major inputs into the new colonial economy, along with the construction of a floating dock at Dar es Salaam and the introduction of lighters and riverain vessels. Other foundation works for the export-oriented economy included the issue of coins and notes, the establishment of government-controlled market halls and the spread of customs posts.

Trade between German East Africa and the outside world came under closer German control, this being one of the primary reasons for colonisation. By 1912, Germany supplied over half the imports of its East African colony, and the proportion was higher with regard to exports. This meant a doubling of the German share of import/export as it stood in 1895.[3] Since Zanzibar for many years retained its nineteenth-century dominance in trade with the coast, the DOAG and subsequent German administrations sought their share of the movement of goods to and from Zanzibar. Nor could India be easily eliminated from the Indian Ocean trade network. In order to cash in on African/Indian trade, the German East Africa Line ran a special shipping service to Indian ports.[4]

Although German colonial preparations were thorough, and although Germans captured a large proportion of the trade to and from German East Africa, they remained restricted to the coast and to the trade routes which connected the interior and the coast. The Germans at first concentrated on ousting Arabs and Swahilis from the pre-colonial export trade which tied up with the Indian Ocean network. Hence, there arose the conflict with Abushiri in 1889–90. For years thereafter, the main concern of the German administration was to improve caravan roads. Thousands of porters were still used, experiments to introduce animal-drawn wagons being timid and unsuccessful.[4] When the Usambara Railway was projected to start from Tanga in 1891, the aim was to reach Mombo and use it as an entrepot for up-country caravans, especially from Lake Nyanza (Victoria). The progress of this railway was extremely slow and after the British completed their railway from Mombasa to Fort Florence on Lake Nyanza in 1901–2, commerce was diverted into British hands. To succeed in their self-appointed task of extracting surplus from what is now mainland Tanzania, Rwanda and Burundi, the Germans hastened to implement their own major railway project—the Central Line, starting from Dar es Salaam in 1905 and reaching Morogoro by 1907.

African resistance was a decisive factor in the late start of the colonial economy. Many areas were not subdued until the early years of this century, especially in Kigoma and Rwanda/Urundi. The launching of colonial activities, such as the building of roads and government *bomas*, was intertwined with violent conquest; and forced labour was prominent everywhere. Then came the laws imposing taxes on the subject African population, although in some districts tax was not collected until a few years before the First World War. Often the drive to collect hut and poll tax was thinly-veiled prolongation of the aggression of conquest, involving hut-burning, the seizing of cattle and the snatching of women.[5]

Both the slave trade and the institutions of slavery as introduced by the Arabs stood in the way of colonial ventures, and they were eliminated by the Germans. However, a different form of forced labour was introduced, comprising short-term service on construction sites, on private European estates and on collective *shambas* whose produce went to the Germans. This coercion was set in train by German civilian and military authorities; and it was usually supervised by paid Swahili/Muslim agents, who became the *jumbes* and *akidas* of coastal and inland African communities. The front line of German colonial authority was also manned by Africans: namely, the *askaris* of the military and police units. They were originally drawn from Somalia, Sudan and southern Mozambique to ensure non-fraternisation with local Africans. Subsequently, Manyema from the Congo were favoured for the same reason, while recruits from within German East Africa were posted outside their own areas.[6]

A great deal of the dirty work of German colonialism was necessarily implemented by the jumbes, akidas and askaris. They saw to the requisitioning of forced labour, the collection of taxes and the punishment of default and insubordination. Through a relatively high wage in the case of the askaris, and through having their salaries tied in tax collection in the case of the jumbes and akidas, these particular Africans were given a stake in the colonial system. They had a relatively free hand when they were dealing with fellow Africans, and therefore they frequently resorted to intimidation and extortion. Many hereditary rulers were also reduced to the status of overseers on behalf of German masters. This applied even to the developed politics of Bukoba, Ruanda and Urundi, whose rulers were given only a slightly greater measure of freedom than others. In most parts of the country, the traditional law enforcers such as the *ruga ruga* and the Mnyaparas became in effect colonial askaris, who brought force to bear on their own people to get them to work for the Germans.[7]

The widespread resort to coercion to initiate colonial production relations is largely explained by the fact that labour was not usually a commodity within the indigenous African economies; and there was little reason for this process to take place spontaneously. So tens of thousands of central Tanzanians had become accustomed to portergae in the pre-colonial period. These (mainly Nyamwezi) were often willing to continue in this occupation or to make the transition to other forms of hired labour. But, without force, the Germans could not fill the ranks even of the porters; and violence was frequently necessary to get Nyamwezi to work on plantations.[8] Besides, German East Africa was a typical colonial situation in which taxes were imposed on Africans not so much for the revenue which resulted but as a means of propelling them into the labour market and the money economy, and thereby drawing off the surplus. Such mechanisms for alienating the product of peoples' labour were few and weak in pre-colonial East Africa. Their introduction inevitably evoked African bewilderment and hostility, which in turn were met by European force exercised in the name of law and order.

Colonised Africans were required to produce more and to produce new commodities. To gain access to exportable surplus which would immediately repay colonising efforts, the Germans forced or encouraged Africans to persist with the hunting of ivory and to intensify the collection of beeswax and rubber. Tax at this early stage was often in kind, utilising these very products. However, by the late 1890s the cultivation of sisal and of new varieties of cotton, rubber, groundnuts and coffee were demanded of Africans—either in the capacity of peasants or as paid labourers.

Havi ıg no special reputation as a producer of valuable minerals, East Africa was looked upon within the imperialist production system as one of the providers of agricultural raw materials to service increased human and industrial consumption in the metropoles and particularly in Germany. For instance, the demand for oil seeds and coffee was tied up with the growth of a large consumer market as the petty bourgeoisie and the organised proletariat of Western Europe made successful demands for higher living standards. Therefore, rubber from East Africa was consequent upon the growth of European technology, which put rubber to novel uses and found better methods of coagulation and processing. The promotion of cotton and sisal constitute another variant on the theme of metropolitan market dependence. These fibres were required of East Africa by Germany to lessen industrial dependence on raw material sources such as the United States (for cotton) and Mexico (for sisal and henequen).

The colonial political economy was given its distinctiveness not so much by the new export commodities but by the socio-economic forms introduced for their production. The Germans experimented with communal farms which bore a superficial resemblance to the traditional African shambas, but the labour was coerced.[9] Alternatively, they charged the Africans with the task of organising African labour on African land and exploitation was effected through price mechanisms when the crop was sold. In this way, a market-oriented peasantry arose out of the self-sufficient communities. Africans near the coast in southern Tanganyika were the first to move to peasant production, with cotton as their staple. Those inland areas which were part of the earlier export connection involving ivory and slaves were also quickly tied to the metropoles by the cash crop nexus. Previous familiarity with a given crop or a similar species would obviously have made the transition easier, as with cotton on the Lakes, robusta coffee in Bukoba and groundnuts in central Tanganyika. However, the cultivation of a strange plant could not be readily mastered—as happened with arabica coffee in Kilimanjaro from the 1890s. The presence of missionaries and white settlers in this area facilitated the acquisition of seeds and relevant techniques.

White settler agriculture was limited mainly to the Usambaras during the first two decades of German rule. A certain pro-settler strain had characterised German colonialism since the time of Carl Peters, but the practical results were few. There were only eighty-six settlers in the colony in 1900, and so the three-fold increase to 284 by 1905 was not really impressive.[10] Plantations were far more significant than settler farms. They were distributed in the Usambaras, Tanga, Pangani, Lindi, and along the first stage of the Central Line from Dar es Salaam to Morogoro. Coconuts, rubber, cotton, and sisal were all 'plantation crops' during the early years. By 1904, there were some five million to seven million rubber trees, constituting the largest plantation sector. Sisal was not far behind in acreage and value. Cultivation having started in the 1890s, mature sisal leaves were being cut at the turn of the century, and by 1905 production was up to 1 397 tons, worth 1.1 million marks.[11]

The plantation was the most important innovation in the formative period of the colonial political economy under German hegemony. It was socio-economic entity ideally suited to metropolitan capitalist investment in the colony, and it fitted in well with notions of racial and cultural supremacy which went hand in hand with the desire to exploit Africa's resources. Combining both field agriculture and a degree of first-stage processing, the plantations required large amounts of land, capital and African labour, along with a small elite corps of non-African supervisory staff.[12] This particular form of the organisation of labour and capital was deliberately chosen and applied. There was nothing intrinsic to any crop which made it botanically or otherwise a 'plantation crop'. Rubber was cultivated on plantations, by settlers and by African peasants; copra was produced by Europeans, Arabs and Africans (sometimes within a semi-feudal framework); while cotton was already being grown by several Tanganyikan communities in the pre-colonial period.

As would be expected, striking differences existed between the political power of African peasants and that of the settlers and plantation owners. Indeed, peasants exercised no political power during the years in question. With regard to the other two groups, there was an interesting disparity in their relative access to power. Settlers wielded more political influence than their numbers would suggest. The communities were given legal status with representatives on District Councils from 1901, and they were represented on the Governor's Advisory Council and other boards. There were close ties between settlers, the administration and the military; they were allocated half of the income from African hut tax, along with other subventions.[13] Nevertheless, the settlers were at best small capitalists or petty bourgeois, and sometimes they ranked merely as impecunious farmers and adventurers. Neither within the colony nor outside could settler influence measure up to the power of the capitalists who owned plantations and who were associated with bankers, industrialist, shipping and railway magnates, big commercial houses and rich capitalist landlords in Germany. In 1901, absentee plantation owners living in Germany founded the Union of German East African Plantations, an organisation which exercised quasi-governmental functions with respect to colonial policy.[14]

Settlers, farmers, absentee plantation owners and plantation managers made common cause on the issue of labour. Their agricultural operations meant both the alienation of African land and the reduction of part of the local population to the status of wage labourers. Without African labour, colonial capital investment was valueless and the forcibly acquired land was also useless. Therefore, farmers and planters used the colonial state to secure the coercion of African labour. The population in the actual plantation sites resisted plantation work, going there under constraints such as famine conditions. Otherwise, they found it more convenient to grow food for sale to the estates. Between 1900 and 1902, Tanga planters got the government to start settlement schemes to relocate some Nyamwezi labour near the plantations, but these failed, leading to dependence on short-term recruitment from considerable distances: notably from Songea, Unyamwezi and Sukumaland. Coercion and abuse were rampant in the sphere of recruitment, with a African chiefs playing a role very similar to their middleman role during the slave trade.[15]

Wages for plantation labourers and other workers were initially low, and they were depressed as soon as the colonial state machinery pushed more Africans on to the labour market, as had occurred by 1903. Living and working conditions were extremely poor, and any attempt to escape was branded as 'desertion' and treated as a criminal offence liable to imprisonment. Africans who were in the employment of Germans suffered day-to-day abuse and brutality, and these first decades of the German East African colonial regime were notorious for the frequency and severity of whippings applied by private employers and by state officials.[16]

Reform, entrenchment and surplus generation, 1906–1914

Even where Africans had been 'pacified', they did not acquiesce in loss of sovereignty when this assumed the form of forced labour, taxation and brutality from Germans and their African minions. The Maji Maji wars provide conclusive evidence to this effect. Subsequent to and partly because of this resistance, the Germans sought to reform the worst excesses of exploitation and oppression.[17] The German working class was strongly represented in the German parliament by the Social Democrats, who led the exposure of the kinds of abuses introduced into colonial territories by imperialist expansion. They voted for the creation of a formal political organ in Germany which would be answerable to parliament in governing the colonies; while in German East Africa itself the most important reforms tended to remove the power of coercing labour from the hands of private individuals and to emphasise Government's role in supervising labour relations. For this latter purpose, District Commissioners were appointed. Forced labour was partially curbed, and so too was the arbitrary behaviour of government jumbes, akidas and askaris. As a complement to this lessening of coercive measures, a significant amount of encouragement was given to peasant production in the era of post-Maji Maji reforms.

A more liberal phase was a prerequisite for the entrenchment of colonial capitalist relations. The colonial economy was entrenched when it incorporated the majority of the African population, and when it set in motion a series of factors which caused Africans to accommodate to the new order peacefully, willingly and even enthusiastically. Coercion remained throughout a critical element within the colonial situation, but once the self-sufficient African economies had been penetrated, Africans themselves sought to participate in the emergent colonial economy and to influence the terms on which they participated. In this way, the maintenance and extension of colonial relations became spontaneous.

Given a choice, Africans preferred to meet their taxes and cash needs by growing a crop which was marketable for money—usually with the overseas market as the ultimate destination. Cash crop farming was the least onerous form of meeting the demands of an economic system which Africans were powerless to reject and which they increasingly accepted as offering certain rewards in goods and services. The moment that transport became available in a locality in German East Africa, it was usually the African population which took active steps to bring commodities to a wider market.[18] This involved initially little disruption to their previous agricultural cycle. They still grew their basic food and provided for their own subsistence. They knew their own environment and they were not very vulnerable to market fluctuations. For these reasons, African peasants were usually more efficient producers than the European newcomers, in spite of utilising only hand tools. They competed successfully with plantations and more so with settlers, who lacked capital in the amounts which would have been necessary to outweigh the advantages of peasants operating at near subsistence level. Recognising these facts, the Germans after 1906 turned to persuasion to augment the numbers and output of the cash crop peasantry.

Cotton was first grown as a plantation and settler crop at the Rufiji delta, at Sadani and around Morogoro/Kilosa, but the returns were poor as compared to the crops which peasants brought to market at little economic cost to the colonisers. After 1906, in spite of protests from farmers and planters, the Imperial German Government and its agents promoted peasant-grown cotton through seed distribution, technical advice, increase of ginneries and small credit distributed in Kilwa, Rufiji and Lindi, and up to 500 tons went to Bagamoyo, Moshi, Arusha, Mwanza and Morogoro/Kilosa. Already in 1908, Africans accounted for two-thirds of the cotton exports, and by 1912 their share had reached five-sevenths of the total.[19] The story of coffee was somewhat similar. Coffee ceased to be a plantation crop from 1909, but it proved to be one of the very few crops which settlers could successfully grow and contribute to the export-oriented economy which the metropole envisaged. The German colonial authorities came to discourage settlers with small capital, and gave their backing to the white coffee growers who had large farms in the Kilimanjaro area.[20] Nevertheless, African peasant production of coffee was also promoted and it caught up with settler output by 1912. Coercion and taxes were still used to extend African cash crop farming of coffee in Bukoba and cotton in Mwanza and Musoma.[21] On the other hand, the alternative of cash crop farming was clearly preferred to such things as porterage and migrant labour.

Apart from the major export crops, Africans furnished the Germans with a variety of agricultural products which could either be exported or consumed locally: notably, groundnuts, sesame, maize, millet, rice and beans. A large proportion of the labouring population was engaged in plantation or peasant production of cash crops which were not destined for the local market, even when they were edible. Therefore, some areas specialising in food were welcome. The German authorities regretted the importation of rice from India and favoured the commercialisation of rice in Ulanga, Mwanza and other parts of the colony.[22] After 1908, the amounts of hut and poll tax recovered increased steadily in all areas and markedly in others, such as Mwanza and Lindi. This was a good index to the growth of the peasantry.

Settlers, who numbered about 880 in 1914, remained too few to decisively shape the political economy of German East Africa, although their local influence spread to Kilimanjaro, Nbulu and the Southern Highlands. Those growing rubber fared disastrously when world prices fell in 1913. Rubber plantations also performed badly. For all practical purposes, sisal became the sole 'plantation crop', and it proved immensely successful. On the eve of the First World War, sisal output was nearly 20 000 tons per annum valued at 10.3 million marks, and it accounted for thirty per cent of total exports. A characteristic plantation economy such as existed in the Belgian Congo was usually sharply differentiated from a characteristic peasant-based colonial economy such as the one which developed on the Gold Coast.[23] The Tanzanian colonial political economy had acquired a unique duality before the end of the German regime, comprising plantation and peasant sectors which were fairly evenly rated with regard to output and value to the metropolitan production system.

Plantation sisal and settler-grown coffee were usually described as 'non-native agriculture'. In reality they were possible only because of African labour. In the German East African context, plantations tapped the labour of as many Africans as were reached by capitalism indirectly through peasant cash crops. By 1913, the wage-earning labour force comprised 172 000 Africans, estimated to have been about one-fifth of the able-bodied male population at this time. Porters accounted for a substantial proportion of this figure, and the Central Line railway was also a major employer during its period of construction up to 1914. But it was the plantation sector which did most to destroy self-contained family labour and to replace it at least partially with wage-earning. Between 1910 and 1914, the area under plantation cultivation increased by 110 per cent to over 100 000 hectares. The rate at which new workers were created could not keep up with this jump, and further extension was constrained by the non-availability of labour. Nevertheless, in the last years before the war, some 14 000 Africans were brought to the plantations annually; and the total increased from 32 000 in 1908 to about 92 000 in 1913.

Reformist labour legislation favourable to Africans was not always implemented, due to lack of supervisory machinery. Settlers and plantation managers often paid less than the agreed contract wages, and they exacted illegal fines. Some officials and missionaries complained to the German Government and public about continuing abuses. After 1909, charges were brought against employers for assaulting workers, and several convictions were made. Nevertheless, although the legislation after 1906 was an improvement as far as labourers were concerned, the law was still an instrument of the employing class between whom and the government the contradictions were secondary. Relics of forced labour were still permitted as in west Usambara, and the legally permissible punishments for workers' 'desertion' were harsh. Wages never ranged higher than 12–14 rupees per assigned task or *kipande*, and they were often depressed through combination of employers to as low as 6–7 rupees.[14] This means that the labourer completed thirty full working days over a period of six weeks or more, before he would earn the amount in question.

Because the migrants and the local labour worked on short contracts for six or nine months, there was a high turnover of the labour force. Besides, the daily absentee rate was high and a marked tendency to run away completely was always evident. A small number of skilled Africans were to be found in the sisal factories, but the vast majority were unskilled and could not accumulate any skills, apart from the expertise of wielding a *panga* to cut sisal leaves. The productivity of labour was necessarily low, given lack of skills, high turnover and little motivation. Yet it was a profitable system under colonial conditions, because (in contrast to the metropoles) the employer was not responsible for giving the worker a 'living wage' which would feed himself and his family from one generation to the next. In the first place, the plantations robbed the indigenous economies of fully-formed male labour.

Secondly, the colonial employer on farm or plantation left the burden of subsistence on those parts of the countryside from which the labourer was recruited. The migrant engaged in subsistence agriculture before and after his stint on the plantation, while his wife and family fended for themselves while he was away. These were the bases for the huge profits made by the capitalist plantations. Sisal companies almost invariably registered huge profits four or five years after they went into production, as soon as the first crops of mature leaves were reaped. In 1907–8 prices were down to 600 marks per ton, but Tanga planters cleared profits of 400 marks per ton. Little wonder that companies capitalised at about one million marks could in a single year make a profit of half a million marks and declare dividends in the region of fifteen and twenty per cent, especially in the years 1910 to 1914. Rubber investment suffered a severe setback in 1913, but prior to this the returns were so high that speculation was rife. In 1910, for instance, settlers were keen on preparing rubber estates for sale at considerable profit to larger enterprises—including English buyers. Up to 1912, the big rubber plantations were also declaring healthy dividends of five to ten per cent.

All elements of the German population who were involved in colonial enterprise, from the settler to the Kaiser, were guaranteed some profit by the imperial German state and the specific colonial state machinery which was created for German East Africa. State support took the form of direct grants and loans as well as duty exemptions, tax concessions, freight rebates and other indirect subsidies. One author of a study on German colonies remarks as follows:

> To a small section of the (German) population the colonies were doubtless a source of profit; the merchants and planters who exploited the natural and human resources of overseas possessions, the shipping companies which received subsidies, the civil and military officials who received posts—all have every reason to support colonial enterprise.[25]

Yet the same author misleadingly concludes that Germany gave more to the colonies than it received. The central point of the colonial relationship was the transfer of surplus to strengthen the capitalist class and the capitalist mode of production. Ultimately the bill had to be paid by many European workers whose labour was exploited at the point of production and more so by Africans whose entire way of life was brutally disrupted so as to integrate them into the global capitalist system.

When subsidies originated in Germany, they were transferred not to Africans but to German capitalists in East Africa. German shippers were granted subsidies to secure them a greater share of the freight to and from East Africa. The railway building concerns received even wider privileges, such as guaranteed credits and heavy payments when the constructed enterprises were taken over by the government. The nexus of exploitation stretched from African labour to firms such as Philip Holzmann of Frankfurt, Lenz and C. of Berlin, the Krupp combine and the Deutsche Bank. Above all, it is the history of the DOAG which consistently reveals how the colonial state nurtured and protected the interests of the big capitalists. After losing its political franchise, the DOAG was 'compensated' with loans and grants which were taken from East African customs revenues and which were therefore met through the exploitation of African labour. By 1903 there was another dimunition of the extensive privileges of the DOAG with regard to land, currency and banking but it continued to enjoy a lucrative near-monopoly of import/export trade and associated activities such as warehousing and lighterage at the Dar es Salaam harbour.

Between 1905 and 1913, the DOAG made over seven million marks net profit. No other private company so completely dominated a colonial economy as the DOAG with respect to German East Africa.[26] Starting with a base in plantations and commerce, it spread its tentacles into every area of the growing colonial economy. Indeed, it was often pioneering the extension of the embryo export-oriented economy, and for this it was handsomely rewarded. It had a monopoly of buying cotton and rubber; and settlers sold exclusively to the DOAG, from whom they borrowed money at six to eight per cent interest. It was part owner of two local banks; it operated the largest retail agency (in Tanga) from 1908; it bought the Hotel Kaiserhof and gained the concession to sell food to the railway; it secured shares in the mining industry; it founded a timber company in 1908; and by 1912 it had expanded into the Belgian Congo.[27] Such economic power can be understood only in relation to the political power of the class which controlled both the German state and the colonial state of German East Africa.

The coercive arm of the colonial state of German East Africa was strengthened after the colonialists received a fright in the scope of Maji Maji. By 1913, the *Schuztruppe* or protectorate force comprising 2 500 Africans commanded by 1 152 Germans. In addition there was a police force of 2 140 under sixty-five officers. Their weapons were not the most up-to-date, but they were good enough for their principal function—'to deal with local risings'.[28] Several small local risings did occur until about 1911, and they were all promptly quelled. For the most part the suppressive apparatus could from this point onwards stand in reserve while the economy spontaneously expanded.

Economic activity in German East Africa was at a much higher level than in British East Africa on the eve of the First World War. It was also more varied—with a small mining sector, obtaining gold from Sekenke and Mwanza and mica from the Uluguru, and with several minor manufacturing establishments making consumer goods. The extractive colonial economy was strengthened day after day as Africans took a variety of steps, such as the Gogo bringing cattle to market or the Nyaturu accepting employment in mines. Many areas remained superficially 'traditional' because they were not directly under plantations or cash crops and they were remote from towns and mines. But these were often deeply penetrated, especially when their labour was drawn off to serve colonialism in other districts.

By 1914, labour utilisation in German East Africa had been redirected, the overall social product had been increased and the surplus was being channelled outwards to the colonial power, and especially to its dominant class. As part of this process, there was a change in African consumption patterns which in turn affected the pre-existing African production and distribution of certain commodities. African-made cloth and iron tools and the trade in these items were already on their way out in German times, with only a few resistant pockets.[29] The increased import of cotton piece-goods was the single most important index to the spread of new consumer habits. The African population was being condemned to produce that which it did not consume and to consume that which it did not produce.[30]

It cannot be said that colonialism determined all social changes in German East Africa or in any other colony; nor can it be said that Africans completely lost control of their own environment and society, but they were well on their way to so doing. Rinderpest epidemics (only incidentally connected with the coming of the colonialists) had severely undermined the indigenous political economy of the whole territory in the late 1890s. Animal husbandry was never restored to its former pre-eminence, with all that this implied for environmental control.[31] Similarly, diseases seriously affected millet during the early years of German rule[32]. Millet was never re-established as the principal staple of the African people, and the population thereby lost the advantages of their own experience in its cultivation as well as the crop's proved resistance to drought in the Tanzanian and African environment in which it was domesticated. There was no possibility of resuming the former trend of development in the context of European colonial power. Famine, havoc and suppression associated with Maji Maji further clinched this fact. The African people were effectively disarmed. Without a licence, they could scarcely hunt game or even defend their homes from wild beats. Issues such as the choice of crop and the method of protection against tsetse fly were removed from African jurisdiction before the end of the German colonial regime.

To the purely economic phenomena, one must add the evolution of a formal colonial educational system and the considerable presence of the missionaries. Islam continued to spread at least as rapidly as the officially-sponsored Christian religion; but Christianised Africans were usually more closely involved in colonial economic activities.[33] Missionaries did a great deal to initiate the colonial economy, especially in Kilimanjaro and the southern highlands; and of course they were in the forefront with regard to education and cultural imperialism. They helped reinforce a pattern of personal dependence imposed on Africans by employers and the colonial state—and symbolised by the necessity to salute all Europeans by bowing from the west and saying *jambo*. This behaviour merely reflected the dominance of the intrusive capitalist mode of production in a colonial situation.

War and the change of masters, 1914–1930

Many historians pass lightly over the period of the First World War in East Africa. In reality, it was a period of intense suffering. Since the British and the Germans fought their African campaigns mainly with African askaris, the majority of the casualties were sustained by African combatants. More staggering still were the losses among African porters. The record of the Carrier Corps attached to the Kings African Rifles (KAR) is a frightening one. Men toiled for long hours, with heavy loads, on empty stomachs along barely passable roads. Through a combination of ignorance and indifference to African welfare on the part of the British, the preparations for food and for preventive and curative medicine for the porters were scandalously poor. By 1917 the Carrier Corps employed some 150 000 porters; and at any given time at least 15 000 of these were so ill as to be confined to bed. Porters suffered severe hardships and casualties on the quagmire Dodoma/Iringa road, in the swampy Rufiji Valley and on the cold mountain paths from Nyasa into Songea—to mention the worst of their 'battlefields'. Over a period of twenty-four weeks in 1917, known deaths among porters were recorded as 11 484, which was an average of more than sixty-eight per day.[34] In the end, the war statistics did not bother to account for porters dead and maimed.

Most parts of Tanzania felt the pinch of the war through having to supply provisions. Sometimes. Africans were induced to sell more food than they ought to have done in the light of their own requirements. At other times, the food was forcibly requisitioned; a procedure which could mean nocturnal raids and seizing of women as hostages. In a district as famous for food surpluses as Ulanda, famine resulted after the Germans exploited it as a food supply base for their armies. In central Tanzania, impressive herds of cattle, goats and donkeys were decimated; and the adverse effects were compounded because the area was already prone to drought. The Gogo in particular suffered tremendous hardships when famine struck, forcing them to abandon their homesteads. Understandably, disease claimed innumerable lives. Influenza, smallpox, diarrhoea, plague and cerebro-spinal meningitis killed tens of thousands. Influenza alone took an estimated 50 000 to 80 000 African lives from 1917 to 1919.[35] Epidemics were the consequence of armies spreading infection from one end of the country to another, often bringing new diseases against which the population had no immunity. The colonialists were not capable of doing much about this, but in addition, they were not motived to do the best they could. Because of war-time disruption of European trade and because of campaigns fought on East African soil, the export-oriented economy was set back. Peasants gave up cotton growing; settlers and missionaries abandoned their farms; and plantation production came to an early half because Tanga was one of the first battlefields. However, the war did give a fillip to industrialisation and technological experimentation. When cut off from Europe, the German civil and military administration turned to the local manufacture of cloth, dyes, rubber tyres, benzene, soap, ropes, bags, alcohol, jams, boots, quinine and cigarettes. The last governor of German East Africa boasted that

> We get all we require from the country. We find all our food supplies, materials and necessities in our German East Africa . . . we find we have an adequate supply of such things as previously we have thought it necessary to import.[36]

Such self-reliance went far beyond the petty manufactures, permitted within a colonial economy in that period, and of course it ceased with the coming of peace and 'normality'. This helps strikingly to illustrate why colonialism has been referred to by some scholars as 'lop-sided' and 'perverse'.[37] Industry in Tanganyika during the 1920s was confined either to the extraction of minerals or to the immediate processing of raw materials to facilitate export—and hence the profusion of ginneries. The colonial economy was not geared to maximise African control of the environment. On the contrary, it inverted the order of priorities followed in any system of production in which the people have some say in their own destiny.

The foundations laid by the Germans were unaltered when the British took over Tanganyika. The change of masters and the change of judicial form from colony to mandated territory were superficial ones. The British argued the superiority of their colonialism over that which had been practised by Germany in East Africa and eslewhere. As a justification for annexing German colonies, Britain amassed evidence concerning brutality, forced labour and other malpractices by the Germans with regard to Africans. Some charges were exaggerated and, in any event, the patterns were typical of colonial rule everywhere, as brought out in the counter charges launched by the Germans against the British.[38] On the other hand, superstructural differences were bound to emerge between one colonial regime and another, having their origins mainly in metropolitan traditions. For instance, the strong militaristic element within the German ruling class was well represented in the colonies. Parts of German East Africa remained under military jurisdiction throughout the German stay. But the British were extremely reluctant both at home and in the colonies to allow military power to intervene where the ruling class considered civilian administration to be sufficient. As their armies advanced into Tanganyika, civilian administrators were brought in from British East Africa and Nyasaland, and they assumed total control over conquered areas as soon as it was feasible. An interesting element of continuity is that these political officers collected taxes as laid down by the Germans and they administered German law, modified only by martial proclamations.[39] Up to the mid-1920s akidas appointed by the Germans remained in several districts.

Since the British regarded their first task as the establishment of law and order, great importance attached to the army and police, as seen from their share of the budget in early years.[40] Nevertheless, the KAR and the police were not as dominant as their German counterparts. Conversely, the bureaucrat was prominent in the British colonial context. Even in the immediate post-war days when matters were most unsettled, the administrative corps numbered 108 as compared with the maximum of seventy-eight officials in German East Africa (Ruanda/Urundi included). These corps had international experience.[41] They brought with them the norms, administrative procedures and laws which had been fashioned in other British colonies. India played a special role as a model, while some colonial political institutions had their roots in the 'old colonial system' maintained since the seventeenth century in the Americas. One such was the Legislative Council, which was introduced into Tanganyika in 1926.

Continuity and change must also be measured in terms of the metropolitan economic institutions which were set up in Tanganyikan Territory. British firms naturally sought to inherit from their German rivals; and the transfer of ultimate political authority to Parliament in Whitehall was matched by the transfer of economic power to Mincing Lane, London's import/export centre. As a consequence of the changeover, several differences in economic organisation were noticeable. Firstly, no single British company acquired the pre-eminence of the DOAG. Secondly, many more non-nationals were allowed to invest and participate in the Tanganyikan colonial economy, largely because British capitalists were less interested than the Germans had been. Thirdly, Tanganyika was merely a part of the British colonial sphere in East Africa, subordinated to Kenya through customs arrangements and through the fact that the link with the metropole was maintained by firms which had their East African head-offices in Nairobi or Mombasa. Nevertheless, the function of the banks, import/export houses and plantation companies remained the same.

The typical post-war reconstruction goal of the British in Tanganyika was to catch up and surpass pre-war production—as expressed mainly in import/export indices. Government departmental reports and the Governor's addresses to the Legislative Council in the late 1920s indicated steady recovery as well as some original developments in sectors of the colonial economy.[42] For instance, the mining of mica in the Ulugurus and of gold in north Mwanza, Musoma and Sekenke was fairly well re-established by 1927–30; while the Lupa alluvial gold field was brought into operation after its recovery in 1922. Thc new government extended the infrastructure of roads bridges and the telegraph; while the completion of the rail link from Tabora to Mwanza in August 1928 was a vital step, further integrating the densely peopled Lake Zone which had already shown its potentialities under the Germans.[43]

Much of the economic recovery was due to peasant effort—notably to the production of cotton in Mwanza and Musoma and to the extension of coffee growing in Bukoba and Kilimanjaro. Groundnuts, sesame, rice, hides and ghee were also among the peasant commodities which originated from the north-west and the centre of the country. Increased output was achieved by taxation (increased in 1925), by force and by 'administrative persuasion' bordering on force. Cotton, which was accorded high priority by the British textile industry, was the crop which usually required a considerable element of force before it was taken up by Africans. Coercion reappeared in the post-war years because the war had created a situation in some ways analogous to that faced by the Germans on their arrival. Nevertheless the British were not starting absolutely anew. They could, for instance, point out with satisfaction that bark cloth had practically disappeared from Bukoba and the Haya were demanding cloth.[44] This and other imported items acted as a stimulus, apart from the coercion which was applied to have the Haya grow more coffee. The same holds true for other cash crops elsewhere and for the process of going out to seek employment.

As the tempo of colonial activities quickened in Tanganyika in the late 1920s, Africans found themselves faced with a range of choices as to how to enter the colonial economy. The range comprised options as varied as becoming an askari, opening a butchery, and (for a few women) becoming prostitutes in the towns. Naturally, individuals and groups seized whatever option appeared to be most advantageous in their own circumstances, and their priorities did not necessarily coincide with those of the colonialists. The most dramatic illustration of this fact concerns the cultivation of arabica coffee. Coffee was consistently the best priced of the agricultural staples which were exported from Tanganyika, and arabica fetched the highest prices which were given for mild coffee. White settlers perceived this, and tried to make arabica their own preserve. However, in spite of vigorous settler efforts and in spite of the opposition of the colonial administration between 1925 and 1931, Africans in Kilimanjaro, Arusha and Tukuyu decisively frustrated efforts to keep them from growing arabica. In the end the Tanganyikan colonial Government gave up the campaign of discouraging African coffee cultivation, stating that nothing short of force could achieve this objective.[45] It was not that Europeans wanted to keep

Africans out of the money economy but they wished to dictate the terms on which they could join. Settlers in the Northern Province and in the southern Highlands wanted African land and African labour rather than the rise of an African peasantry. They failed in this. The victory won by the respective African populations were not insignificant, but they ultimately strengthened the export orientation.

Meanwhile, recovery was also taking place in the plantation sector. The pre-war peak figure of some 20 000 tons of sisal was surpassed in 1926. By this time the area under sisal was extended, especially along the Central Line in the Morogoro region. Equally significant was the corresponding increase in labour and the sources of migrant labour. By the latter part of the 1920s, Kigoma and Njombe had joined Songea in making major contributions to plantation labour supply. Ufipa, Tukuyu, Singida and Biharamulo were also important in this respect. Recovery in the sisal industry was due mainly to labour inputs, with the profits from exploiting African labour being ploughed back to achieve sustained growth.[46]

By the end of the first decade of British rule in Tanganyika, the dual plantation/peasant economy had re-asserted itself, with settler production coming a poor third—as seen from the accompanying table of the value of agricultural and pastoral products exported. It is important to bear in mind that if an area did not supply labour for the plantation sector or cash crops for export, it tended to grow food for these two sectors and for the towns—as in the case of Ulanga, Upare and Uluguru. So that while (say) Tanga or Bukoba were peripheries of the metropole, other parts of the country were doubly peripheral.[47]

Table 4.1

AGRICULTURAL AND PASTORAL PRODUCTS EXPORTED FROM TANGANYIKA

VALUE IN £	1922	1925	1928	1929
African production	623 654	1 477 078	1 111 000	1 475 07
Sisal	289 388	688 451	1 336 000	1 485 593
Other European production	231 283	465 651	495 000	391 82
Total	1 444 325	2 632 103	2 942 000	1 352 492

Source: TNA 18699, memo to the Governor, 5/2/1930.E.

As the administering authority of a mandated territory, the British claimed to have initiated in Tanganyika a policy of the 'paramountcy of native interests'. In practice, the above plantation/peasant dichotomy was reflected in two different systems of political control, neither of which was addressed to African interests.

Plantations required land alienation. Government authority was totally behind land alienation in the four sisal zones—Tanga, Morogoro, Lindi and Moshi/Arusha, in order of priority. In these same areas, other African rights associated with land usage were trampled upon, as in the case of access to water free from the pollution of sisal waste. The colonial state assured conditions for the exploitation of labour with very little investment of metropolitan capital. This they did, firstly, by inducing labour to move to the plantations from *de facto* labour reserves, and secondly by guaranteeing the exploitation of the worker while on the estate. The Masters and Native Servants Ordinance (1923) was one of the earliest pieces of major legislation passed by the British in Tanganyika. It borrowed a great deal from German East African labour legislation, and continued to impose penal sanctions for breaches of civil contracts. Under its authority, labour officers could and did frequently order workers to receive lashes.[48] Desertion from the estate still merited imprisonment, while the migratory and piecework characteristics of the labour system were maintained to the detriment of the workers. Similar observations apply to the settler farms in the few areas where they were encouraged.[49] And, finally, the control of the employers and the colonial government in the plantation/settler district was uncompromisingly backed by the regular police force.[50]

Labourers on the plantations and elsewhere struggled determinedly against exploitation and oppression, but they could not readily organise themselves. Estates had changed hands, after having been seized as enemy property during the war. They were sold cheaply not only to Englishmen but also to Greeks and Asians. Irrespective of nationality, plantation owners hastened to organise themselves, as had been done in German times. The Tanganyika Sisal Growers' Association was formed in 1923, and for decades thereafter it was the most powerful pressure group in the colony. There were undoubtedly differences of opinion between the TSGA and the government from time to time. These sprang from the fact that the colonial state had to represent the interests of the whole metropolitan and colonial bourgeoisie and not just a part of it. The state had also to operate on a long-term basis, while the employers were tempted to pursue short-term gains. In the final analysis, however, their positions were perfectly reconcilable.

Outside of the towns, plantations and settler districts, Africans were guaranteed possession of their land so as to cultivate cash crops and provide sustenance for producing cash crops in the peasant and plantation context. Here the political system was 'indirect rule' aimed at silencing the vast majority and using a few indigenous authorities as instruments for disciplining the peasant masses. It was a means of exacting tribute with the minimum of overt political change, although some supposedly indigenous authorities were expressly created to serve as British spokesmen.[51] Recent scholarship on colonial Tanganyika has invariably exploded one aspect or another of the myth that indirect rule sponsored African development and self-expression, and it is perfectly clear that real power never left the hands of the Governor, the PCs and the DOs.[52] In another sense, however, the politico-administrative device of indirect rule was successful, since it helped secure the maximum surplus extraction from the peasantry. With the regular police held in reserve, the structures of indirect rule were particularly successful during the depression of 1930–33.

Dependence, differentiation and stratification, 1930–1939

To suggest that the international depression of 1930–33 was a turning point in Tanganyikan history may well appear 'Eurocentric'. Yet the simple fact is that the Tanganyika economy was by then dependent on the capitalist metropoles, and no more vivid proof of this was needed than the spread of the depression from America and Europe. The moment that Tanganyika or any other part of Africa became integrated into world capitalism, it became subject to the same remorseless economic laws as the metropoles themselves. The sharp contradictions between production and consumption and between capital and labour, leading to periodic crises and recessions in America and Europe, also affected East Africa: notably, in 1907–8, 1921 and 1925. Then came the most decisive slump of all in 1930–33, casting ripples even into the most peripheral corners of a peripheral economy. Not only were Tanganyikan sisal, coffee and cotton affected, but the marginal involvement of pastoralists was hit by falling prices for hides, while areas producing food for sale locally also found that the market had disappeared.

Overwhelmed by the extent of the great depression, Europeans were forced to cut back in some areas of the colonial economy. Large import/export houses closed their Dar es Salaam branches and restricted themselves to a single Nairobi office.[53] Sisal estates ceased expanding and instead reduced production and the labour force drastically. Even the government bureaucracy had to accept reductions in their salaries and fringe benefits. The manifest inability of Africans to pay taxes when no money was available led to some relaxation in tax collection, but on the whole Tanganyika survived the depression by placing the brunt of the burden on the African workers and peasants. One of the indices to this effect is that the social services for Africans (which were miniscule enough to begin with) were the first to be sacrificed, they were cut most severely, and they were the last to be restored to pre-depression proportions many years afterwards.[54]

Events on the sisal estates followed a parallel course. Up to 1930, workers earned from shs. 18 to shs. 36 per assigned task or labour card (*kipande*). With the slump, wages fell to shs. 10 or shs. 12 and the size of the tasks were increased. No benefits were offered to the labourers after the slump ended, except that a bonus of shs. 3 was offered to certain categories of workers who completed the kipande within forty-two working days. When another recession emanated from Euro-American and hit Tanganyika late in 1938, the employers quickly withdrew the bonus and also reduced the numbers of workers receiving rations.[55] It was not until after the Second World War that sisal wages were again comparable to what they were in 1930, in spite of the fact that both the employers' profit levels and the workers' cost of living were known to be sky-rocketing during the period 1940–45.[56]

Many Tanganyikan wage earners returned to the land, rejoining those who were being exploited by incredibly low prices being offered for agricultural produce—when there was a market. In this crisis, the Colonial Government once more resorted to thinly-veiled coercion in the form of a 'Grow More Crops Campaign'. Its object was to get Africans to expand the area of production and to increase output in spite of unremunerative prices. Throughout 1932 and 1933, the Governor made speeches on this topic, the Chief Secretary issued circulars, the DOs held numerous conferences with their respective PCs and above all the Director of Agriculture propagandised and exhorted. This official conceded in October 1933 that 'in the past far too much of the slump has been thrown on the shoulders of the primary producer'; but he nevertheless went on to urge 'larger areas per man and more men working on the land'. Knowing that prices were too low to serve as an inducement and that they were still falling, he instructed his subordinates not to mention any price as likely to be paid for any given commodity; and he concluded with the workmen that 'any tendency to slack off and have a breather after this season's efforts should be checked and reported to my offices and to the Senior Agricultural Officer of the Province.[57]

Years afterwards, other agricultural officers reviewed the 'Grow More Crops Campaign' as having been technically unsound. It sacrificed quality for quantity and encouraged extremely poor land usage. But it achieved its primary purpose of maintaining the level of surplus extraction in the midst of the greatest recession in the history of capitalism. Similar techniques had been tried on a smaller scale for earlier slumps in 1921 and 1925. When the next periodic crisis came along in 1938, the colonial state in Tanganyika, and elsewhere in Africa was fully prepared to deal with it in the manner which had proved its efficiency: namely, by forcing Africans to paddle harder against the current, so that they might at least stay in the same place.[58]

The depression induced permanent growth in the Tanganyikan peasant sector. Many migrant labourers never returned to plantation employment, especially in the case of the Sukuma.[59] The TSGA complained bitterly against what seemed to have been a peasant-oriented colonial policy which was encroaching on their sisal labour reserves. Government response was indeed to protect the enlargement of cash crop growing in Sukumaland, but it also took steps to guarantee a larger inflow of migrant labour to the plantations and the mines. They were helped in this by the backwardness of the political economy of Portuguese East Africa, which forced thousands of Makonde and some Yao to stream across the border. They sought employment in the Lindi sisal plantations, they walked on to Dar es Salaam and Morogoro, and by the early 1940s they had become a mainstay of the Tanga industry.[60] A somewhat similar development took place with regard to the Warundi, except that recruiters and the Belgian Government itself took a more active part in supervising Warundi labour migration to Tanga and Central

Line estates. Inside Tanganyika itself, Kigoma became a classic instance of the labour reservoir, maintained as such through the discouragement of other alternatives by which the population might have earned cash, to meet their taxes and other monetary demands.[61]

Therefore, the cash crop peasantry expanded throughout the 1930s side by side with the plantation and not at the expense of the latter. White settlers did not do so well. Many foundered during the depression; and settler coffee growing was virtually wiped out in the southern Highlands.[62] On the other hand, they were helped to re-establish themselves with new crops such as tea and pyrethrum. Returned Germans came to dominate the settler field until the outbreak of the Second World War.[63] Their own government served as a sponsor, along with an offshoot of the DOAG known as the Usagara Company. Boers continued to be encouraged, particularly in Arusha where they were heavily subsidised to grow wheat and maize. Settlers were always given preferential treatment—in terms of acess to agricultural credit, grants, technical services and markets. Taxation, grading and price structures also discriminated in their favour is the peasants; while the police and the courts helped them to victimise African agriculturalists, and pastoralists with whom they came into conflict. Paradoxically, however, the very necessity to provide such massive state support to a handful of settlers proved even to the colonialists themselves that (apart from the plantations and mines) the cash crop peasantry were the ideal form for continued metropolitan penetration, so as to ensure the expatriation of surplus from the colonial periphery.

The 'Grow More Crops Campaign' was in effect part of a programme to ensure that African did not opt out of the money economy; however much it hurt them to remain. Other aspects of this programme included tighter control over marketing and insistence on currency transactions to counter the tendency to engage in barter.[64] In this connection, the Asian middlemen traders proved to be indispensible allies of the colonial state and the metropolitan bourgeoisie. This association goes back to the earliest days of German colonialism, because Asian merchants were already pursuing the caravan trade in the nineteenth century. They did a great deal to help establish the colonial economy in German East Africa as in British East Africa by supplying porters, by providing small specie coins, by distributing imports and by making the innumerable small purchases of primary commodities which were necessary.[65] The leading Asian merchants in German East Africa were Ismailis; and the Aga Khan was a firm friend of both the Germans and the British in turn, urging his followers after the First World War to open up the furthest recesses of the territory.[66]

Asians outnumbered Europeans two to one in German times. Their population remained at about 95 000 during the war, while that of the Europeans dropped to 2 500. By 1931, Asians were enumerated at approximately 23 500 in Tanganyika.[67] Even before the British took over, the Asians had made the whole of East Africa their sphere of operations, with their capital at Mombasa. Therefore, they had no problems making the transition to British rule and becoming closely integrated with British banks and commercial firms on the well-known ninety-day credit arrangement. Asian middlement constituted the clearest expression of the dependent nature of the colonial economy in Tanganyika and they were at the same time one of its strongest props. Their presence in itself meant that new stratification and class differentiation was taking place, coinciding roughly with the racial distinction between Europeans, Asians and Africans. The distinction was highly visible because of residential segregation within the towns, differences in lifestyle and inequalities in access to social services and government institutions. For a more precise analysis, one would need to distinguish between the Asian comprador capitalist and the small retailers or *dukaswallas*, between those who came to own huge sisal estates and those who hired themselves out as a *fundis* or craftsman, and between contractors or bus-owners and lesser government clerical employees.[68] But it was as a link in the import/export trade that the Asians were most valued by the system. Writing in 1934, one Tanganyikan colonial official put the matter succinctly as follows:

> On the whole the Indian of the frugal, petty shop-keeping class which is the most numerous—serves as a useful and necessary link between the European and the Native. Dealing as he does mostly in cotton-piece goods and in hardware, he acts as a retailer for the manufactured products of Europe which are distributed by the large firms at the coast and elsewhere.[69]

A few members of the Asian community had sufficient ready capital to purchase sisal estates cheaply from the Custodian of Enemy Property in 1920–21. These increased tremendously in value before the end of the decade, and a firm such as Karimjee Jivanjee Estates

Ltd. was a multi-plantation venture which was soon to be as powerful and as influential within the TSGA as the foreign-owned plantation companies like Bird and Co. Meanwhile other smaller Asian capitalists became owner-managers of individual estates operating on low overheads. They were found in Tanga but more so in the Morogoro/Kilosa region, where they cultivated both cotton and sisal. The capital invested was neither from Europe nor from India. It was generated locally, 'ploughed back' and multiplied. Credit arrangements made with European banks served not so much to bring in fresh capital but to maintain capital in circulation and ultimately to export a significant proportion of it to Europe [70] Asians made their profits in the interstices of the system. This was well illustrated by their role in buying and reselling primary commodities. They not only purchased cotton but also established ginneries which processed the raw cotton for export which also provided a base for more energetic Asian entrepreneurs to engage in soap and oil manufacture.

Conflicts arising out of the Asian middleman position in the economy often presented themselves in racial terms. From German times, settlers and other Europeans treated Asians in a disparaging fashion. European resentment increased with the growth in the economic strength of the Asians in the inter-war years, reaching a peak during the depression when Asian merchants were accused of sharp and underhand business methods—more so than usual, that is. The government stood firm against proposed discriminatory anti-Asian legislation, recognising their indispensability as a class.[71] Besides, Asians had the capacity to organise and defend their class interests. They proved this in 1921 when they fought off government efforts to get more tax from them; and it is significant that they were allowed representatives in the Legislative Council when Africans were not. From the African viewpoint, there was also a tendency to denounce Asians as a racial group because of their activity as retailers. Popular 'anti-Asian riots' were found from time to time from the 1920s until the latter part of the colonial period. '*Wacha huyu Muhindi*' and '*piga huyu bamiani*' were typical cries.[72] Such anti-Asian riots were really aspects of the class struggle—inevitable once the colonial society began to stratify, but primitive because of the inability of exploited Africans to see or strike at the real controllers of the colonial political economy.

Meanwhile, African society did not remain homogeneous. There was a considerable disparity between the amount of colonial activity carried on in the southern parts of the country as opposed to the north, due mainly to the transport infrastructure which concentrated attention on the Central Line and districts lying to the north. Up to about 1926, the convenient way of getting to Tukuyu from Dar es Salaam was via Beira and Nyasaland.[73] After this changed, communications south of the Central Line were still poor, and the links with the rest of the territory were tenuous. This basic sectional difference became more pronounced during the British period than it had been before, as large parts of the Southern province never recovered from the effects of Maji Maji.[74] Cash crops and other economic activities were more easily promoted elsewhere, and the 'South' in Tanganyika acquired a significance comparable to the 'South' in the USA or Italy—that is, one of backwardness. It actually became a place to which civil servants were posted as a form of demotion or punishment.[75]

More usually, regional differentiation is taken to mean the contrasts between the indices of growth from one district or another[76]. Kilimanjaro, Bukoba, Mwanza and Tukuyu showed high growth characteristics compared with Songea, Biharamulo, Musoma and Dodoma in terms of the money generated and circulated, the availability of roads, the type of houses and the provision of social services such as schools and hospitals. The growth areas correspond partially with the better endowed ecological areas: and they were usually more closely integrated into the colonial economy than the non-growth (subsistence) or low-growth areas. For instance, this applied to Bukoba as compared to Masailand or Dodoma. Contrasts also came about because of the particular way in which sections were integrated. Songea and Kigoma were no less closely involved in the colonial economy than Kilimanjaro and Mwanza, considering the proportion of adult male labour affected. But the first two were labour suppliers, a role which did not bequeath the population with any tangible growth in their home areas. Neglected zones were indirectly disadvantaged by being isolated from interactions with other parts of the country. Ultimately, even Africans within the most fortunate pockets of peasant production were not developing any control over the environment, and they became more vulnerable to external forces as they increased their acreages. Growth and non-growth areas together constituted the dependent underdeveloped economy.[77]

Further inequalities were to be found if one pursued the matter at a micro level. Thus, within Kilimanjaro, Rombo was a supplier of paid agricultural labour and a location with few amenities. Conversely, there were in Songea 'islands' of tobacco and coffee, whose inhabitants boasted more cash and did not have to migrate seeking employment.[78] These finer distinctions lead on to the most decisive of the forms of differentiation: namely, class stratification within the African community.

Regional differentiation was mainly an expression of class stratification. To state that one place was more advanced than another within the Tanganyikan context was really to say that it comprised more of those individuals who came to be loosely referred to as the African elite and who, properly speaking, constituted the embryonic African petty bourgeoisie. These were the Africans who alienated land from their fellows, hired labour and (increasingly by the end of the Second World War) used ploughs and tractors to specialise for the market. With them were associated those who could invest small capital in a retail store or a bus or a coffee huller or some such venture which would help in the process of capital accumulation and a higher level of consumption. Above all, the large proportion of this class achieved its position not directly through economic means but because of access to education, especially to upper primary or secondary level. They were thereby guaranteed jobs in the lower ranks of the civil service, and their salaries went to reinforce such activities as purchase of land cattle and so on.

Kilimanjaro, the best known of the growth areas in Tanganyika, serves as a useful specific illustration of the process of class formation from as early as the 1920s and 1930s. Statistics referring to Kilimanjaro coffee production in this period usually mention only the gross and average figures. Thus, one might read that in 1932 the total number of coffee growers was about 13 000, the average number of trees per grower was 350, the average acreage was less than one acre and the average annual returns were about shs. 100. Such figures in themselves are useless and even misleading, because the 'average' hides the wide gap which had already risen between the few coffee *kulaks* and the vast majority for whom it was still a supplementary activity earning them a few shillings per year. Fortunately, the above figures were explained by the colonial authorities in the following manner:[79]

Table 4.2

PERCENTAGE OF GROWERS	SIZE OF FARMS
60%	½ acre or less
24%	½ to 1 acre
8%	1 to 1½ acres
4%	1½ to 2 acres
4%	over 2 acres

A half-acre plot could contain 250 coffee trees at nine foot spacing; and it would bring an annual income of shs. 50 to shs. 75 if well tended. Therefore, sixty per cent of 7 800 of the 13 000 families then said to have been growing coffee would have earned no more than shs. 75 at the end of the year, and possibly much less than shs. 50. This was a year of low prices, but at the best of times the eighty-four per cent with one acre or less would not have derived any livelihood from coffee. On the other hand, four per cent or about 520 growers had 1 000 trees or more. Within this group, there were a few persons with 10 000 trees or more, while one individual with over 20 000 trees was expected to realise well over shs. 4 000 (at the same depression prices). The top 500 were the ones who were buying pulpers and competing with settlers in hiring labour.[80] Many were chiefs, making use of customary privileges and of advantages which derived from being part of the structure of British indirect rule. But these better-off Africans clashed with the colonial administration and with the officially sponsored chiefs, since they were seeking recognition as a given socio-economic class and not as gazetted hirelings. This accounts for the constant conflicts in the 1930s between the colonial administration and a few favourite chiefs on the one hand and the embryonic petty bourgeoisie of Kilimanjaro on the other hand. This was the time when the Chagga residents of the area were called turbulent and undisciplined by the colonial regime.[81]

Missionaries invaded Kilimanjaro in great numbers during both the German and the British periods. By direct encouragement, they helped bring out clearly the capitalist ethic implicit in cash crop production and other colonial economic activities. It was the missionary who was most likely to praise 'as an example of progress among the Wachagga' an individual who kept 'a small shop in addition to his farm and cattle.[82] Since the so-called elite came to think of success along such lines, they challenged the colonialists in order to participate more fully in the colonial economy. These points are applicable to other growth areas, especially to Bukoba, although no classes had fully crystallised in any part of the country before the Second World War.

The architects of indirect rule openly stated their distrust for an evolving African intelligentsia or a class which might challenge colonial rule as happened in West Africa in 1920 and in India before that.[83] The promotion of Asians was partly a conscious gesture to maintain an alien (and hence politically more docile layer) to perform functions which otherwise would certainly have been carried out by Africans—in commerce, in the skilled trades and in the junior civil service. For instance, the African Credit (Restriction) Ordinance of 1923 and subsequent amendments ensured that Africans could not be advanced sufficient credit to allow them to compete with Asians, whose greatest strength lay not in the capital they possessed but in their links with the banks and big commercial houses. Tanganyika (and east Africa generally) lay far behind West Africa in the rise of African traders in the 1920s and 1930s, as a result of the above policy as well as the relatively slow growth of the money economy and the peasant sector. Thoughtful spokesmen of British colonialism noted that capitalism in Tanganyika needed African representatives in the countryside in order to advance more rapidly.[84] From the 1930s onwards, there were sporadic settlement schemes aimed at creating 'progressive' or 'yeoman' farmers. Thus, the claims of an aspiring African minority were eventually to be favourably considered by the more far-sighted section of the colonial state. The process was not planned: it derived from the conditions of production and it worked itself out through political struggle.

Notes

1 It is generally accepted that a period of twenty years was required for conquest and 'pacification' of German East Africa. See, e.g., John Iliffe, *Tanzania under German Rule 1905–1912*, London, 1969; and Detlef Bald, *Deutsch-Ostafrika 1900–1914, eine Studie über Verwaltung, Interessengruppen und wirtschaftliche Erschiliessung*, Munich, 1970.

2 German Annual Reports are available in English translation at the Department of History, University of Dar es Salaam. In this paper, references to the German Reports are derived from the said translation.

3 W.O. Henderson, *Studies in German Colonial History*, London, 1962, pp. 2, 37, 51, 53.

4 J.S. Mangat, *A History of the Asians in East Africa, C. 1886 to 1947*, London, 1969, p. 93.

5 L.E. Larson, 'A History of Ulanga District, 1860–1957', Ph.D. thesis, University of Dar es Salaam, in preparation.

6 German Annual Report, 1907/8.

7 *Ibid.*

8 Rainer Tetzlaff, *Koloniale Entwicklung und Ausbeutung, Deutsch Ostafrika 1885–1914*, Berlin, 1970, p. 252. (I am grateful to Mrs A. Arnold of the German-African Friendship Society (GDR) for translations into English of large sections of this book and that by Detlef Bald.)

9 Gilbert Gwassa, 'The Outbreak and Development of the Maji Maji War, 1905–1907', Ph.D. thesis, University of Dar es Salaam, 1973.

10 German Annual Reports, 1900, 1905. The figures jointly include 'settlers, planters, farmers, gardeners'.

11 Tetzlaff, pp. 90, 123.

12 George Beckford, *Persistent Poverty: Underdevelopment in Plantation Economies of the Third World*, London, 1972 (for a general discussion of plantation structure); and A.C. Mascarenhas, 'Resistance and change in the sisal plantation system of Tanzania', Ph.D. thesis, UCLA, 1970.

13 German Annual Report, 1901.

14 Bald, p. 121.

15 Iliffe, *Tanzania under German Rule*.

16 F.S. Joelson, *The Tanganyika Territory*, London, 1920. (He indicates on p. 197 that Germans were known to the Swahili populace as *Watu wa hamsasheri* (sic.)—referring to the reputation for administering twenty lashes as punishment.)

17 Iliffe; Bald; and review of Bald by Ralph Austen in *International*

Journal of African Historic Studies, vi, 1, 1973.

18 German Annual Report, 1907/8.

19 Bald, p. 212.

20 German Annual Report, 1908/9. Kilimanjaro settlers were said to have had 'plantations' of 300 to 700 hectares (about 750 to 1 700 acres).

21 Ralph Austen, *Northwest Tanzania under German and British Rule: Colonial Policy and Tribal Politics, 1889–1939*, Yale, 1969, p. 126; and C.K. Magoti, 'The Development and Impact of the Money Economy on Musoma District, 1939–60', M.A. thesis, University of Dar es Salaam, 1974.

22 For Ulanga, see L.E. Larson. See also German Annual Report, 1907/8.

23 Samir Amin, 'Underdevelopment and Dependence in Black Africa—Their Historical Origin and Contemporary Forms', IDEP, Dakar, 1972.

24 Bald, pp. 133, 134.

25 Henderson, p. 40.

26 Other comparable ventures were the South Africa Company and the United Africa Company.

27 Tetzlaff, pp. 164–8.

28 Heinrich Schnee, *German Colonialism Past and Future*, London, 1928, p. 81.

29 German Annual Report, 1907/8.

30 For a scientific elaboration of this concept, see Clive Thomas, *Dependance and Transformation: The Economics of the Transition to Socialism*, New York, 1974.

31 H. Kjekshus, 'Ecology Control and Economic Development', Mimeographied, University of Dar es Salaam, 1974.

32 German Annual Report, 1900/1; and 'The Economic Development of German East Africa', *Bulletin of the Imperial Institute*, Oct., 1903.

33 John Iliffe, *Agricultural Change in Modern Tanganyika*, Historical Association of Tanzania, Paper No. 10, East African Publishing House, 1971, p. 22.

34 David F. Clyde, *History of the Medical Services of Tanganyika*, Dar es Salaam, 1962, pp. 51, 59.

35 J.P. Moffett, *Handbook of Tanganyika*, Dar es Salaam, 1962, p. 91.

36 Brian Gardner, *German East: The Story of the First World War in East Africa*, London, 1963, pp. 58–9.

37 See especially Justinian Rweyemamy, *Underdevelopment and industrialisation in Tanzania: a Study of Perverse Capitalist Industrial Development*, London, 1973.

38 Schnee; and W.H. Rodemann, *Tanganyika, 1890–1919, Selected Aspects of German Administration*, Chicago, Ill., University, 1964.

39 G.P. Fendall, *The East African Force*, 1915–1919, London, 1921, p. 177.

40 *Tanganyika Territory, Proceedings of the Legislative Council*, Dar es Salaam; 1st, 2nd and 3rd sessions, 1926–9. (To be cited hereafter as *Legislative Council* of the relevant year).

41 Alexander Gilchrist, *Tanganyika Memories: a Judge in the Red Kanzu*, London and Glasgow, 1936, p. 8.

42 *Legislative Council*, 1926–7.

43 M.F. Hill, *Permanent Way: the Story of the Tanganyika Railways*, vol. II, Nairobi, 1957.

44 Bukoba District Book, report of 22 Jan. 1924, TNA 1733: 8 (microfilm).

45 TNA 11160, 'Arabica Coffee Growing by Natives'; and 11918, 'Coffee Cultivation by Natives'.

46 C.W. Guillebaud, *An Economic Survey of the Sisal Industry of Tanganyika*, London, 1958 (revised) p. 46.

47 J.R. Mlahagwa, 'Agricultural Change in the Uluguru Mountains During the Colonial Period, with Particular Emphasis from 1945–60': M.A. thesis, University of Dar es Salaam, 1974.

48 TNA 13657, 'Flogging—general correspondence' (1929).

49 Primarily the Northern Province and to a lesser extent the southern Highlands.

50 W. Rodney, 'Policing the Countryside in Colonial Tanganyika', *Proceedings of the Annual Social Science Conference of the East*

African Universities 1973, Dar es Salaam, 1974.

51 A considerable amount of research on the authenticity of 'traditional' rulers under Indirect Rule is associated with the sociologist, Hans Cory.

52 See, e.g., Austen, op. cit. and Walter Morris-Hale, *British Administration in Tanganyika, 1920–1945*, University of Geneva, 1969.

53 See, e.g., TNA 34277 'Leslie and Anderson Ltd.'

54 Morris-Hale makes a strong case concerning the deliberate withdrawal of educational services from Africans in the 1930s.

55 TNA 652/12, Reports on Tanga area labour.

56 See, e.g., Registry of Companies, Dar es Salaam, T20625, Bird & Co.

57 TNA 215/694/1, 'Lake Province—Increased production and development of Native Economic Crops'.

58 This metaphor is used by President Nyerere discussing cash crop prices of the 1960s. See J.K. Nyere, *Freedom and Socialism*, London 1968, p. 161.

59 TNA 23217, Annual Report 1935 (Labour section).

60 TNA 21484, 'Native Immigration from Portuguese East Africa'. (Treats the phenomenon in its early stages in the 1930s.)

61 I. Sago, 'A History of Labour Migration in Kasulu District, Tanzania, 1928–1960', M.A. Thesis, University of Dar es Salaam, 1974.

62 TNA 13205, 'Coffee Cultivation, Iringo Province', and 77/2/44, 'Iringa Agriculture—Co-operative Societies'.

63 D.R. McDonald, ed., *Enemy Property in Tanganyika*, Cape Town, 1946, p. 5.

64 *Legislative Council*, 1932–4.

65 Mangat, pp. 50–60.

66 J. Listowell, *The Making of Tanganyika*, London, 1965, p. 68.

67 L.W. Holingsworth, *The Asians of East Africa*, London, 1960, p. 68.

68 See, e.g., Agehananda Bharati, 'A Social Survey' in D.P. Chai, ed., *Portrait of a Minority: Asians in East Africa*, London, 1965.

69 Eric Reid, *Tanganyika Without Prejudice*, London, 1934, p. 144.

70 Steward Symes, *Tour of Duty*, London, 1946, p. 173.

71 See, e.g., TNA 13986, 'Native Disturbance in Dar es Salaam', 1929.

72 *Stations in Tanganyika Territory*, Dar es Salaam, n.d. (ca. 1926).

73 Clyde, p. 36. (Refers to signs of deformity and infertility seen 30 years after and as a consequence of Maji Maji.)

74 It is commonly acknowledged that this practice survived into the post-independence period.

75 Iliffe, *Agricultural Change*, p. 30.

76 This position is of course incompatible with the more orthodox distinction between so-called 'traditional' and 'modern' sectors of a 'dual economy'.

77 P.H. Guliver, *Labour Migration in a Rural Economy*, Kampala, 1953, pp. 3, 16.

78 TNA 11908, 'Coffee Cultivation by Natives'.

79 *Legislative Council*, 1929. (See representations of Hon. N.F. Howe-Browne of 29 April).

80 Margaret Bates, 'Tanganyika Under British Administration 1920–1955', St. Hilda's College, Oxford, 1957, p. 187.

81 Anza A. Lema, 'The Impact of the Leipzig Lutheran Mission on the People of Kilimanjaro, 1893–1920', Ph.D. thesis, University of Dar es Salaam, 1973.

82 *Legislative Council*, 1926 (address of the Governor, Sir Donald Cameron).

5. The Political Economy of Colonial Tanganyika 1939–61

B.D. Bowles

The state, in other words the institutions of government, has a tendency to operate against the interest of the majority of the governed. That is a theoretical statement which one may deduce from a variety of sources. If one applies a Marxian class analysis one may conclude that an economically dominant class is likely to control the organs of government and operate them in its own, separate, interests. If one begins from a nineteenth-century liberal viewpoint, one may arrive at the same conclusion through the argument of Acton that 'all power tends to corrupt and absolute power to corrupt absolutely'. Similarly from a Christian doctrine of sin one may derive the conclusion that the possession and operation of power by a sinful man does not make him good, but rather multiplies the effects of any evil acts he does.

A colonial government has an even greater tendency to operate against the interests of the majority than an indigenous one. Having been imposed obviously by force and being operated obviously by members of an alien community, the government is clearly differentiated from the people. The ruling class is obvious from its wealth and style of living and from, in Tanganyika, its colour. The tendency to corruption is demonstrated not so much by the embezzlement of money as by the claim to superiority and its use as a justification for the most high-handed actions. The volume of propaganda is very likely to be inversely proportional to the amount of activity undertaken for the welfare of the governed.

The major theme of British Government propaganda in the period under consideration was 'development'. This was thought of as an increase in economic activity, but it was also argued that an increase in the amount of economic activity would benefit the people of the territory by raising the levels of individual incomes and of government revenue available for services to individuals. With a theory of comparative advantage in mind, colonial officials conceived the 'advantageous' form of economic activity of a tropical area to be the export of articles it could produce, in the case of Tanganyika, the export of sisal, raw cotton, coffee and cashew nuts, all of them impossible to grow in temperate climates. Since these were the articles which the Tanganyikan environment was best suited to produce, according to this theory, 'development' consisted of the the increased production of them for the benefit of the 'whole world'.

But the historical evidence suggests that what was for the benefit of the 'whole world' was not for the benefit of Tanganyikans, the vast majority of whom remained poor. Cash crops were grown in Tanganyika as a result of actions of a colonial government representing the interests of relatively rich countries where industries and hence markets for raw materials already existed. Additional sources of raw materials would reduce the reliance of those industries upon these sources, while the producers of the raw materials would become more dependent on the markets. The theory of comparative advantage merely serves to justify in the eyes of German or British industrialists the increased production of tropical raw materials in tropical colonies so that they may compete with each other and keep down prices, benefiting the industrialist and impoverishing the producer. It is an argument that the poor countries should serve and continue to serve the rich. It is argued here that this process of increased dependence is not, and cannot lead to, true development, that is, a movement towards the conquest by Tanganyikans of their own environment for their own benefit, and that the process can be more usefully referred to as one of underdevelopment, for it worked to prevent Tanganyikans conquering or benefiting from their own environment. The political economy of Tanganyika during the period 1939–61 was, according to this argument, one in which the colonial state operated to create and maintain dependence, not least on the part of those individuals who received higher incomes as a result of it.

Evidence for this argument will be presented in the following pages. An attempt will be made to describe and analyse economic changes occurring in Tanganyika in this period. The policies of the colonial government will be considered in relation to these changes and with regard to the theoretical points made earlier.

The colonial government was already accustomed to a larger measure of regulation in certain aspects of Tanganyika's economy before 1939 than would have been acceptable at that time in Britain itself. The distinction between those aspects in which direct regulation was considered justified and those in which it was not, can be shown to be a racial one. Sisal was grown almost entirely by immigrants on plantations. Here, direct regulation was not attempted. Cotton and coffee were grown primarily by Africans. Rules related to the cultivation of coffee were so numerous (and often wrong-headed) that they led to a serious riot in Bukoba in 1937. A similar riot in the other major coffee-growing area, Kilimanjaro, opposed the imposition of a market monopoly for the government-sponsored Kilimanjaro Native Co-operative Union on the growers. Similar interventions in the cultivation and marketing of cotton were planned, notably in zoning regulations, preventing competition between ginneries by allocation to each ginnery an area in which all raw cotton had to be sold to it alone. The colonial state was moving towards monopoly marketing of both the main African-grown crops. In addition, neglect of food crops had become an offence punishable by the chiefs, whose powers were extended to include the insistence on certain minimum areas of 'famine reserve' crops. In this as in the case of many other economic regulations, the chiefs were relied upon to enforce regulations devised by the colonial state.

During the war period state intervention increased. This appears to have been for three reasons. First, the existing system for the exporting of crops became difficult to work, and in some cases broke down altogether. Second, the war provided a justification for harsher measures to bring an increase in production which was already required. Third, the war demanded a reassessment of the state's priorities and an attempt to plan production in accordance with these priorities.

In late 1939 there were already difficulties in the shipping of sisal, compounded by the internment of those producers of sisal who happened to be German. In 1940 the cotton markets did not open in June as scheduled because no buyers appeared. The state stepped in to purchase the whole of the first-grade crop. In 1941, the normal cotton markets in Britain closed and the London government took control of all cotton imports through the Raw Cotton Commission.[1]

The war brought to British officials a willingness to sacrifice and especially to impose sacrifices upon others, in order that the war with Germany should be won. A British administrator wrote of 'still greater production' being required from producers for the sake of the 'Empire to which they belong'. What this implied was clearly stated by an agricultural officer, newly entitled the Director of Agricultural Production, in 1942. He said that it was necessary for the 'entire exportable surplus' to be available for the war effort. This was said to justify compulsion on both the chiefs and the growers because 'we are all together in the struggle for freedom'.[2] Extraction of the surplus was being openly advocated, and the use of the penalties of the legal system to enforce on Tanganyikans participation in a war for Britain's continued possession of empire followed. That participation was to take the form of labour to increase production.

Though in the 1930s British officials had sometimes said that economic production of any crop was justified merely by the need to pay taxes and therefore provide revenue, the war forced those same officials to consider once more which crops were vital to the British economy and which were not. They recognised that cotton for the moment was not, since it could be imported from the United States. Throughout the 1930s the United States held a cotton surplus over two hundred times the size of Tanganyika's annual production. British manufacturers generally imported from the United States, treating Tanganyikan production as a reserve supply which could normally be allowed to go to India. This reserve supply could not be a British priority during wartime. It became clear, on the other hand, that sisal was of vital importance. Through the capture of Indonesia and the Philippines by the Japanese in 1941, the world production of sisal and its competitor, manila, was greatly reduced. Since sisal twine was an important raw material in the mechanical reaping of Britain's corn, and since the British Government was making a major effort to increase food production, Tanganyika's sisal became vital to Britain's economy, in a way in which it had never previously been. Since sisal was a plantation crop grown by non-Africans employing African labourers, it became more important to the colonial state to recruit labourers and to ensure food supplies for them than to insist on production of cotton. This, together with a demand for food for British soldiers stationed in Kenya and in the middle east, was the reason for an emphasis by British officials on the production of food crops by Africans during the war.[3]

Having considered the motivation of state regulation of agricultural production, it remains to discuss the methods and content of this regulation. It rapidly becomes clear that methods differed from producer to producer. The sisal industry, run by Europeans and Asians, was left largely to regulate itself, while government intervention included the negotiation of a contract with the Ministry of Supply in London and the fixing of prices. Because European farmers, largely in the northern area of Tanganyika, were considered to be the most reliable producers of food, generous guaranteed prices for wheat, maize and beans were offered. Though the legislation did not name Europeans, it prescribed large amounts in new bags as the criterion for the payment of the prices. Similarly, planting subsidies were allowed, guaranteeing a minimum return of shs. 100 per acre for large areas planted. Export taxes were also reduced. It was clear that European farmers were not expected to make financial sacrifices for the sake of the war effort.[4]

But the state's normal method of attempting to ensure greater production by Africans was force. Immediately on the outbreak of war officials in the Lake Province were discussing how to extend their powers of compulsion. This was eventually achieved through the Defence Regulations of 1940 and a further Native Authority Ordinance of 1942. But it was also clear that in practice in many areas growing of cash crops had been compulsory for many years. Compulsory growing of cotton had been justified as a famine relief measure, on the grounds that cotton was less likely to succumb to drought than maize or groundnuts. A particularly interesting admission was made by British officials with regard to Musoma District. In 1941, when it was decided that the production of cotton was not a priority, the District Commissioner of Musoma was asked how much cotton would be grown if its cultivation were made voluntary. The answer, in an area within fifteen miles of Musoma town, was none at all, though pre-war production had been approximately 1 000 bales. When District Commissioners in the Lake Province were asked in 1942 how much cultivation they proposed to enforce, the response varied from one to two-and-a-half acres per household. One DC replied that he already enforced the cultivation of one acre of cotton per adult male, and one acre of groundnuts and a quarter of an acre of rice per household. In addition he was insisting that every able-bodied African should be working in his fields during normal hoeing hours. The Governor in 1943 introduced the conscription of labour for sisal and other essential industries and, in African agriculture, proposed to use 'such compulsion as can be legally and effectively employed', including an increase in taxation in agricultural areas as a 'stimulus' to production.[5]

Measures to enforce a certain quantity of cultivation have been considered. There were also attempts by British officials to prescribe the crop cultivated. In the Lake Province, for example, it was announced in 1942 that groundnuts and rice should be grown in preference to cotton, for reasons stated earlier. Some British officials had doubts about the wisdom of changing the pattern of cotton-growing; they feared tax revenue would be reduced. It was true that the system for distribution of cotton seed and the buying and ginning of the crop had taken some trouble to build up; British officials did not like to see their efforts wasted. One District Commissioner commented that efforts to tell African growers what to plant had led in the past 'not only to dissatisfaction but to disaster'.[6] He was concerned with the climate problem, since it was likely to be either too wet for groundnuts or too dry for rice, and a wrong decision could lead to crop failure. But in spite of these dangers the policy was pursued. It is significant that the main method used was price incentives. While in the past there had been talk of peasants' 'perverse' reaction in producing less if the price was higher, now officials clearly calculated that, as with the European farmers, African growers would react positively to price incentives. In early 1942, growers were offered guaranteed minimum prices of 10 cents per pound for groundnuts and 4 cents per pound for rice. Later maize was added, at 4 cents per pound. These prices were based on a calculation of the man-days required at a rate of 35 cents a day, which was the normal daily wage labour rate. The cotton price by an equivalent calculation would have been 21 cents per pound, but no guaranteed minimum price was offered and the actual price paid was 10 cents per pound. The result was a decline in the production of cotton which lasted for the rest of the war period and for some time afterwards, in spite of a subsequent reversal of British policy[7]

The figures quoted indicate something of the impact of the system upon the farmer. His income was extremely low, and even then much of it was taken away in taxes. This fact may be illustrated in two different ways. One is by examining the income of an individual grower. The rate of taxation was, in 1941, shs. 10 a year. In the same year British officials calculated the average income per tax-payer in Musoma as shs. 26 a year, and Zanaki chiefdom, shs. 7 a year. They also calculated that the annual income from an acre of cotton was shs. 15. Another way of illustrating the problem is from the provincial point of view. In the cotton area of the Lake Province as a whole in 1941 income from cotton was£300 000, while tax receipts were£190 000.[8] It would appear that the cultivator who could make an income greater than shs. 10 a year excluding tax was relatively fortunate, and that tax rates (on the poorest) were of the order of fifty per cent. In addition, food shortages were liable to occur, as in Kwimba district, because of the insistence on early planting of cotton during the period when food crops had to be planted. Further, cassava, whose cultivation interfered less with cotton planting and was often insisted upon to provide a famine reserve, was unpalatable to many and known by those who insisted on it to be deficient in protein.[9]

By 1945 the Tanganyikan economy had become dependent, part of the economic system of another, stronger, country. Although Britain was measurably weakened by the fighting during the Second World War, this made no difference at that time to the relative positions of Britain and Tanganyika. Indeed, as the leaders of the British Government gradually realised the extent of the damage done by the war to the British economy, they turned more and more to the colonies for 'help' in rectifying the situation. Much of Britain's weakness was financial, or, more specifically, inability to pay for imports, and was especially apparent in relation to the United States. Imports from the United States, which included all categories of goods from food to machines, vastly exceeded Britain's exports to the United States. Since the difference had to be paid for in dollars, there was a 'dollar crisis' in Britain. The British Government wished to use the Empire, and parts of the former Empire in the shape of the Commonwealth, all euphemistically named the 'sterling area', to help it overcome the 'dollar crisis'. Specifically for Tanganyika this meant that Tanganyika should reduce dollar imports (of which there were few anyway) and increase exports which could either be sent directly to the United States, sent to Britain to be re-exported, to the United States, or sent to Britain as a substitute for imports from the United States. Tanganyika's three major crop exports, coffee, sisal and cotton, fell quite neatly into these three categories. The dependence of Tanganyika's economy upon external markets, which had already been established at a time before the war when Britain's need for Tanganyika's products was relatively small, now enabled Tanganyika's exports to be used for Britain's advantage when Britain's need for them was relatively great. Tanganyika's 'reserve' resources were now to be called upon. The control of Tanganyika's exports instituted during the war in state-controlled marketing arrangements and bulk-purchase contracts was also to be turned to peace-time purposes. The propaganda for war effort on behalf of the Empire was modified to become an appeal for export effort on behalf of the sterling area.[10]

Such was the attitude of British administrators in Tanganyika at that time, that at first they considered only European agriculture capable of a quick expansion of output. When asked to justify this, they argued that African agriculture was inefficient. They spoke of African systems of land tenure as leading to an impersonal attitude to land with no incentive to improvement, and African systems of land use, for example, shifting cultivation and burning, as leading to reduction of soil fertility and decreasing yields. It was the attitude of Europeans who believed that European capitalist methods of cultivation adopted since the agricutural revolution were a model for the world. Only such methods would lead to 'development' they argued, and only Europeans were immediately capable of using them.[11] If European farming using European machines was the efficient way to expand output it followed, for example, that if a great increase in the production of groundnuts was required, a groundnut 'scheme' managed by Europeans and using machines designed in Europe was the solution. Similarly if beef was required for export, it was assumed that Europeans must produce it.

The groundnut scheme was prepared at a time when the British Government desired a rapid increase in the production of vegetable oil in the sterling area. The urgency of this led planners very early to reject the idea of African-grown groundnuts. British planners believed that with the injection of capital and the provision of machines vast areas of then unproductive land could be made productive. If African methods had caused loss of fertility and a lowering of the hydrological level, European methods could avoid these problems, and even allow cultivation where Africans had failed. The glib assumption that Europeans could produce a yield per acre from thousands of acres as great as, if not greater than, an

African farmer from half an acre, illustrates British attitudes to methods of 'development'. It means the extension of European 'experience' to African conditions. Its failure illustrates the inapplicability of these atitudes.[12]

Similarly, over the Meru ranching scheme, British officials assumed that Europeans in private possession of land would rapidly produce an exportable surplus of food, on this occasion meat. Tanganyika Packers was being established as a meat-canning concern in Dar es Salaam, and officials wished to ensure adequate supplies of animals. An area between Mount Kilimanjaro and Mount Meru and adjacent to already alienated land had been recommended for alienation by a land commission. The government now decided to alienate the land in thirteen plots to European ranchers. But on the land were 3000 Africans of the Meru tribe, some of them occupying a farm which had been in an unusual case 'alienated' to them. These Meru were told that their land was 'required' for 'development'; they were offered land lower down the slope, where water supplies were lacking and tsetse clearance doubtful. The Meru refused to move and were in 1951 forcibly ejected. The removal further illustrates the meaning of 'development' so far as the colonial government was concerned. This scheme also failed.[13]

Other British officials in the late 1940s began to discuss changing their methods of approach to African farming. Consideration was given to the ending of compulsion and the modification of the marketing system to make it self-supporting and voluntary. Accordingly, ideals were expressed about growers receiving the 'full' price or 'best possible' price for their products and being allowed some participation in marketing them. These ideals should be seen in the light of the British desire to maximise production, and also of the fact that the system of cash-crop growing for export was considered to be sufficiently established. Growers' control of marketing appeared to have been a major influence in increasing the production of Kilimanjaro coffee. The Kilimanjaro Native Coffee Union had functioned well, even during war-time, and the tensions of the 1930s appeared to be part of the past. Although in Bukoba coffee production had been variable and generally declining since 1936, it was believed from the experience of Kilimanjaro that this was due to the lack of a co-operative union, and the government proposed to introduce one. So far as cotton growing was concerned, during the war methods of compulsion with low prices and detailed government direction had not worked well. Production had drastically declined and it was clear that some change of method was necessary. Fear was another important motivation. Realistic administrators knew that troubles in the coffee-growing areas in the 1930s were directly related to compulsion, and that organised cash crop growers could do much to disrupt the system if they wished, as they had in the Gold Coast cocoa-growing areas before the war. They believed that government-sponsored non-political co-operatives, like the KNCU, would both satisfy the growers and be more efficient than the system which had operated in the Bukoba coffee area and the Mwanza cotton area before the war. Direct concern with the 'political repercussions' of obviously oppressive measures was expressed, and heightened by experiences in Uganda in 1949, where Baganda growers rioted against low cotton prices which they knew had been imposed by the government.[14]

There were two reasons why such a policy (that is, the ending of compulsory measures and the payment of a higher price to the growers) was not put into practice at once. One was the habits of agricultural and local government officials in Tanganyika, who had been schooled in the old methods, and administrators who continued to accept racial myths of African laziness and lack of desire for monetary rewards. The other was the continued desire of state officials to retain the surplus resulting from African cash crop production. Even on small turnovers in Bukoba coffee and Mwanza cotton during the war, government profits had been shown to be possible, and this was too good a source of revenue for officials to give up easily. Further, rising prices in the post-war period made it possible both to make a profit and to raise growers' prices slightly. Many rationalisations were circulated to explain these profits. It was argued that Europeans had contributed their share of taxation for a long time while no satisfactory method of taxing African peasants had been found until now. It was said that government profits were for the good of the people since the government used them for 'development'. It was argued that to release the 'full' price would cause uncontrollable inflation since consumer goods were not available in sufficiently large quantities.[15] But it is more probable that opposition to inflation was opposition to any basic change in the cheap labour policy, and resulted from a fear that cash crop incomes would become greater than prevailing wage rates. Even when the surplus was used to finance 'development' in the cotton-growing areas, this was the forced provision by the growers themselves of the investment necessary to expand production for the sake of the metropolis.

The result of administrative reluctance tended to be a compromise or a mixed policy. Policy-makers in London, for example, argued that cotton prices for Africans and non-Africans must be equal. In Tanganyika officials, faced in 1951 with the situation that non-Africans were being paid more than twice as much for cotton as Africans (who were receiving 34 cents a pound), replied that to reduce non-Africans' prices would cause them to cease production, and to raise Africans' prices would have serious repercussions among African growers in Uganda. The result was a rise to the Uganda price of 50 cents for African growers in 1952 and a later reduction in price for non-Africans when world prices dropped. Similarly, over marketing boards, the ideas put forward were that marketing boards would temporarily be necessary in order to enable growers to obtain the 'best possible' prices for their products, that African growers should be represented on them, and that co-operatives would eventually become 'responsible for the control of the marketing of their own product'. But Tanganyika officials allowed this to happen only in the case of coffee, where from 1952 the KNCU was reluctantly allowed to auction its own coffee. So far as cotton was concerned, the Lint and Seed Marketing Board was set up in 1952 before cotton co-operative organisations were established, and it continued to be run by Europeans. In the field of profits, there were suggestions at various times that the government should use the profits for the benefit of the producers. As a result, profits were paid into a fund named the Agricultural Development Fund. This was used (among other things) to recruit, house and pay several European agricultural assistants (at £700 a year) and many African instructors (at £40 a year) who enforced cotton cultivation regulations. It also helped to finance the Sukumaland Development Scheme begun in 1948, a large part of which was intended to remove a number of Sukuma from an exhausted cotton area to a virgin area where better cotton could be grown.[16]

As far as the growers were concerned, the result was that much of the value of what they produced was kept from them. Consciousness of this situation was sooner or later likely to be aroused. The leaders of the Kilimanjaro Native Coffee Union complained that in 1951 they had received only two-thirds of the value of the crop. This was so, and it was the result of relatively fixed price contracts with the British Ministry of Food at a time of quite sharply rising world prices for coffee. But cotton growers undoubtedly suffered more. For their cotton the Tanganyika Government consistently received less than the world price during the period 1943–52 of long-term contracts with the Raw Cotton Commission in Britain. But in addition the growers often received less than half of the low proceeds the government received. The government itself decided, as we have seen earlier, what those prices should be. The tendency in the late 1940s was for it to calculate its likely receipts and to divide these, approximately two-fifths to the growers, two-fifths to the central and local government and one-fifth to the ginners. When its receipts were higher than anticipated, which they quite regularly were as prices rose before 1951, the proportion received by the grower was even smaller. We can follow in some detail the process by which the cotton price was fixed for the 1950–51 season. Government profits for the previous season, when the growers' price was 25 cents per pound, had been approximately 30 cents per pound. Government officials considered an increase in the growers' price for the following season, but discussion ranged between prices of 32 and 35 cents, at which government profits were expected to be 33 cents and 29 cents respectively. The price was eventually fixed at 34 cents, at which profits were in fact 30 cents. Growers' reaction was at first to reduce planting in favour of crops whose prices were relatively higher, or to smuggle their cotton to Uganda. Later they turned to political methods.[17]

The ways in which the British Colonial Government of Tanganyika operated the finances of the country will repay further attention. Talk of 'development' was in the air after 1945, and British government grants (or government investment funds) were available under the Colonial Development and Welfare Acts passed in 1940. Capital expenditure in the ten and a half years from 1947 (January) to 1957 (June) was approximately £33 million. Of this, £8 million was contributed by Colonial Development and Welfare Grants. In the same period budget surpluses amounted to £14 million. Of these, £6 million were devoted subsequently to capital expenditure, leaving by 1957 a balance of £8 million, which was invested in Britain. In other words the grants were equivalent to the reserve held in Britain. In addition the Tanganyika Government was obliged to allow the East African Currency Board to keep sterling securities almost equivalent to the total currency in circulation in Tanganyika. These funds, available from Tanganyika's trading surpluses, were invested mainly in Britain, and the Tanganyika Government was unable until 1956 to borrow from these funds itself in order to finance expenditure.[18]

In addition to its reserves, the government also handled a further fund, acquired from trading in cotton and coffee in the period 1943–52. Having taken over the marketing of these two export crops, as we have seen, it made profits on them, especially on cotton, due to the difference between the price it paid to the growers and the price it received when it exported the crop. The profits amounted to approximately £9 million in the eight years from 1945–52, being particularly great when cotton prices were high in the period 1949–52. The Agricultural Development Fund received £2.5 million profits from government trading in the period 1945 to 1948. Profits from cotton trading for the period 1949 to 1952, which amounted to £5.2 million, were almost entirely credited to the Lint and Seed Marketing Board in 1952. Profits from Bukoba coffee, which accounted for the remainder, were paid into the funds of the Bukoba Native Coffee Board. £3 million of the Lint and Seed Marketing Board's balance was designated a Price Assistance Fund, but the fact that much of this was lent to the Tangankyia Government indicated that it was regarded by the latter as useful source of temporary revenue. £1 million was lent to the government for capital works in the cotton-producing areas, to be repayable only after twenty years. A further large fund was needed in order to finance the purchase of the cotton crop (i.e. to provide the money with which it was bought, normally the function of a commercial bank). With these commitments the Lint and Seed Marketing Board did not undertake any element of risk in its pricing policy and in 1953 and 1954 further large profits were made. Most of the income from this source was invested overseas, again in Britain.[19]

A major motive of the colonial system in this period appears to have been the bolstering of Britain's sterling balances. It has been noted how funds from three sources, budget surpluses, East African Currency Board reserves and finally cotton marketing profits, were invested mainly in Britain. Private organisations such as banks and insurance companies acted in much the same way. It has already been noted how the Lint and Seed Marketing Board credit policy relieved the banks of providing finance for the purchase of the cotton crop, leaving them freer to keep their balances in London. Such 'assistance' in Britain's financial difficulties, the latter illustrated in the devaluation of sterling in 1949, paralleled the attempts to use Tanganyika and other colonies to solve Britain's balance of trade difficulties. In addition there was a net drain of capital whenever (as often occurred) the Tanganyika Government invested money in British government securities at rates of two and a half to three per cent and at the same time borrowed three and a half to four per cent from other sources. Other drains of capital occurred whenever the British Government through the Raw Cotton Commission or the Ministry of Food paid a lower price than the world price for the purchase of cotton or coffee, which it almost invariably did during the period 1945–52. There was nothing new in this drain of capital; government bodies were merely participating in it more obviously than private bodies in this particular period. At a time when, for once, the terms of trade were moving in favour of commodity producers, the colonial state ensured that the growers received only a little of the benefit, and that much of it was siphoned back to the consumer of the commodities.[20]

Turning now from finances to matters which were somewhat less under government control, we will briefly consider trade unions and co-operatives. The appearance of trade unions, often preceded by growing strike activity, was caused by the growing resentment of town workers against the cheap labour policy. In the absence of manufacturing industry the number of town workers was relatively small. The towns existed to service the export economy, and service workers, such as those concerned with transport, predominated. Dockworkers and railway workers were important groups in Dar es Salaam and coastal towns elsewhere. They lived in overcrowded and chaotic conditions and during the 1939–45 war rising prices had worsened their plight. The colonial government, fearing something more radical, did not altogether oppose trade unions. The administration wanted to guide them along the 'right lines'. The 'right lines' meant the practice of techniques of moderate collective bargaining as used in Britain by workers somewhat cowed by the aftermath of the General Strike of 1926. 'To guide' meant the use of the power of the state to register and withdraw registration from unions and to impose certain rules of 'responsibility' in such matters as control of funds and decisions on action. The Labour

Department conceived its function as the erection of a system which would absorb complaints and produce little activity. In practice its rules proved to be so rigid and difficult to obey that its effect was virtually to suppress union activity in the period before 1952. The most notable exception was the Dockworkers and Stevedores' Union formed in Dar es Salaam in 1947 after an important dockers' strike. Attempts by the Labour Department to insist not only on the registration of the union but on the registration of individual dockers, and the use of the system to discipline workers by the employers, led to a further strike in 1950. After the strike the union was dissolved by High Court Order and its assets confiscated.[21] The union had proved too radical for the Tanganyika Government.

Co-operatives were in a similar position. In the late 1920s and 1930s they had begun to emerge in certain cash crop producing areas in order that the grower could strengthen his own position as against the buyer. They emerged first in the coffee-growing areas of Kilimanjaro and Bukoba, probably because the income from coffee-growing, though small, was sufficient to differentiate a group of better-off farmers of kulaks who had common interests as against both merchants and chiefs. In the early 1950s the movement spread, notably to the cotton-growing areas of Sukumaland. Here buyers were very clearly the focus of discontent. After prices were fixed in 1943, buyers turned to cheating illiterate growers over weights and payments. Co-operatives, which could organise the selling of cotton direct to the ginneries, and could check weights and payments, grew up in response. Like trade unions, these were not completely opposed by the government. Indeed, the government favoured the removal of the middlemen buyers, and encouraged co-operatives, provided they were run on the 'right lines'. Its real interest was of course in encouraging higher production, and, since production had fallen alarmingly in the 1944–6 period, it was considered that something drastic needed to be done to 'restore the confidence' of the growers in the marketing system. But administrators were reluctant to give up control of the system. A typical example was over the issue of independent weighers. In order to protect themselves against cheating over weights, peasants had been willing to pay for double weighing, first by an independent weigher and later by the buyer. But the government insisted that it should license the independent weighers who would then have to use approved scales and charge approved fees. Initiative on the part of African growers or workers had to be carefully restrained and its effects limited. The government refused to register cotton-growers' co-operatives until an official from the Co-operative Development Department was stationed in Mwanza in 1952. It wished to ensure, among other things, that co-operatives should not be mixed up with 'politics'.[22]

Family incomes, in the cotton-growing areas of Sukumaland, were estimated by the 1951 United Nations Visiting Mission to be shs. 148 a year. This compared with shs. 600 claimed by KNCU for each of its members, and 630 estimated by the mission to be the average town worker's yearly income. These figures were considerably higher than in 1945, but at shs. 50 a month neither the town worker nor the coffee-grower could clearly be said to have escaped from the cheap labour syndrome, while the cotton-growers were still distinctly poor. Not only did the system expect cheap labour from its participants, but also compulsory labour lingered on during this period. The 1948 United Nations Visiting Mission noted that compulsory labour of up to sixty days a year existed for those not otherwise employed, and that 8 000 persons had been called for compulsory labour in the year 1946–7. Legally enforceable contracts for sisal workers were still normal; it was therefore a criminal offence for a sisal worker to leave his employment. In 1949 the enforcement of cash crop growing as such was ruled '*ultra vires*', but in the same year a Legislative Council committee on agricultural production policy recommended that Provincial Commissioners should have power to direct Native Authorities to issue orders with regard to methods of cultivation, for example to specify the methods of preparation and manuring, and to ensure that soil conservation measures were taken. These became the more usual form of forced labour during the early 1950s: the enforcement of measures, said to be in the peasants' own interest, which involved effort, the peasants could not be persuaded to make voluntarily, such as terracing, ridging, manuring and spraying. Agricultural 'instructors' were expected to bring to prosecution those who failed to carry out these measures. They were the new agricultural policemen, paid for by the growers themselves, carrying out a policy whose object was simple: to increase the production of 'high quality' exportable crops.[23]

The period 1953–61 was one of further increased production with some relaxation of government pressure. It is probable that this relaxation was planned, even that government policy in Tanganyika in this period was far-sighted enough to plan for a period of transition to constitutional independence, because in that way the economy would continue to operate in Britain's interests. Statements made in 1951, such as this one arguing that government officials were 'responsible throughout the territory for fostering development until such time as the African producer is in a position to play a larger part in the actual administration of his own economic affairs' appear to suggest that bureaucrats planned a devolution of power. But before we accept the interpretation that there was a neo-colonial strategy consciously pursued by British officials, we should consider on the other hand the changes forced upon the British by the non-co-operation and resistance of Tanganyikans. These suggest that we should explain British policy in terms of a neo-colonial solution rather than an autonomous strategy.[24]

Table 5.2 COTTON PRICES AND PRODUCTION

	PRICE IN CENTS PER LB.	THOUSAND TONS EXPORTED
1945	14	7.0
1946	15	4.5
1947	16	6.8
1948	24	10.0
1949	24	10.8
1950	25	7.0
1951	34	8.3
1952	50	11.1
1953	50	14.8
1954	62	12.1
1955	62	20.4
1956	62	27.9
1957	54	27.2
1958	54	32.1
1959	52	30.7
1960	54	38.9
1961	59	29.7

Source: *Annual Reports of the Department of Agriculture: Annual Trade Reports.*

Many changes occurred in spite of rather than because of British efforts. Measures of compulsion in agriculture were not so much withdrawn as forced out of existence by mass refusal to follow regulations. It was after this that government agricultural officials began to talk more about the advantages of enclosure and individual tenure for Africans, of the progressive 'master' farmer, in other words the capitalist farmer. Similarly higher prices were not so much paid in order that production should increase, but paid with the result that production did increase. Production of cotton rose most remarkably in the period 1952–6; previous export records were broken in 1953, 1955 and 1956. A major cause of this was the rise in price to 50 cents in 1952. Though the existence of co-operative societies clearly contributed, a major motive in their formation was the desire to secure a better price. Even Peat, the agriculturalist who had proposed the intensive effort to increase production by massive supervision and the imposition of 'scientific' methods, recognised that price levels and not new methods were responsible. Officials who had previously argued that a higher price would result in lower production had to swallow their words.[25]

Another important subject is the relationship of the colonial state with the providers of capital. Once it was accepted that it was unwise to continue to finance 'development' from profits on the sale of African-grown cash crops, it was assumed that capital would come from outside the country, provided certain guarantees were offered. These guarantees which the government set itself to provide were primarily political, that is, guarantees of political stability and assurances against nationalisation without compensation. This explains many of the government's tirades against 'irresponsible' politicians. But there is no evidence that the government was right in its diagnosis. Capital poured into Kenya in spite of Mau Mau. A significant advantage Kenya had was cheap power. Electricity was actually exported from Tanganyika to Kenya at a cheaper price than was charged to consumers in Tanganyika. However, Shell BP spent £1 million prospecting for oil in Tanganyika in 1957, and a similar amount must have been spent in an abortive search for uranium in the period 1955–8 when atomic energy appeared to be the primary source of power for the future. A Dutch company invested in a pilot production plant for pyrochlore in Mbeya, and an American group helped to set up a lead processing mill at Mpanda. On the other hand, no finance was forthcoming to extract and use the vast coal and iron deposits known to exist in the Songea area. The government decided not to build a railway, and without a railway it was clear that extraction of coal and iron would not be 'economic', in other words, the large investment which would have to be made could not be expected to yield quick, large profits. The level of profits expected was revealed in an interesting controversy between the government and a South African company named Huletts. They had been promised, they said, every assistance in the setting up of sugar plantations and a refinery in the Kilombero valley. When such assistance, primarily the building of a railway, was not forthcoming, the company sued the government for damages of £0.75 million. Counsel for the plaintiff argued that the company had in fact expected to make profits of £2 million in three years, but was prepared to settle for only £0.75 million damages for loss of profits. Large profits of this order of magnitude were in fact made by some companies. Bird's, a sisal concern, made profits of over £1 million in 1951–2, a year of high sisal prices, and paid a 70 per cent dividend. Dalgety's, a merchant group, made profits of this order fairly regularly throughout the 1950s. Capital was not unavailable therefore. It was forthcoming whenever capitalists believed they could make quick profits. Government policies were relevant when they directly assisted profits through tax concessions or the building of infrastructure.[26]

There was some change of attitude towards industries on the part of British administrators, but without something much more positive industrialisation itself could not be expected to follow. The British Colonial Secretary said in 1954 that industry in colonies must not be prevented or delayed, implying that there was a danger that it would be. The President of the British Board of Trade said in 1952 that the establishment of secondary industries in Commonwealth countries would create new demands which British exports could satisfy. He recognised that the pattern of British exports was changing, that the days when the major British export had been cheap cotton textiles were ending, and that Britain was more likely to be able to sell machines and other capital goods. But such perception was rare. In Tanganyika until the late 1950s British officials attempted to boost Lancashire's textile exports by banning or restricting the entry of Japanese textiles, instead of allowing tariff protection from all imported textiles to a potential manufacturer. Their talk of encouraging investment meant investment in mineral extraction and not in industry. They did not see even Britain's interest, let alone pursue Tanganyika's. To establish cotton manufacturing was clearly in Tanganyika's interest. Criteria of profitability rather than need at first prevented such an establishment at all, and later prevented the spinning part of the operation being set up on Tanganyika soil. One of the earliest textile mills, Tanganyika Textiles, was founded in 1959 to weave imported rayon yarn. All of Tanganyika's own cotton, which was in any case of too long a staple to be suitable for the manufacturing of cheap materials, continued to be exported. Further, lack of capital was not the reason for the low level of industrialisation. Capital formation was taking place in this period as we have seen. Where Asian capitalists wished to invest, they were often discouraged by the government. It would appear therefore that decisions were taken against the investment of such capital in Tanganyika. When the government did bring itself to act favourably towards investment it was almost always multinational companies, spreading outwards from Britain or Kenya, which it favoured. In this way British-American Tobacco was granted a licence in 1960 when such licences had previously been refused to local Asians.[27]

Interpreting the principle of comparative advantage through criteria of profitability, the government saw its main task as encouraging agriculture for export. It is noteworthy that even here British administrators were slow to appreciate the importance of African agriculture from their own point of view. Impressed by the fact that from 1948 to 1951 sisal comprised more than 50 per cent of the total value of Tanganyika's exports, they continued to think of African-grown coffee and cotton as subsidiary matters. European agriculture was considered more valuable than African agriculture. Their blinkered thinking on this issue led to the continuation of both guaranteed minimum returns, and of the payment of prices for wheat and maize which were higher than world prices, to European farmers until 1955. At the same time, as we have seen, prices for African products were *below* world prices. The so-called efficient farmers were subsidised, the so-called inefficient peasants were taxed. It is therefore possible to see on a minor scale a process familiar in Kenya—a direct transfer of the products of their labour from African peasants to European farmers. There was, it is true, a shortage of food in Tanganyika in many years in the period 1945–54, which might have justified subsidies to good producers. But such was the inadequacy of storage facilities in Tanganyika that when, in 1955, more than sufficient maize was produced, it had to be exported (at the low world price) at a loss to the Tanganyika Treasury of more than £1 million. This at last brought the government down to earth, the guaranteed minimum return was abolished and the subsidies were phased out. Another example of the results of the government's belief in the value of European agriculture was the continued alienation of land throughout the 1950s. The total alienated land (not all of it for agriculture, it is true) reached 3 million acres in 1956, having been below 2 million acres in 1949. While the usual justification that this was only 1 per cent of Tanganyika's land area is well-known, the figure should perhaps be compared with the total land under African cultivation, estimated to be $4\frac{1}{2}$ million acres in 1956. The number of holders of the 3 million acres was not quite 1 500. It should also be noted that a sizable proportion of non-African held land was not used; in 1961 this amounted to 29 per cent of land alienated for agriculture or ranching. One of the lesser known facts about the notorious Meru alienation is that European farmers did not succeed in producing beef cattle in the area alienated. A committee considering the results of the alienation in 1955 found that four of the six units they investigated were vacant and the other two were not being used 'properly'.[28]

Meanwhile in African agriculture slow and reluctantly applied changes were being made, often as a result of African pressure. The tradition that African production was induced by propaganda and the threat of legal penalties dies hard. It was comfortable to believe that African peasants did not react to money incentives and that it was therefore useless if not counter-productive to pay more for their services. But prices had risen in the period before 1954, profits by government marketing agencies had been declared unsuitable, and the government feared the political repercussions of putting them down again when world prices began to drop in the late 1950s. Cotton growers for whom prices were decided by the Director of Agriculture on the advice of the Lint and Seed Marketing Board, were now given special treatment. At least partially as a result of the part played by Mwanza cotton growers in the foundation of TANU, and the subsequent incipient trouble in the area, prices were not allowed to drop below 50 cents a pound, the level reached in 1952. At this price growers were prepared to cultivate cotton voluntarily, and there was a continuing increase in total production. The government however continued to expect that growers would only cultivate and reap if constantly hounded by agricultural officials, who operated, as we have seen, at the growers' expense, and the number of such officials did not decrease. After 1955 much of the government's powers of interference were allowed to devolve on the newly formed South East Lake County Council. Far from being representative of the growers, this was one of Twining's experimental multiracial councils, the African section of which was nominated and consisted mainly of chiefs. It did not finance itself but was given grants partly by the central government, partly by the Sukumaland Development Fund, and the Lint and Seed Marketing Board. Since the latter two (which together provided more than half of the revenue) had raised their money in the first place from cotton profits, the old system was continuing whereby the growers paid for their own supervision. It is interesting to note that much of the LSMB grant was spent on salaries and housing for 'extension' staff.[29]

It is not surprising that during this period Tanganyika's position as exporter of agricultural products did not change. Though sisal, due to a decline in prices greater than that in coffee, did not play the same dominant part, other crops, especially cotton and cashew nuts, filled its place. Even the attempt to make Tanganyika an important exporter of minerals falied. Though diamonds, in which the government inherited an interest in lieu of death duties, remained important, gold declined and the lead mine at Mpanda was exhausted and closed in the same year as Independence. No uranium or oil was found, pyrochlore was not found profitable and the coal and iron were not even touched. But in 1956 and again from 1959 until Independence Tanganyika's exports were greater in value than Uganda's or Kenya's. A little over a third of these exports actually went to Britain. But Britain's gold and dollar reserves continued to benefit from the export of Tanganyika's coffee and sisal to the United States, for which Tanganyika received almost nothing directly in return. What in fact happened was something like this. Britain could not export cars, bicycles and tractors to the USA. But she could export these things to colonies like Tanganyika who could then export their agriculutral products to America. Britain could then import short-staple cotton, wheat and other essential items in turn from the United States. Not all the value of Tanganyika's exports was returned in goods, in any case. The total balance of trade surplus in the years 1951 to 1961 inclusive was £77 million. The balance not expanded on services became the government's or the currency board's reserves, invested largely in London. In 1958, for example, these amounted to £20.6 million. Since Britain's balance of payments problems, and the related problem of the value of sterling as an international currency, were perennial, any such investments assisted Britain. Attempts to justify this state of affairs by British officials, politicians or bankers stressed the mutual interest of the Commonwealth or the sterling area in upholding the value of sterling or even of upholding Britain's position as a manufacturing country, the workshop of the Commonwealth. This use of the doctrine of comparative advantage, even expressed sometimes as the duty of the colonies to make sacrifices for the good of the industrial centres, and the praise of the sterling area as a mutual benefit society, show us how Tanganyika's economy was treated as part of a larger economy, and we may conclude that it was still in fact part, and a peripheral part, of an economy dominated by Britain.[30]

Table 5.2

GOVERNMENT AND MARKETING BOARD RESERVES INVESTED OUTSIDE TANGANYIKA

AMOUNT IN £ MILLION	INTEREST PAYABLE	SECURITY	SOURCE
1.8	2%	British Government	EACB
3.4	2½%	British Government	EACB
5.2	3%	British Government	EACB
2.7	3%	British Government	LSMB
1.0	4¾%	British Government	EACB
8.9	n.a.	British Government	Tanganyika Govt.
0.3	3–4½%	Other Commonwealth Governments	EACB
0.3	4–6%	Other bodies	LSMB
23.6			

EACB East African Currency Board, 32½% of its currency reserve, representing currency in circulation in Tanganyika.

LSMB Lint and Seed Marketing Board Price Assistance Fund.

Sources: *East African Currency Board Annual Reports Lint and Seed Marketing Board Annual Reports Tanganyika Standard*, 1 May 1959.

So far as the effect on the workers and peasants of Tanganyika is concerned we may note some slight increases of income for some of them during the later years of colonial rule. For workers the improvements came remarkably late and as a result of trade union action. The employers of Tanganyika, in agreement among themselves to keep wages down, made almost no voluntary changes. Militant strike action, having begun with the Dar es Salaam dockworkers' strike of 1947, reached a crescendo in the years 1957–9. Sisal plantation workers were among the last to receive significant increases, in 1960, though even these brought them up to only around shs. 75 a month. Town workers, at around shs. 100 a month, became somewhat less poor, though not an aristocracy in any sense of the word. Many employers, and especially sisal plantation owners, tried to reduce the numbers of their employees as a result, and the strange situation of relatively capital-intensive production in a capital-starved but labour-rich country began to follow.[31]

For the much-abused peasant, provided he was a cash crop grower, some increase in income occurred during the 1950s. But in some cases this increase was of the order of from shs. 50 to 100 a year, not a month, as was the case with town workers. Such was the position among cashew nut growers in the southern region. Growers of rice, considering the intensive cultivation especially weeding required, were not much better off, and the cultivators of one acre of cotton could expect to gain little over shs. 20 a month. Most cultivators had begun to plant more than one acre of cash crops, but the pressure on land in the 'favoured' acreas was such that expansion was not always possible, and differentiation between those who possessed the land and labour to cultivate larger areas, and those who did not, began to appear. British administrators wished to encourage this differentiation, since they saw it as the way to an agricultural revolution such as had occurred in Britain. That it did not occur to any greater extent was, however, due to their own policies in the past. Extremely few African farmers had been able to accumulate capital which they could invest in machines and other 'improvements'. However, the relative wealth and satisfaction of kulaks in Kilimanjaro contrasts greatly during this period with peasants in Sukumaland, Mbulu, Uluguru and the Usambaras. Peasants in these areas had been the focus of intensive efforts on the part of British administrators to change methods of cultivation to prevent soil erosion. Except in the case of the Sukuma, the peasants had little income from cash crops. Yet they had been constantly interferred with by agricultural officials. Peasants had been imprisoned in many areas for not planting a sufficient area of cassava. Others had been prosecuted for not carrying manure on their way to their fields or for not being present in their fields during the 'normal' cultivating hours. Some of these regulations had actually worsened the yield of crops as for example in the Uluguru Mountains where rice on the regulation terraces grew less well than on unterraced land. It had been assumed that peasants did not understand their soil, and were incapable of making rational choices. Popular resistance occurred in all four places, linked up inextricably with dissatisfaction with the African chiefs, who had been made responsible for punishing offenders. The effect of this resistance was remarkable. The peasants by mass disobedience made the regulations unworkable, and the government had simply to withdraw and decide to rely on persuasion.[32]

Such peasant action was often, but not always, tapped by TANU, and played its part in the coming of Independence. But it should be noted that it was not, and it did not bring, a revolution. The peasants, like the workers in the trade unions, were seeking a more acceptable place in the system, not a change in the system itself. In a sense peasant action had forced the British into the position to which their own arguments should have led them. They had talked of seeking peasant co-operation but they had to be forced to do it. Ultimately they were forced to allow Independence as a means of securing co-operation. Some think out a neo-colonial strategy, some have a neo-colonial solution forced upon them by otherwise insoluble problems. To achieve willing adherence to an economic system, a certain measure of freedom is necessary. The political economy of colonialism was being modified, not drastically changed.

Notes

1 *Annual Trade Report* 1939; *Tanzania National Archives* (hereafter TNA) 215/694/11/388 and 400; 10037/VI/424 and 44A. I would like to thank the staff of the Tanzania National Archives for permission to see the documents cited.

2 TNA 215/694/II/254 and III/653.

3 *Ibid.* 728 and 741–4210037/VI/7A, IIA, 20A and 26A; 19496/I/54 and 104–5; *Annual Trade Report*, 1941. On the concept of reserve supply, see Mahmoud Mandani, *Uganda: Economic*

Policy between the wars, unpublished paper, University of Dar es Salaam, -973.

4 *Annual Trade Reports*, 1939, 1941 and 1942; N. Fuggles-Couchman, *Agricultural Change in Tanganyika*, 1945–60, Stanford, 1964, pp. 50 and 60.

5 TNA 215/694/II/237, 254 and 255; III/516, 554, 558, 561, 674–81 and 685; Anse Tambila, *A History of Tanga Sisal Labour Force 1936–64*, M.A. thesis, University of Dar es Salaam, 1974, pp. 21–3.

6 TNA 215/694/III/557, 562, 572, 574 and 674.

7 *Ibid.*, III/515, 552, 667, 684 and 686.

8 *Ibid.*, III/450, 493 and 552.

9 *Ibid.*, III/734, IV/740; C.K. Magoti, *The Development and Impact of the Money Economy on Musoma District 1939–60*, M.A. thesis, University of Dar es Salaam, 1974, p. 57.

10 TNA 215/694/IV/806A, report of a speech by Sir Stafford Cripps, British Chancellor of the Exchequer.

11 See, for example, *Tanganyika Standard*, 1 February 1949, leader, and *United Nations*, T/L/301, report of a speech by a British representative in the Trusteeship Council.

12 Alan Wood, *The Groundnut Affair*, London, 1950; *Tanganyika Standard*, 5 February 1947, leader and 28 May 1948, report of a speech by Strachey, British Minister of Food.

13 A. Nelson, *The Freemen of Meru*, London, 1967; *Tanganyika Standard*, 19 April 1948 and 23 March 1956.

14 TNA 35783/24A; 37746/II/85A; 40657/87 and 125; 40868/42; 41735/13 and 18.

15 *Ibid.*, 23420/137; 31301/III/822A; 41735/9, II and 16.

16 *Ibid.*, 215/AG/18/25 and 35; 35783/24A; 41735/18, 30, 33. The 'full' price in 1951 was said to be 90 cents a pound.

17 TNA 5/25/II; 23420/II/56, 60, 63A, 68, 74, 82, 95 and 95A; 43679/9. On coffee prices, see below, footnote 20.

18 International Bank of Reconstruction and Development, *The Economic Development of Tanganyika*, Baltimore, 1961, pp. 35, 46–50, 332–4; East African Currency Board, *Annual Reports*, 1945–61.

19 TNA 40657/87; 41735, *passium* 43679/17. Most of these figures can be seen in Tanganyika Government, *The Cotton Industry 1939–53*. Dar es Salaam, 1953.

20 TNA 41735/55 and 56; International Bank, *op. cit.*, p. 405, table 82. The United Nations Visiting Mission of 1951 noted that during its visit the British Ministry of Food was paying the Tanganyika Government £296 per ton for coffee when the world price was £450.

21 John Iliffe, 'A History of the Dockworkers of Dar es Salaam', in J.E.G. Sutton, ed., *Dar es Salaam, City, Port and Region: Tanzania Notes and Records*, 71, 1970, pp. 134–8.

22 G. Andrew Maguire, *Towards Uburu in Sukumaland: The Politics of Participation*, Cambridge, 1969, pp. 82–99; TNA 215/AG/18/23 and 93.

23 United Nations Visiting Mission to Tanganyika, *Report 1948* and *Report 1951*, p. 36; TNA/5/25/11: 215/694/IV/833.

24 *Ibid.*, 40657/87.

25 *Ibid.*, 215/AG/18/113; 215/694/V/944; and 1067: *Annual Trade Reports, 1945–61*. The argument is not that price is always the only detriment of production. If so, it would be impossible to explain the continued rise in production after 1956. It is that price was the major detriment for the level of voluntary production in the period 1945–56. This period was itself vital in the establishment of a voluntary habit of cotton production which continued for at least another decade. Continued increased production when prices fall can be explained by increased dependence on income levels attained in years of higher prices. This is very different from the explanation using a theory of perverse reaction, which suggests that in addition production drops when prices rise.

26 *Tanganyika Standard*, 1 October 1952, 26 April 1954, 19 August 1955, 30 April 1956, 28 February 1958, 14 July 1959; *East Africa and Rhodesia*, 2 October 1952.

27 *Ibid.*, 24 July 1952, 15 July 1954; *Tanganyika Standard*, 5 April 1952, 25 November 1955, 16 September, and 29 October 1957, 9 December 1961; Martha Noney, *Asian Industrial activities in Tanganyika*, East African Universities Social Science Conference Paper, 1973.

28 Annual Trade Reports, 1945–55; *East Africa and Rhodesia*, 18 August 1955; *Tanganyika Standard*, 4 June 1954 and 21 November 1955; J. Clagett Taylor, *The Political Development of Tanganyika*, Stanford, 1963; International Bank, op. cit., p.

29 TNA 215/2995/205 and 344. While the Lint and Seed Marketing Board did not make large profits on the sale of cotton lint after 1954, it sold the by-product, cotton seed, with no compensation to the grower. This was worth £$\frac{1}{2}$ million in 1957–8.

30 *Annual Trade Reports*, 1954–61; *Tanganyika Standard*, 1 May 1959; Justinian Rweyemamu, *Underdevelopment and Industrialisation in Tanzania*, Nairobi, 1973, pp. XI, 34–5.

31 A.C. Mascarenhas, *Resistance and Change in the Sisal Plantations of Tanzania*, Ph.D. dissertation, UCLA, pp. 197–9; William H. Friedland, *Vuta Ramba: The Development of Trade Unions in Tanganyika*, Stanford, 1969.

32 Tanganyika Government Department of Agriculture, *Annual Reports*, 1953–61. Joseph R. Mlahagwa, *Agricultural Change in the Uluguru Mountains during the Colonial Period*, M.A. thesis, University of Dar es Salaam, 1974, pp. 41–50, 61–4; John Iliffe, *Agricultural Change in Modern Tanganyika: An Outline History*, Nairobi, 1971, pp. 34–43.

6. Colonial Ideological Apparatuses in Tanganyika under the Germans

Karim F. Hirji

Missionary activities before colonialism

Before the influx of missionaries in the latter half of the nineteenth century, some European and American companies were already trading along the East African coast. Based on the island of Zanzibar, these companies purchased goods like ivory and gum and sold guns, cloth, brandy, etc. British gunboats patrolled the coastal line in order to curb the export of slaves. The slave trade had become an impediment to the development of capitalism. Africa was no longer required to provide cheap labour for American and West Indian plantations. Capitalist industry now required sources of raw materials and markets for its manufactured goods.[1]

It was at this historical juncture that European missionaries appeared on the East African scene. Not surprisingly, the first missionaries came from Britain, the most advanced capitalist nation of the time. The missionaries preceded and prepared the groundwork for the complete colonisation of the area.

However, it would be a distortion of facts to say that all missionaries consciously identified themselves with imperialist ambitions.[2] But whether they did so or not is beside the point. For history is rarely preconceived and very few men ever act with an awareness of their objective historical roles. The missionary pioneers did, however, possess some clarity about their historical mission. Although Livingstone, the inspirational architect of missionary endeavour, protrayed Africa as a place full of suffering souls to be saved from sin and damnation, his conception of redemption was both material and spiritual. In his view, Africa needed commerce as well as Christianity. The latter need served to rationalise the former. Influenced by him, the dignitaries of the Anglican Church founded the University Mission to Central Africa which planned to set up 'centres of Christianity and civilisation for the promotion of true religion, agriculture and commerce'.[3]

Such ventures received the support of the merchant bourgeoisie in Britain. After Livingstone's death, a group of Glasgow businessmen raised £10 000 to finance the setting up of such ventures. Two missions were set up near Lake Nyasa and a steamer served to stimulate trade. The Livingstonia Central African Trading Company was established by James Stevenson of Glasgow, 'with the dual object of supplying the two missions and of bringing out ivory at a price which would undercut the Arab merchants'.[4]

Livingstone's death provided further impetus to missionary penetration. The UMCA and the Church Missionary Society (CMS) spread further inland. On the other hand the French Cardinal, Lavigeri, toured a number of European capitals to promote a similar movement in the Catholic Church. Thus in 1868, the Holy Ghost Fathers (HGF) set up a mission station at Bagamoyo. In 1872, it comprised twenty-four European priests and nuns and 324 ex-slaves, including 251 children. By 1885, five missionary societies had established themselves in Tanzania, namely the UMCA, CMS, HGF, the Lutheran Missionary Society (LMS), and the White Fathers (WF). On arrival, they stayed in the coastal areas and later spread out over the various parts of the country and established their respective spheres of influence.

Idealised versions of missionary settlements depict a picture in which missionaries encountered a friendly reception from the 'suffering natives' and their chiefs who later fell under the 'civilising' influence of the missionaries and adopted Christianity. In reality:

> the missionary who set out with a few dozen porters and tried to settle in a native village had to set up what amounted to a small independent state. He was recognised as a kind of chief by the headmen round about and to a greater or lesser extent the Sultan of Zanzibar and the British or French consul were felt to be behind him, as they were felt to be behind any other caravan manned with porters from the coast.[5]

The early missionary followed the established trade routes and settled in the proximity of some trading centre. He established a more or less self-contained station which grew its own food, had its own laws to regulate life on the mission and even some sort of a police force to maintain order and, in some cases, for defensive purposes. The supreme authority at the station would, of course, be the chief European missionary. Thus, for example, the White Fathers' station at Kibanga on the shore of Lake Tanganyika, had by 1890 vast plantations which grew rice, maize, sweet potatoes, oil palms, bananas, sugar cane, vegetables, etc. The work on the plantation was done by converts. They worked for three days a week on the mission plantation; the rest they could spend on their own plots. As wages, they received a few pieces of cloth.

The principal aim of the missionaries was to propagate their faith. Most of their initial converts had in fact no choice but to adopt Christianity. These were the former slaves 'freed' by the British and passed on to the mission—for cultural and ideological enslavement. Due to the fear of being recaptured and lack of means to go back to his home area, the ex-slave was compelled to remain on the mission. Also, the fact that many of the slaves who were captured and handed over to the mission were young children made them easy victims of the missionaries. Some missions even bought slaves to swell the ranks of their converts! Once on the station the ex-slave was required to accept the Gospel and follow the rules governing life on the mission. The villages which sprang up in the vicinity of the early missions stations were quite often started by former slaves or refugees from various tribes in the area. Besides being taught elements of the Gospel, these potential converts helped to build the station and maintain production.

After an initial period of settling down, the missionaries looked for converts beyond the immediate surroundings of the mission. They gained their initial foothold in the indigenous societies in various ways. The initial reception accorded to the missionaries and the extent of their success depended largely on the concrete economic and political situation in the various areas. In places ravaged by famine or disease or where the population had been dislocated by inter-tribal warfare, the missionaries could, in general, penetrate easily, while they would find it more difficult to penetrate prosperous tribes which had strong links with coastal traders. In other areas such as Mahenge, the first missionaries faced vigorous opposition, and the mission was ransacked by the people.

A common strategy of the missionaries was to try to establish links in order to convert the tribal chiefs. Once this was done a major obstacle was removed and they could work more freely in the area. Carefully chosen presents were enough in some cases to win favours from some chiefs. In other cases the chiefs themselves desired a mission in their area for reasons of diplomacy. Also the superior technology and scientific knowledge which the missionary possessed assisted him to establish his reputation among the local people.

Gradually the missionaries realised that provision of elementary educational facilities was useful to accelerate the rate of conversion. A literate congregation can more rapidly absorb religious ideas through reading the Bible and can participate effectively in activities like hymn-singing.[6] Moreover, facilities like health and education would attract more people to the mission. Then they could be used to spread religious ideas. Thus, for example in January 1885 at Kipalapala mission there was still no public preaching although every opportunitv was taken to talk to adults individually at, for example, the dispensary. Besides these attractions, some missions served to provide a sanctuary, because of the comparative safety they offered, to refugees in times of tribal conflict.

The WF mission set up near Tabora in the 1890s, gives a generally representative picture of the evolution of early mission stations. The initial years were mostly spent in building a church, a school and residential houses for the European priests. The African Christians and their families lived in areas not very far from the mission and regularly came to participate in the various activities. They did the construction work and cleared the surrounding areas for farming. Gradually a complex emerged in which activities like construction, agriculture, evangelical work, literacy training and nursing sick patients were carried on. Besides, the missionaries also visited nearby villages to extend invitations to chiefs to come to the mission.

It was in such a context that the educational activities of the missions emerged and mission schools developed. Literacy was taught as a means to impart Christian beliefs and rudimentary education gradually became the principal means for conversion. An integral feature of mission education was manual work and training for practical jobs. Hence the pupils also engaged in productive and construction activities. For example, at the HGF station in Bagamoyo the school pupils spent five and a half hours a day in the classroom and five and a half hours in practical work which was either agricultural work or craftsmanship. Some pupils were trained to be carpenters or masons in order to meet the requirements of the mission for such skilled workers. In the same school, some children, who were categorised as 'unfit for literary training had only one hour of elementary studies; the rest of the day was spent in the field.[7]

An individual missionary or even a group of them, however fanatical they might have been about spreading the Gospel, could only cover a small area and influence a small number of people, so they needed local manpower. This need for local 'priests' was acutely felt as mission activities began to expand. Besides, the problem was not just one of numbers. As Nolan points out: 'in many areas where the chiefs were hostile to the Fathers, the visits of one or two catechists would make friendly relations possible.'[8] The utilisation of catechists would also ease the communication problems of the missionaries.[9]

Missionaries had emphasised catechist training right from the early days. Many of the initial converts, mainly ex-slaves, were trained to be carriers of Christianity to the people. The best pupils at the HGF school in Bagamoyo were selected and sent for further training to a seminary in Zanzibar. At the WF mission near Tabora catechists were trained for a period of four years. The training comprised for the most part elementary literacy and Bible study, as well as productive work on the mission. On completion of the course, the catechists were sent to distant villages to spread the word of God. This represented a qualitative change in missionary endeavour. In the past conversion was solely through contact with European missionaries. But now the process was localised insofar as it was the local churchworker, who had internalised the Christian ideology, who diffused it among the people. Conversion was no longer a restricted affair centred on the mission but much more widespread.

Normally a catechist was someone who had, through extensive contacts with the missionaries, rejected the customs and beliefs of his tribe, adopted Christianity and memorised a few Biblical texts. The missionaries tended to emphasise that a catechist should be a self-sacrificing and devoted Christian not so much concerned about material rewards and comforts but about propagating the faith. This was in most cases a justification for the hard work, with meagre pay, that was expected from the catechist.[10] However, the catechists were in fact one of the first groups of Africans to receive regular cash remuneration without doing manual work.

The catechist was an important weapon in the missionaries' crusade against Islam and local religions. In their endeavours, the missionaries inevitably came up against local customs and traditions. Their efforts to demolish them resulted in many conflicts with the people. However, the tactics of the missionaries in combatting the local customs and religious practices tended to vary from place to place. In some areas, especially in the initial stages, they appeared to be adaptable in order not to alienate the chiefs and the villagers. Some even tried to interpret local beliefs in Christian terms. Some used their scientific knowledge either to mystify the people or to disprove their beliefs. In other areas they directly tried to suppress traditional practices. In Ungoni area, for example, 'Father Lenther, head of the Peramiho mission had ordered the destruction of Nkosi Mputa's *mahoka* hut. The mahoka worship came to be regarded by the missionaries as mere idolatry.'[11]

Whatever their tactics, the missionaries came into conflict everywhere with traditional customs and ideas which could not be reconciled with Christian precepts. The missionaries' interference began to arouse more and more hostility. Many of the customs had a material basis in the concrete conditions of the tribal societies and could not just be wished away. It was the use of catechists that was partly instrumental in overcoming this hurdle. The catechist was looked upon by the people as someone who had learned the ways of the white man. He represented a future image of themselves. Being one of them he encountered less hostility and was more able to move and work among them. A catechist's session with a group of villagers would often be a combination of recitation of holy verses and singing hymns with denunciation of customs frowned upon by the missionaries such as polygamy, folk dances, superstitious practices, etc. The function of the catechist was thus, both to deculturalise the people and to imbue them with a foreign ideology.

In areas where Muslim influence was strong, the missionaries were not able to make much headway. This was the case along the coastal areas as well as in places such as the shores of Lake Tanganyika where the LMS had constructed its stations. But besides the idealogical conflict between the Muslims and the missionaries there was a deep-rooted material conflict as well. At the time of missionary intrusion, the Muslim traders from the coast had entrenched themselves in many parts of the country. In some areas they were allied with the big chiefs. The coastal traders, in alliance with and backed by the Sultanate of Zanzibar, dominated the territory's internal and external trade.

Initially the coastal traders and the European merchants required each other's services and did not interfere in each other's domain of activities. The European trader brought his commodities to Zanzibar to exchange them for goods brought from the interior. The inland import of western manufactured goods and export of local items was monopolised by the coastal merchants, who used porters to carry the goods. The major area of conflict was over the export of slaves which was being curbed by the British navy. But by this time ivory trade had become more important than slave trade and in fact the porters used by the coastal traders were mostly wage-workers rather than slaves.

The penetration of missionaries into the interior slowly upset the détente existing between the two merchant classes. In spite of their initial policy of peaceful co-existence with the coastal traders, the activities of the missionaries slowly undermined the ideological, economic and political positions of the coastal traders. Objectively, the missionaries represented interests of European capital.[12] As Oliver puts it, the missionaries.

> were employers of labour and therefore dispensers of calico and trade goods. For the erection of their stations, even the simpler ones, they required the assistance of hundreds of Africans, and for their daily existence they needed food and firewood, cooks and gardeners, and many other services. The transport of their supplies alone became quite an industry. Hore employed more than 1,000 porters to carry an open steel boat overland to Ujiji in 1882; a figure of two or three hundred was quite common for the routine caravan, bringing up tinned food and missionaries' chattels, European building material and barter goods.[13]

The weakening of the monopolistic position of the coastal merchants occurred simultaneously with the erosion of their political standing *vis-a-vis* the various chiefs in the interior. For the missionaries could, and did, supply to the chiefs the manufactured goods previously supplied by the coastal traders. They employed the chiefs' subjects. Furthermore when they managed to convert some of the chiefs or their subjects their position was further enhanced.

To cap it all, the missionaries were followed by the European trading companies. German trading concerns had been operating from Zanzibar since 1849 and by the early 1870s about a quarter of 'Zanzibar's trade was with Germany'.[14] Now these firms penetrated inland to establish trading outposts. The consequence was a sharpening of the contradiction between the coastal traders on the one hand and the European companies and missionaries on the other: the former struggling to retain their established positions and the latter attempting to make further advances.[15] In some places the conflict assumed violent proportions right from the initial days. For example, 'Karonga in 1891 was like an armed fort, with three cannons and a garrison of over a hundred men, its stockage being guarded by watches of four men each night to warn of attacks from Mlozi, the Swahili trader with whom the African Lake Company had a commercial feud'.[16]

The struggle reached its climax and assumed territorial proportions after the German East Africa Company was granted the charter to administer Tanganyika. Besides the ruthlessness of the company's agents, the principal contradiction between the two merchant classes was the basic cause underlying the uprising against the company which erupted in 1889 in the coastal districts. The uprising was led by Bushiri, a prosperous merchant, and Bwana Heri, a big trading chief. As Lubetsky puts it, the leaders of the uprising were 'town notables'.[17] The company's trading posts as well as some missions such as the Benedictine mission at Pugu, which were thought to be outposts of the company, were attacked.

The suppression of the uprising resolved once and for all the question of the political and economic position of the coastal traders, who were relegated to a subordinate position in relation to the European colonisers. Bushiri had led a popular resistance movement against the German invaders, but the uprising ended with a compromise between the local commercial class and the Germans. For the Germans realised that they could not completely dispense with the services of the coastal traders. As Iliffe puts it,

> As (the resistance) collapsed, the Germans negotiated with a peace party of Omani aristocrats, who then became the agents of a bureaucratic system of government, providing each major coastal town with a *liwali* (governor) and the

hinterland with subordinate administrators called *Akidas*.[18] Company rule was abolished and the era of direct German colonialism over mainland Tanzania began.

Colonial conquest and consolidation 1885–1905

The initial two decades of German colonialism were marked by the colonisers' efforts to consolidate their political hegemony over the territory. These were also the years which witnessed the inception of the fundamental elements of the colonial socio-economic structure[19]. Land was alienated from the people in various parts of the country and was either given to the missions, the incoming tide of settlers and German enterprises or appropriated by the colonial administration. Production of cash crops on a large scale commenced and the people were, directly or indirectly, compelled to work on plantations for miserable wages. Taxes were imposed and an infra-structure and communication network was created to serve the colonial enterprise. This was the era in which the colonial state (which must be considered as an extension of the German metropolitan state) was taking shape and entrenching its authority.

The basic problem was to establish law and order. The 'recalcitrant native' must be made to submit to the colonial system. But the people did not submit readily to the invaders. They fiercely resisted the imposition of colonial rule. First against the German East Africa Company and later against the colonial government, the struggle continued in various parts of the country, culminating in the Maji Maji war of 1905. The principal instrument of the coloniser in this pacification campaign was, of course, the repressive apparatus of the colonial state. *Askaris* recruited from the coast and other parts of Africa, led by German officers, engaged in bloody battles with resisting tribes. A common tactic used by the German commanding officers was to play off one chief against another to conquer both.

However, pacification was not purely through military means. It was considerably facilitated by judicious utilisation of the ideological apparatuses which the Germans found in existence, and whose further growth they promoted, after coming to Tanzania. These were the missionary and the Muslim religious/educational apparatuses as well as some elements of the tribal social structure. The missionary ideological apparatus was instrumental in creating the psychological climate for colonisation whilst the Islamic apparatus assisted in ensuring the functioning of the colonial state apparatus at administrative level. We shall first examine the role of the Islamic apparatus.

Of course, the Germans did not adapt and utilise the Islamic apparatus as a result of any particular liking for Islam as such, but for reasons of political expediency and practical administration. This utilisation by the Germans of the Islamic apparatus offers a classic example of how an emergent social formation can modify and adjust the superstructural elements of a previous social formation to suit its own needs. In fact, the adaptability of ideologies and ideological institutions in the transition from one class society to another class society has been a common historical occurrence. Anything which finds a root in a social formation tends to become integrated into it by the very dynamics of the system. So even if later on the political conditions which made the Germans utilise the Muslim bureaucrats from the coast were no longer there, they had become part and parcel of the colonial administrative machine.

As has been mentioned earlier, the uprising against the German East Africa Company ended with a compromise between the coastal merchants and the Germans. For the Germans realised that they would not only need the commercial services but also political assistance from these coastal 'aristocrats' in their campaign to pacify and govern the interior. The Germans also used the political institutions which had existed along the coast before their arrival, to serve their own interests. In the coastal towns, Liwalis continued, as before, to be the civil administrators; the difference being that now they were under the colonial governor. As the number of Europeans available was too small, the Germans recruited the Swahili-speaking personnel from the coast to be junior administrators, tax-collectors, clerks, interpreters, etc., in the coastal and interior districts. The 'aristocratic' elements, namely those from or associated with the merchant class became liwalis and akidas, while the commoners joined the ranks of the colonial askaris. Many of these agents of the Colonial Government, especially those in the middle echelons, were products of the *Quran* schools which had spread along the coast.

These Quran schools had been the first institutions to provide formal literary training in the territory. Its pupils were mainly taught to recite and read the Quran in Arabic. But in the process they learnt how to read and write and do simple arithmetic. Their literary skills as well as the knowledge they possessed of the interior areas were to prove useful to the Germans.[20] But the importance of these Quran schools was rapidly to decline soon after the colonial government started its own schools;[21] first along the coast and later in the interior districts. So although the akidas and liwadis continued to be recruited mostly from the coast, they were now increasingly people who had passed through the government schools rather than the earlier group whose literary skill was an outcome of attendance in Quran schools.

The use of Swahili-speaking agents to man the colonial administration machine had several important consequences. Not the least among these was promotion of Swahili as the *lingua franca* for the territory. Swahili had evolved over centuries as a result of fusion of Arabic and Bantu languages and its usage was common along the coast. The decision of the colonial administration to use Swahili, together with German, as one of the official languages certainly accelerated its spread into the interior. In the long run it may even have promoted the further secularisation of Swahili. After a time most of the official correspondence came to be conducted in Swahili. The colonial administrators were taught Swahili at the Orientiale Seminar in Berlin before they took up their posts in Tanganyika.

Thus the Germans utilised three aspects of the Islamic ideological apparatus; personnel, political institutions and the language. An inevitable corrolary of such judicious utilisation was the spread of its religious aspect. It is an historical fact that conversion to Islam gathered momentum in the German era. Whatever the other forces propelling this process, the German policy, in spite of its intentions to the contrary, was also a contributing factor.

The Christian missionaries and the colonial government came into prolonged conflict over this issue. The missionaries accused the government of favouring Islam—an allegation which the government flatly rejected. They also opposed the importance accorded to Swahili, giving preference either to German or local vernacular language.[22] However, despite disputes over these and other issues these was a fundamental objective unity between the missions and the colonial authorities. Their relations may have been marred from time to time by conflict over specific issues, but in the long run their objective goals complemented one another. We shall now turn our attention to this relationship between the missionary ideological apparatus and colonialism.

The upsurge of overseas activities of German missionary societies coincided with Germany's attempts to acquire colonial possessions. In Tanganyika, a number of German missionary societies followed in the footsteps of the German East Africa Company. The Benedictine mission was founded in 1885 with financial assistance from Freiherr von Gravenreuth—one of the principal shareholders in the German East Africa Company. Its first station was set up in Dar es Salaam, and later it went inland as far as Peramiho and Madibara. Berlin III, a German missionary foundation, was set up around this period with one of its aims being to teach the 'natives' to work on plantations. Not surprisingly, its penetration in Tanganyika 'followed exactly the line of colonial occupation'.[23] The Moravian Missionaries went towards Lake Nyasa while the Leipzig missionary society replaced the British CMS on the slopes of Mount Kilimanjaro as the latter had been accused of inciting the Chagga against the German administration.

The leading spokesman for colonialism in Germany tended to take a rather crude view of the entire exercise of colonialisation in general, and the role of the missions in particular. In the same manner as they preferred the use of strong-arm methods to 'discipline the native', they adopted a pragmatic and utilitarian attitude towards the missions. Thus Count Pleil, one of the founders of the German Colonisation Society, advised a missionary congress in Germany in 1886 that in the colonies 'they should teach less of the dangerous doctrine of brotherhood and equality and give all instruction in practical tasks'.[24] In other words, their only role was to train the colonised people to work for the government and the settlers.

Of course the missionaries could not accept such a crude characterisation of their 'civilising mission', and in fact, the director of Berlin III sharply criticised Count Pleil's views. The missionaries took a much broader view. Thus the congress resolved that:

> German missions, Evangelical and Catholic alike, should be encouraged to take an active part in the realisation of a national colonial programme; in other words, they should not restrict their activities to mission work but should help to establish German culture and German thought in the colonies.[25]

The missionaries' objective role was not simply to make the

colonised person work but to make him *consent* to work for the colonisers; to make him accept the colonial system. Ideological enslavement perpetrated by the missionaries was essential for colonial exploitation to be practised smoothly. The *kiboko* (a whip made from hide) alone was not sufficient. It had to be supplemented by ideological work.[26] Here lay the fundamental task of the missionary apparatus; to ensure the spread and reproduction of the colonial ideology; to justify and rationalise colonialism as 'a will of God', to inculate Christian morality; to preach submissiveness and humility as prime virtues, and so on. Nowhere more fitting than in the colonial situation is Marx's description of religion: 'the sigh of the oppressed creature, the sentiment of a heartless world and the soul of soulless conditions'.[27]

In the field, the missions and the colonial administrators soon realised their identity of interests.[28] In the Ungoni area, for example, the missions were on good terms and co-operated with the district authorities right from the start. Where the people put up vigorous opposition to the imposition of colonial rule, missionaries were used to win them over. Thus in order to subdue the militant Wahehe, 'the governor (Von Soden) urged the Berlin mission to penetrate the Uhehe to make peaceful contact'.[29] The Wahehe, under Mkwawa, however, fought bitterly until they were defeated by better armed and better organised German forces. This struggle had its side effects on the missions as well: 'The vicissitudes of the Hehe resistance had a more direct effect upon the Moravians in the mid 1890s, for they became involved with the allies of the German forces, the Sangu'.[30]

In those areas where missions had been operating for some time before the advent of colonial rule, the German forces found it relatively easier to establish their authority. For the people did not find the demands made on them completely new. To some extent they had already been conditioned to work for, and accept 'the white man's ways'. There was a difference of course; for life now was much more difficult. But those who had come under the missionaries' influence had learnt to accept and participate in the commercial culture and submit to colonial discipline.

> At a time when law and order, the introduction of currency, the promotion of local trade and the beginnings of taxation were the main preoccupations of government, mission

> employees and adherents stood out from the rest as prosperous and orderly. They paid their taxes and understood (?) the new regime.[31]

The missionaries derived numerous benefits from their alliance with the colonial authorities. In some areas the missionaries came into conflict with local chiefs as the political power and social status of the latter were being undermined by the presence of the former. At times, the alienation of large tracts of land by the missions exacerbated this conflict.[32] Without the backing of the colonial authorities, the missionaries would have found it difficult to maintain their positions *vis-a-vis* the chiefs. In some cases, the district authorities enlisted the missionaries, assistance in carrying out land surveys and vaccination campaigns.[33] This enhanced the prestige of the missionaries in the eyes of the people, and also provided them with opportunities to come into direct contact with a large number of people, thus increasing their numbers of converts. In Tanga, an area with a strong Muslim influence, the Evangelical mission operating there found it rather difficult to obtain converts. But in 1903, they were assisted by the district authorities and allowed to preach the gospel regularly 'to prisoners in the Boma'.[34]

Some district authorities considered work on mission lands as a substitute for payment of taxes.[35] As a direct recognition of the contribution of the Church, the administration exempted the catechists, the indigenous diffusers of colonial ideology, from *corvees*.[36] The colonisers undoubtedly realised that in carrying the 'Word of God' to the 'native', the catechists were also assisting in making him submit to the rule of capital. The catechists' role was especially crucial since they often 'assumed leadership in civil and political affairs in the village'.[37] In some areas, such as Mahenge and Bukoba, the district commissioners gave encouragement and assistance to the growth of mission schools. Thus under the protective umbrella of colonialism missions and missionary activities grew rapidly. Their influence, too, spread proportionately.

There were undoubtedly some contradictions between the missionaries and the colonial authorities. The main issue at stake was the exercise of political power by the missionaries. When the missionaries encroached upon the functions of the administrators a clash was inevitable. Also, the colonial authorities could not tolerate the unlimited authority exercised by some missionaries in their mission stations.[38] Eventually, however, all missions came to accept the necessity of working under the colonial authorities.

The missionary educational apparatus experienced a rapid growth under colonial rule. The increasing output of catechists led to the rapid expansion of 'bush schools'—which were open to all and run by a lowly-paid catechist—in villages near, and far from, the mission stations.[39] Gradually, the following system took shape.

The bush schools fed the central mission school, which was often a boarding school, the missionaries realising that these were much more effective than day schools, since the pupils were under their supervision all the time. Local teachers and churchworkers were also employed to assist in running the school and the mission. For example, Lutheran missions in Iringa district employed African aides who conducted sermons in villages, and taught in mission schools. Besides their task was also

> to help the missionary in carrying out the station orders; they mediate in the intercourse between the missionary and native (Christians and pagans) residing in the area of the station; they collect donations to the church and keep accounts on them, at the acceptance of applicants for baptism and their eligibility for admission to the Church by baptism, these aides are being consulted.[40]

The mission schools gradually developed into fully fledged primary schools which also imported vocational education. Besides crafts and agricultural training, catechists and primary school teachers were also trained here. The promising pupils were earmarked for the priesthood and sent to a seminary. Crafts education helped to meet the need for artisans required by both the missions themselves and the European settlers, while literary education qualified its recipient for a clerical job with the government or the plantations.[14] Subjects taught in mission schools included religious instruction, Bible history and hymn singing as well as reading, writing and arithmetic. Instruction was mostly in the vernacular, though some missions taught German and Kiswahili too. Practical skills which were taught included carpentry, masonry and shoemaking. The UMCA also gave training in printing work.

On top of this, pupils were required to work for the missions.[42] They participated in road construction, building of schools, churches, houses for missionaries, large-scale commercial farming of coffee, cotton, vegetables, and looking after cattle and poultry. As the Trappist Mission reported in 1901:

> The black people must be taught through work and prayers. The natives must learn that work and prayers are essential for them, they must realise that work is an honour, that they cannot prosper without it and the necessary education. The one who does not work will be chased away and will never get the benefit of Christening.[43]

According to one estimate, by 1912 there were 171 mission stations scattered all over mainland Tanzania. These had a European staff of 616 and 1 694 African aides. The latter figure includes catechists and primary school teachers. These missions ran 1 119 schools, including bush schools and the total number of pupils in these was 105 197.[44]

Besides the mission schools and the Quran schools, there was also a government system of education during the colonial period. The government demand for literate and skilled personnel could not be completely satisfied by either of the first two systems. Much of the output of mission schools remained within its own ambit as catechists, teachers and mission workers. Another portion went to the plantations and the settlers. Only a small percentage was left, and there too the Swahili requirement posed a problem for the mission-educated clerk in the early stages. The Quran schools clearly had many limitations. Thus the colonial administration found it imperative to start its own schools after some time.

The governmental demand for trained manpower was basically of two types: artisans and white collar workers. The latter were needed to man the lower and middle ranks of the administration. Skilled craftsmen were needed, *inter alia*, 'in the workshops of the "Kaiseriche Flottille", the imperial navy, the railways where coppersmiths, boiler makers, turners and casters were employed'.[45] Also in demand were blacksmiths, masons, leather workers, carpenters, etc. In general, colonial economic policies led to a decline of traditional crafts and skills, both along the coast and in the interior. However, those traditional craftsmen that were utilised proved to be either insufficient or unqualified to meet the demand. Thus in the early years, in fact, the demand was met by importing craftsmen, mostly from the Indian sub-continent. These imported craftsmen were also employed in government schools as teachers, teaching their respective trades.[46] Only later did the government and mission schools produce enough local artisans and craftsmen to meet these demands.

The first government schools were started, not unexpectedly, along the coast where the administrative apparatus was firmly set up and the demand for trained manpower was greatest. Schools were set up first in Tanga and then in Bagamoyo, Dar es Salaam and Lindi. The majority of the pupils were Swahili speakers. An official circular clearly spelled out the aims of these schools:

> (a) To enable the native to be used in Government administration.
> (b) To inculcate a liking for order, cleanliness, diligence and dutifulness and a sound knowledge of German customs and patriotism.[47]

The language of instruction was Swahili, and the curriculum included the following subjects: Swahili, German, Arithmetic, Geography, Natural History, Drawing, Singing, Music and Gymnastics.[48] The education provided was functional, that is it was directly related to the jobs the pupils were expected to take up after completing school. Thus the pupils were given different types of training and had to engage in manual labour. A brief review of the evolution of Tanga school will illustrate these points.

The Tanga school was opened in 1892. Initially it comprised a single room, a few pupils and a teacher, a German who spoke fluent Swahili—an outcome of training at the Orientiale Seminar in Berlin. Initially only reading, writing and the German language were taught. The curriculum was determined by the demand for literate clerks and interpreters. It was enlarged and modified accordingly as the school began to supply a more diverse category of office personnel and junior administrators. By 1897 the school had 96 pupils. It was then converted into a boarding school. The pupils were supplied with basic necessities and shelter. The food was cooked by themselves. A further expansion of the school was planned and the construction of new buildings was started in 1890. 'The building operation was largely done by the boys who marched to and from the beach carrying stones on their heads, and at high tide had to wade into the sea to get them'.[49]

In 1899, the school started to train *fundis*. By the end of the century, there were more than 400 pupils at the school attending classes in standards I to VI. The school also had a teacher training and a technical department. By 1904 the technical department was producing carpenters, printers, bookbinders, tailors, blacksmiths and bricklayers.

By 1902, the government had three main schools at Tanga, Bagamoyo and Dar es Salaam, and three subsidiary schools at Kilwa, Pangani and Lindi. The set-up of these schools was not, in principle, very different from what has been described above. In addition, there were a number of small hinterland 'schools', run by district authorities.

An important feature of the government education system that needs to be emphasised is the contribution of the pupils towards the cost of their own education and to the development of the colonial economy.[50] The value of the work done by the pupils while still at school was, in general, of the same order as, if not more than, all the expenses incurred in construction of the school, buying teaching material, maintaining school facilities, paying the teachers, etc. Besides, in coastal townships, special levies were imposed to meet costs not covered by the pupils' labour. Thus the direct financial contribution of the government towards developing and running the education system was insignificant. The hinterland schools in Tanga district were each allotted a coconut plantation so that 'the pupils acquire already from their youth an interest in and liking of plants and soil; and the revenues enable the schools to obtain financial means for their equipment and enlargement'.[51]

The annual report of the Craftsmen School in Kilwa for the year 1907–8 mentions the following:

> All expenses for material and so on, wages for coloured workers, as well as the living expense of the apprentices could be covered by its own revenues.[52]

What remained was the salary of one European teacher which was paid by the residents of Kilwa town.

In the same year residents of Lindi town contributed about 5 500 rupees to cover the expenses of running the government school.[53] The contribution of the pupils of the Technical School in Dar es Salaam to the colonial economy during the year 1908–9 amounted to the following:

> the completion of furniture of various styles, also the repair

> of buildings, furniture; turning and wagon building; also the construction of a bridge over the Simbosi at Kissarawe, three bridges on the Kissarawe to Kassi road and a bridge on the road to Magogoni.[54]

All this was accomplished by only 19 pupils! The contribution of Tanga school pupils was even greater. Besides working in the school farm, they transported, using only their hands and feet, things like timber, stones, limestone, sand and clay from the source to building sites. While some pupils went daily to the local meteorological station to record instrument readings, others assisted in 'the administration of the savings bank and town library. Seven senior pupils ably lent assistance in accountancy, book-keeping and stocktaking'.[55] To cap it all, by this time all the government printing was being done at Tanga school.

The pupils of Tanga school also assisted in the expansion of the education system. Besides printing books and making equipment for schools, some pupils, like carpentry apprentices, for example, were sent to interior schools. 'There, they have to furnish the school building and the teacher's flat, according to their own plan and specifications, with professionally constructed doors, windows, tables, school-benches, and with everything else the school needs in wooden untensils.'[56]

If one could compile a balance-sheet of all this, the myth of colonialism being an 'educational enterprise' would soon be exploded. Let alone the fact that education was meant to assist exploitation,[57] it was the pupils themselves who put up a large part of the educational edifice.

Table 6.1 OUTPUT OF SOME GOVERNMENT SCHOOLS, 1908

LOY

SCHOOL	EMPLOYMENT OF SCHOOL LEAVERS
1 Kilwa School	3 telegraphists, 1 postman, 1 clerk, and 2 sent for further training as craftsmen.
2 Lindi School	5 clerks, 3 assistant teachers, 2 houseboys.
3 Tang9 School	6 assistant teachers, 2 as writers with district administrators, 1 with meteorological station, 4 as assistants in the hospital, 6 postmen, 2 with railways, 11 as clerks with planters, merchants and *Akidas*, 8 carpenters, 7 compositors and 7 printers.

Source: Annual Report, 1907/8.

As can be discerned from the above descriptions, life in the government school was tough. The discipline was strict and punishments severe. In the early years at Tanga school some pupils protested that they were being kept at school by force. In order to discipline them, the school authorities put them 'in the chains' for a week! Flogging was quite common. The scale of punishment at Tanga school was as follows: minor offences—six strokes, major offences—twelve strokes. In some places, even African teachers who were found to be absent from duty were thrashed 'in front of the whole school'.[58]

The teaching methods in the schools also reveal the disciplinarian and oppressive character of the colonial administration. The following example is a case in point. In 1903, Bishop Weston of the UMCA visited the government school at Lindi where the boys were being trained to become minor government officials. One of the lessons he watched dealt with 'the laws governing the action of native magistrates'.

> I heard small boys recite the laws dealing with the powers of *majumbe* or village magistrates, and the master showed me the book itself, a most formidable volume which each boy must get by heart. Then on Wednesdays and Saturdays the school attends the Government Court, listens to all the cases, witnesses all the flogging.[59]

What a combination of education in the theory and practice of oppression!

By 1902 there were about 4 000 pupils attending various government schools throughout the territory. However, it is a fact that during the entire period of German colonial rule in Tanganyika not a single girl studied in any of the government schools. Only a few girls were educated in some mission schools.

The children of the colonial administrators and settlers received their education in the metropole. But later on two schools for Europeans were set up in Dar es Salaam and Meru area.

The Maji Maji war

The year 1905 witnessed the culmination of the struggle of the people against the establishment of colonial rule on mainland Tanzania. In the initial two decades there had been hardly a year in which the colonial armed forces were not fighting in some places or another. But the resistance had been localised and isolated. Now almost the whole of the southern part of Tanzania rose to oppose colonialism. The immediate cause of the uprising was the cotton scheme being forcibly implemented in the coastal and southern areas.[60] Under this scheme each village was compelled to cultivate cotton in an allocated area. The scheme was financed by a group of German textile manufacturers seeking an alternative source to the high priced American cotton. The workers were paid meagre wages and had to suffer the harsh treatment meted out. So the Maji Maji war erupted and the colonialists as well as their agents faced the bitter onslaught of the people. The officials and the settlers as well as the akidas, traders and some missionaries who were closely identified with the district authorities were attacked.

The class base of the struggle was the peasantry but the leadership was provided from the dissident and discontented elements of the traditional ruling groups and the lower sections of the emergent petty bourgeoisie.[61] The uprising was brutally suppressed and the leaders who were caught were executed. In some areas it was only widespread and prolonged famine, caused by the ravages of the war and reinforced by deliberate measures of the colonial authorities, which sapped the fighting spirit of the people. The mobilising ideology of the struggle was based on superstition. But the people were defeated mainly due to inferior technology and lack of organisation.

The unfolding of the Maji Maji struggle served to underscore an important historical truth: the necessity to complement physical repression by ideological obfuscation in order to perpetuate exploitation. It revealed that the ideological apparatuses, especially the missionary ideological apparatus, had not functioned in vain. The ideological impact of the missionaries can be discerned by noting first that missionaries in affected areas were, in general, spared during the uprising and secondly, that 'several mission-educated groups refused to participate in the uprising'.[62]

Lubetsky elaborates the same point in a more comprehensive manner[63]. According to him, it was the 'Akidaless' areas which were also the areas more fully integrated into the colonial socio-economic network which did not participate in the Maji Maji war. This was a consequence of complementary material and ideological forces set in motion by colonialism.

However, considerations regarding the non-participation of

various areas of mainland Tanzania in the Maji Maji war must bear in mind that in no part of the country had people willingly consented to the establishment of colonial rule. Wherever they had gone, the Germans had encountered resistance. The Maji Maji war was but the last and the major battle in this struggle against the establishment of colonialism. Areas like Uhehe (Iringa district) had put up a prolonged fight as a consequence of which the leadership had been decimated, subservient chiefs installed, the people demoralised and firm colonial administration imposed, thus making it impossible for it to participate in the Maji Maji war.

The war was sparked off in the Rufiji area because of the cotton scheme mentioned above. This scheme had not only alienated the mass of the people but also the lower sections of the petty bourgeoisie, who provided the leadership in the struggle. The spark, once kindled, spread like a prairie fire over the southern half of Tanganyika. It did not spread into the northern areas because not only was there a fire-proof barrier preventing its spread (the potential leaders had been co-opted into the colonial system) but also the grass was greener with less susceptibility to ignite (the mode of life had been transformed as a result of colonial economic policies making the people more responsive, because of the dependence relationships, to the demands of the colonial system rather than to a call of rebellion against the system). Thus one reason for non-participation in Maji Maji was that the elements who elsewhere provided the leadership to initiate the struggle were, in these areas generally more integrated into the colonial system. It was precisely in these areas where cash crop production had developed extensively that there was a greater concentration of the colonial educational facilities. Having had the 'benefits' of education and Christianisation as well as the crumbs from colonial exploitation, the emergent petty bourgeoisie was unable at this stage to provide the masses with the necessary leadership. Thus areas like Bukoba, Sukumaland, Kilimanjaro and the Usambara did not participate in Maji Maji. Although the intensity of exploitation in areas such as Kilimanjaro was higher, the effectiveness of the colonial ideological apparatus deprived the masses of the catalyst which would arouse them. In the southern areas, the chiefs who had sided with the colonialists during Maji Maji were generally the ones who also exhibited greatest enthusiasm for Christianity and education.[64] As we shall see further on, this important lesson of the Maji Maji war was not lost on the colonial policy-makers.

The post Maji Maji era

The reverberations accompanying the suppression of Maji Maji resounded throughout the territory leading to the onset of a new phase of colonialism. It was a phase characterised by political stability and the virtual absence of violent struggles against the colonial rulers. The people were convinced, by the gun, that it was 'futile' to oppose the colonial system. They had to live and struggle within the system.[65] This is no better illustrated than by the fact that after Maji Maji more and more people came to terms with and accepted the three major ideological symbols of colonial domination, namely education, Christianity and Islam, and considered them as a means of economic advancement.

Iliffe notes that the post Maji Maji period was one of 'rapid Christian expansion in Tanzania'.[56] This was particularly true in the southern areas where the struggle had taken place. In areas devastated by famine large sections of the population had come to be dependent on the missions. Oliver talks of the rapid increase in demand for education and Christianity after the failure of Maji Maji giving examples of the Usagara and Ugogo areas where increasing numbers of villages began to ask for teachers and schools[67]. Marcia Wright mentions 'the burgeoning congregation in southern highlands after Maji Maji'.[68] In areas such as Mahenge conversions to both Islam and Christianity took place. 'Substantial conversion to Islam occurred . . . only among those people who had fought against the Germans'.[69]

Thus in general attendance in various schools increased rapidly. Local demands for educational facilities grew fast. Chiefs and villagers in various areas spontaneously built schools and asked missions to provide them with teachers or acquired their own paid teachers, as in Tabora.[70] In the government schools, too, the attendance rose and more schools were opened in the interior districts. 'In certain schools the pressure was so great that there were not enough teachers to cope and some pupils wishing to gain admission had to be turned away'[71].

Partly as a consequence of spectacular demand for education and Christianity the colonial ideological apparatuses expanded and came to the forefront while the repressive apparatus of the colonial state receded into the background. Force, of course, remained the ultimate means of domination throughout the period of colonial rule and violence was exercised on the people whenever it was felt necessary. But now it was more a question of policing the colony as opposed to conducting military campaigns. Furthermore, the ideological movement reflected the fact that people had come to be dependent on a way of life imposed on them by colonialism, that more and more were involved in cash crop production and in the migrant labour system, and that the colonial economy was giving rise to a specific social structure which created its own ideological demands. It was not a simple question of transformation of ideas, as the Tanzanian economy became more integrated into the global capitalist system, it internalised the conditions for the reproduction of the colonial social formation, and internal social, political and ideological conditions were created for the perpetuation of colonial rule. Thus to understand the expanding role of the ideological apparatuses, and in particularly of the education system, within this framework one has to examine the other relevant changes which were simultaneously taking place in Tanzanian political economy after the failure of the Maji Maji uprising.

An important 'exogenous' factor in the post Maji Maji period was the struggle between a section of German monopoly capital and the European (mainly German) settlers for political and economic domination over Germany's colonial possessions in general, and over Tanganyika in particular.[72] The large German banks, industrial enterprises and commercial concerns were interested in making the colonies a lucrative field for investment, an expanding market for their manufactures, as well as a reliable supplier of raw materials and foodstuffs. The latter was seen as a means to solve 'Germany's balance of payments problems'.[73] Hitherto, the German state had been granting subsidies to both the colonial administration and the German firms like the German East Africa Company; William O'Swald and others had been subsidised to the tune of around 1 000 000 marks annually.[74] The subsidies to the colonial administration could be justified considering the expenditure involved in conducting military campaigns and setting up the administrative apparatus, as well as in building roads, railways, etc. Of course, the labour of the colonised peoples was exploited to the maximum extent, both directly and indirectly through taxation, in these activities but still the colonial deficits had been rising.[75] The subsidies to the business firms could be justified considering the impact of social and political instability on their operations, the lack of a developed infrastructure, the long gestation period before the investments became profitable, and the state of the international market. But now that two major colonial uprisings, in East Africa and Southwest Africa, had been ruthlessly put down the position had to be reversed. Not only must the labour of the colonial people contribute the revenue to run the colonial administration but it must also provide profits for the German companies.[76] Irrational policies which hindered this goal must be done away with and replaced by 'sound economic management' of the colonies.

It was over the issue of economic policy in the colonies that a political conflict between the settlers and the monopoly capitalists arose. The battle was fought out in the German Reichstag as well as in the colonies. In Tanganyika the fundamental question around which these conflicts revolved was whether the territory was to be a settler economy or a predominantly smallholder peasant economy. What land and labour policies should be enforced to encourage the development of one or the other? The big German bourgeoisie favoured the latter alternative. In the words of their chief spokesman, Dernburg: 'We have not gone to East Africa to found plantations for 3–400 people, but to make a vast country bloom, to find raw materials and create markets for German trade and German industry'.[77] Since the performance of the plantation and settler sector had been unsatisfactory and their prospects were not promising either, the only source of revenue and profit lay in the encouragement of African peasant cultivation. Besides, this policy would be conducive to the promotion of political stability thus avoiding the costly consequence of another uprising.

The settlers' interests were promoted by the German Colonial Society the chauvinistic parties in the Reichstag as well as by pressure groups within the German Government. The monopoly capitalists besides being supported by the National Liberals, traditionally 'a party of big business'[78] and the powerful Catholic Centre party, also had a substantial representation in the German state and the colonial administration. To promote the interests of monopoly capital, 'a prominent banker, Berhard Dernburg', whose 'speciality was the reorganisation of business failures' and who 'occupied a place on thirty-eight different boards of directors' was appointed as the Colonial Director in the German Government in September 1906.[79] His counterpart in Tanganyika was the new

Governor appointed after Maji Maji Baron von Rechenberg.[80] Dernburg toured Tanganyika with a group of ten businessmen, including a prominent industrialist, Walter Rathenau, in 1907. He encountered strong hostility from the settlers and refused to give in to their demands. The Dernburg group together with Rechenberg worked out an economic policy which emphasised the need to make the colony financially self-sufficient, rapid construction of railways together with maximum involvement in economic activities, and better treatment of the indigenous population.[81]

For Tanganyika, the new policy[82] implied a programme which would encourage small peasant production and utilise Indian and Arab traders as middlemen.[83] The main stimulant would be the completion of the central railway line which would assist the transportation of crops to the port and manufactured goods to the interior as well as facilitate the movement of troops in times of trouble. Moreover, the railway would help to ease 'the existing labour shortage since (it) would substantially reduce the need for caravans'.[84]

On the other hand, the European settlers wanted the primary emphasis to be given to their economic activities. Besides the construction of infrastructural facilities to serve their enterprises, they wanted to restrict the local population from growing cash crops so as not only to induce them to look for wage employment in settler plantations in order to pay taxes but also to reduce competitors and obtain better prices. The settlers wanted stringent labour regulations and *apartheid*-type control to be imposed. They opposed the policy of encouraging Indian traders, whom they viewed as commercial competitors. While the settlers would have preferred to continue with 'the horrors of almost unrestricted flogging'[85] the farsighted Governor instituted reforms, having no doubt assimilated the lessons of Maji Maji.[86]

In the eyes of the German Government and monopoly capitalists the new economic policy was a success. Not only did political stability prevail over the colony but also subsidies from the metropole were reduced. In the later years, even the plantations prospered. But it was the monopoly capitalists who reaped the largest profits. For example, in the construction of the central line, '(t)he monopoly capitalist involved was the Deutsche Bank, the most aggressive financial institution in Germany at this date, which underwrote the necessary loan and owned the under-employed subsidiary which built the line'.[87]

Consequently, it is not surprising to note that by 1914 'no less than 32 per cent of local revenue was used to service loans for the railway construction'.[88] Between 1905 and 1912, textile imports into Tanganyika more than doubled while the total value of foreign trade trebled. A large share of profits from this increased trade went to the German East Africa company which had

> the widest trading network, the only land concession, and the largest plantations, and which controlled the only two banks and conducted most mortgage business. From 1906 to 1908 it paid dividends of 5 per cent; in 1909, 6 per cent; in 1910 and 1911, 8 per cent and in 1912, 9 per cent.[89]

The settlers, no doubt strengthened by the rubber boom in the latter period, tried to make a comeback after 1910. However, policies instituted during the governorship of Rechenberg were never substantially reversed.[90] The outcome of the struggle was made irrelevant by the outbreak of the First World War in 1914.

The struggle between the settlers and the monopoly capitalists, and the economic policies adopted in the post Maji Maji era have been described at length precisely because of the importance of its outcome and the subsequent economic policies in determining the form of ideological domination and the organisation, function and content of ideological apparatuses in colonial Tanganyika. Had the struggle been settled in favour of the settlers, the liberalism and reformist policies of the post Maji Maji period would not have been implemented. In this case, the settler sector would have expanded at the expense of small-holder peasant cultivation, there would have been further land alienation, stricter labour laws, etc. Consequently even the educational policies and role of the missions would have been oriented to meet the requirements of a predominantly settler economy. Basically this would have implied the strengthening of the repressive apparatus of the colonial state, extension of its active role in carrying out economic policies and relatively diminished role of the ideological apparatuses. Direct force rather than economic incentives and pacification through ideology would have been the predominant means of implementing colonial policies.

Education policy after Maji Maji

The education policies after Maji Maji reflected the policies and changes in the political and economic spheres. Of course, there was a continuity from the past and many policies were carried over from the pre-Maji Maji era. We shall quote extensively from a report prepared by Martin Schlunk[91] in 1911, after a comprehensive survey of the education system in the German colonies, to illustrate our points. This report has been regarded as representative of both the official and missionary opinions of the time.[92]

Firstly, Schlunk fully endorsed the idea that the African must be educated for work[93]—for the coloniser, of course! The German Government was not interested in education for its own sake but to serve its primary purpose of turning the colonies into useful economic dependencies.[94] Hence the emphasis on vocational training. However, functional education should not be to the exclusion of character training. For

> colonial schools are the cradle of German culture in Africa . . . The true process of civilisation (underdevelopment!) has to be internalised if it is to be effective. The purpose of the schools cannot be merely to teach a trade to a few people. Rather it must be to bring up a new generation that will have accepted the new civilisation (*sic*!) internally as well as externally.[95]

Perhaps what he had in mind was something like what was taking place in the drawing classes of the government school in Pangani. Here the pupils drew '(i)llustrated pictures of German history from Germany's greatest era (which) deepened their grasp of Germany's strength and greatness'.[96]

But this was not all. Colonial education must also emphasise the training of leaders.[97] Schlunk clearly saw that the pupils graduating from colonial schools constituted 'a special class between us (i.e. the colonisers) and the rest of the natives'.[98]

Their central importance lay in the fact 'that those natives who have received education will then become leaders of their people in the struggle against us. The only chance of averting this is to use schools for character training'.[99] Clearly the lessons of Maji Maji had been assimilated thoroughly. These potential leaders must not come into contact with subversive ideas, especially socialist ideas. Having clearly in mind Marxist literature, Schlunk advocated the complete exclusion of 'that undesirable literature which preaches internationalism instead of patriotism'.[100]

This policy of appointing educated leaders was implemented, for example, in the Ungoni area where the traditional political system and the ruling groups had been completely destroyed with the suppression of Maji Maji. In their place the Germans appointed people who had received education in mission schools.[101] The akidas appointed after Maji Maji were usually those who had been through either government or mission schools.[102] Also some school teachers were appointed as akidas.[103]

Other features of the education policy included a reduction in the harsh punishments meted out to the pupils. By order of the Governor, the use of the kiboko on African pupils under sixteen as well as on Arab and Indian pupils and African teachers was forbidden.[104] Furthermore, the relations and co-operation between the missions and the government in the field of education improved after Maji Maji.[105] Rechenberg not only encouraged increased school attendance but also advocated the raising of the standards of mission schools to match those of the government schools.[106] A number of missions gradually shed their hostility to the usage of Swahili as the medium of instruction. Rather than oppose Swahili as such, the missionaries proposed to Christianise it.[107] Axenfield, a pre-Rechenberg missionary, later to become director of the Berlin mission, was quite straightforward about it: 'The new classes could be captured positively by full missionary participation in the Swahili medium education'.[108] By the end of 1906, both the Berlin mission and the Moravians operating in the Southern highlands had introduced instructions in Swahili.[109] Some of the other missions who had not already introduced Swahili gradually did so.

In 1910, the government issued an order making it compulsory for all chiefs and their progenies to learn to read and write.[110] The objective effect of this was to increase the enrolment in mission schools. And by 1913, the colonial government began to grant subsidies to missions for training pupils for government posts.[111]

Colonialism and class-formation: the contribution of education

Before the advent of colonial rule Tanganyika was not a unified entity—economically or politically—although the process of unification had commenced as a result of commercial penetration long before colonial rule. One can broadly describe the social structures in Tanganyika before colonial rule as follows.[112] There were scattered tribal groupings comprising communal cultivators or pastoralists in which little differentiation had taken place and no particular group in society had come to dominate the means of production. Out of this conglomeration of communal groupings some had already undergone significant differentiation. A particular group appropriating the social surplus and exercising political power over the rest had made its appearance. In a few of these latter societies, the social structure which emerged can be characterised as nascently feudal or semi-feudal. For example, among the Bahaya an institution resembling serfdom enabled the chiefs to expropriate surplus from others.

Along the coast Arab, Indian and Swahili traders had dominated the scene for a long time, from their base in Zanzibar. The penetration of these traders into the interior in search of slaves,[113] ivory, gum, etc., all of which were exchanged for western manufactured goods hastened the process of differentiation in the societies with which they came into contact, and set in motion the process of integration of these societies into the commercial network of international capitalism. The import of large quantities of guns served to consolidate the power of the indigenous ruling strata who had by this time formed alliances with the coastal traders.[114] The surplus exacted as a result of these trading activities went to the chiefs, the traders and the western companies operating along the coast.

This arrangement was threatened when the European companies and missionaries penetrated inland, as were the economic position and political power of the coastal traders and their chiefly allies. A violent struggle ensued culminating in the Bushiri uprising, the outcome of which was victory for European commercial capital. Simultaneously with this penetration, German imperialism strove to establish political hegemony over the entire territory and impose its economic designs. In this endeavour, imperialism was assisted by various chiefs, but in general encountered vigorous resistance wherever it went. This culminated in the Maji Maji war of 1905 from which imperialism emerged triumphant. After Maji Maji the class struggle between sections of German monopoly capital and the settlers intensified. In the initial period the monopoly capitalists secured commanding positions but just prior to the first imperialist war, the settlers appeared to be regaining lost ground.

Having briefly outlined the class struggles under German colonial rule, we shall summarise the social structure which evolved during this period. The characteristic features of this structure were the dominance by foreign ruling classes, emergence of intermediary classes, or proto-classes (that is, strata which would evolve into fully-fledged classes) and the formation of basic oppressed classes. This process did not occur overnight, it continued even after the demise of German colonialism and it occurred unevenly at different times and in different places.

The fundamental role of the ideological apparatuses was to assist the formation of and reinforce the colonial class structure. Thus the operation of the ideological apparatuses implied certain relationships between itself and the various classes in colonial Tanganyika, relationships which were also a reflection of relationships between the various classes. The relationship between the ideological apparatuses and a particular class was one of four types: either the class dominated other classes through the ideological apparatuses or it was dominated through the apparatuses, or it was central to the apparatuses or it was incidental to them. The following summarises the relationship between the various classes as mediated through the ideological apparatuses and gives a brief description of each class.

The dominating class

The class which dominated the ideological apparatuses was also the ruling class in the territory. This was the metropolitan bourgeoisie. Its dominance was expressed by the fact that the ideological apparatuses basically functioned to serve its interests and justify its rule. This absentee ruling class resided in the metropole and its interests in the colony were taken care of by managers and agents of large European firms, civil servants, military officers and the European missionaries. The missionaries, considering the amount of land they alienated and labour force they employed, could be regarded as settlers in their own right. But because of the paramount importance of the ideological function, which complemented the functions of the state apparatus, they are considered as agents of the metropolitan bourgeoisie.

The European settlers in Tanganyika comprised a potentially dominant class. In their unsuccessful struggle against sections of the metropolitan bourgeoisie, described earlier on, they strove to establish their dominance. The settlers had come to Tanganyika to establish agricultural enterprises and had acquired and settled on large tracts of the best lands. However, their economic role was not very significant until the final years of German rule. In 1907, there were 479 adult male settlers in Tanganyika, seventy per cent of whom were Germans. By 1913, their number had increased to 882.[115]

As the settlers remained in a subordinate position *vis-à-vis* the metropolitan bourgeoisie, their influence on the ideological apparatuses was insignificant. Moreover, the settlers generally held very backward attitudes towards education for not only the local population but also their own children. However, in the process of serving the interests of the ruling class the ideological apparatuses also partly served the interests of the settlers.

The dominated classes

These were the classes against whom the barrage of ideological propaganda was directed, the classes to whom the ideological apparatuses sought to justify and rationalise the rule of the colonisers. These were also the most exploited classes in the colonial society, namely the peasantry and the proletariat.

Colonialism accelerated the process of peasantisation already at work in some areas, and extended it to other places. This process entailed the drawing of cultivating groups which, hitherto, had produced mainly for their own subsistence and had perhaps engaged in barter exchange with neighbouring groups, into a commercial orbit. Now the peasant produced export crops for the world market or foodcrops for towns and plantations, and was involved in a money economy. He was exploited through unequal exchange and his fate was decided by the state of the world market. Introduction of taxation as well as direct compulsion were instrumental in hastening this process.

The proletariat comprised those who sold their productive labour power in return for wages. Prior to colonialism wage labour had existed in Tanzania. The thousands of porters working in caravans which transported goods to and from the coast were employed as wage workers. As wages they mostly received cloth and other articles. With the onset of the colonial rule, cheap labour was required for the plantations, the railways, roads and building construction, the few manufacturing enterprises, workshops, etc. This emergent proletariat comprised two types: unskilled migrant labourers who, due to lack of another alternative, were forced to seek wage employment in order to pay taxes, and a small skilled labour force, the *fundis*, mostly a product of mission and government schools.

The reforms instituted during the Rechenberg era had the effect of increasing the size of the labour force. By 1913 there were about 146 000 wage labourers in Tanganyika.[116]

The role of the ideological apparatuses in relation to the dominated classes was not just one of making these classes submissive to the colonisers as, for example, was the role of the Church in feudal Europe in making the serf submit to the lord. What is involved here is to make the colonised person accept the domination of capitalist mode of production, to make him respond 'positively' to its demands, to make him believe the limitations imposed by peripheral capitalism to be unchangeable. After the end of formal colonial rule, it is precisely these aspects of ideological domination which are preserved and further developed.

During the historical genesis of capitalism in Europe, force had to be used to deprive the producer of his means of production and turn him into a seller of labour power. Also during the genesis of colonialism it was brute force which ensured the subordination of the colonised to monopoly capital. Under metropolitan capitalist formations 'the organisation of the capitalist process of production, once fully developed, breaks down all resistance . . . . The dull compulsion of economic relations completes the subjugation of the labourer to the capitalist'.[117] Under peripheral capitalist formations, however, the capitalist mode of production does not become the universal mode of production.[118] Rather, it dominates and preserves, in distorted forms, other pre-colonial modes of production. It is precisely this enforced co-existence of the various modes of production which impedes the 'automatic' reproduction of the relations of production through 'the dull compulsion of economic relation'. Thus in peripheral formations, the colonial state continues to play an *active* economic role throughout the colonial period in order to ensure the subordination of the producer to the metropolitan bourgeoisie.

It is these quantitatively different roles of the state as well as the difference in the level of development of productive forces which determine the different modes of operation of the ideological apparatuses within the metropolitan and the peripheral capitalist formations. In the metropolitan formations, the apparatuses are multifarious, embedded in all spheres of social life and basically operate at economic level. In the periphery, especially under colonial rule, the apparatuses are few, restricted in scope and basically operative at political level. Their basic function is, however, the same as under metropolitan formation, namely to ensure the continuous subordination of the producer to the metropolitan bourgeoisie. Paraphrasing Marx: 'The advance of (colonialism) develops (working and peasant classes) which by education, tradition, habit look upon the conditions of (peripheral capitalism) as self-evident laws of nature'.[119] In this connection it is not surprising to note that the stated purpose of the first taxation ordinance issued by the Germans in Tanganyika was 'educational' in nature. As Iliffe says 'it was intended to oblige Africans to accept paid labour and accustom themselves to European administrative discipline.[120]

The petty bourgeoisie

The petty bourgeoisie was central to the ideological apparatuses in the sense that not only was it a product of the functioning of these apparatuses, but it was also crucial to ensure the functioning of the apparatuses. Not only was the petty bourgeoisie ideologically dominated through the ideological apparatuses but it also had to ensure the ideological and political domination of other classes in the colonial society.

The characteristic feature of the petty bourgeoisie was that its members had benefited from colonial education. They received a regular income without engaging in manual labour. The growth of the petty bourgeoisie was fostered by the development of cash crop production, and the expansion of the colonial state apparatus and the colonial ideological apparatuses. At this historical juncture, the petty bourgeoisie does not constitute a class but a stratum. It can be subdivided into two sub-strata:

Upper level: this consisted of the liwalis, akidas and other higher civil servants as well as the chiefs and the kulak farmers. Lower level: included here were church workers, teachers, clerks, interpreters, lower ranks of the armed forces, etc.

The upper level of the petty bourgeoisie was recruited mostly from chiefly or well-to-do families.[121] In the early years, the petty bourgeoisie employed in the state apparatus tended to be drawn from the coastal areas, the upper levels probably from the wealthy families. Later on the interior areas provided their share as well.

The nature of selection for the upper level of the petty bourgeoisie was decided by two factors: preferential education and unequal benefits from cash crop production.

Mission schools for sons of chiefs were quite widespread during the German era. The schools in Bukoba district[122] and in Tabora, the Catholic Lutheran schools among the Chagga[123] and the Peramiho school in Ungoni[124] catered for sons of chiefs.

Mission schools in Sukumaland and the Malangali school near Iringa were also mainly meant for sons of chiefs.[125] St Andrew's College in Zanzibar established by the UMCA drew most of its pupils from chiefly families on the mainland.[126]

Government schools also gave preference to sons of chiefs, for example, the school at Songea boma.[127] Along the coast the wealthy families were induced by the government to send their children to school.[128] About one third of the pupils of the government schools in Dar es Salaam in 1908 were of Indian origin, mostly from trading families.[129]

Von Gotzen, the Governor before the outbreak of Maji Maji, encouraged education for sons of chiefs.[130] But this received more emphasis after Maji Maji, especially after the government made literacy compulsory for all chiefs and their sons.[131]

Not only did the chiefly families have preferential access to educational facilities, but they also received disproportionately large benefits from commercial agriculture.[132] Thus the chiefs tended to be kulak farmers as well. Consequently, the upper layer of the petty bourgeoisie was filled from chiefly and wealthy families.

The petty bourgeoisie acted as political intermediaries between the people and the colonisers. At this stage, they struggled for betterment within the colonial system. For example, in the latter years of German rule, there was conflict between European missionaries on the one hand and the African priests and church workers on the other over the question of pay and status.[133] Faint beginnings of the struggle between the commercial bourgeoisie and the petty bourgeoisie that was to unfold after half a century[134] could be detected in this period.[135] In the same period, educated Africans began forming self-help associations, which were at first based on tribal lines.[136] These were the precursors of civil servants, associations that were formed during the British period and which led to the formation of the nationalist parties that struggled for independence. Thus the colonial education system, despite intentions to the contrary, was producing the grave-diggers of the colonial rule. Shaban Robert, the prominent nationalist poet and author, was a student of Tanga School in 1914, while Martin Kayamba, the political activist of the 1930s, was a graduate of St. Andrew's College.

The commercial bourgeoisie

This class which was central to the process of surplus appropriation was only incidental in relation to the ideological apparatuses. The commercial bourgeoisie which had dominated the coastal areas before colonial rule was converted by colonialism into a dependent commercial bourgeoisie. The ranks of this commercial bourgeoisie were swelled by migrants from the Indian sub-continent. By 1910, there were 6 923 Indians in Tanganyika, most of them traders.[137] This class consisted of owners of large trading firms, like, for example, Alidina Visram, who conducted most of the trade in Mwanza during the latter years of German rule,[138] or Sewa Haji, who donated money for schools and hospitals 'in order to promote his commercial interests'.[139] This class forged strong links with the Colonial Government and the European companies.

Rechenberg considered these traders as indispensable 'commercial intermediaries between European firms and the natives'.[140] But the commercial bourgeoisie faced strong hostility from the European settlers who considered them as competitors.

Conclusion

The principal ideological apparatuses during German colonial rule were the religious apparatuses and the colonial education system. Their chief function was to reinforce the colonial class structure. This was done through:

(i) mass ideological work, ie, spreading the ideology of the colonisers;
(ii) training of cadres for the colonial administrative system;
(iii) assisting the distorted development of the colonial productive forces by:
  (a) training craftsmen;
  (b) imparting agricultural education;
  (c) spreading cash crop production;
(iv) ensuring their own reproduction by training local priests and teachers.

The ideological apparatuses also contributed significantly to the evolution of the colonial class-structure. They further produced the future grave-diggers of the colonial rule. These products of colonial education, however, were also qualified to man the neo-colonial state apparatus.[142]

Notes

1 The search for overseas investment outlets, and the consequential export of capital was to become significant later and become one of the driving forces behind the establishment of colonies.

2 For an interesting analysis of the differing attitudes of German missionaries towards imperialism see Marcia Wright, *German Missions in Tanganyika, 1819–1941; Lutherans and Moravians in the Southern Highlands*, Oxford, 1971, p. 7.

3 Roland Oliver, *The Missionary Factor in East Africa*, London, 1952, p. 13.

4 *Ibid.*, p. 37.

5 *Ibid.*, p. 50.

6 L.Y.C. Mgonde, *Mission Education and the Kaguru*, History Students' Research Papers, University of Dar es Salaam, 1966, p. 2.

7 F.P. Nolan, 'The Changing Role of Catechists in Tabora' in D.B. Barrett, ed., *African initiatives in Religion*, Nairobi, 1971, p. 51.

8 *Ibid.*, p. 52.

9 Oliver, p. 181.

10 The WF paid their catechists 6 shillings a month in 1919.

11 Mapunda and Mpangara, *The Maji Maji War in Ungoni*, Nairobi, 1968, p. 14.

12 See chapter 2.

13 Oliver, p. 69.

14 R. Lubetsky, *Sectoral Development and stratification in*

Tanganyika, 1890–1914, 1972 Universities Social Science Conference, Nairobi, mimeo, p. 7.

15 Oliver, p. 117.

16 Marcia Wright, p. 44.

17 Lubetsky, p. 8.

18 J. Iliffe, *Tanganyika under the German Rule, 1905–12*, Nairobi, 1972, p. 13.

19 For details consult ch. 4.

20 Iliffe, p. 181.

21 *Annual Report on Development in German East Africa*. Hereafter cited as AR, 1901/1902, p. 19.

22 A. Smith, 'The Missionary Contribution to Education (Tanganyika) to 1914', *Tanganyika Notes and Records* (*TNR*), March 1963, p. 99. There were some exceptions to this. See Abdurlaziz, 'Tanzania National Language Policy and the Rise of Swahili Political Culture', in J. Saul and L. Cliffe (eds.), *Socialism in Tanzania*, Vol. 1, Nairobi, 1972, pp. 156–7.

23 Oliver, p. 96.

24 A. Smith, p. 99.

25 C.J. Hellbert, *Missions on a colonial frontier west of Lake Victoria*, Uppsala, 1965, p. 92.

26 The colonial administration's crude views were, however, in line with their priorities in the early years, and reflected as well the relative inexperience of the Germans, say, compared to the British, as colonial masters. The latter employed a more subtle method of domination and had learnt from experience the long term value and benefits of ideological work.

27 Quoted in T.B. Bottomore and M. Rubel, eds., *Karl Marx, selected writings in Sociology and Social Philosophy*, London, 1967, p. 41. The above description, to some extent, also applies to the role of Islam in coastal areas where missionary influence was marginal.

28 As Oliver puts it: 'Europe invested capital in great enterprises like the railway, only to find that the 'raw' African so far from being able to make them pay, was unemployable, that he worked under the whip for a fortnight and then slipped silently

away to his village. Where the missionary found African customs wicked, the administrator found them a barrier to progress (*sic!*); and in breaking down their solidarity he saw the missionary as an ally'. p. 178.

29 Wright, p. 50.

30 *Ibid.*, p. 67.

31 Oliver, p. 177.

32 Wright, pp. 55–6, 78, 101.

33 *Ibid.*, pp. 72, 102.

34 AR, 1902/3, p. 20.

35 Wright, p. 102.

36 Nolan, p. 56.

37 *Ibid.*, p. 56.

38 Wright, pp. 78–80.

39 Not infrequently a bush school would be a catechist providing oral instruction under a tree.

40 AR 1901/2. Supp. A. IV. p. 26.

41 See A. Smith, pp. 100, 108. Also see K. Schadler, *Crafts, Small scale Industries, and Industrial Education in Tanzania*, IFO Africa Studies, 34, Munich, 1968, p. 111.

42 See AR 1901/02, AR 1902/3.

43 AR 1901/2, Supp. A. IV. pp. 39–40.

44 Smith, p. 107.

45 Schadler, p. 52.

46 AR 1900/01, p. 5.

47 Quoted in Cameron and Dodd, *Society, Schools and Progress in Tanzania*, Oxford, 1970, p. 56.

48 AR 1901/2, p. 61, Besides there were requirements such as 'Each pupil in the first grade must be capable of independent compilation of lists and tables concerning payments, taxes, etc'. *Ibid.*, p. 61.

49 G. Hornsby, 'A Brief History of Tanga School up to 1914', *TNR*, 62, p. 148.

50 This was, of course, true for the mission schools as well.

And the rationalisation for the exploitation of the pupils' labour was also the same: 'These works of the school are of great value in accustoming the natives to regular physical labour from youth onwards'. AR 1908/9, p. 189.

51 AR 1901/2, p. 56.

52 AR 1907/8, p. 95.

53 *Ibid.*, p. 96.

54 AR 1908/9, p. 189.

55 *Ibid.*, p. 189.

56 AR 1901/2, p. 56.

57 To cite an obvious example: 12 pupils were trained to join the heliography unit of the colonial armed forces at the Tanga school in the year 1901/2. AR 1901/2, p. 55.

58 G. Hornsby, 'German Educational Achievements in East Africa' *TNR*, 64, p. 89. African teachers were given a salary of one rupee per month when they started teaching, and were entitled to annual increments of one rupee a month. After some years of teaching, they were accorded the status of a qualified teacher, with a monthly salary of twelve rupees.

59 *Ibid.*, p. 85.

60 Iliffe, p. 23.

61 For example, some of the village headmen who had suffered as a consequence of the cotton scheme led the struggle in their areas. *Ibid.*, p. 23.

62 M.J. Mbilinyi, 'The Decision to Educate in Rural Tanzania,' University of Dar es Salaam, unpublished Ph.D. dissertation, 1972, p. 40.

63 Lubetsky, p. 14.

64 Iliffe, p. 153.

65 For example, cultivation of cotton, which had sparked off the struggle, was spontaneously taken up by the people after Maji Maji. See Lubetsky, p. 15.

66 John Iliffe, 'The Age of Improvement and Differentiation (1907–1945)' in Kimambo and Temu (eds.), *A History of Tanzania*, Nairobi, 1969, p. 131.

67 Oliver, pp. 197–8.

68 Wright, p. 108.

69 Communication with L. Larson, 1974. Larson, however, disagrees that in Mahenge the increased opportunities for education were a consequence of the Maji Maji. According to him, the coincidence was purely accidental, explained by the availability of African catechist teachers in 1906. But the reasons he gives to explain the demand for education, namely official pressure and the prestige accorded to the educated, are precisely the factors which began to operate vigorously (perhaps in a different form than in Magenge) after Maji Maji over the territory as a whole. For example, support for mission education became official policy after Maji Maji.

70 AR 1908/9, p. 13.

71 AR 1908/9, p. 12.

72 For additional details supporting arguments advanced in this section, see G.C.K. Gwassa, *On Colonial Labour Force and Labour Market in Tanzania*, 1890–1961 and W. Rodney, ch. 4 in this volume.

73 R.V. Pierard, 'The Dernburg Reform Policy and German East Africa,' *TNR*, 67, p. 33.

74 Lubetsky, p. 9.

75 We have already seen how the labour of the pupils contributed to setting up and running the education system.

76 Pierard, p. 34.

77 Quoted in Iliffe, *Tanganyika Under German Rule*, p. 91.

78 *Ibid.*, p. 40.

79 Pierard, p. 31. Derburg was involved in the management of the Deutsche Bank, the Siemens organisation, the giant Bank of Darmstadt.

80 Rechenberg's anti-settler newspaper was financed by the German East Africa Company, of which Krupp was a principal shareholder. Also Rechenburg 'co-operated closely with the big trading firms . . .' Iliffe, *Tanganyika Under German Rule*, p. 97.

81 When attacked in the Reichstag, Dernburg said that his policy was not one of 'loving the Negro', but one of 'preserving the Negro'—to generate profits, no doubt! Pierard, p. 36.

82 Marcia Wright in 'Local Roots of Policy in German East Africa', *Journal of African History*, ix, 4, 1968, and Lubetsky, are correct to point out that to some extent, Rechenberg's policies were a continuation of previous administrators' policies but what they both fail to see is the qualitative leap after *Maji Maji* when these policies received primary emphasis. Moreover, the question is not one of 'local roots' versus 'overseas roots' of policies, but one of class interest and class struggle.

83 These traders would act as agents for the German East Africa company, and other trading firms.

84 Pierard, p. 35.

85 Iliffe, *Tanganyika under German Rule*, p. 106.

86 For a summary of these reforms, see Lubetsky, p. 15. Also Iliffe, pp. 106–7.

87 Iliffe, p. 73.

88 *Ibid.*, p. 76.

89 Iliffe, p. 97. For further details see Walter Rodney, ch. 3.

90 Wright, pp. 628–9.

91 M. Schlunk, 'German Education Policy: The School System in the German Colonies', in D.G. Scanlon. (ed.), *Traditions of African Education,* New York, 1964.

92 Scanlon, p. 29.

93 Schlunk, p. 47.

94 *Ibid.*, p. 34.

95 *Ibid.*, p. 32.

96 AR 1908/9, p. 12.

97 Schlunk, p. 32.

98 *Ibid.*, p. 43.

99 *Ibid.*, p. 43.

100 *Ibid.*, p. 42.

101 Mapunda and Mpangara, pp. 28–9.

102 Iliffe, p. 186.

103 *Ibid.*, p. 183.

104 Hornsby, 'German Educational Achievements in East Africa', p. 89. This order reflected the policy of making Arabs and Indians as economic and educated Africans as political intermediaries.

105 Marcia Wright, *German Missions in Tanganyika*, pp. 123–133. See also AR 1908/9, p. 14.

106 Lubetsky, p. 15, and Wright, *German Missions in Tanganyika*, p. 83.

107 Wright, *German Missions in Tanganyika*, p. 113.

108 *Ibid.*, p. 122.

109 *Ibid.*, pp. 114–5. See also Oliver, p. 206.

110 Lubetsky, p. 18.

111 Smith, p. 100.

112 For a comprehensive picture, consult ch. 1.

113 As Lubetsky points out, most of these slaves went to European plantations abroad. Lubetsky, p. 3.

114 Lubetsky, p. 5.

115 Lubetsky, p. 18.

116 Lubetsky, p. 24.

117 Karl Marx, *Capital*, Vol. I, Moscow, 1971, p. 689.

118 For an elaborate discussion, see Samir Amin, *Modes of Production and Social Formations*, University of Dar es Salaam, 1974, mimeo.

119 Karl Marx, p. 689.

120 Iliffe, p. 160.

121 Iliffe, p. 149.

122 Lubetsky, p. 12.

123 Oliver, p. 213.

124 Mapunda and Mpangara, pp. 28–9.

125 Lubetsky, p. 12.

126 Iliffe, pp. 176–9. It appears that in Mahenge area more or less all sections of society had equal access to education. Communication with Larson.

127 Wright, 'Local Roots of Policy . . .', p. 626.

128 AR 1901/2. p. 19.

129 AR 1908/9, p. 187.

130 Wright, 'Local Roots of Policy ...', p. 627.

131 Wright, *German Missions in Tanganyika*, p. 124.

132 See Lubetsky, p. 13, and Iliffe, p. 170–1.

133 Wright, *German Missions in Tanganyika*, pp. 131, 134–5, and Iliffe, pp. 206–7.

134 For an analysis of this, see Issa Shivji, *Class Struggles in Tanzania*, Dar es Salaam, 1975.

135 Iliffe, p. 179.

136 Lubetsky, p. 24.

137 Iliffe, p. 94.

138 *Ibid.*, p. 97.

139 Wright, 'Local Roots of Policy . . .', p. 626.

140 Iliffe, p. 96.

141 See K.F. Hirji, 'School Education and Underdevelopment in Tanzania', *Maji Maji*, 8, Tanu Youth League, University of Dar es Salaam Branch, 1973.

7. African Education during the British Colonial Period 1919–61

Marjorie J. Mbilinyi

The colonial mode of production established under the German colonial administration gathered momentum during the British period of colonisation. As Rodney shows in chapter 4, production in British Tanganyika was oriented towards the imperial metropole, England. Export crops such as cotton, coffee, tea and sisal were produced in ever-increasing quantities by African labour, either in the form of small-holder peasant production or in the form of hired labour production on settler or corporation plantations. The surplus which was produced by African labour was under the control of the metropolitan bourgeoisie. Agents in London and elsewhere fixed the prices and bought up the crops. Other primary goods such as gold, mica and diamonds were likewise mined by Africans, but the surplus accrued was controlled by the English bourgeoisie. The colonial state represented the interests of the imperial English state, and therefore the English metropolitan bourgeoisie, and functioned to develop and maintain the colonial mode of production through coercive and ideological structures. The colonial police and colonial army, the judiciary system of courts and laws represented the coercive structure, geared towards promoting greater production of goods exported to the metropole.[1] The African formal educational system under the government and the missions, and missionary activity in general represented essential parts of the ideological structure of the colonial state. It served the objective function of providing the African with the skills and knowledge necessary to be productive peasant producers, workers or petty-bourgeois servants of the state, and shaped his willingness to accept his place in the colonial social structure.

> (Our objective is) ... an educational system which will provide for African needs and at the same time produce a virile and loyal citizen of the Empire ... where character, health, industry, and a proper appreciation of the dignity of manual labour rank as of first importance ... the school ... is the centre of all Government propaganda work.[2]

At the same time, the colonial administration and missionary agencies had to contend with the demands of different social groups in the African population.

This chapter will attempt to relate the development of formal education as a state apparatus and the struggles over education to the development of the colonial economy, in particular to the development of the colonial division of labour. Special attention is given to the demands of the African petty bourgeoisie for higher education of a certain kind, since the post-independence bureaucratic bourgeoisie have emerged from this stratum. The influence of native authorities and the struggles between them and the educated petty bourgeoisie *and* the colonial administrators and missionaries are also given some focus in order to understand the process of class formation. The demands of the poor peasants and the workers are masked in the kind of material relied upon as sources. Department reports written by colonial administrations and most historical writings reflect the interests of colonialists and petty-bourgeois forces. Much more work is needed to dig deeper into written records and to go out to talk to the people about the past, in order to find out more about the form and content of the struggle waged in the field of education by peasants and workers.

Three different school systems developed, African, Asian and European, separated on a racist basis from each other, and in turn divided internally into education for the 'leaders' and education for the 'masses'. The European and Asian communities both had a much more highly developed education pyramid than the African; the European one was rooted in the metropolitan system itself and European children received their higher levels of schooling in Europe, and often primary as well. Primary and secondary education was developed earlier for Asians, with a greater proportion of primary school leavers entering secondary school. The Asian school system(s) developed primarily through the financial support of the Asian communities themselves, separated internally by religious and other differences. African education was limited to Standard VI until 1937, with very limited expansion beyond Standard VII thereafter. The content of the three education systems was also different, though more investigation is needed in this area. European colonial schools were literary and used the English language. African schools were vocational, and used vernacular as the medium of instruction at the elementary level, and Swahili for most Central School advanced courses (Standards IV to VI) until 1945.

The structure and content of the different education systems differed in specific ways because the racial groups being served by these schools, and the classes or strata *within* these groups, occupied different places in the developing colonial mode of production. The African was the producer of the surplus, but had little if any control over the surplus. A bare minimum of skills and knowledge was therefore necessary to be an effective producer—too much knowledge would lead the African to question his place in the set of social relationships into which he was being drawn or forced. The role learning or attitude learning which arose through the rituals of schooling—flag-raising, caning, standing at attention when the teacher entered the classroom—was given as much attention by colonial educators as the subject matter, and they called it 'character training'. The African system was intended to produce submissiveness, a sense of inferiority, and an orientation towards extrinsic rewards and punishments.

The Asian community primarily occupied positions in the colonial bourgeois class (for example, sisal estate owners, large scale commercial houses) and in the petty bourgeois class (clerks, teachers, middle-level civil servants, self-employed craftsmen, retail traders). Despite some ownership of large-scale means of production as estates, Asians were not in the position of surplus controllers. Cut off from control in the colonial context, they played a vital middleman role in siphoning off the surplus from the African producers and passing it on through the colonial administration to metropolitan buyers.

Europeans included settlers, missionaries and the colonial administrators. The colonial administrators represented the interests of the metropolitan bourgeoisie, the true controllers of surplus, a surplus produced increasingly more cheaply by African smallholder peasant producers than by European settlers, from the administration standpoint. Conflict between European settlers and the colonial administration occurred, sometimes with respect to African education. The settlers' purposes were best served by producing an African class of labourers with limited skills and knowledge. As the colonial economy developed, and the international political situation changed, colonial administration interests (the metropolitan bourgeois interests) were better served by also producing a more highly educated African petty bourgeoisie.

It is important to understand the division of labour found in the colonial mode of production outlined above, which includes the metropolitan bourgeoisie, in order to understand the meaning of the form and content of African education as it developed and the struggles which took place between Africans and the colonisers over education. The different groups or classes mentioned above are defined by their relationship to production and represent the social relations of production.[3]

The economic division of labour was paralleled in the political superstructure which included the Colonial Government's policy of 'divide and rule': divide leaders and masses, Asians and Africans, Native Authorities and emergent African petty bourgeoisie. The colonial administration devised several tactics to maintain control over the colonial economy, and foresaw that the greatest threat to their control would lie with an African petty bourgeoisie. The action and demands of the African petty bourgeoisie and colonial administration behaviour towards this group are of particular concern here because the bureaucratic bourgeoisie emerged from that stratum of colonial society.

The themes raised in the above paragraph expressed themselves in struggles over formal education as in struggles over other social institutions. The interests of the different parties to the struggle at any given point in time and place were increasingly determined by their position in the colonial relations of production. The dominant capitalist mode of production and class relations which exist today developed out of the transformation that occurred in the colonial period.

The period between 1919 and 1945

During the First World War German teachers were withdrawn and non-German missionaries evacuated or restricted. All government schools were disbanded and most, but not all, mission schools were closed. After the war, in 1919, Tanganyika was handed over as a

League of Nations Mandate to England. Given the uncertainty over the political status of a 'mandate', the new colonial administration was slow in 'picking up the pieces'. The British defined the mandate in practice as a part of the British Empire.[4] Tanganyika mainly represented a source of raw materials and a market for manufactured goods, some of which were produced in Nairobi. Nairobi was the financial and commercial centre of East Africa, Tanganyika its periphery. This partly explains the much lower development of education in Tanganyika.

The British applied the principles of indirect rule in Tanganyika. At the local level, 'native authorities' were relied upon, either traditional chiefs or headmen, or else individuals selected by the colonial administration to fill the position. Tribalism was deliberately promoted in order to facilitate domination and hamper the growth of militant detribalised 'natives' who might define themselves as future citizens of a nation, rather than a tribe. The intention was to establish a pattern of Native Authority rule for Africans separate from the colonial territorial government apparatus which later included a Legislative Assembly. The architect of Tanganyika's indirect rule, Governor Sir Donald Cameron, gave the following rationale for the policy of indirect rule.

> If we set up merely a European form of administration, the day will come when the people of the Territory will demand that the British form of administration shall be passed into their hands . . . we have India at our door as an object lesson . . . If we aim at indirect administration through the appropriate Native Authority . . . Chief or Council . . . founded on the peoples' own traditions and preserving their own tribal organisation, their own laws and customs purged of anything that is repugnant to justice and morality, we shall be building an edifice with some foundation to it, *capable of standing the shock which will inevitably come when the educated native seeks to gain possession of the machinery of Government and to run it on Western lines*.
>
> We shall have the sound answer to our critics that we are already administering the country through the people (I am, of course, not writing of the European settled areas) and endeavouring to teach them to develop on their own lines. If we treat them properly, moreover, we shall have the members

of the Native Administration on our side rather than on the side of those desiring to destroy them.[5]

There are two notable things in Cameron's statement: first, an awareness of, and an anticipation of, African struggle, identified particularly as a struggle emanating from the African petty bourgeoisie against the colonialist system; and second, the tactic of playing off one one stratum or class in African society against another, in this case, the Native Authorities and the petty bourgeoisie. The educational system reflected the policy of indirect rule. Elementary levels were all in the vernacular. Special schools were established for sons of chiefs, often the same schools begun by Germans, in order to ensure the development of a local leadership indoctrinated with British values and at the same time capable of handling the minor administrative responsibilities of local government.

Prior to the widespread effects of colonialisation, each African tribe had its own indigenous formal and informal educational system which helped to maintain the culture of the people and to reproduce the social relations of production. The mode of production at this time in most places was characterised by subsistence agriculture based on household production. The division of labour was mainly by age and sex. The means of production such as land and tools were owned by the family or clan, and controlled by the elder men of each household. Women were often the main food crop producers, whereas men hunted, fished and provided military defence of the area.

Vestiges of the indigenous system of education have persisted until today, although they have changed as the historical and material conditions of different groups have changed. Young girls were instructed by their mothers and elder sisters on proper techniques of crop cultivation, on the processing and preparation of food, on child care, and some learned special skills and knowledge of medicine and ritual, basket-weaving and pottery-making. Young boys were taught animal husbandry, house construction, tools manufacture and some also learned special skills and knowledge of medicine, of government, of blacksmithing and many other things. Certain aspects of these areas of knowledge and technology were taught informally while the child was actively engaged in doing what he was to learn about. The girl learned about crop cultivation by helping her mother cultivate in the fields. The boy learned animal husbandry by tending calves at an early age.

Most ethnic groups also had formal educational institutions, usually the 'schools' set up separately for boys and girls at puberty to initiate them into the adult ranks of their society. Certain elders were assigned to teach the boys or girls their own history, religion and all the skills and knowledge which an adult man or woman was expected to know to function intelligently in his or her life. The period of instruction lasted for as long as three years in some places, and was never less than several weeks' duration. The young people and their teachers resided together in separate 'camps' or temporary villages isolated from the community. The whole time could therefore be concentrated on intense instruction, though much of it involved physical endeavour at sports, and the practical elements of the knowledge being learned. Circumcision was the final stage in most of these initiation schools, after which the boy or girl returned home with a new status – a young adult.

Later we shall discuss how the British, often together with the Native Authorities, deliberately attempted to model some of the government or the Native Authority schools set up during the colonisation period on indigenous African educational institutions. These efforts to adapt western schools to African institutions were nearly always rejected in the end by Africans themselves. Tied as such experiments were to vernacular education and vocational training, Africans perceived this kind of education as a way of keeping them in their place in the colonial economy.

The policy of 'divide and rule' also applied to the colonial Government's policy towards Asians and Africans. The colonial administration deliberately maintained a racially segregated school system to reproduce the division of labour. The administration attempted to control staffing, structure and curriculum of Asian as of African education, and insisted, for instance, that assisted Asian Secondary (formerly central) schools should use English rather than vernacular medium of instruction.[6] When the Director of Education, Rivers-Smith, was asked by Cameron to state his opinion on integration of the Asian and African schools (Europeans were never included), the Director noted the greater economy of integrating the schools. The same buildings, books, teachers and school equipment could then be used. The director opposed integration in spite of its economic advantages for political reasons:

But . . . there is the political aspect which in all schemes of education should be kept constantly in view. With the knowledge of political developments during the last few years in India, we cannot affort to ignore the possibility of an unfortunate African political repercussion in future years as a result of the development of a closer liaison between the two races which might be a result of co-education.

At present we have a healthy rivalry and a growing race-consciouness among the Africans and a certain feeling of resentment that the Asiatics get so many of the 'plums'. In my opinion, co-education might conceivably weaken this healthy and natural rivalry and eventually lead to make common cause for political ends . . .

For facility of educational administration and from the financial point of view, co-education offers many advantages. There is, however, this political aspect, whether in years to come it may deprive the Administration of a *very valuable asset.*[7]

The colonial administration was always skilful in manipulating and perpetuating whatever conflicts already existed or which developed during the colonial period among the groups under its rule. To set African against Asian, and African against African, suited the interests of the state very well.

The metropolitan framework of colonial education

A major consequence of the colonisation of Tanzania is that the economy of the people was transformed on the basis of capitalist relations of production and drawn into dependency relations with the worldwide capitalist system. The bourgeois ruling classes in the industrialising capitalist nations developed and consolidated power as well as wealth through the exploitation of the workers and former slave labourers in their own countries and the peasants and workers in the colonies.

In both the United States and England, mass education became a major tool, to 'shape' the labouring classes so as to be more adaptable to capitalist forms of organising production and to be more productive. Special schools were created for English and American labouring classes in order to create a literate and numerate proletariat 'taught' to accept group confinement and routine chores and to submit to authority. Ideas about special schooling for different classes in society were implemented in Tanganyika, based partly on the advice of British and American experts in education, such as Thomas Jesse Jones and the other members of the Phelps-Stokes Commission. At the same time, social classes were created in Tanzania, based on production relations of the colonial economy. A certain form of school education finally developed and was inherited at Independence, which functions to perpetuate capitalism and therefore capitalist social relations, to maintain the rule of the bureaucratic bourgeoisie. In order to understand the Tanzanian system of education, it is therefore important to examine briefly the historical development of education in the metropolitan countries which had the most direct influence on Tanzanian educational development, namely England and the United States.

The evolution of English education

The basic pattern of education in Tanganyika was devised in London, just like the decision-making about the economic development of the colony. Even more important, however, was the fact that the colonialist administrators, the government teachers and the English missionaries shared a similar ideological background, rooted in the rigid class structure of Britain.[8] The government educational system imposed on Tanganyika by the colonial administrators reflected definite aspects of the English system of formal education.

The most significant aspect of the history of English educational development was the class structure of the educational system itself. Another important aspect was the dual role of government and religious institutions in the educational system. Education was the major ideological apparatus for ensuring the reproduction of productive relations in England, that is, the workers received a special kind of education different from that of the petty bourgeoisie and different again from that of the ruling class. Each class had its own kind of education to prepare its members for their future places in society. In this way, the class system was to be maintained and strengthened, with the ruling class ensured of its position on top and the working class perpetually relegated to the bottom.

In 1870, a dual system of education (church and state) and a national system of elementary schools were established in England. Until 1870, formal education had been mainly restricted to the upper class. As British capitalism was transformed into imperialism, a 'public school colonial ethic' emerged. The upper-class young men were taught gentlemen's etiquette complemented by the structural organisation of the institution itself. The prefect and House systems were deliberately intended to socialise the youths within a particular framework. On the one hand, the class structure of society was symbolised by the prefect system, and on the other, the spirit of group loyalty of the upper classes grew out of the House and School mystiques. At this stage, the only truly national 'group' was the upper class, the bourgeoisie, partly because of the public school system which set them above and beyond all other Englishmen, in a way that wealth alone could not.

The curriculum of the public schools befitted the colonial gentlemen. Lessons were drawn from the Classics, especially Greek and Roman. This was coupled with pedagogical beliefs that the mind needed to be disciplined through rigorous drill and memorising, and that the subject matter itself made no difference: the harder, the better.

By the late nineteenth century in England, traditional socialisation systems were no longer adequate to create the kind of labour force needed in the developing industrialised economy. Elementary education was considered necessary and sufficient to produce a literate and effectively socialised labourer. Elementary education was in fact working-class education, based on a curriculum of reading, writing, arithmetic, some vocational training and a good dose of Scripture to pacify and mould 'good character'. Religious institutions controlled the field of elementary education until the early decades of the 1900s. The children of the bourgeoisie and petty bourgeoisie attended private, public and grammar schools.

In 1902, the Balfour Act established Local Education Authorities who had control of secular education in voluntary (denominational) schools, and at the same time established local taxes for the use of these voluntary schools. In the same act, a government secondary education system of grammar schools was established separate from other education systems, specifically for the needs of the middle and petty bourgeois classes. The curriculum of the grammar schools was utilitarian, with less emphasis on Classics. Entry into the grammar schools was eventually based on performance in a selective examination (the 'eleven plus'). Children of the working class had less chance of passing this examination, due to the nature of the examination process and content, the nature of home and community facilities and reinforcement for school learning, and the motivational effects of the low expectation of the working class for upward mobility in England's rigid class society. Even if they did pass, however, most working-class children had to leave school to work in factories to help their families. Only a few rose above their working-class origins, although these were significant in legitimising the system.

The most significant aspect of the 1902 Act was the sharp distinction made between elementary (working-class education) and secondary school (petty bourgeois and middle-class education) systems. Higher elementary schools were established as extensions of the working-class education programme, wholly geared to vocational study. Their students left school at the age of fourteen years. Grammar schools, in contrast, were literary and non-vocational, as pointed out above, and led to higher levels of education.

> The public schools comprised the first class, grammar schools and private schools comprised the second class, while elementary schools made up the third class. Each class of schools served a different social class and prepared its pupils for different occupational levels.[9]

The Education Act of 1944 officially required religious instruction in all government schools, and established a three-tier system of education (primary, secondary, higher). Until this time the British Government had been reluctant to affirm any 'national' responsibility for maintenance of the educational system. This was partly due to the conflict between church and state over control of education. However, the need for expansion of secondary and technical education was recognised as vital in order that England 'keep up' with its competitors after the Second World War; that is, in order that the English bourgeoisie could control more surplus through increased labour productivity. State investment in education was necessary to fulfil the required expansion, and the petty bourgeoisie entered academic streams and grammar schools.

American education: education for adaptation

The Phelps-Stokes Commission was significant in popularising the principle of 'education for adaptation' in East Africa. The Commission was led by Dr Thomas Jesse Jones, a white 'leader' of Negro education in the United States. Two major reports were published on Africa, in 1922 and 1925. The principles of the Commission's approach were based on the form and content of 'Negro education' in the United States most often identified with Booker T. Washington. Agriculture education was the central focus of the educational system in Southern United States, and was justified statistically by showing that most African Americans were in agriculture – so therefore, African Americans should receive agriculture education. Despite attacks from progressive African Americans such as W.E.B. DuBois, this became the most prevalent form of black education.

The curricular content consisted of health, home like training, industry (which meant agriculture in particular) and recreation. As noted by King, 'Industrial education had originally been introduced as a guarantee that the Negro would continue to provide a low-level labour supply for the white South . . . .'[10]

Education for adaptation in the United States applied to the white working class as well as to African Americans. The majority of white working-class children in the Northern industrial states only attended elementary school in the late nineteenth century, whereas petty-bourgeois children entered the public high schools and bourgeois children attended private schools. As education expanded, working-class children were compelled to remain in school until they reached a certain age. At the same time, a growing number of bourgeois and petty-bourgeois children began to attend public schools. A differentiated school system developed to handle the 'mixing' of the classes. Working-class students were primarily directed into vocational and commercial streams and schools, whereas bourgeois and petty-bourgeois children entered college-preparatory academic streams and schools. This was called the 'progressive' education movement in the United States in the early 1900s, which demanded that education be tailored to suit the 'needs of the child'.[11] At the same time, 'objective' testing devices were developed and used, which tended to mask the growing reification of the class structure in the educational system. The form and content of academic examinations grew out of bourgeois class values, and referred to subject matter which was unfamiliar to working class children. Usually students in the non-academic streams did not take the examinations for selection to university at all. The use of ability measurement as a device for legitimising unequal access to higher education has become an essential part of the ideological structure of the capitalist system.

Education for adaptation in Tanganyika

Certain elements of the English and American education systems oriented towards working-class and black children were directly transposed by missionaries and colonial administrators to Tanzania. It is essential to note, however, that the contexts in which the educational systems developed were totally different. On the one hand, the former relate to industrial capitalist societies at already high stages of development. In colonial Tanganyika they were set in the context of a colonial economy at a very low level of productive forces, where the emergent dominant mode of production, capitalism, was developing in interaction with pre-capitalist modes of production. The objective function of mass education in the developed capitalist system, to reproduce labour power as well as to maintain capitalist relations of production, is therefore different from that set in an underdeveloped colonial economy where the labour force fed, housed and clothed itself through semi-subsistence agricultural production and where production did not depend upon school-manufactured skills. The objective function of formal education in the colonial context will be seen to include:

1 producing a small group of skilled, literate workers and administrative subordinates to work in the colonial government departments and for settlers and missions;
2 pacifying all those who enter the formal school system, both those who receive 'higher' education and the majority who receive only one or two years of vernacular education;
3 later, especially in the 1950s, producing a stratum of literate progressive capitalist farmers who would be highly productive cash crop producers and well-endowed with capitalist ideological tendencies.

Despite statements and memoranda *ad nauseam* about mass education, the formal educational system never functioned to produce a literate, more productive peasantry. The colonial economy depended completely upon the labour of an illiterate unschooled peasantry.

Educational development in Tanganyika: 1919–45

The majority of schools in Tanganyika under the British colonial administration were established and run by missionaries, who were to influence the educational system far more than under German rule. There was also greater heterogeneity in national origin of missionaries in the British period. There were twenty-one missions and mission orders in the field by 1933 and eighty per cent of all missionaries were not British, which affected government mission relations and educational policy. The uniformity in mass education development among the missions is notable, given the diversity of ethnic and class origins of the missionaries. All of the missions were responding to one context defined by the colonial mode of production, and were a part of the colonial ruling strata. Most missions had a string of bush schools and a few village primary education schools. Mission emphasis was on primary education, for education still retained the original function which was proselytisation, the conversion of the people to the foreign religion. Standard I to II level was considered adequate for a layman to participate in the church and Standard III to IV adequate for a churchworker. The missions were initially hostile to development of higher education, partly because the most highly educated youth did not remain in the mission but rather got jobs in government or private business.[12]

An important consequence of having such diversity in missions was the intense competition for converts and local power in some areas like Bukoba which led to even greater regional differentiation in educational development.[13] Missions were frequently concentrated in areas which were also commercial crop production centres, and therefore reinforced the pattern of regional differentiation in the territory. Missions directly contributed to commercialisation of agriculture production by providing seeds or seedlings to converts, encouraging modern farm practices and wealth accumulation, and by engaging in commercial agriculture and trade themselves.

The spread of Christianity depended on African catechists and church leaders. The number of European missionaries attached to any given mission was very small. An essential part of their proselytisation programme was therefore based on training African catechists who later left the mission centre to establish bush schools. The catechists taught in these schools themselves, often without European supervision for many years. This helps to explain the great suspicion that colonial administrators had for bush schools. They were not recognised as legitimate education institutions deserving of registration and possible government aid until the close of the colonial period. The reason given for this stand was lack of qualified teachers and inadequate curriculum. The degree to which Africans controlled the content, methods and student recruitment of such schools as well as their material base (land, house constructions, food for pupils and teachers, etc.) was another and probably more significant contributing factor requiring investigation.[14]

By 1936, the enrolment in mission-unassisted schools (Standards I to IV) had reached 191 061 and 30 596 in mission-assisted schools (Standards I to IV), the latter including government and native authority as well as mission grant-aided institutions.[15]

During the initial period of British rule, the government concentrated its efforts solely on elementary education. By 1924 there were seventy-two government primary schools in rural areas, two central schools in Tanga and Dar es Salaam respectively, and schools for sons of chiefs in Tabora and Bukoba (up to Standard VI) and Mwanza (Standards I to IV). The central schools primarily consisted of 'industrial' courses (carpentry, tailoring, ploughing, masonry, boot-making and occasionally 'road construction') together with reading, writing and arithmetic. The central schools were mainly the old German schools, and were similarly focused on vocational training (see chapter 6).

A clear distinction between 'elementary' (early primary) and post-elementary levels of education was observable from the beginning in the government system. Elementary education was mass education for the peasants, whereas the early post-elementary central schools were directed towards sons of chiefs to be prepared for local administrative positions and others to become clerks and semi-skilled labourers and craftsmen in the government.

> The development of the elementary education schemes . . . is becoming firmly established on vocational lines and in accordance with the policy of teaching the native child the three Rs while keeping him as closely as possible in touch with the life he is accustomed to, and at the same time to introduce as the industrial influence during his school life the work which . . . he would do at home . . . Agriculture shall be the keynote of our educational programme.[16]

The education structure was clearly based on assumptions of class as well as racial differences.

> It is generally admitted that free elementary education is the right of every child who can benefit by it, but it is also clear that the child cannot benefit unless, as a result of his education, he is better *equipped for the life to which he is entitled by birth and upbringing.*[17]

Class divisions were perceived to be instrumental not only in dividing elementary education from higher levels of schooling, but also with respect to streaming within the central schools themselves, as 'commoners' joined others in the central school. Two distinctly different curricula were developed for the two classes of students, as shown in the 1923 Report for Bukoba Central School.

> Two broad divisions have been made in the school, forming a 'general side' and a 'special side'. The first consists chiefly of sons of sultans, chiefs and wealthy land-owners, who receive a general all-round training consisting of academic subjects such as English, Mathematics, Geography, Hygiene and practical subjects such as Agriculture, Animal Husbandry, Elementary Carpentry and Tailoring and Native Handicrafts (such as Drum-making, etc). The second will consist of apprenticeship to various trades, carpentry, tailoring, etc.[18]

Central Schools

Central schools were an important focus for struggles between Africans and the colonialists. Africans continually demanded more 'English' courses, which really meant English was taught as one subject, and later became the medium of instruction at higher standards. Literary or academic course-work was characteristic of the English course, rather than vocational education. By the 1930s a graduate of the English course was able to get higher pay than the graduate of the industrial course. Looking at this conflict over English versus vocational education in terms of the division of labour/vocational education was tied to the African's place as semi-skilled worker or rural producer in the colonial economy. To struggle against this place was to struggle against certain aspects of the colonial social and economic relationships taking root in the territory. Just as African Americans struggled against negro vocational education in Southern United States, Africans in Tanganyika and elsewhere in Africa struggled against native vocational education (or bantu education in southern Africa).

The contradiction inherent in this struggle, however, was that it was not a struggle against the capitalist mode of production, per se, but rather a struggle over the appropriate place of the African within capitalist social relations. As noted by Walter Rodney in chapter 4,

> Africans themselves sought to participate in the emergent colonial economy and to influence the terms on which they participated . . . The victory won by the respective African populations were not insignificant, but they ultimately strengthened the export orientation (and development of the colonial mode of production).[19]

Tanga Central School was as typical of English colonial ideas about 'higher African education' as it was typical of German. A British head took over the school in 1922. By 1924 there were 304 day pupils; ten African teachers, eight industrial instructors in addition to the European head. The school had six elementary classes (three years), two advanced classes (three more years), and one night class for apprentices in the school workshops. Industrial streams of students taking carpentry, tailoring, book-making, blacksmithing and masonry existed side by side with the English literary stream.

Tanga school had a school board which included some local Africans, an outcome of the Director of Education, Rivers-Smith's programme for local responsibility and 'community participation' in the government school system. In 1924, the School Board raised shs. 900 to finance the development of secondary education at the school. The headmaster 'persuaded' the Board to spend the money on scholarships for needy students instead.[20] This incident illustrates the opposition between African demand for higher education and colonial efforts to limit African education to a minimum. The colonialist point of view, reflecting the place of African labour in the colonial economy, is exemplified by Rivers-Smith's statement of objectives in a 1922 minute:

> We must be careful to avoid the production of the type of the cultivated little gentleman and to aim at the robust industrialist able by demonstration to teach his people how to do things.[21]

The colonialists had an ideal image of the 'good African' not cut off from his traditional roots. What the 'good African' really meant is best defined by one of the colonialists themselves, the Chief Secretary John Scott, who defined him when challenged by referring to his opposite, 'a bad imitation of a European . . . a half-educated African who considered himself quite as good as, if not better than, the white man who governed him'.[22] Here again we find reference to the threat of an emergent African petty bourgeoisie.

The significance of knowledge of English in the colonial ideological structure is expressed by Cameron when inaugurating the Tanganyika Legislative Council in 1926. Africans were not allowed on the council: 'The native community cannot be directly represented because for the present a native cannot be found with sufficient command of the English language to take part in the debates of the Council—indeed to understand what is being said'.[23] In a meeting of the Permanent Mandates Commission in the same year, it was pointed out that there were two Africans on the Territorial Central Advisory Committee on Education and the Chief Secretary was asked, 'Did these natives not speak English?'. His reply was that speaking English was a necessary but not sufficient qualification.[24]

During the depression retrenchment of personnel was carried out. The colonial administration of Tanganyika was criticised by the Retrenchment Commission in 1931 of 'too rapid expansion of social services to the African population'[25]—namely education. The judgement is certainly remarkable, given the small number of Africans who received even two years of primary schooling. Expenditure on African education was reduced drastically and for a much longer period than other social services, and remained low long after the economy picked up again in the late 1930s. Isherwood, the new Director of Education, spearheaded the drive to expand vernacular elementary education (Standards I to IV) and diminish the few post-elementary levels of education that existed. The number of English courses was reduced and several former central schools were downgraded to become vernacular elementary schools or else became specialised agricultural schools. For example, the Bukoba Central School was dropped and Nyakato Central School later became an agricultural school. The Native Authorities in Bukoba, as well as the local branch of the African Association, representative of petty-bourgeois interests, attacked this change in policy as a move to further the oppression of the African. Dissatisfaction with the course at Nyakato grew among parents and students and culminated in student efforts to block the return of the first Head, A.E. Haarer. The following report of the acting Provincial Commissioner on the pupils' reasons for dissatisfaction are a valuable key to the reality of the African school.

> Pupils had complained that instead of receiving scheduled lectures they had been given manual work of a non-instructional nature, that many of Haarer's carefully polished lectures had in fact been delivered in translation by the African teacher, Benedict, of whom Haarer thought highly but who lacked standing among the pupils and the personal knowledge to interpret the lecture material, that Haarer had spent too much time with the higher classes, and that he had apparently led them to believe that he would assist all who passed the course satisfactory to obtain paid employment.[26]

The elementary school syllabus was eventually extended to include six years, with a strong handicraft bias, to be followed by a three-year rural industrial course at some schools. A definite policy switch had occurred, from specialised industrial courses which might lead to wage employment or urban self-employment to village handicrafts, better fitting the African producer in the rural areas.

Tabora Central School was established in 1925 as a special central school. Although the school has often been defined as an elitist institution like the public schools of England, there were important differences. The elite of Tabora were trained to be a subordinate group of administrative officers within the colonial structure, not *the* ruling class. Whereas at Eton a deliberate effort was made to develop national *esprit de corps*, at Tabora the colonialist educationists intended their students to identify themselves according to tribal divisions. They were housed along tribal lines and tribal customs were taught specific to each group's affiliation. As noted already, one of the greatest fears of government administrators and missionaries was threat of detribalisation. To have promoted a *national* ruling class ideology would have been contrary to the interests of the colonists, and to the principle of indirect rule. Nevertheless, the objective outcome of the 'sons of chiefs' school system was the development of a nationalist group who would later provide the leadership for the independence struggle.

Another important difference between the public schools of

England and the 'chiefs schools' of Tanganyika was the content of the course. Whereas the youth of Eton learned Classics, the Tabora students learned 'book-keeping, typing and office routine in preparation for taking up jobs in government offices'.[27]

At the same time, it was to the colonial interests to have an African dominant local ruling class who had been socialised to fit a capitalist set of social relations, if they were to be integrated smoothly into the system. Similar structural aspects of the public school in England were therefore used at Tabora, and at most boarding schools then and thereafter. House competitions and the prefect system, and the nature of teacher-student relationships and teaching methodology promoted a hierarchical, competitive system. This was partly because it was easier to accept a model already tried and tested, as the English public school was, but at least some educationists were consciously aware of the relationship between the organisation of the school and attitudinal change. For example, the advantages of the prefect system were pointed out in a 1947 Annual Report from Bukoba: 'Several *bolsy* [*sic*] problem pupils have proved loyal and resourceful when made prefects'.[28] Musgrove, while Headmaster of a prestigious Ugandan secondary school for Africans, pointed out the significance of socialisation within the secondary school system in this way:

> Loyalties unknown outside the school are now felt to the class, the team, the informal group, the House (which stirs strong feelings of rivalry in inter-house sports and games) and to the school.[29]

The significance of such loyalties is that they separated pupils from 'others', those who were not participants in the school process, and helped to create a sense of group loyalty upon which class consciousness could be based. The organisation of the school in this respect worked against the 'indirect rule' principle outlined above. The individual was the basis of the educational system. The structure reinforced a sense of comradeship and elitism that rose above tribal differences. Special uniforms and the style of life characteristic of boarding school served to enhance the 'superiority' of these students *vis-à-vis* the rest of the society. It was therefore inevitable that *in spite* of colonial educationists' intention, at this time the upper primary schools and later the secondary schools produced a national educated group who would later oppose the colonial system.

Colonial administration control of missions

Administration efforts to control mission education began as early as 1927. The Education Ordinance of that year institutionalised government grants-in-aid to mission schools that fulfilled government standards (i.e., the use of Swahili, appropriate secular instruction, sufficient and qualified teachers, and sufficient students). At the same time, the principle of state control over mission education was established. Since the missions were perpetually short of funds, it was necessary for them to seek government assistance, and in this way they had to submit somewhat to the state's objectives in education. The colonial administration directly represented the interests of the English bourgeoisie, whereas the majority of missions did not. State control over mission schools was necessary to ensure that they fulfilled the desirable ideological functions of the former school system.

Specific conflict between missions and the colonial administration arose from several different sources. The missions at first resisted the state's growing demand for higher education (i.e. post-Standard IV, later post-Standard VI), and for state control over the curriculum and the medium of instruction of the schools. Swahili, as under the German period, was still considered to be a Muslim language and representative of the detribalisation force which the missionaries resisted. Urbanisation and detribalisation were perceived to be corrupting influences, and Islam represented a competing religious force. The expansionist tendency of missions, limited to multiple bush schools, conflicted with the states growing interest in a hierarchical, pyramid structure that was adjusted to the needs of the colonial economy, and which provided some expansion at higher levels of education. Another 'innovation' which threatened the hegemony of the missionaries in the rural areas of the interior was the growth of Native Authority committees responsible for administering all the schools. The Native Authority Ordinance of 1926 encouraged Native Authorities to set up their own primary schools. The response was enthusiastic enough in some areas to raise questions over the 'proper function' of Native Authority Schools. By 1939, there were 141 Native Authority elementary schools in the territory, as many as government schools.[30]

After the depression, the *Memorandum of the Education of*

African Communities (Advisory Committee on Education in the Colonies) stressed that education must provide low level manpower for government and commercial enterprises so the colonial regime could 'sustain' itself. The growing emphasis on the need for education to serve economic development coincided with increasing government pressure on peasants to produce more cash crops.

Native Authorities and community participation

Colonialist statements on education continually emphasised the need for community 'participation' in the primary school; 'community education' received special attention, however, at this time. To appreciate the meaning of community participation in schools in the colonial context, it is essential to examine the colonial administration's response to African efforts to influence if not control educational development. The conflicts over the central schools described above provides one set of examples.

African reaction to western schooling is often described as following a pattern of indifference or suspicion, then acceptance and finally enthusiastic demand.[31] As Ranger pointed out, many African societies first welcomed western education, and even invited missionaries to settle in their area with the proviso that schooling be provided for their youth.[32] The early demand was for technical education, not literary education. In the Department of Education Annual Reports during the 1920s, enthusiasm for technical education is reported, but also dismay at the shift from enthusiasm to apathy or hostility towards the schools in general, especially the Native Authorities in certain localities. And whereas earlier it is reported that parents and students demanded technical education and rejected literary education at central schools due to employment prospects, later there is reference to a rising demand for English literary education.

Here we can only speculate on the reasons for this shift, given the absence of concrete data. Traditional or indigenous leaders in some areas recognised the significance of modern western technology and wished to adopt it. Their actions indicate the false belief that they and their people were still in control of the indigenous economy. As the colonial capitalist mode of production developed and permeated every aspect of African life, the leaders and their people became aware of the fact that they were not in control of the new mode of production, that they had been relegated to the bottom in colonial social relations, and that different school courses led to different positions within that bottom 'layer' of social relations. Technical education led to subservient menial labour, English education led to subordinate petty-bourgeoisie-type positions, positions of dominance among the oppressed Africans as a total group.

The renovation of German government schools depended more on the efforts of the African people than of the British Government. Between 1919 and 1923, Native Authorities were financially responsible for more elementary schools than the Department of Education, though this does not show up in the records of that time because they were all called government schools.[33] In Bukoba, ten government schools were established and running by 1921, before any English Government Education Officer was posted to the district. In Shinyanga in the 1930s, 'Kaya' boarding schools were set up under Chief Wamba, who provided land, cattle, food and payments for teachers.[34] Blumer, a government inspector of schools in Mwanza, pointed out in 1941 that the aims of the Kaya schools were 'rural education for boys and girls on *strictly tribal lines* . . . the principal object of the school is to give an education which will not take the youth of Usukuma away from the land' (Blumer's emphasis).[35] Mason noted that these schools 'should be considered as purely agriculturals schools, designed to meet the requirements of children of rich cattle owners, progressive peasants, headmen and the like'.[36] The Kaya schools were serving the interests of the rich peasant stratum and traditional rulers of the area, and to the extent that their interests coincided with those of the colonial administration their interests were met.

The conflict between Mumford, the first English Government Education Officer in Bukoba, and the Bukoba Native Authorities exemplifies conflict of class interests. Mumford arrived in Bukoba in 1923 and found the well-organised system of district schools mentioned above, known as the Sultan's schools or 'camp' schools. The children were housed and fed by the chiefs and were supervised by African teachers. In 1924, Mumford notes 'a change of policy occurred by which Sultans were relieved of all responsibility with regard to the upkeep of schools buildings and the maintenance of pupils.[37] Mumford established a curriculum reflecting the government policy of vocational education for Africans: agriculture, industrial education and handicrafts. Mumford then reported that the chiefs had become indifferent to the government school programme, and many parents hostile to enrolment of their children in the school. He explained this by saying that chiefs had originally only had a superficial interest in schools; parental response was due to the fact that their children were previously forced to go to school by the chiefs. Griffith, the District Officer in Bukoba, argued instead that the chiefs' reaction was due to their loss of control over the school system. Moreover, another Bukoba government official noted, 'in respect of his revival of basket and mat weaving, chiefs and parents were later reported as expressing the view that they did not send their children to "European school" for such instruction'.[38]

The Native Authorities of Bukoba consistently struggled for higher levels of education for the African and for more English literary education, which was mainly preserved for whites and Asians. For example, in 1928 they invested £2 250 to build the new Nyakato Central School. It could be argued that the Native Authorities were serving their own interests by demanding more higher education, just as before their reaction to Mumford had been due to a recognition of their own interests. However, this is an example of the situation where the dominant stratum of the oppressed population represent their own interests as identical to the interests of the whole population, and where objectively speaking their interests and those of all the oppressed are indeed identical.

By 1931, 40 per cent of the vernacular teachers employed by the government in the whole territory were in fact working at the thirty-seven Native Authority schools operating then. Two years before that, however, the government began to clamp down on NA schools, alarmed by the amazing speed with which they were established and the fact that they were not under tight colonial supervision. In 1935, the provincial commissioner of Western Province wrote that for some time,

> The Native Authorities will be of little real value in any campaign for social progress. The African native community, from top to bottom, is inclined to treat all our efforts to change its mode of life with the suspicion that we are inspired by desire to benefit ourselves; only visible results will convince them to the contrary.[39]

This was stated at the same time the colonial administration was designing a more rigid system of agricultural and vocational education for Africans restricted almost completely to elementary level, a change which Native Authorities and the masses in several areas protested against. For example, it was reported in Moshi by the Education Secretary of the Holy Ghost Fathers that people would attend the Catholic school only if English was taught. In Mwanza Province the chiefs of the Bukwimba Federation applied for the appointment of English teachers to NA schools. The application was rejected 'on the grounds that to accede would be to invite a deluge of further applications'.[40] Stephone Mgalwe, senior African teacher at Tabora School, stated at a Provincial Education Committee Meeting that 'demand for English was no product of the educational system confined to schoolboys but arose from the widespread desire of the people'.[41]

The following exchange between Martin Kayamba, an African member of the Tanganyika Advisory Committee on African Education, and other members at their tenth meeting in November 1934 raises many of the issues discussed above.[42] Notable in Kayamba's argument is the acceptance of the division of labour of the colonial capitalist mode of production—his struggle, and that of the petty bourgeoisie group he belonged to, was for entry into the higher levels of the division of labour and not a struggle *against* the system itself.

> When discussing the new syllabuses, the questions of student promotion from one standard to the next, the establishment of higher standards and English language instruction were brought up. Kayamba said, 'The Government appeared to be considering only the supply of clerks and employees for commercial firms, but since there were many higher branches of employment such as doctors, lawyers, etc, the facilities for higher education should not be restricted. Isherwood (Director of Education) replied, 'Only a very few would be in a position to achieve the standard required for such professions at the present time.' Canon Broomfield expressed the opinion that, 'It would be a waste of time of the teaching staff to promote pupils who were not fit for promotion.' Kayamba pointed out that if the children were properly taught, no more than one per cent of them would fail in the promotional examinations. Bishop Byren expressed his opinion that,

'However well taught pupils may be it did not at all follow that they would all be able to profit by teaching to the extent that Mr Kayamba thought they would'. Kayamba doubted that the children were being pushed to their intellectual capacity. Mr. Isherwood assured him that the headmasters were only too anxious to help their pupils progress to the full extent of their capacity . . . Isherwood asked the other members if any thought they had pupils who were being unjustifiably held back. None of them thought they did. Kayamba said that many Africans believed that their children were being held back. Isherwood promised to look into the matter.

Kaymba proposed that English language instruction should be introduced as a subject in Standards III and IV. Since Africans had such difficulty in learning English correctly, he believed that by introducing it at any early stage in the primary schools, Africans would be better equipped for secondary and higher education where English was the language of instruction. Isherwood pointed out that this suggestion was in conflict with the principles upon which the new syllabus had been drawn up.

We have already presented above the essential aspects of the shift in policy which occurred at this time of 'retrenchment'. The numbers of central schools was reduced drastically, English teaching was eliminated almost completely from the curriculum, and English-speaking African teachers had not been trained for several years.

Kayamba's demands went right against the social structure underlying the colonial state, consisting of the mass of producers at the bottom and a small dominant class of controllers of surplus at the top, namely the metropolitan bourgeoisie represented in Tanganyika by the colonial administration. The structure of society was reflected in structures of education for Africans, Asians and Europeans, all of which were pyramid in shape, but with the pinnacle of the African pyramid resting midway up the pyramid structure for the other races. Moreover, the majority of Africans did not receive any formal education in the colonial school system, government or mission, nor was it essential at that time for peasant producers to have formal education in order to fit their place in the colonial economy. The colonial state depended far more on the coercive apparatus of police, army and laws to maintain control. The purpose of the whole African education system was in fact to produce the very small number of African semi-skilled workers, clerks, native police force, primary teachers and rich peasants or capitalist smallholders. The ideology of the pyramid bourgeois educational structure is clearly stated by Turner, the former Principal of Makerere University College, in a review of secondary education in East Africa in 1946: 'In any country where education standards deserve respect the proportion of students that passes from primary to secondary and later from secondary to higher education, is small'.[43]

The stand of the colonial administrators and missionaries in the exchange quoted above with Mayamba also reveals the way concepts of individual differences and inherited ability which underpin racist and class structures were manipulated to explain the form and content of African education.

Underlying the policy of African 'education for adaptation' were fundamental assumptions about the innate nature of the native's mentality, and the 'natural' economy he was best suited for. And these assumptions were in turn grounded in the colonial division of labour. For example, one Agriculture Officer in Shinyanga criticised schooling because it was too academic, 'and divorced the pupils from *normal* native agricultural pursuits'.[44] Clearly, it was not necessarily 'normal' for African peasants to maintain shifting hoe agriculture based on hand cultivation, even if it was the prevalent form of production. The African economy is a historical phenomenon to be explained, not to be taken for granted.

In 1925, the Director of Agriculture in Tanganyika stated that only five per cent of all African students had 'sufficient intelligence to profit from academic instruction'.[45] The Superintendent of Education for Bukoba stated in the *1931–32 Annual Report* that 'No Native I have met can teach English or Geography. The limits of their mental experiences prohibit them'.[46] In 1931, the Director of Agriculture stated that 'the African is a peasant farmer at heart and should be trained rather than educated'.[47] That 'Education for Adaptation' was tied to the particular place of the African in the colonial mode of production is shown in the questions raised by A. Murray in 1929.

It is said by many people that the Native must be 'educated

> for industry'. The question is, whose industry? If it is his own, of what value is it, if owing to labour conditions, he does not know whether he will ever see the profits of his own labour? If it is not his own, how does it benefit the Native to make him simply a superior tool for the white man?[48]

At the same time as the impliementation of the retrenchment policy of African education, the colonial administration was faced with increasing demands for better qualified Africans to work in government departments and in private business. It was therefore decided to improve the quality of those central school courses which were remaining in order that some Africans could finally enter Makerere Secondary Level course. In 1934 Tabora Central School and St Mary's School at Tabora were upgraded to junior secondary schools. In 1936 six out of eight candidates passed the Makerere entrance examination. Secondary courses also began at Kibosho, Tosamaganga and Minaki, soon to be followed by courses at other schools. The curriculum of the secondary level of education was literary and used the English medium. 'Adaptation of Education' principles of vernacular and vocational education only applied to lower levels of education.

African education in Tanganyika was examined by the Commission on Higher Education in East Africa, which reported on Makerere College and the development of the school systems which would feed into it in 1937.[49] The commission stressed the need for greater expansion of secondary education in Tanganyika. The fact that Tanganyikan students would now take the Makerere entrance examination reinforced a more literary education. Tanganyika, Uganda and Kenya depended on the Cambridge Syndicate for creation and marking of examinations, which greatly influenced the content of secondary coursework.

The Colonial Government also considered strengthening the role of local authorities by increasing the rebate of hut and poll taxes to Native Authorities and promoting school councils which would include representatives of Native Authorities, parents and teachers. The policy was not implemented at this time, partly due to the outbreak of the Second World War. Nevertheless, Para Native Authorities went ahead. The actions taken at this time re-established the foundations of uneven regional and district development, 'changes would be introduced whenever the people in an area had demonstrated their competence and willingness to accept them'.[50] Those areas such as Kilimanjaro, Pare and Bukoba which were more developed in terms of commercial agriculture were better able to finance schools, so that by Independence, the majority of school-aged children were already in schools in these areas.

The period between 1946 and 1961

By 1945, there were 1 000 primary schools, eighteen secondary schools and twenty-four teacher training centres in Tanganyika. The total secondary school enrolment was 1 000 and the teacher training enrolment, 1 100, and there were twenty-seven students at Makerere following a pre-senior secondary course. The responsbility for these schools was divided between the government and voluntary agencies as shown in Table 7.1 below:

Table 7.1 THE AFRICAN EDUCATIONAL SYSTEM IN 1945*

	GOVERNMENT AND NATIVE AUTHORITY	MISSIONS
Primary schools	200	300 (assisted)
		500 (unassisted registered)
Secondary schools	8	10
Teacher training centres	8	16
Makerere	1	

*Source: J. Cameron and A. Dodd: *Society, schools and progress in Tanzania*, London, 1970, p. 71.

A pyramid structure was clearly established; moreover, the educational system was racially segregated, with different schools and different curricula for Asian, European and African children, especially at primary and middle school levels. The opportunities for education were much greater for Asian and European children. By 1945, there were seventy-nine Indian assisted schools run by 'voluntary agency' groups and three government schools for Indians, with a total enrolment of 8 000 pupils. There were two European government primary schools and four assisted European schools with a total enrolment of 300. European children were usually sent to the UK for post-primary education, as were children of wealthy Asian families.

The inbalance in expenditure for the racially segregated educational systems are indicated in the figures provided in the table below. It must be stressed that nearly all the few Africans in school received only one or two years of primary education.

Table 7.2 NET EXPENDITURE ON EDUCATION IN 1946

	TOTAL POPULATION	STUDENTS IN SCHOOL	ENROLLED STUDENTS AS % OF RACE (APPROX)	GOVERNMENT NET EXPENDITURE	GOVERNMENT NET EXPEND. PER STUDENT
African	5 242 167	105 050	2%	£201 000	£ 1.9
European	7 926	792	10%	30 000	38.0
Asian	31 801	8 824	30%	39 000	4.4

Source: *Annual Report of Education Department (1946), Tanganyika,* cited by S. Nkonoki, 'A Study of the Philosophy of Education for Self-Reliance and Its Implementation in the Tanganian Secondary Schools', University of Dar es Salaam, pp. 63–64.

The percentages only make sense if we recognise that the majority of Europeans were adults, which draws the percentage in school down.

Education: The Ten Year Plan 1946–55

In 1945, the first vigorous planning operation for the Tanganyika territory was achieved with the Ten Year Plan. The focus of the plan was deliberately on primary education, with a stated objective of getting thirty six per cent of the primary school age group enrolled in Standards I to IV. District day/boarding middle schools were planned to include Standards V and VI, whereby one-fifth of the Standard IV output would enter Standard V. In 1958, the pyramid structure of today was established: Lower primary (Standards I to IV), middle school (Standard V to VIII), and secondary (Standards IX to XII). In 1946, there were only 917 students enrolled in Secondary school, and all of them were boys. There was a high degree of wastage throughout the system, so that in 1948 two-thirds of the Standard I intake had dropped out by Standard IV.[51]

An agriculture syllabus was officially introduced in all rural primary and middle schools in 1952, but was withdrawn by 1959. The policy met with growing resistance from parents and students alike, related to the growing political consciousness in the territory and the growing antagonism concerning agriculture production and marketing in the rural areas.

Nkonoki[52] provides some specific reasons for the failure of the agriculture syllabus:

1 it applied only to Africans;
2 it was imposed in most places with no consultation among African leaders or else 'Native Authorities' agreed to the syllabus, but their political legitimacy in the local areas was already suspect;
3 the syllabus seemed to be designed to perpetuate the colonial class structure;
4 parents expected their children to get jobs and thereby provide a 'return' on their investment in education;
5 the land tenure system did not provide a framework in which youths could apply new agricultural ideas on a large scale;
6 agriculture was never an examined subject, therefore belittling its importance in the educational structure;
7 agricultural work had always been doled out as punishment and therefore represented a negative valence;
8 agriculture instructors had less educational qualifications, and therefore were considered 'inferior' which also meant that their subject had diminished prestige;
9 the syllabus was too rigid and therefore did not allow for specific ecological and social factors to be considered;
10 agriculture instruction tended only to be work, with very little scientific content.

In addition, a dual system of middle schools aggravated the situation; most middle schools in the rural areas were agriculture-oriented, but all urban middle schools were academically-oriented. The examinations for secondary school entry were based on academic coursework and therefore objectively favoured students in the academic-oriented urban middle schools.

There was also a division of opinion about agricultural education within government circles. As a result, the Departments of Agriculture and Education often conflicted over delegation of responsibility for the syllabus. Inadequate training facilities were developed to cater for the special needs of agriculture instruction. By 1956, out of 232 middle schools only eighty-five had even one trained agriculture instructors.[53]

The Ten Year Plan's emphasis on primary education partly grew out of the Colonial Government's need for a counter-revolutionary mechanism. The Advisory Committee on Education in the Colonies pointed out in *Mass Education in African Society*, a 1944 policy paper, that growing political consciousness among the natives was of primary concern. Character training (i.e. socialisation of behavioural characteristics such as obedience, submissiveness, passiveness, etc) in the mission schools was praised. Moreover, British missionaries as well as the government educational system had carefully geared the content of instruction in history, current events and other subjects to British history and British culture. In the words of the Director of Education in the Central Education Committee Report in 1943,

> . . . it seems important in a world of conflicting ideologies that it would be less than just to our tradition not to ensure that the English way of life and the English conception of education shall be presented to the people as vividly and as widely as accords to our position.[54]

The emphasis on primary education to the exclusion of secondary education was another measure meant to perpetuate very low educational levels among the majority of the population. References were frequently made to India in correspondence among government officials, as an example of what could happen if a fully-developed educational system were established.[55]

The pyramid structure of education is shown by the enrolment figures for 1956 given in Table 7.3. The unequal educational opportunities for girls are also indicated.

Table 7.3 ENROLMENT IN THE EDUCATIONAL SYSTEMS IN 1956 (VOLUNTARY AGENCY, GOVERNMENT NATIVE AUTHORITY COMBINED)

	TOTAL	GIRLS
Primary school (Standards I to IV)	336 000	105 000
Middle school (Standards V to VIII)	28 000	4 900
Secondary school (Standards XI to XII)	2 409	204

Source: D.R. Morrison 'Education and Political Development', University of Sussex, 1970, for total enrolment figures; J. Cameron and W.A. Dodd, *Society, Schools and Progress in Tanzania*, New York, 1970, for girls' enrolment.

By 1956, local decisions on education were increasingly under the control of district education committees, which consisted of missions, Africans (frequently the former Native Authorities) and government officials. This followed a move to consolidate division by the establishment of African District Councils in 1949, whereby representatives were 'indirectly' selected to handle certain administrative tasks.[56] District Education Officers (formerly Assistant Provincial Education Officers) were posted through the territory, resulting in more centralised control of all educational systems in the country. This led to renewed friction between government and missions, especially since the District Education Committees now had powers to determine the location of schools, the arrangement of school terms and even the payment of teachers' salaries in missions as well as government and Native Authority schools.

Mission rivalry together with uneven economic development and differential local response to the school led to definite provincial imbalance in educational development. Table 7.4 shows the targets for enrolment of primary school age children in school in 1953[57]. Non-Christians were barred from entry into most mission schools, and at the same time many Traditionalist and Muslim parents refused to send their children to western schools, knowing they would be converted to Christianity. As Rodney points out, this pattern of uneven development was related to social class formation.

Table 7.4 PERCENTAGE TARGETS FOR ENROLMENT OF CHILDREN AGED 7 TO 11 AND PERCENTAGE ENROLMENT BY PROVINCE, 1953*

PROVINCE	PERCENTAGE TARGET FOR 1956	PERCENTAGE ENROLMENT IN 1953
Tanga	50	53
Northern	50	46
Southern	40	39
Eastern	40	29
Southern Highlands	30	23
Lake	30	20
Western	30	20
Central	30	18

Source: Department of Education, *Annual Report 1953*, cited in Morrison; p. 107 (Table 3.6.).

Five Year Development Plan: 1956–61

In 1954, Governor Sir Edward Twining was provoked, presumably by growing African demands for participation at all levels of government, for work and for more educational facilities, into complaining in the Legislative Council that Africans 'have lost their sense of values and appear never to have heard of such a phrase as "dignity of labour", and who seem to expect themselves to be regarded as fully educated and entitled to well-paid employment for which they are inadequately equipped'.[58] The shift in emphasis from lower primary education to middle and post-primary education in the Five Year Plan is partly an indication of growing African demand for a more equitable education system. The changes taking place internationally were also important. Independence of the territory had become a possibility the colonialists could no longer deny. Primary expansion was restricted so that by 1961 only 45 per cent of the primary school age population would be enrolled (compared with 40 per cent in 1957). Middle school places were to be increased by 50 per cent, secondary enrolment (especially Standards XI and XII) expanded and a Higher School Certificate course introduced. However, the Plan was never implemented, ostensibly due to lack of funds.

A committee on integration of the schools was established in 1958, and by 1960 a White Paper on the subject had been presented. The policy of integrated schools was only established, however, after Independence.

By 1959, there was a secondary enrolment of 4 200 and middle school enrolment of 44 700. There were 200 Tanganyikan students at Makerere, and Royal College (Nairobi), by 1960 three secondary schools offered Higher School Certificates, and there were 1 000 students overseas, primarily in university programmes. Whereas the middle school curriculum still retained a somewhat vocational agricultural bias, the secondary and higher school curriculum was bookish and academic. The content was geared towards England, and the majority of post-primary teachers were English, as were principals and Department of Education officials. The Cambridge 'O' and 'A' levels ensured that the system retained its peculiar class and cultural bias. There were also a number of post-primary institutions geared towards occupational training (for example, teaching, medical assistants and nursing).

By the end of the colonial period, the pyramid education structure of today was firmly implanted, and its specific relationship to the hierarchical occupational structure cemented. As Table 7.5 below shows, there was a severe shortage of highly trained Africans to take over the future independent government, a result of deliberate colonial policies discussed above and a reflection of the colonial mode of production.

Table 7.5 MANPOWER IN 1961 BY ETHNIC GROUPS AND CATEGORY

	AFRICANS	ASIANS	EUROPEAN	TOTAL
Category I	598	1 947	1 932	4 447
Category II	3 870	6 418	2 377	12 665
	4 468	8 365	4 309	17 142

Source: Hunter, *Education for a Developing Region*, London, 1963, p. 58

These policies reflected the objective place Africans were allocated in the colonial economy: unskilled and semi-skilled labourers, subordinate government officers and peasant producers, and the petty bourgeois teachers and priests/catechists who trained their fellows to accept and fit productively into the capitalist system created under colonial rule.

One of the first major policies of the newly independent government was to integrate the school system, thus doing away with the racial basis of separate schools for Europeans, Asians and Africans. As noted above, this action was based on a White Paper initiated at the end of the colonial period. In the first Five Year Development Plan (1964–9), expansion of secondary and tertiary levels of education was predictably given top priority as part of the policy of localisation of high and middle level manpower. Despite the recent efforts to expand primary schooling so that all seven-year-old children can enter Standard I, much more money is spent per student at secondary and higher levels of education. Basic classroom facilities, laboratory apparatus and teaching materials, and teachers' qualifications are lowest at primary level, and yet by 1989 it is estimated that only two per cent of the school-age population will benefit from higher levels of education. Occupational opportunities depend upon formal educational attainment, which really means 'success' in the examinations which lead to paper certification. The 'paper qualifications' that are won are the keys to high income and status; more than that, they determine an individual's or group's place in the structure of social relations. The education structure, therefore, contributes to the reproduction of class relations in Tanzanian society. Investigations of the organisation of knowledge (curricula, examinations, etc.), teaching methods and social organisation of school and classroom at all levels and the differential access to and benefits from different levels of the educational structure would confirm the fact that the educational system functions to perpetuate capitalism and control of the economy by the international bourgeoisie. Efforts to alter the educational system in line with the 'Education for Self-Reliance' policy have not modified the basic capitalist and class nature of the educational system which was established under colonial rule.[59] Even though education is not the primary determinant of the mode of production and production relations, a critical analysis of class struggles in education in the past contributes to a better understanding of the state in an underdeveloped society *in process*, and may provide clearer insight into the nature and strategy for the struggle of peasants and workers to take command of the state in the present.

Notes

1 W. Rodney, 'Policing the Countryside in Colonial Tanganyika', paper presented to Annual Social Science Conference of the East African Universities, Dar es Salaam, 1973 (Paper No. 51 – mimeo).

2 Education Department, Tanganyika Territory, *Annual Report, 1924*.

3 I have drawn heavily on lectures given by Jim Breeden in the Department of Education, First Year Foundation of Education course, 1974–5, University of Dar es Salaam, for the framework given above. See J. Breeden, 'The Struggle for Socialist Education in Tanzania', *Papers in Education and Development, No. 1: Policy and Practice in Tanzania Education*, July 1975, Department of Education, University of Dar es Salaam, pp. 23–34.

4 Pledges to maintain the territory as a permanent English fixture were frequently made. For example, Sir Donald Cameron, Governor of Tanganyika, said in 1925 while laying the founda-

tion stone of Tabora School, 'that Tanganyika was definitely and forever embodied in the framework of the British Empire'. (S. Nkonoki, 'A Study of the Philosophy of Education for Self-Reliance and its Implementation in Tanzania Secondary Schools', unpublished draft dissertation, 1972.)

Throughout, the colonial administration actively promoted the economic exploitation of the territory on behalf of metropolitan interests.

5 Taken from a circular from the Chief Secretary to Administrative Officer, 18 May, 1925 and quoted in W. Morris-Hale, *British Administration in Tanganyika from 1920 to 1945*, University of Geneva, Ph.D. Dissertation, 1969, p. 265.

6 See Morris-Hale, 'Indian Education in Tanganyika', *op. cit.*, pp. 162 passim.

7 *Ibid.*, p. 167. Confidential letter from Rivers-Smith to Chief Secretary 24 July 1925. My emphasis.

8 This does not mean that all shared the same class origins. The colonial administrators were all upper-class public school 'old boys'. Missionaries and even mission groups represented different class origins (e.g. Anglican High Church was upper class; German Evangelicals were working-class). Nevertheless, the majority adopted an upper-class style of life, given their objective place in the colonial social structure as the white colonial rulers.

9 D. Wardle, *English Popular Education 1780–1970*, Cambridge, 1970, p. 73.

10 K.J. King, *Pan-Africanism and Education: A Study of Race Philanthropy and Education in the Southern States of America and East Africa*, Oxford, 1971.

11 Bowles (S. Bowles, 'Unequal Education and the Reproduction of the Social Division of Labour,' *Cambridge Policy Research in Education Reprint Series* No. 25, Harvard Center for Education Policy Research, 1971, no. 19, 0. 9), quotes a superintendent of schools in Boston, Massachusetts, who stated in 1908:

'Until very recently, (the schools) have offered equal opportunity for all to receive *one kind* of education but what will make them democratic is to provide opportunity for all to receive such education as will fit them *equally* well for their particular life work.'

12 In 1922, a Reverend Davis planned to start a school to reach Standard X, but the plans were opposed by other missionaries and stopped. In 1935, an American pastor tried to set up a school reaching secondary level of instruction, and he had to relinquish his idea and leave the territory. D.R. Morrison, 'Education and Political Development. The Tanzania Case', This was published by Heinemann in 1977, but page references are to the dissertation.

13 C.J. Hellberg, *Missions on a Colonial Frontier West of Lake Victoria*, Gollerups, Uppsala, 1965.

14 See T. Ranger, 'African Attempts to Control Education in East and Central Africa, 1900–39', *Past and Present*, 32, December 1965, pp. 57–85.

15 Morrison, p. 82.

16 Education Department, *Annual Report*, 1923, Dar es Salaam Government School, p. 5.

17 Education Department, 1923, *Ibid.*, p. 5 (my emphasis)

18 Education Department, *Annual Report*, 1924, p. 28.

19 W. Rodney, 'The Political Economy of Colonial Tanganyika, 1890–1930', ch. 4 in this volume.

20 A.R. Thompson, *The Adaptation of Education to African Society in Tanganyika Under British Rule*, London University Ph.D. Dissertation, 1968.

21 *Ibid.*, p. 95.

22 Morris-Hale, p. 268.

23 *Ibid.*, p. 284.

24 *Ibid.*, p. 284.

25 Thompson, p. 191.

26 *Ibid.*, p. 231.

27 Nkonoki, p. 56.

28 Educational Annual Reports, 215/787, vol. 1, Nyakato, 1947.

29 F. Musgrove, 'A Uganda Secondary School as a Field of Culture Change', *Africa*, xxii, 3, 1952, pp. 234–49.

30 A.R. Thompson, 'Ideas Underlying British Colonial Education

Policy in Tanganyika', in I.N. Resnick, ed., *Tanzania: Revolution by Education*, Arusha, 1968.

31 B.A. Yates, 'African Reactions to Education: The Congolese Case '*Comparative Education Review*, XV, 3, June, 1971, pp. 158–71.

32 Ranger.

33 Thompson, ch. 9.

34 TNA SMP 215/1552, vol. 1, p. 217.

35 TNA SMP 215/1655, vol. 1, letter from Blumer to Senior Agriculture Officer.

36 TNA SMP 215/1552, vol. 1, p. 220.

37 Annual Report 1924, Appendix III, p. 26.

38 Thompson, p. 107.

39 *Ibid.*, p. 257.

40 *Ibid.*, p. 258.

41 *Ibid.*, p. 258.

42 Morris-Hale, pp. 213–4.

43 Thompson, p. 379.

44 TNA SMP, 251/1552, vol. 1, my emphasis.

45 P. Saul, 'Agricultural education in Tanganyika: the Policy, Programmes and Practices, 1925–55', in S. Mbilinyi, ed., *Agricultural Research for Rural Development*, Nairobi, 1973, p. 35.

46 TNA SNS 215/787 vol. 1, p. 787.

47 See Saul.

48 A.V. Murry, *The School in the Bush*, London, 1929, p. 10.

49 Thompson, ch. 14.

50 *Ibid.*, p. 85.

51 J. Cameron and William A. Dodd, *Society, Schools and Progress in Tanzania*, New York 1970, p. 348.

52 *Ibid.*

53 See Saul.

54 TNA SMP 2115/1552, vol. 1, p. 340.

55 For example, in 1939 an education official in Tanganyika referred to the 'present tragic state of the Indian rural comminutes' as the basis for arguing against a fully developed primary and secondary educational system. See letter to King from Mason, 21 April 1939, TNA SMP, 2115/1552, vol. 1, p. 233.

56 S.O. Odede, 'Dialectical Process of Colonial Politico-Administration Penetration, the Case of Tanzania and Kenya', University of Dar es Salaam, Department of Development Studies, n.d. (mimeo).

57 At that time, Tanga Province included Pare, Northern Province included Arusha-Moshi, Lake Province included Bukoba and Mwanza, Southern Highlands included Mufindi and Iringa Districts.

58 Morrison, p. 117.

59 For discussion of the education system in the context of present-day class formation and class struggle, see K.F. Hirji, 'School Education and Underdevelopment in Tanzania', *Maji Maji*, 12, September 1973, pp. 1–22.

8. Wage Labour and Urbanisation

John Iliffe

When people work for others, it is normally because they are under some compulsion.[1] The compulsion may be obvious and violent, as when a slave is held to his task by the whip or a forced labourer is constrained by the law. More subtle forms of political and social exploitation are possible, as when a chief exacts tributary labour from his subjects or a family head commands the labour of his wives and children. And compulsion may be economic, when a man works either because he has no property and will otherwise starve or because he wants certain goods which he can obtain only by working for others.

During the colonial period in Tanganyika there was a general tendency for political and social means of exploiting labour to give way to economic means. The change was by no means total. Some men worked for economic returns before colonial rule, and some still exploited their wives in 1961 as their ancestors had in 1885. But by 1961 economic need had become the normal rather than the exceptional motive among those who worked for others. This is another way of saying that during the colonial period capitalism increasingly penetrated Tanganyika's social relations, for the exploitation of labour by economic means—wage labour, 'the cash nexus'—is the essence of capitalism. The growth of capitalist relations in colonial Tanganyika is the main subject of this chapter. Two subsidiary topics accompany it. One is urbanisation; for going to live in towns was an important way in which some Tanganyikans became dependent on wage labour for their very survival. The other topic is the history of labour organisation; for trade unions, strikes, and the like are the means by which workers protect and advance their interests once they have entered into capitalist relations, so that the penetration of capitalism and the emergence of a labour movement were two aspects of the same process.

The nineteenth-century legacy

At the time of the German invasion Tanganyikans knew four methods of exploiting labour. One was the exploitation of weaker family members—women and the young—by senior men. This was probably very widespread, even among stateless and apparently egalitarian peoples. Senior men had superior strength, possessed the agricultural experience necessary to a society's survival, controlled its legal system and public opinion, and owned whatever scarce and coveted goods the society possessed. As fathers and uncles they monopolised the supply of marriageable women and used them to extort labour and deference from younger men seeking wives. In nineteenth-century Unyakyusa, for example, there were two forms of marriage: a wealthy bridegroom paid bridewealth in cattle and thereby obtained legal control over the resulting children, whereas a poor man obtained a wife by working for her parents who kept the legal rights over any offspring from the marriage. Dr Shorter has described brideservice in Ukimbu:

> The period of uxorilocal residence [i.e. residence at the bride's parents' home] lasts from three to five years . . . . In the homestead the attitude demanded of the son-in-law to his parents-in-law is described as *uxuvatija*, fearing or obeying them. He must perform services for his wife's father, must greet her parents at the doorway of their hut with great respect every morning, and must stand or sit at a distance when addressing them . . . . Eventually he is allowed to move away with his wife to another village.[2]

Antagonism between generations was probably the most widespread and important form of social tension in pre-colonial Tanganyika. It was often institutionalised in age-grade systems.

The second method of exploiting labour was the exaction of tribute by political leaders, which naturally occurred only where state institutions existed. In Buhaya, for example, not only did each clan perform a particular service at the chief's court, but each family had to undertake a certain quantity of labour each year on the chief's fields, while Haya chiefs also maintained their agents and rewarded their favourites by granting them the right to tributary labour from the occupants of areas which became known as *nyarubanja* estates, Tanganyika's closest approximation to feudalism. Merere of Usangu made his conquered Safwa subjects build a great stone fortress at Utengule Usafwa in the 1870s, and tributary labour may have become increasingly common in the nineteenth century as standing armies of musketeers made chiefs more powerful and increased their need for food supplies. But against this must be weighed the increasing prevalence at this time of a third method of exploiting labour: slavery.

The history of slavery—as opposed to the slave trade—in Tanganyika is still almost completely unknown. Until the nineteenth century, it appears, slavery existed among inland peoples only where state institutions were strong, and there it was more a relationship of personal dependence than the ownership of one man by another as property. Shambaa or Kerewe slaves were people without descent groups who had become attached to a chief's court: prisoners of war, men unable to pay fines, or men so uncontrollable that their kinsmen had disowned them and given them to the chief. Such slaves could usually marry, acquire wealth, cultivate their own land, redeem themselves, and gradually be assimilated over the generations into normal society. Slavery was thus an outgrowth of political rather than economic power; it did not exist in the small chiefdoms of Usukuma or Unyakyusa. On the coast, slavery was probably rather different, because slaves were more numerous—in 1977 a visitor guessed that more than half the inhabitants of Kilwa Kisiwani were slaves[3]—and Islamic law and custom probably distinguished slaves more sharply from freemen, but later evidence nevertheless suggests that coastal slaves were followers and dependents of powerful men rather than mere property. During the nineteenth century, however, the position of slaves probably deteriorated. On the coast their numbers increased greatly and a clear distinction grew up between slaves born on the coast, who were regarded as assimilated and civilised, and *watumwa wajinga*— 'ignorant slaves'—newly imported from the interior and good only for the plantation work which became increasingly common after 1873, when slave exports were prohibited and Arabs began to establish plantations whose labour regime was more rigorous than anything Tanganyika had previously seen. Meanwhile, both slavery and coastal notions of slave status became increasingly common inland. Many peoples were net importers of agricultural slaves. Zaramo headmen had gangs working their fields. Gogo exchanged ivory for slaves to cultivate their land, as did the Nyamwezi of Unyanyembe. Ngindo bought slaves from Ulanga, Ha from Manyema, Haya from Buganda, Kerewe from Lake Victoria's eastern shore. In nineteenth-century Ukerewe the redemption of a slave became increasingly rare. With no tradition of slavery and little regard for cultivation, Gogo were said to treat their slaves harshly. For many Tanganyikan peoples, the idea of working in large groups on fields belonging to a man from outside one's own community became closely associated with slavery.

Wage labour was already quite common among certain Tanganyikan peoples at the time of the German invasion, but it was labour of particular types. Only rarely was it labour for other Africans. Caravan porters often cultivated fields for those through whose country they passed, usually in return for food, and various specialists—masons, carpenters, secretaries—found paid employment with chiefs. But most wage labourers were caravan porters employed by Arabs, Swahili, or Europeans, and it was through the caravan trade that capitalism first entered most Tanganyikan societies. Very many caravan porters were Nyamwezi, both on the central route to Tabora and in the north and south, where few local peoples were prepared to carry loads. Some porters were lifetime professionals, but most were occasional migrants. When Richard Burton traversed Tanganyika in 1856–7 he was struck by the youth of his porters. Many of them were probably earning bridewealth, although Nyamwezi later recalled that on a porter's return his father often took the cloth he had earned and distributed it among the family[4]. It is difficult to gauge the total numbers of porters, but they were probably very large. A missionary reckoned that 15–20 000 Nyamwezi visited the coast annually in the 1880s.[5] Other observers guessed that more than 100 000 Africans travelled the central caravan route each year around 1890.[6] Often, it was said, Bagamoyo contained 30–40 000 porters.[7] If correct, these figures suggest labour migration as widespread as in the colonial period. Wages were also comparable. Unskilled labourers in Tanga in the late 1880s earned about thirteen shillings a month.[8] Thirty years later they would earn roughly the same, and only a few shillings more in 1935.

Junior family members, subjects rendering tribute, slaves, and migrant porters made up Tanganyika's labour force on the eve of

German invasion. Scarcely any had been driven to work by plain economic need. They were the subjects either of social compulsion in the case of women, political compulsion in the case of slaves and subjects, or the desire for scarce goods in the case of aspiring bridegrooms and caravan porters. Given Tanganyika's sparse population and ample land, more than purely economic pressures were needed to make men work for others. That was the dilemma which, together with the existing pattern of labour, was passed on to the first German colonists.

The creation and character of the colonial labour system

As the Germans gained control of Tanganyika after 1885 they gradually reorganised its economy to Germany's advantage. Slave exports, already rare, were banned entirely. Slavery itself was treated more cautiously. Slaves were allowed to buy their freedom and officials had power to free any who were maltreated. Between 1891 and 1912 the Germans issued 52 313 certificates of freedom.[9] They also declared that all children born after 31 December 1905 were automatically free, but there were still several thousand slaves in Tanganyika when the institution was finally abolished after the First World War. The Germans also replaced the caravan trade by a cheaper and less wasteful form of transport: the railways which they built along the northern and central caravan routes. In 1900 some 35 000 porters arrived at Bagamoyo and 43 880 left the town for the interior, according to official figures, but in 1912 – when the central railway reached Tabora – only 851 arrived and 193 departed.[10] Yet porterage still flourished on the southern route, where there was no railway, and human labour remained the chief means of local transport throughout the country until motor vehicles became common in the 1920s, so that the amount of labour freed for other purposes in German times was probably small.

The Germans' main economic activity was to establish European-owned coffee, rubber, and sisal plantations, chiefly along the valley of the River Pangani in the north-east of the country. Together with the towns, the construction industry, and a small plantation area around Kilosa and Morogoro, the estates of the north-east were Tanganyika's chief market for wage labour until independence. In 1906 plantations employed an estimated 20 000 men; in 1912, 91 892. In 1913 the total number of people in paid employment of all kinds was 172 100.[11] The First World War replaced this demand by a massive conscription of porters and labourers, of whom something approaching a million were recruited from all parts of eastern Africa.[12] During the 1920s the British reconstructed the plantation industry and a new demand for labour came from emerging African cash-crop farmers. In 1937 some 244 000 Africans were in wage employment, excluding those working for other Africans.[13]

In German times a proportion of workers were men who lived close to employment centres. The plantations of the Pangani valley were deliberately interspersed with African 'native reserves' in order to ensure a labour supply. When tax was introduced in 1897 it was designed to have the 'educative' function of compelling Africans to work for Europeans. Yet neither of these measures succeeded in making local people work for Europeans because the plantations also needed food, so that local people could earn their tax by growing food on their own land and selling it to the planters. In the 1890s some Bondei people of the Pangani valley did work on the plantations, but after the turn of the century they concentrated instead on growing food and even employed migrant labourers to help them. Of the 14 000 plantation workers in Tanga district in 1910, only 1 200 were local men.[14] To meet this problem, the Germans used more openly political methods of compulsion. One system originated in West Usambara, where the mountain climate both deterred migrant labourers and made the Shambaa easy to exploit because they feared to leave their homes. Moreover, the mixed farms which the Germans established in West Usambara grew their own food and so offered no market for African produce. In the late 1890s each settler entering West Usambara was allocated villages whose headmen had to provide a daily quota of workers. This led to such abuses that the governor banned the system in 1904, with the result that 'not a worker can now be found'.[15] In 1907 the district officer began to issue each Shambaa with a card obliging him to work for a European for thirty days every four months, at a fixed wage, on pain of otherwise being conscripted for public works. As a result wages were much lower in Usambara than in Tanga and local workers outnumbered migrants, but the system did spread the burden relatively evenly and enable workers to choose their employers. These advantages led officials to introduce card systems elsewhere. Moshi district adopted one in 1912. 'Our people can no longer be regarded as free cultivators,' a missionary wrote of the Chagga. 'They are all apportioned among the farmers and in some way dependent on them. If one walks through the fields, one meets mainly old people, women, and girls. The men and boys are away on the farms and at best come home on Sundays'.[16] In 1914 government acknowledged that compulsory labour existed in Lushoto, Dar es Salaam, Rufiji, Morogoro, and Lindi districts. It was probably becoming more rather than less common as European enterprises multiplied. But it had critics. In 1914 the Reichstag insisted that Dar es Salaam's district officer must be transferred for organising an unauthorised card system.

Thus the Germans could obtain local labour only by exercising political power. The same was true of African employers. Among the Chagga, it was said, 'people . . . work for fellow-tribesmen only reluctantly'[17] and only political leaders who controlled tribute had access to a regular labour supply. The same was true in Buhaya, where it was common knowledge that the only way to obtain workers was to pay a chief for them. In 1907 Chief Mutahangarwa of Kiziba joined a partnership with two Europeans to open a plantation. 'Bwana H. Rehse and Bwana Weber will each contribute £1,500,' he explained. 'I myself shall not contribute anything because I shall supply workers until the plantation is ready'.[18] Only in the 1920s did there emerge African capitalists employing workers by purely economic means. Two reasons for this were the British Government's refusal to coerce workers for private employers and its decision to replace tributary labour for chiefs by higher taxes. Another reason was a great expansion of African cash-crop farming in the 1920s in response to high world prices and the introduction of motor transport. The old political and social compulsions began to give way to economic pressures. 'Important men are no longer prepared to give anything to help the weak as they once were,' a Chagga teacher complained, 'for they see that among the weak every man relies on his employer, be he white or black.'[19] In 1924 the Haya were said to employ at least 20 000 workers, mainly to lay out coffee plantations, pick the crop, and carry it to buying centres.[20] Some 45 per cent of Nyiha coffee growers were said to employ seasonal hired labour in 1944.[21] Social anthropologists working in Unyakyusa in the 1930s noticed that chiefs and rice growers were just beginning to employ poor young men for wages.[22]

Yet from the beginning both European and African planters relied less on local workers than on migrant labourers. Migration was the essence of the colonial labour system in Tanganyika, as in most areas of Africa. There were several reasons for it. European plantations were concentrated so heavily in the north-east that local people could not possibly supply their labour needs, especially after a succession of epidemics and famines in the 1890s which may have halved the region's population. Whereas people in the plantation districts could earn cash by selling food, those who lived on the peripheries of the colony were often too remote from transport to market crops, so that they had to sell their labour in order to earn the tax which in the early days was the essential reason for seeking employment. Moreover, caravan porterage had made migratory labour familiar, and it had important advantages for both workers and employers. Migration enabled workers to escape proletarianisation by committing themselves to wage labour only briefly while retaining their property rights and family ties in their home areas, for at this time the number wanting to become lifetime employees was probably small. At the same time planters found migrants relatively easy to exploit and control because they lacked experience and solidarity, while employers did not have to bear the costs of migrants' families, who normally remained at home, and could easily increase or reduce their labour forces by hiring or laying-off these short-term workers as economic circumstances dictated. The disadvantages of the system were its wastefulness and inefficiency, the misery of long journeys to work, the effects on many labour-exporting regions, and the fact that so little positive social progress resulted from so much exhausting labour. Yet the migration system was not simply a European conspiracy to prevent the emergence of a labour movement. It was a logical corollary to the whole structure of the colonial economy.

There were three phases of labour migration in German times. During the 1890s most migrants were Nyamwezi or related peoples from western Tanganyika who thus passed on to the colonial economy the labour patterns of the caravan trade. Between 1900 and roughly 1908 these peoples still predominated but tax and other pressures began to compel other peoples into regular migration, especially from the south. After 1908 migration expanded very rapidly, notably through the building of the central railway, which not only required large numbers of unskilled workers from the areas through which it passed—it was this, for example, that first drew the Ha into wage-labour around 1912—but also enabled the labour recruiter, tax-collector, and Asian shopkeeper to penetrate more deeply into the countryside. By 1914 the only peoples still untouched by labour migration were pastoralists, agriculturalists unusually wealthy in cattle (for example Gogo and Iraqw), peoples with access to marketable forest produce (for example Ngindo rubber-collectors), cash-crop producers, those still largely untaxed (for example Nyakyusa), and those living close to German estates. Moreover, Tanganyika was already part of a migration network which came to cover the whole of southern and eastern Africa. By 1908 Nyamwezi were working in South African gold mines, while men were recruited from Mozambique to help build the northern railway. After the First World War these trends continued, with the more remote peoples—Ha, Rundi, Bena, Bemba, Nyakyusa, Makonde—increasingly supplanting the Nyamwezi as the core of the labour force, a pattern which survived until the end of colonial rule.

Since it was only those with access to alternative sources of cash who did not need to migrate, it is clear that the need for cash – for tax, bridewealth, schoolfees, imported goods – was the essential stimulus to migration. When other cash sources became available men abandoned migration, as did Sukuma cotton growers, Ndendeuli tobacco producers and Matengo coffee planters. Among unskilled men it was the poor who left their homes. 'All . . . Nyamwezi who live on the coast as workers . . . belong to the lowest classes,' a German observer stated,[23] and investigations in Songea and Tukuyu in the 1950s showed a direct correlation between poverty and frequency of migration. To have worked at a distance carried little prestige; that came from not having to migrate. Most migrants were young men without family responsibilities who needed capital to set up homesteads. They often travelled to work in parties under a leader who had made the journey before. Most walked, often for several hundred miles, along routes which became as familiar as the caravan trails, but this was so exhausting for those without money to buy food on the way that some traded their freedom to choose their own place of employment for a labour recruiter's ticket to a lorry or the closed goods or cattle wagons in which the Ha travelled their hated 'middle passage' to the coast.[24] Either way they became *manamba*, 'numbers', as migrants were known throughout the colonial period.

Studies of labour migration in many parts of Africa have shown that its effects on labour-exporting societies varied according to their socio-economic systems and the character of the migration in different areas. This was certainly the case in Tanganyika. The withdrawal of labour from Unyamwezi and its environs in the late nineteenth and early twentieth centuries was probably a reason for the massive loss of formerly cultivated land to tsetse-infested bush which occurred at that time. In the twentieth century the areas which suffered most from migration were probably the remote, quasi-feudal highland regions of the north-west—notably Buha and Bugufi—where the absence of many men made the cultivators' tenure even less secure, impeded the introduction of permanent crops like coffee, and provided income which landlords could extort without needing to encourage commercial agriculture. By contrast, many parts of Central Province suffered little by exporting migrants to Moshi and Arusha for the four or five months of the dry season, while fertile and densely-peopled Unyakyusa could supply many young men without damaging its agriculture. In the 1950s Professor Gulliver concluded that migration was harmful to the Ngoni but on balance profitable to the Nyakyusa.[25] Tanganyika's rural innovators—pioneers of new crops, of Islam, or of voluntary associations—were often former migrants.

This highlights the most important point about labour in Tanganyika before the Second World War. Only rarely did men work for others as a result of economic compulsion. Some worked as a result of political compulsion through tax, others in order to acquire coveted goods. Given Tanganyika's vast resources of land and the paucity of European enterprise, scarcely any Tanganyikan was a true proletarian compelled to labour for others or starve. Migratory labour was the system of a country still in transition towards capitalism.

Urbanisation and the emergence of a labour movement

As capitalism penetrated Tanganyika's social relations it was accompanied by the gradual emergence of a specifically capitalist pattern of labour relations: that is, free and organised workers in conflict with their employers for the proceeds of capitalist production. During the colonial period this pattern gradually replaced the more paternalistic relationships of earlier periods, where antagonism between master and servant was to some degree masked by social and political ties between them. The transition to capitalist relations was obviously a consequence of Tanganyika's general economic transformation, but it was more specifically a result of urbanisation and of the crisis which the country experienced during the economic depression of the 1930s and the Second World War, although the labour movement which grew up at that time was to be checked after the war by government action.

Just as nineteenth-century slavery preserved elements of personal protection and dependence, so labour relations in the caravan trade retained strong elements of paternalism. Custom and practice determined the length of marches, the weight of loads, the bonuses for extra duties, the relationships between different grades of personnel. The employer appointed the *virangozi* (guides and leaders) and they were the normal spokesmen for the workers, but when these spokesmen were ineffective the porters quite frequently struck, ensuring that their actions were collective and ostensibly leaderless in order to prevent victimisation. This distinction between appointed spokesmen and anonymous collective action is common in the early stages of labour organisation, indicating a solidarity which was instinctive but fragile, so that men avoided the risks of leadership unless selected by the employer. This pattern of action was carried forward to the early colonial plantations.

A great sisal plantation was a social unit as well as an economic enterprise.[26] A few—notably Amboni, near Tanga—were 'model' estates with their own schools, mosques, churches, hospitals, and welfare centres. Others were notorious for their squalid rows of hovels, their high rates of disease and death, their attempts to defraud workers of their wages, and, in German times, their sadistic use of whipping. But most estates were more casually organised, with workers' huts and fields scattered in tribal clusters and only a factory and office acting as a central focus. Among the workers the highest status was held by clerks, dressers, schoolteachers, and the like. The most influential manual workers were headmen, overseers, and factory workers who often spent their lives on one estate. The heavy and painful task of cutting was done by long-distance migrants who boasted their toughness, while the lighter, low-paid cultivation was left to local casual workers and women and children. The cutters were the key element in the whole operation. The size of their daily 'task' largely determined the estate's output and profitability. Their wages were the guideline for semi-skilled and unskilled wages throughout the territory. Consequently, cutters were responsible for most of the very widespread unrest on sisal estates in the early colonial period.

Six main forms of labour action can be identified on estates at this time. The least sophisticated was intertribal fighting, invariably involving migrants and sometimes escalating into a labour dispute, as at Kidifu in 1938 when Makonde workers beat up a non-Makonde headman who refused to sign their wives' *vipande* to show that they had completed their tasks. More common was 'desertion', a criminal offence under colonial law. Normally individuals deserted, but occasionally an altered task or brutal overseer dispersed a labour force overnight. Most common of all was the day-to-day protest by slacking or small-scale sabotage which characterises every large capitalist enterprise. Workers quickly learned to defend the strict terms of their contracts, and in British times they often called in government labour officers to weigh rations, measure tasks, or check wage records. But by then the most common response to an employer's breach of contract was to down tools. No true plantation strike is recorded from German times, which probably indicates how colonial power and plantation discipline made the workers' position weaker than it had been in the caravan trade. By the later 1930s, however, strikes and stoppages were very common. There were twenty-two in Tanga Province in the second quarter of 1937 and thirty-two in the first nine months of 1938.[27] With one exception these actions were of the anonymous, ostensibly leaderless type designed to prevent victimisation, the most common pattern being for cutters to demonstrate outside the estate office, brandishing *pangas* and shouting for their rights.

Apart from accumulated experience, the main reason for the militancy of the later 1930s was a sharp decline in real earnings. It is very difficult now to calculate changes in real wages during the early colonial period, largely because it is so hard to make the necessary allowances for changes in the cost of living. Broadly speaking, however, it appears that real plantation wages fell slightly during German rule, declined sharply after the First World War, rose again in the 1920s, probably at least maintained themselves in the early 1930s when the international depression cut prices even more than wages, but then fell very seriously in the later 1930s and during the Second World War.[28] Measured in terms of real wages, the fifteen years of crisis between 1932 and 1947 were almost certainly the worst that Tanganyikan workers have experienced, chiefly because prices rose rapidly while wages were held down to depression levels by non-economic means: first by combination among employers—the Tanganyika Sisal Growers' Association was formed in 1930, partly to fix wages—and then by wartime government policy which for the first time permitted the conscription of workers for the plantations.

Protest against wage-fixing appeared in the rash of sisal strikes in the late 1930s and especially in the most important of them, which took place at Amboni in August 1939. With its 'model' conditions, Amboni had the most stable, and therefore possibly the most conscious and organised, estate labour force. It was also close to Tanga, whose dockworkers incited the strike in order to win support for their own industrial action. Urged on by emissaries from the port, the cutters stopped work, attacked and halted Amboni's factory, and set out for Tanga, demanding a wage of thirty shillings for thirty tasks, 'the old rate of pay before the depression in the sisal industry'.[29] They eventually returned to work with nothing gained, but the strike demonstrated a higher level of consciousness than any earlier plantation protest, both in its collective memory of conditions in the 1920s and especially in its connections with urban protest.

Pre-colonial towns had existed on the coast and at such royal capitals as Merere's. European conquest led to the abandonment of the capitals and the decline of many coastal ports, but two—Tanga and Dar es Salaam—flourished as administrative centres and outlets for railway traffic, while further inland small townships—Mwanza, Arusha, Dodoma, Mbeya, and the like—grew up at the focal points of colonial government and communications. Urbanisation remained very limited throughout the colonial period: in 1952 only 2.75 per cent of Tanganyikans lived in the thirty-three gazetted townships.[30] It was naturally, however, in the expanding colonial towns, especially the capital, that urban workers were concentrated and labour organisation emerged.

Because Tanganyika had a colonial economy, the history of its labour movement differed from that normal in an industrialised country. In Britain, for example, labour organisation began in skilled trades and led through factory workers and transport industries to the service sector and finally to white-collar workers and civil servants. In Tanganyika the sequence was almost exactly the reverse, beginning in the 1920s with civil servants and moving through service and transport sectors to reach industrial workers only in the 1950s.[31] Many of the difficulties faced by Tanganyika's first trade unions were due to their operating in occupations like domestic service and motor transport which were peculiarly difficult to organise, while others resulted from the fact that so many workers were short-term migrants. Nevertheless, over a period of thirty years small organisations of workers were created in several industries. With the protection which these provided, leaders gradually emerged in the place of management-appointed headmen and ostensibly leaderless demonstrations. This was a crucial advance in labour organisation, and it went together with growing communication among organised groups in different industries. The chief interest of labour history in Tanganyika is that one can see how workers gradually felt their way towards these advances in organisation and consciousness.

The country's first organisation of African workers was the Tanganyika Territory African Civil Services Association, founded in Tanga in March 1922 in imitation of similar societies existing among European and Asian civil servants. In Tanga TTACSA became chiefly a social club for educated men, but a similar association formed in Dar es Salaam was active between 1925 and 1927 in championing the interests of African clerks, ending with a carefully-documented petition to the Colonial Office which brought a curt rejection. When the quasi-political African Association was formed in 1929 most TTACSA members joined it and the older association withered. It was revived in 1944 under the name of the Tanganyika African Government Servants Association. Like other labour organisations of that period, TAGSA was a reaction to wartime economic pressures, notably the failure of civil service wages to keep pace with inflation. By October 1944 TAGSA claimed 1 820 members in Tanga, Mwanza, Arusha, and Dar es Salaam. By utilising the government's communications network, another twenty-three branches were formed at district centres during the next year.[32]

Less is known of two other organisations of public employees. An African Teachers' Association was formed in 1944, claiming 210 members in thirty-five branches by the end of the year.[33] More important was the Railway African Association. An organisation of African railway workers may have existed as early as 1929, but effective action began during the war when a series of stoppages in protest against inflation led the railway administration to encourage the formation of a staff association. By 1945 the Railway African Association was Tanganyika's most powerful workers' organisation, with some 2 000 members under a Kenyan president named George Ogilo.[34] It was very loosely organised, with much trouble over money and a tendency for the senior African at each station to treat his branch as a private empire, but railway workers drew strength from their relatively high levels of skill and permanency and from their excellent communications system.

Tanganyika's first trade unions—as opposed to staff associations—were formed by Asians in response to a Trade Union Ordinance which a Labour Colonial Secretary forced the territorial government to issue in 1932. The Union of Shop Assistants of Tanganyika was registered in 1933 and lapsed in 1940. The Asiatic Labour Union, composed of Sikh carpenters, was formed in 1937 and organised Dar es Salaam's first serious strike in that year before disappearing. The earliest African trade union took shape during the war among domestic servants. The *Chama cha Wapishi na Maboi* was created in Dodoma in August 1939, probably at the initiative of the lively local branch of the African Association. Two years later a similar body came into being in Dar es Salaam, where domestic servants were the most numerous category of workers. Their rules, drafted in January 1944, showed their desire for solidarity. 'Members should not cheapen themselves as regards wages paid to them by their employers,' they decreed; 'Each man must remember what befalls another will react on him'.[35] As their leader they enlisted Saleh bin Fundi, who had almost certainly led a widely-popular and highly-desciplined dance society known as the Arinoti. During 1945 he held several public meetings to inculate solidarity:

> 'If [the government] . . . lock up all committee members next time they call us and tell us that we are teaching you wrongful ways, what are you going to do?'
>
> 'If that happens we shall refuse to work.'
>
> 'No', said Salehe, 'if you do not know, I will tell you.'
>
> 'In such a case, all of you, boys employed by Europeans as well as those employed by Indians, should go to the Chief Secretary and ask to be locked up'.[36]

By deliberately assuming the risks of leadership, Saleh bin Fundi was Tanganyika's first real African labour organiser. Recognising that a permanent organisation was his best protection against victimisation, he was already creating one of territorial scope. It was registered with government in August 1945 and at one time or another had at least twelve branches, but so large an organisation in so unstructured an occupation proved unviable and in June 1949 it was deregistered for persistently refusing to obey the Registrar of Trade Unions. Shortly afterwards government also deregistered the Amalgamated African Motor Drivers and Commercial Road Transport Workers' Union. Societies of African lorry drivers existed in Moshi as early as 1927 and in Dar es Salaam in 1940, but the union was created in 1944 by drivers working for the railways administration in the southern highlands. Apparently they had learned of the idea while serving in the army. The difficulty of organising so scattered and individualistic a labour force again proved their undoing.

Thus during and immediately after the Second World War a number of small organisations were created among workers in clerical and service occupations. They were clearly reactions to the declining real wages of the period. They were also responses to the enormous influx into the towns during the war. Dar es Salaam's population, for example, increased between 1939 and 1948 from 25 000 to 69 227.[27] Not only did this undermine living conditions—the number of houses in the capital actually fell slightly during the war—but it threatened the jobs of those Africans who were employed. It is striking that much wartime trade unionism took place in occupations like motor transport and domestic service where the levels of skill required were relatively low—the army alone trained over 6 000 drivers.[38] Such unions were largely concerned with job protection and often tried to assert a right to control entry into their trades. The drivers' union, for example, urged that employers must recruit drivers only through the association, while a branch of the domestic servants' union demanded that non-members 'may be made to cease to work'.[39]

All these pressures acted also on the most important work groups of the period: the dockworkers of Tanga and Dar es Salaam. Those of Tanga were the earlier to mount industrial action. In 1937 they struck for two days. Two years later another strike developed into a serious riot, but subsequent enquiry found 'no directing brain: indeed impartial observers could not pick out ringleaders',[40] for these actions retained the anonymity of sisal estate protests. By contrast, it was in the port of Dar es Salaam that more sophisticated patterns of labour action developed. Between 1939 and 1947 the capital's dockworkers mounted three major strikes, each more extensive than its predecessor. The first involved only a section of the dock labour force. The second brought out almost every African in the port. The third developed into a general strike embracing large areas of Tanganyika, and in its wake the dockworkers created the territory's first powerful trade union. The sequence is a classic example of the growth of consciousness among workers.[41]

Dar es Salaam was a small port where the work available varied greatly with the arrival of ships. Employers therefore paid a few skilled men a regular wage but hired most workers on daily terms when needed, giving preference to picked men who formed a 'pool' of registered casual workers. The dockworkers' first strike, in July 1939, was confined to casual workers. Its demand—as in the almost contemporary strikes at Tanga and Amboni—was for a return to the daily wage paid before the depression of 1929. No identifiable leaders emerged. Solidarity was very slender, some men returning to work on the second day. Moreover, since only casual workers struck, the employers could break the strike by threatening to recruit other unskilled workers. The strikers eventually returned with virtually nothing gained.

The next strike, in August 1943, showed a higher level of consciousness. Wartime inflation had hurt all workers but especially the permanent employees, who this time joined the strike and probably led it. The only workers who did not participate were headmen, who at government's request acted as intermediaries and even signed the letter stating the strikers' demands—an indication that the line between workers and management was not yet entirely clear. After the stoppage had lasted ten days, wartime necessity caused the government to break the strike by declaring it illegal and arresting 142 permanent employees. Although permanent workers gained small wage increases, the most important result of the strike was that in the absence of a trade union the workers who had been conspicuous as strike leaders became highly vulnerable. Several were dismissed.

The third strike in the sequence, in 1947, both showed a further advance in the dockworkers' consciousness and also drew all the other groups of newly-organised workers into Tanganyika's most widespread and militant protest since the Maji Maji rebellion. The immediate causes were continued inflation, shortages, and urban squalor at a time when everyone had hoped that the end of the war would bring relief. The dockworkers struck first, on 6 September, even the headmen joining. Other casual workers joined, partly as a result of intimidation, and on 10 September the railway workers came out and passed the strike along their communications network. Morogoro, Dodoma, and Tabora struck on 11 September, Kigoma and Mwanza on 15 September, the railway employees spreading the movement to other urban workers and to neighbouring plantations. The final stoppage took place at the Uruwira lead mines in Mpanda on 6 October, exactly a month after the strike began. In the meantime other workers had returned after government had appointed a tribunal of enquiry. This awarded dockworkers forty to fifty per cent wage increases. Other industries gradually followed suit until urban real wages began to outpace inflation for the first time since the early 1930s.

It is indicative of the low level of labour consciousness at this time that the general strike did not lead to any attempt to create a general union, such as was simultaneously being planned in Kenya. Instead, the Dar es Salaam dockworkers, who had been the spearhead of the strike, were those who gained from it a permanent organisation. Warned by victimisation in 1943, the informal committee which led the strike of 1947 transformed itself into the nucleus of a trade union which was registered in January 1948. Its original leaders were mostly illiterate headmen, but during 1948 they hired an educated, full-time general secretary to handle the business of an organisation which by late 1949 had 2 259 members. Together with government it worked out a scheme which effectively restricted dock work to union members, whose wages were now substantially above the territorial average. By 1950 the union possessed £3 250, partly invested in a half-completed clubhouse which was designed to be the first two-storey building owned by Africans in Dar es Salaam.

This achievement collapsed in February 1950 in a further dock strike which developed into the worst riot Dar es Salaam saw before Independence, two men being killed, several seriously injured, and at least eighty-seven convicted of criminal offences. What exactly lay behind these events is still unclear. The union was widely considered authoritarian and corrupt. It was increasingly angry that its system of job protection was being used by government as a means of weeding out irregular workers. On the other side, government's response to the strike—the port was immediately guarded by steel-helmeted police and the employers were permitted to hire black–

legs—supports the widespread belief that the authorities suspected the union of falling under left-wing influence. Be that as it may, the events of February 1950 destroyed the dockworkers' slowly-accumulated solidarity, for many feared to resume their jobs in the port, and also destroyed the union, which was dissolved by court order in June 1950. With it ended the whole phase of labour history which had begun in the nineteenth-century caravans and culminated in the general strike of 1947.

The breakdown of the colonial labour system

The last fifteen years of colonial rule saw a very rapid penetration of capitalist values and relations into many areas of Tanganyikan life as a result of a general increase in prosperity, a substantial growth in production for the market, and deliberate government policy to prepare the territory to govern itself along lines acceptable to the British. Although superficially paradoxical, it was really in the nature of the situation that colonial values and institutions should be accepted most fully by Tanganyikans at the moment when colonial rule was collapsing. Similarly, it was in the nature of the situation that the growth of an effective trade union movement in the 1950s was both a cause and a consequence of the replacement of paternalism and migrant labour by more purely capitalist relations and the nucleus of a true proletariat. By 1961 economic reasons chiefly explained why Tanganyikans worked for others.

After 1947 Tanganyika experienced several years of unprecedented prosperity. The chief reason was an enormous increase in the world prices of primary products owing to economic recovery in the industrial nations and political crises such as the Korean War. One result was a rapid expansion of export production. Between 1945 and 1961 sisal output doubled, the production of coffee on Kilimanjaro multiplied three times, and the Sukuma cotton crop increased five-fold. This expansion helped to increase government expenditure between 1949 and 1956 from £8 700 000 to £22 600 000 a year,[42] although part of the increase also came from British economic aid. Much of the money was spent on better roads, which in turn extended commercial agriculture still further.

Postwar prosperity led to an increase in wage labour. One area of growth was probably the employment of hired labour by African capitalist farmers, although there are no figures by which to measure the expansion. African farmers had hired labour in this way since the 1920s in such prosperous cash-crop areas as Buhaya and Kilimanjaro. After 1945 the demand for hired labour declined in these regions because local population growth and land shortage provided enough family labour to work the farms. In 1964, for example, only six per cent of agricultural labour in Buhaya was hired.[43] By contrast, there was a very large demand for wage labour in new cash-crop areas pioneered after 1945, notably the grain farms of Ismani, Mbulu, and Arusha, the cashew nut plantations of the south, the tobacco farms of Urambo, and the cotton-growing areas of Geita, Maswa, and Shinyanga. The pattern appeared clearly in an analysis of the economics of cotton-farming in the Lake Region during 1963. Whereas in densely-populated Ukerewe district the average cotton farmer could rely on family labour and spent only shs. 9 on wages, the figure was shs. 32 in less crowded but still intensively-cultivated Kwimba district, while in Shinyanga district, an area of recent pioneering and large farms, average expenditure on wages rose to shs.110.[44] In these pioneer regions most workers were migrants. Makonde cashew nut growers, for example, employed fellow Makonde immigrants from Mozambique. In the more densely populated districts, by contrast, workers were the poorer members of the local community, but studies of these regions agree in stressing that class antagonism was rare, partly because almost everyone still possessed at least some land, partly because capitalist values and aspirations were so pervasive in areas like Kilimanjaro and Rungwe, and partly because ties of kinship, neighbourhood, and patronage cut across nascent class divisions.[45] No Tanganyikan rural society was to any marked degree polarised on class lines before Independence.[46]

For a decade after the end of the war the sisal estates were able to expand production rapidly without significantly altering their structure. Planters reckoned that to produce a ton of fibre required the labour of one man for one year. An increase in exports between 1946 and 1960 from 111 521 to 207 225 tons therefore indicates the scale of expansion in the sisal labour force.[47] When conscription ended in 1944 employers for the first time formed an effective recruiting agency, the Sisal Labour Bureau (Silabu), which during the next ten years generally satisfied the demand for labour and acquired almost a territorial monopoly of recruiting. Sisal wages were raised in 1951 and 1954 to keep them broadly in line with inflation, but unlike urban wages they probably still remained lower in real terms than those paid in the 1890s or late 1920s. During the war certain traditional sources of migrant labour were lost to the expanding industries of southern Africa. The Nyakyusa, in particular, abandoned the sisal estates for the higher wages of the Rand and the Copperbelt, the latter paying underground miners shs. 110–133 a month in 1954, compared with the shs. 39 plus food earned by sisal cutters.[48] In that year—probably the peak of southward migration—there were thought to be 7 400 Tanganyikans working in Northern Rhodesia, 3 150 in Southern Rhodesia, and 10 080 on the Rand[49]. The sisal estates, in their turn, relied increasingly on migrants from remote regions. In 1956 12 per cent of workers in the Korogwe area were from Rwanda or Burundi, 11 per cent from Mozambique, and seven per cent from Nyasaland or Northern Rhodesia.[50] Among Tanganyikans the most numerous group were still the Ha. 'Bring WAHA BACHELORS', a planter instructed Silabu in 1954, '... they can live four or five in a house.[51] Two years earlier government had promised employers not to 'press' inhabitants of labour reservoirs to grow cash crops, and the local provincial commissioner had declared bluntly that Buha's function in the territorial economy was to supply labour.[52] The old order still ruled.

Compared with the very large numbers working in the sisal industry, employment in manufacturing remained small: only 75 000 men in 1958, and more than half of those were in agricultural processing.[53] Yet in structural terms the non-agricultural sector was the most important area of postwar economic change. Although Tanganyika did not experience Kenya's or Uganda's postwar industrial development, a small manufacturing enclave grew up along the Pugu Road in Dar es Salaam. Several early factories supplied furniture or materials for the postwar construction boom consequent on rapid urbanisation. Others serviced motor vehicles or machinery for the Groundnut Scheme, while others again were processing industries: important flour-millers like Chande Brothers (1946), a subsidiary of the Metal Box Company (1947), the local licensee for Coca Cola (1950), together with a brewery, cigarette factory, and the like. In 1956 deep-water berths were opened at Dar es Salaam and the port became a modern industry. These enterprises were important not because of their scale but because their technology, organisation, and labour patterns were vastly more sophisticated than the crude, old-style methods of the sisal estates or the wartime port industry. Not only did they need permanent, moderately skilled, and relatively high-paid workers, but it was through these new enterprises, together with the Groundnut Scheme and to a lesser extent the government, that the labour relations machinery of modern 'welfare capitalism' entered Tanganyika.

As an enthusiast later described it, the new style of industrial relations was 'the opposite of the gospel of Karl Marx'.[54] It stressed ordered negotiation through pyramids of works committees, staff associations, and joint industrial councils, with trade unions confined to small groups of craftsmen. The object was precisely to prevent the formation of large, ill-organised, unpredictable, and dangerous unions like the Dockworkers' and Stevedores' Union, and when that was proscribed in 1950 a frightened government seized the opportunity to move against trade unionism generally, so that by the end of 1951 there was only one union, with 372 members, in the whole of Tanganyika.[55] Policy at that time was clear:

> The majority of workers cannot be considered as permanent members of a wage earning class and show little apparent interest in trade unionism: past experience also indicates that any union which is formed tends inevitably to collapse because of lack of administrative ability and integrity. In fact, the experience of the post-war years shows that the evolution of a responsible trade union movement must inevitably be a slow process and that the structure of industrial relations based on the principle of joint consultation will require to be built up in well defined stages. It is believed that in the existing circumstances a start can only be made at the lowest (e.g. workshop) level . . . . Present policy is directed therefore to the encouragement of the formation in individual concerns of a simple form of joint consultative machinery . . . . It is thought possible that the existence of joint consultative machinery and the experience which it will provide for Africans may assist in the development of a more mature attitude on their part towards industrial negotiations.[56]

It was against this background of maddening paternalism that a new unionism was pioneered during the 1950s, at first chiefly by clerks working in Dar es Salaam's private commercial firms who in 1951 founded an African Commercial Employees' Association, possibly modelled on an existing Asian organisation.[57] The most active pioneers, notably M.M. Kamaliza, M.M. Mpangala, and a Kenyan, Domie Okochi, had close ties with TAA and TANU, whose headquarters they used as their base until 1955. Their object was to found a Tanganyika African Trade Union Congress on the lines of an organisation then fighting to survive in Kenya. Government obstructed their plans, while the tiny groups of organised workers scattered throughout the territory proved keen but difficult to coordinate when approached in April 1955. The breakthrough came two months later when Tom Mboya, the Kenyan trade unionist, visited Tanganyika on behalf of the International Confederation of Free Trade Unions and organised a seminar to which he invited leaders of the ACEA, TAGSA, the Railway African Union (a recent reconstitution of the old Railway African Association), and a staff association representing African clerks in the Dar es Salaam port. Mboya defined the problem with characteristic clarity:

> The Civil Servants Association . . . was the only union which was then national in character . . . . [The others] had in almost all cases tried to build from the bottom upwards, and each one was trying to form a little union, in some cases merely a group of workers in one factory or shop struggling to create a union . . . .
>
> The British concept, that a trade union should develop from the bottom and that experience should be gained by a man as he moves up the ladder, is impossible to adopt in Africa. The whole emphasis has to be given from the top.[58]

This analysis set the tone for the movement. The leaders present at Mboya's seminar decided to create a central organisation, the Tanganyika Federation of Labour, which was formed on 7 October 1955 with Rashidi Kawawa of TAGSA as general secretary. The TFL was designed as a general union to which all workers would belong as individual members, but government rejected this plan and the leaders eventually compromised by making the TFL a loose federation of industrial unions on the British model. Fearing repression, and because civil servants were prohibited from joining political parties, the TFL did not formally affiliate with TANU but encouraged trade unionists to exercise their political rights 'while preserving the independence of the labour movement from political control'.[59] The issue of subordination to TANU policy was to divide TFL leaders bitterly in the years immediately before independence.

Under the TFL's leadership trade unionism spread in Tanganyika at a pace 'probably unequalled in Africa'.[60] By 1961 there were thirty-five unions with 203 000 members, representing forty-two per cent of Tanganyika's workers, compared with the twelve per cent who were then unionised in Uganda and eight per cent in Kenya.[61] Mpangala was responsible for persuading Dar es Salaam's apprehensive dockworkers to form a new union in 1955 and for creating a Domestic and Hotel Workers' Union. Lorry drivers were organised in 1956, while a year later TAGSA was opened to unskilled workers and converted into a Government Workers' Union. This activism was accompanied by a wave of strikes which demonstrated the TFL's solidarity. When hotel workers struck in 1956, for example, building workers and commercial employees came out in sympathy. Public support was shown in a boycott of Dar es Salaam's buses and in a TANU-backed boycott of bottled beer during a brewery strike of 1958.

Having been formed rapidly from the top downwards, the new unions had a distinctive character. A study of union leaders made in 1960 showed that only two per cent had been manual workers, fifteen per cent craftsmen, and eighty-three per cent white-collar employees. They were very young—sixty-one per cent were under thirty—with between six and ten years of education. Two-thirds were Christians, four-fifths had been born in the countryside, and more than three-fifths had uneducated parents.[62] Thus, like TANU, the unions were a ladder of advancement for men from unprivileged backgrounds who had failed to enter or to complete secondary school. Manual workers took little part in union affairs. They often paid entrance fees but rarely subscribed monthly dues, assuming that they were automatically union members. The unions were consequently in constant financial difficulty, especially as most of their funds—ninety-four per cent in 1963—were spent on their own administration.[63] The strike was almost their only weapon, and against a colonial regime in full decay it was very effective. Between 1956 and 1959, while prices remained roughly stable, the most common monthly wage among African workers in the Magomeni quarter of Dar es Salaam rose from shs. 76–90 to shs. 91–120.[64]

The new labour movement's character is best illustrated by its impact on the sisal industry.[65] In the mid-1950s the only labour organisations on most sisal estates were councils of tribal or village headmen. The first trade union was formed in the Eastern Province in March 1956 by the joint action of workers led by a lorry driver named Mbwana Salimu and of TFL organisers led by their president, J.B.A. Ohanga of the railway workers. During 1957 Ohanga intervened in other provinces and a wave of local strikes occurred. The sisal planters were divided in meeting the challenge. Most sought to prevent union growth by prohibiting all union activity on their estates, but a number of wealthier and more sophisticated planters urged that the unionists must be domesticated through a joint consultative machinery. Early in 1958 a Central Joint Council for the Sisal Industry was established with equal representation of workers and employers, the majority on both sides being chosen by a pyramid of councils leading upwards from estate committees. At the same time the Tanganyika Sisal Growers' Association recognised a single Tanganyika Sisal Plantation Workers' Union, both bodies securing a small representation on the Join Council.

From 1958 to 1961 a complicated struggle for power took place within the sisal industry. On one level the planters sought to use the estate representatives on the workers' side of the Joint Council to neutralise the trade union, which itself tried to break the planters' authoritarian control of their estates. On another level this conflict involved a struggle for power within the labour force on each estate, a struggle which appears to have taken place within the ranks of clerks, headmen, factory workers, and guards who formed the elite of each estate. The key event was a strike at Mazinde Estate which began in November 1958, lasted sixty-eight days, and provoked much bitterness and low-level violence which led to an enquiry into the industry's labour relations and the strengthening of the union's position on the Joint Council. This it used to oust the other workers' representatives, who complained of 'a kind of dictatorship', and finally to break the Joint Council in September 1961.

In the meantime, however, trade union activity had transformed the structure of the sisal industry. Between August 1958 and March 1960 a sisal cutter's average wage rose from shs. 54 to shs. 111 per working month.[66] In return for higher wages, the employers successfully bargained for larger tasks. This meant that fewer workers were needed, while higher wages made it possible for workers to make a career in the industry and settle on the estates with their families. A train of events was set in motion which happened throughout colonial Africa in the 1950s as low-wage, migrant labour forces were replaced by relatively high-wage, permanent proletariats. For by the 1950s many workers *wanted* to be proletarians. 'What they wanted', a spokesman for the sisal workers' union explained, 'was that . . . local people should be attracted to the Industry by better conditions. Furthermore they wanted money to stay in the country rather than be taken outside by workers returning to Ruanda-Urundi.' The planters heartily agreed, just as they shared the union's desire 'to do away with all recruitment'.[67] In November 1959 the TFL demanded that the word *manamba* should no longer be heard in Tanganyika.

Between 1958 and 1963 trade union action was chiefly responsible for increasing the labour costs per ton of sisal by fifty-nine per cent.[68] Between 1959 and 1964 the number of workers on the estates fell from 133 000 to 83 000,[69] while the average number of workers needed to produce 100 tons of sisal reduced between 1954 and 1964 from seventy-seven to thirty-seven.[70] Similar processes were taking place in other industries. Once the port's deep-water berths were opened in 1956, for example, dock work in Dar es Salaam was decasualised, despite intense opposition and at the cost of adding many hundreds of casual dockworkers to the town's unemployed, who were nearly a fifth of its adult male population in the late 1950s.[71]

Thus it was chiefly as a result of action by the workers themselves that the colonial labour system of low wages, long-distance migration, and quasi-political constraints was ending. Capitalism had largely ousted pre-capitalist elements from the modern sector of the economy and was increasingly, but more slowly, penetrating African rural societies. It was the most important change that took place in the political economy of Tanganyika during the colonial period.

Notes

1 This chapter draws heavily on my forthcoming book, *A Modern History of Tanganyika*, in which many of the statements made here are more fully documented. I am indebted to the Directors

of the Tanzania National Archives [TNA] and Deutsches Zentralarchiv, Postdam [DZAP], the Administrative Secretary of the Tanganyika African National Union [TANU], and the Librarian of Rhodes House, Oxford [RH], for permission to use records in their keeping.

2 Aylward Shorter, *Chiefship in Western Tanzania*, Oxford, 1972, pp. 74–5.

3 G.S.P. Freeman-Grenville, *The French at Kilwa Island*, Oxford, 1968, p. 170.

4 I owe this information to Dr Frank Nolan.

5 François Coulbois, quoted in Norman R. Bennett, *Mirambo of Tanzania*, New York, 1971, p. 12.

6 Paul Reichard, *Deutsch-Ostafrika: das Land und seine Bewohner*, Leipzig, 1892, p. 199; Franz Stuhlmann, *Mit Emin Pascha ins Herz von Afrika*, Berlin, 1894, p. 16 n.

7 H.F. von Behr, *Kriegsbilder aus den Araberaufstand in Deutsch-Ostafrika*, Leipzig, 1891, p. 138.

8 Oscar Baumann, *Usambara und seine Nachbargebiete*, Berlin, 1891, p. 304.

9 Fritz Weidner, *Die Haussklaverei in Ostafrika*, Jena, 1915, pp. 138–9.

10 *Die deutschen Schutzgebiete in Afrika und der Südsee 1912/13*, Berlin, 1914, part 1, p. 48.

11 List in Reichskolonialamt [RKA] 122/139, DZAP; *Die deutschen Schutzgebiete*, 1912/13, part 2, p.79.

12 Ludwig Boell, *Die Operationen-in Ost-Afrika: Weltkrieg 1914–18*, Hamburg, 1951, p. 429.

13 *Report of the committee . . . on . . . native labour*, Dar es Salaam, 1938, p. 9.

14 *Die deutschen schutzgebiete*, 1909/10, part 1, p. 16.

15 Martienssen to Bezirksamt Wilhelmstal, 11 January 1906, TNA Landkommissionsverhandlung Wilhelmstal 77.

16 Jessen, quoted in Johannes Schanz, *Am Fusse der Bergriesen Ostafrikas*, Leipzig, 1912, p. 134.

17 Schone [?] to Bezirksamt Moschi, 15 February 1913, TNA G44/6.

18 Mutahangarwa to Stuemer, 15 July 1907, TNA G34/5.

19 Filipo Njau to Gutmann, 3 April 1921, in Bruno Gutmann, ed., *Briefe aus Afrika*, Leipzig, 1925, p. 10,

20 A.E. Kitching, 'Biharamulo Sub-District: Annual Report, 1924', TNA 215/77/13.

21 Agricultural Assistant, Tukuyu, to DC Mbeya, 3 February 1944, TNA 33/A/3/13/615.

22 Godfrey Wilson, *The land rights of individuals among the Nyakyusa*, Rhodes-Livingstone papers no. 1 (Livingstone, 1938), p. 28; Monica Wilson, *Good Company*, London, 1951, pp. 56, 63.

23 Meyer to Government, 11 May 1906, TNA G1/96.

24 For Ha migration, see especially Laurent Sago, 'A history of labour migration in Kasulu district, Tanzania, 1928–60', M.A. thesis, University of Dar es Salaam, 1974.

25 P.H. Gulliver, *Labour migration in a rural economy: a study of the Ngoni and Ndendeuli of southern Tanganyika*, Kampala, 1955; *idem*, 'Nyakyusa labour migration'. *Rhodes-Livingstone journal*, 21, 1957, pp. 32–63.

26 There is an excellent account in Anse Tambila, 'A history of the Tanga sisal labour force, 1936–1964', M.A. thesis, University of Dar es Salaam, 1974.

27 R.C. Jerrard (ADO Labour, Tanga) to PC Tanga, 17 July 1937, TNA 11168/1/331; Jerrard, 'Labour Report for the 9 months ending 30 September 1938, Tanga Province', TNA 25908/1/202.

28 The sources for these statements are too numerous to list here but will appear in my forthcoming book.

29 'Report of the Proceedings of the Meeting with the Provincial Commissioner, Tanga, . . . on the 11th August 1939', TNA 304/959/1/28.

30 M.J.B. Molohan, *Detribalization*, Dar es Salaam, 1959, pp. 13–14.

31 Agricultural workers were an exception to this generalisation. They were equally late to organise in both countries.

32 See the papers in TNA 11051/2.

33 A.R. Thompson, 'Partnership in education in Tanganyika,

1919–61', M.A. thesis, University of London, 1965, p. 261.

34 *Annual report of the Labour Department* [*Labour report*] 1945, p. 11.

35 'Hizi ndizo Sheria za Chama Chetu cha Maboi', 16 January 1944, TNA 61/679/1/15.

36 'Meeting of Native Domestic Servants at Mbuyuni wa Simba Mwene, Tuesday the 13th February 1945', TNA 61/679/1/32.

37 *Tanganyika Standard*, 2 September 1943; *Recorded population changes 1948–67: Tanzania*, Dar es Salaam, 1968, p. 13.

38 'Employment of ex-servicemen. Meeting held on the 2nd August [1944]', TNA 171/76/10/9A.

39 Jim Mwalemba and Ali Mwasokwa to L.O. Mbeya, 10 October 1944, TNA 134/LAB/63/3.

40 Evidence of CID Superintendent in *Report of the commission appointed to enquire into the disturbances . . . in the port of Tanga*, Dar es Salaam, 1940, p. 10.

41 The following account is based on John Iliffe, 'A history of the dockworkers of Dar es Salaam', *Tanzania Notes and Records*, 71, 1970, pp. 119–48.

42 Cyril Ehrlich, 'The poor country: the Tanganyika economy from 1945 to independence', in D.A. Low and A. Smith, ed., *History of East Africa: volume III*, Oxford, 1976, p. 291.

43 Karl-Heinz Friedrich, 'Coffee-banana farms at Bukoba', in Hans Ruthenberg, ed., *Smallholder farming and smallholder development in Tanzania*, München, 1968, p. 198.

44 Dietrich von Rotenhan, 'Cotton farming in Sukumaland', in *ibid.*, p. 55.

45 See, for example, P.H. Gulliver, *Land tenure and social change among the Nyakyusa*, Kampala, 1958, p. 17; P.M. Van Hekken and H.U.E. Thoden van Velzen, *Land scarcity and rural inequality in Tanzania*, The Hague, 1972, p. 14; Jürgen Schultz, *Agrarlandwirtschaftliche Veranderungen in Tanzania,* München, 1971, p. 256.

46 Except perhaps for antagonism between landlord and tenant in Buhaya.

47 Tanganyika Territory, *Blue Book*, 1946, p. 206; *Annual report*

of the Department of Agriculture, 1960, p. 38.

48 Gulliver, 'Nyakyusa migration', p. 48.

49 *Ibid.*, p. 32.

50 P.H. Gulliver, 'Alien natives in the Tanga region', duplicated paper, 1956, Cory Papers, University Library, Dar es Salaam.

51 Zagorittis Sisal Estate to Silabu, 2 December 1954, quoted in Tambila, 'Tanga sisal labour force', p. 32.

52 Sago, 'Migration in Kasulu', pp. 33, 36.

53 Cranford Pratt, *The critical phase in Tanzania, 1945–68*, Cambridge, 1976, p. 20.

54 Sir Barclay Nihill, in 'Minutes of a Joint Conference between Management and Employees of the Sisal Industry', 10 April 1958, Nihill Papers, RH.

55 *Labour report*, 1951 p. 20.

56 *Ibid.*, pp. 21–2.

57 The following account is based chiefly on A.C.A. Tandau, *Historia ya kuundwa kwa T.F.L. (1955–62) na kuanzishwa kwa NUTA (1964)*, Dar es Salaam, n.d.

58 Tom Mboya, *Freedom and after*, London, 1963, pp. 197–9.

59 'Tanganyika Federation of Labour: Constitution', TANU 23. (For the numbering of TANU files, see John Iliffe, 'A list of certain records in TANU headquarters, Dar es Salaam', typescript, University Library, Dar es Salaam.

60 Roger Scott, 'Trade unions and the growth of nationalism in East Africa', East African Academy symposium paper, Dar es Salaam, 1965.

61 *Ibid.*

62 William H. Friedland, *Vuta kamba: the development of trade unions in Tanganyika*, Stanford, 1969, appendix 3.

63 *Labour report*, 1963, p. 7.

64 J.A.K. Leslie, *A survey of Dar es Salaam*, London, 1963, p. 288.

65 This account is based chiefly on Sir Barclay Nihill's papers in Rhodes House, Oxford.

66 'Minutes of the Second Meeting of the Central Joint Council of the Sisal Industry', 14 August 1958, and B. Leechman, 'New

Wage Rates and Increased Tasks', 15 March 1960, Nihill Papers, RH.

67 'Minutes of the Fifth Meeting of the Central Joint Council of the Sisal Industry', 26–8 November 1959, Nihill Papers, RH.

68 C.W. Guillebaud, *An economic survey of the sisal industry of Tanganyika*, 3rd edn, Welwyn, 1966, p. 72.

69 *Ibid.*, p. 78.

70 *Ibid.*, p. 135.

71 *Labour reports*, 1958 p. 5, 1960 p. 5, 1961 p. 5.

9. The Political Economy of Health and Medicine in Colonial Tanganyika

D.E. Ferguson

When Tanganyika became independent in 1961, malnutrition was widespread, infectious diseases were common, infant mortality was extremely high and the average life expectancy was short by international standards.[1] The medical facilities built during the colonial period were inadequate and understaffed. The new nation was faced with a major task of improving the medical and health care available to the people.

The problems of ill-health and disease which existed in the newly independent nation were those common to all ex-colonial countries. We do not share the assumption, held by some, that these health problems are the natural consequence of the tropical environment. We have reached the conclusion, through historical investigation, that the socio-economic system under which a people live, produce and reproduce, is more determinate of a people's ill-health or well being than is the natural environment. In this chapter we present the view that many of the health problems confronting Tanzania in 1961 were a product of the demands and priorities of the colonial economy under which the people lived for more than two generations.

The nineteenth century background

There is no evidence at present which would enable us to conclude that the pre-colonial population of Tanganyika was any more unhealthy, or healthy, than the population of other regions of the world in the early nineteenth century. Nor is there evidence that would enable us to conclude that diseases were more widespread or fatal in Africa than on other continents. Certain areas of the world had diseases peculiar to them while there were other diseases that recognised no regional boundaries. Certainly, in the early nineteenth century, no region of the world had made much progress towards containing common infectious diseases.

It does appear, however, that the nineteenth century was a period of change in Tanganyika as far as the introduction and spread of disease is concerned, and the pattern that was established in that century was carried much further under colonial rule in the twentieth century. In the nineteenth century there were an increasing number of infectious diseases found in the coastal ports which were carried inland along the trade routes to the previously uninfected peoples of the interior. In the twentieth century the economic demands of the colonial system created the conditions for the further spread of these diseases throughout the colony.

Cholera was one of the diseases introduced to the coast from India in the nineteenth century. A physician to the Sultan of Zanzibar, James Christie, recorded four epidemics on the island between 1836 and 1876.[2] Each was associated with outbreaks in other Indian Ocean ports and each epidemic subsequently spread to the mainland ports from Zanzibar and then inland along the caravan routes.

Venereal diseases were introduced at an earlier date to the coastal cities by sailors, traders, and merchants from other Indian Ocean ports and Europe. By 1900 the Germans noted a high incidence of syphilis among the *askaris* of the coastal cities while peoples of the south-west were complaining bitterly to the German administrators that syphilis was brought inland to them by traders.[3] The Wahehe claimed that it was introduced to them by soldiers from the caravan centre of Tabora during the Maji-Maji war in 1905–7.[4]

A third disease which was localised in the coastal ports during the nineteenth century was tuberculosis.[5] It is a disease which is spread by human contact in overcrowded living conditions. During the nineteenth century the conditions necessary for the spread of this disease were only found in the ports and the major settlements of the caravan routes. That is why the majority of the population, living as they did in villages outside these centres, remained relatively unaffected.

All pre-colonial African societies had medical practitioners, or doctors, who treated the diseases, ailments and injuries of their people. In each society there was both general and specialised medical knowledge. Women seem to have shared the general knowledge which enabled them to perform the role of midwife and treat common childhood diseases. They were the gynaecologists and paediatricians of their day, and they invariably knew medicinal plants which were effective abortifacients.

Men were usually specialists, or full-time practitioners of medicine in most pre-colonial societies of the nineteenth century. This may not always have been the case, however, for there is evidence from other regions of the world that this monopoly was usurped from women.[6] We do not know whether this struggle for ultimate control of the practice took place in the African past, but it is a question which merits further attention.

Specialised medical knowledge in early nineteenth century Tanganyika was often limited to a select group of males within each society. This knowledge remained in particular families and passed from the father to a predestined son.[7] There was a lengthy period of apprenticeship in which the secrets and mysteries of the profession were passed on to the novice. The general population was denied access to this specialised knowledge, and thereby the power and influence of the medical profession was enhanced. But it is highly likely that limiting this knowledge to a small select group hindered further progress in the field of medicine. Had the exclusive medical knowledge been available to the general population, further advances would have been made through widespread experimentation and innovation.[7]

Medical treatment practised by the pre-colonial doctor ranged from rational to magical. In the past, the general tendency has been for writers to pursue the magical basis of pre-colonial medical treatment. This is unfortunate for it has prevented us from learning about the rational basis of much traditional medicine. Many of the rational treatments were for common ailments. They were performed by common people, often mothers, through the use of household remedies. Most of the illnesses and diseases treated rationally had a visible pathology: they could be observed, studied, and successful treatment achieved through experimentation. Dr Marley has made the following conclusion about the choice of technique by the traditional practitioner:

> There is a general transition from simple medicine rationally applied for common and external maladies to magical con-

coctions directed against sickness of a rare and dangerous nature.[9]

In south-west Tanganyika, for example, the medical practitioners used both rational and magical cures for more than twenty-five different health problems. Some of the diseases, ailments and complications which they treated were yaws, worms, a disease which appears to have been bilharzia, headaches, toothaches, earaches, hernias, snakebites, miscarriages, and others.[10] Most of the medicines used were made from plants in the environment.

The medicinal plants used by the medical practitioners in a particular society had been selected through a long period of experimentation. There are many cases where a particular medicinal plant was used as a cure for the same illness over a wide region within Africa. There are other instances where the traditional medical practitioners in East Africa used a particular medicinal plant in the same way and for the same purpose as medical practitioners in other regions of the Indian Ocean world to which Tanganyika belongs.

There are literally thousands of medicinal plants that were used though the African continent and the Indian Ocean world. Here we will give a few examples. The trees or shrubs of the plant family *Myrsinaceae* were widely used as a remedy for worms in pre-colonial Tanganyika. Both the Wachagga and Masai people used the fruit of one species for that purpose.[11] The Masai used the bark and berry of another species as a purgative, while the Wachagga preferred to use the roots and dried seed of this species as a remedy for worms.[12] The Wahaya and Wasambaa used the seed of another species found in their area to treat worms, and they shared this remedy with people as far away as Ethiopia and South Africa.[13] The fruit of still another species was commonly used by the Wachagga, Wapare, Wahehe, and Wasambaa as a worm remedy.[14]

Another illustration of the widespread use of a particular medicinal plant is the case of *Abrus precatorius*. The bright red bean with a black spot, often called the love bean, the prayer bean, or lucky bean, was commonly used as a remedy for eye problems. It was used for that purpose in pre-colonial Tanganyika by the Wachagga, Wanyamwezi, Wasambaa, Wasukuma, Wayao, and Waswahili.[15] It was used for the same purpose in other parts of East Africa, as well as Central Africa and West Africa.[16] It was also used by traditional doctors in other Indian Ocean countries, like

Cambodia, as a remedy for eye problems.[17]

The widespread use of a particular medicinal plant would seem to be strong evidence for its efficacy. The colonial rulers were not ignorant of this possibility. Therefore, during the period of colonial rule the government authorities were most anxious to learn the use of African medicinal plants. Government chemists analysed them to establish whether there was any chemical basis for their efficacy. Often there was, as in the examples we have used above. Chemists reported the following active ingredients in one of the species of the *Myrsinaceae* family:

> The plant yields embelin . . . also known as embelic acid, which has been used as an anthelmintic (remedy for worms) in a does of 0.2 to 0.4 gms (in the laboratory).[18]

In the case of *Abrus precatorius*, we have this report:

> A powder of the decorticated seed, or an extract from it, placed in the eye causes an inflammation which European Opthalmic (eye) surgeons have made use of for clearing away opacities of the cornea. This practice commenced in 1888, but has not found favour, being too drastic. The chemical substance, abrin . . . is that which causes inflammation.[19]

Thus, there was, indeed, a chemical basis for these medicines to be effective. But there is one further observation which should be made at this point. Both the bean of *Abrus precatorius* and an overdose of the fruit and root of *Myrsinaceae* are poisonous![20] Therefore, the use of these potentially dangerous medicinal plants was left to the medical specialist whose role it was to regulate the dosage for the good health of the patient.

In Tanganyika, over one thousand traditional medical plants had been analysed by British chemists working at the Amani Research Station in the Usambara mountains by the time of the Second World War.[21] When an active chemical agent was discovered it might then be synthesised in the metropolitan country and sold on the world market, or back to the people of Tanganyika by a British pharmaceutical firm. This practice of tapping traditional medical knowledge in a subject territory, or colony, was a major method used by the European and North American nations to accumulate their wealth of pharmaceutical knowledge over the past four centuries.[22]

While the traditional doctors successfully treated a number of illnesses through remedies arrived at by trial and error, they probably remained ignorant of the causes of most of them. Guesswork attributed the causes to the malevolent practices of gods in the heavens, individuals on earth, or simply fate. This is understandable because the doctors did not have the technology required to discover, for example, that micro-organisms such as bacteria, protozoa and viruses which are invisible to the naked eye, cause infectious diseases.

The level of medical knowledge and practice which we have described for early nineteenth-century Tanganyikan society is, in many ways, comparable with that of the medical profession of early nineteenth-century Europe. In both Africa and Europe medical practice remained pre-scientific. The following description of the early nineteenth century European doctor written by the British scientist J.D. Bernal in 1939 fits the one we have outlined for early nineteenth century Tanganyika:

> The doctor (in Europe) before the middle of the last century, could not in fact have had any knowledge of the physiological and chemical facts on which his practice depended. A few useful things could, it is true, be done in surgery and a certain common sense used in nursing . . . Yet the doctor remained for all his learning a medicine man whose chief function was to give hope to the patient and to relieve his relatives of responsibility. Doctors because of their attendance on persons of wealth and importance were from the beginning among the privileged and intellectual classes.[23]

As the nineteenth century progressed, European medicine moved beyond that of Africa. This was a result of the different economic contexts in which the medical traditions were being practised. European doctors were practising at the centre of the world capitalist system and the African doctor was at the periphery. Wealth and knowledge was being drawn from the periphery to the centre where it was being applied to scientific and technological advancement.

Therefore, it was not by chance that the breakthrough from pre-scientific medicine based on guesswork to scientific medicine based on the germ theory of disease was made in Europe by the scientist Pasteur working with a microscope, one of the most advanced pieces of late nineteenth-century technology. As we look back from the present the process is clear. Vast amounts of wealth were being accumulated by the European bourgeoisie through exploitation of the European workers at home and non-European peasants abroad. This wealth was applied to technology during the Industrial Revolution. Scientists worked with this technology, and took what they wanted from the rich accumulation of scientific knowledge, and then made the advance to scientific medicine.

This advanced medical knowledge made it possible for the industrial nations of Europe and North America to contain certain infectious diseases and, in some cases, practically eliminate some of them by the twentieth century. The principal reason for this progress in health care was not a humanitarian attitude on the part of those who controlled industry; rather, it arose from their material interests. The attitude of the capitalist towards the health of a worker is, in other words, a consequence of the conditions under which the capitalist operates. In late nineteenth-century Europe there was a limited labour supply and thus a pressing need for the ruling class to eliminate contagious diseases in the increasingly unhealthy industrial cities where the work-force was being concentrated.

But the European ruling class could not completely eliminate infectious diseases, for the primary social cause of such diseases is poverty, and the impoverishment of the worker is a basic feature of capitalism.

When capitalism reached its imperialist stage in late nineteenth-century Germany, the colonial war for the conquest of what was to become Tanganyika began. The colonial system was established and the German planters and capitalist firms settled down to producing export crops. In that process, the majority of the people in the colony became impoverished and the social conditions were created for the further spread of diseases.

German colonialism

One of the consequences of European expansion into and exploitation of, the non-European world over the past four centuries has often been a period of population decline or stagnation among the conquered peoples. The decline in population is well documented for the western hemisphere where it is estimated that the indigenous population was twenty times greater before the conquest than after it.[25] For Africa, Rodney suggests, the period of 1650–1850 was one of stagnation in which the total population failed to increase as a result of the slave trade.[26] The population of East Africa throughout the first half of the nineteenth century was probably fairly constant with growth being prevented by the slave trade, and towards the end of the century a downward trend began with the colonial wars of conquest. The demographer, R.R. Kuezynski, examined the population data for Tanganyika, Kenya and Uganda, and concluded that this period of decline began in the late nineteenth century and continued until shortly after the First World War[27]. In the case of Tanganyika there are few official statistics before 1902 when the Germans estimated the population of Tanganyika, excluding Ruanda and Urundi, to be 4622000[28]. During the next twenty years of colonial rule the population showed a decline of more than half a million to 4107000 in 1921.[29]

The evidence further suggests that during the first decade of conquest in the 1890s, for which there are no official statistics, the impact of the colonial wars was very costly in human lives. These wars began on the coast in 1889 and along with the civilian and military casualties in battle there was a great loss of life as a result of famine. Food shortages began with the rinderpest cattle epidemic in 1890. This cattle disease was new to East Africa, having first entered Sudan and Somalia with cattle introduced to feed British and Italian occupation armies during the previous decade[30]. The cattle in East Africa had no immunity to this new disease and it quickly assumed an epidemic level. In 1890 it was widespread in Tanganyika and the cattle fatality rate was ninety per cent or higher.[31] This loss of cattle, combined with famine due to war and drought, led to malnutrition and starvation. Smallpox then reached an epidemic level in 1897–9, among the malnourished population. It is estimated that over 750000 persons died during the five-year period from 1894–1899.[32]

A prolonged plague epidemic also accompanied the wars of conquest. It was widespread in the western half of Tanganyika from 1886–1905. When it first appeared in Uhehe in 1886, preventive measures were taken by Mkwana to eliminate the rats which spread the disease.[33] Wahehe doctors doubled their efforts to cure the sick, but they were not able to combat the epidemic successfully and it continued to menace them until 1904. From Uhehe the plague spread to Ubena where it reached epidemic proportions between 1891 and 1905. Further outbreaks took place on the coast and the outbreak in Zanzibar in 1905 caused great anxiety among German administrators for it threatened troops coming by sea to suppress the Maji-Maji revolt.

Two new diseases which were introduced to Tanganyika during the wars of conquest affected the people directly. The first of these was caused by the sandflea, or jigger, which was introduced into West Africa from Brazil during the early nineteenth-century slave trade. From the Congo it was carried into Uganda and East Africa, perhaps by Stanley's Emin Pasha Relief Expedition.[34] In 1890 the German traveller Oscar Baumann observed its spread into Tanganyika:

> The sandflea larva . . . can cause blood poisoning and death. Particularly in areas where the sandflea occurs for the first time, and where its treatment is unknown, its impact can be devastating. We saw people in Usinja whose limbs had disintegrated. Whole villages died out on account of this vexation.[35]

During the first decade of this century the impact of warfare, famine and diseases on the population is further documented in the case of the Maji-Maji resistance of 1905–7.[36] The following account taken from the Annual Report of the German Administration for 1907 gives us an insight into the effects of German colonial aggression on the population of southern Tanganyika:

> For the natives the period following the rebellion was harder than the period of warfare. In the first frenzy of the war they ate most of the remaining harvest and they slaughtered the cattle. When we advanced and discovered their hidden reserves we destroyed what could not be used by our military expedition.
>
> Farming for the defeated was impossible. The fear of the future forced most of them to surrender. In addition there was a poor harvest and lack of food in some parts of the country. A large number of those who were not troubled by war and hunger were weak and fell victim to all kinds of disease. Intestinal diseases were spread. Mothers suffering from malnutrition could not breastfeed their young in regions which were previously healthy. An enormous infantile mortality was the result.[37]

It was officially estimated that some 75 000 people died in the resistance, but the long-range consequences were certainly much greater. Thirty years later, for example, an investigation of fertility patterns in southern Tanganyika showed a higher degree of infertility among women in the area of Maji-Maji resistance than in neighbouring areas[38].

These examples highlight the initial broad impact that colonialism had in Tanganyika. Warfare not only resulted in the loss of life but it created the conditions for the spread of infectious diseases and famine which further contributed to the population decline. The colonial system was imposed through violence with devastating human consequences.

By the time the wars of conquest were ending the Germans were laying the groundwork necessary to extract wealth from their new possession. The peoples who had resisted so long were now being prepared to produce within the framework of the colonial economy. There were three ways in which they could enter the economy. First they might become wage labourers on the colonial plantations. Second, they might produce cash crops on their own land. Third, they might work as wage labourers in the towns, at the harbours, or on road and railway construction.

The administration used two techniques to get the labour. In many cases physical force was used; either the person's land was taken and he had to go to work for wages, or he was directly coerced. The second method was more pervasive and successful. That was to use monetary incentives which made it necessary for the population to work for a cash return. People were taxed, school fees were imposed, and cheaply produced commodities from abroad were introduced. All of these measures required the peasants to obtain and use money, while the last measure also contributed to the decline of local industry.

The attitude of the colonial employer and administrator was basically one of indifference to the health and reproduction of the work-force. This was in accord with the general behaviour of capitalists working with unlimited supplies of labour. While the pool of labour was seen as limitless, the capitalist faced the problem of getting it flowing at a steady rate to the work-place. Coercion, monetary incentives, and famine could be counted on by the employers to provide a fairly reliable flow of labour out of the villages, but the labour force was very unstable and there was a rapid turnover in its composition due to the low wages and unhealthy conditions of the work place which made it necessary for the labourers to constantly retreat to the villages to maintain and reproduce themselves.

Malnutrition became widespread under colonialism. There are a number of reasons for this development. First there was the uprooting of the formerly self-sufficient food producer who became, of necessity, a cash crop producer or wage labourer. If he engaged in cash crop production, food production was often neglected. In the case of both the cash crop producer and wage worker the income received for their labour was seldom adequate to purchase the requisite food for good health.

Another factor which contributed to the spread of malnutrition was the colonial emphasis on the production of maize as the primary grain staple. During the nineteenth century both maize and rice appeared as new crops in Tanganyika and when colonial rule began they were favoured by the administration over the traditional staples of millet, sorghum and bananas.[39] The government encouraged maize production because of its higher yield per acre. Along with rice, it was to be the staple grain for the labour force in the colony as well as a major export.[40] Nutritionally, however, the shift from millet, sorghum and bananas to maize and rice was not in the interest of the people. Both millet and sorghum are a much better source of protein and many essential vitamins than are maize and rice.[41] Also the regular consumption of maize and rice resulted in vitamin deficiency diseases because they lost much of their vitamin content through milling.[42] Pellagra was caused by regular consumption of milled maize and beriberi was caused by milled rice. Yet local production and milling was encouraged and by the 1940s the mills at Mwanza were turning out triple polished rice which supplemented machine milled maize as the staple food in the capital of Dar es Salaam.[43]

Another consequence of the shift to maize production is that this crop was extremely sensitive to variations in rainfall and it often failed in times of drought. Thus it contributed to famine. There is also evidence that maize contributed to famine by being an export crop. Mascarenhas has noted that the colonial authorities sometimes exported maize during periods of famine rather than transfer it from one district to another to overcome the food shortage:

A striking aspect of the colonial administration is that the food

> commodities, e.g., maize, have been exported to Australia when famine existed in a neighbouring district.[44]

These are a few of the more important ways that health problems were created for workers and peasants under German colonial rule. We will return to this subject when we discuss the period of British rule

Under the colonial state there were both government and missionary medical services. Government hospitals were limited to a few major urban centres where they served the European population and the small Asian and African commercial and petty bourgeoisie. The mission dispensaries were in most cases situated in the rural areas.

The government system began when European doctors were recruited to serve the military in its campaign of colonial conquest. The first doctors arrived in 1889 to care for troops wounded while suppressing coastal resistance and the first hospital was built that year in Bagamoyo.[45] The doctors then prepared to march inland with the troops in 1891. They performed their services at the military garrisons and stations while more permanent facilities were established for the military in the areas of heaviest fighting. A small hospital was built at Iringa after the defeat of Mkwawa in 1894, while others were built at Kilwa and Morogoro in 1905 and 1906 to accommodate troops wounded in combat against the Maji-Maji resistance movement. These medical facilities remained rudimentary.

The colonial administration was headquartered on the coast and it was in Dar es Salaam and Tanga that the most comprehensive government services were to be found. Services were available on a racial and class basis. Expensive, adequately staffed, well-equipped hospitals were the norm for the European ruling class. Inexpensive, understaffed, poorly-equipped hospitals or clinics were built for the Asians or Africans who served the Europeans in administrative, commercial, military or police capacities.

The dual hospital system of Dar es Salaam provides an excellent illustration of this pattern. The government hospital (Ocean Road Hospital) was built for Europeans through funds approved by the German Reichstag in 1894–5. However, the same body would not approve funds for the construction of a hospital for the Asians and Africans in their service. Such a hospital was needed, so the Chief

Medical Officer approached Sewa Haji, one of the most prosperous Asians in the colony, who was in debt to the administration through favours given to him.[46] After a short talk he agreed to donate the the money necessary to build a hospital for 'askaris, military employees and government civil servants', although Asians and Africans less dependent on the administration were to be admitted too. These hospital services were confined to the urban areas which were not easy for the peasants of the countryside to reach.

Throughout the colonial era the mission dispensary played a key role in the rural areas of all the East African colonies, for medicine proved to be an indispensible means for drawing the population under the influence of the Christian church. Perhaps the clearest statement of how medicine was related to the missionary effort was made by Archdeacon Walker of the CMS mission at Mengo, Uganda in 1897:

> I regard the medical work from its missionary aspect . . . I consider how far it is likely to aid our work, not how much suffering will be relieved.[47]

He also believed that it was not worthwhile to provide medicine where it was 'not needed to draw the people under the influence of the mission'.[48]

In Kenya, medicine served the church in the same way. Dr J.W. Arthur of the Church of Scotland mission had the following to say about medical work in 1912:

> The missionary should gain the confidence of the patient through his medical work and in this way prepare him for acceptance of the Christian message.[49]

In Tanganyika the goal was similar, with the missionaries taking advantage of epidemics and famines to spread their ideological influence. In the Southern Highlands, where Moravian and Lutheran missionaries were active, a missionary who had been rejected by the local people used the occasion of a smallpox epidemic to vaccinate the 'lost congregation' and win them back to mission influence.[50] In north-western Tanganyika, it was the policy of the Methodist mission at Bukoba to see that the dispensary did not become 'merely a medicine shop'.[51] In the Usambara mountains the UMCA stated that they won converts by gaining control of the food supply during the famine of 1894–8:

> (Our) missions . . . made good use of this time and bought and sold rice to the famished people . . . . (They) prostrated themselves at our doors, imploring assistance . . . One blessed result of the famine was a great desire to be taught; many came forward to receive the cross.[52]

The missionaries were also in constant struggle against the traditional doctors. The doctors were identified with paganism and witchcraft, and the congregations were exhorted to avoid them.[53] The traditional practitioners were known to have influence in society and they were often in the forefront of resistance to the church and colonialism. For that reason the church attempted to isolate and undermine the influence of traditional doctors.

Thus medicine at the mission station was primarily to serve the missionaries and colonialism. The medical facilities were a means to achieve the ideological goal, and the availability or unavailability of medical services, in many areas, came to depend upon the people's attitude towards the church. The Colonial Governments were well aware of the important ideological role the missions played in the colony, for few institutions were of greater service in preparing people to accept colonial rule. For that reason the Government enacted witchcraft ordinances to be used against traditional practitioners who might resist the authority of the colonial state, or church, and the governments subsidised the mission medical work in order to enhance its ideological influence.[54]

The plantation system dominated the colonial economy, and the number of labourers rose from approximately 5 000 in 1900 to 92 000 in 1913. The work-force was highly unstable because of the deplorable working and sanitation conditions maintained by the planters. Workers were repelled by the plantation rather than drawn to it. The population in the neighbourhood avoided this work while the majority of the plantation labourers came from the regions where there was persistent poverty. Famine and malnutrition pushed peasants out of their villages onto the pathways and roads leading to the plantations. Their physical condition worsened on the trek of a month or more, and planters regularly complained that peasants were arriving in a state of semi-starvation which made them practically useless as labour.

The planters nevertheless often gave the labourers poor food in lieu of wages. Deficiency diseases combined with hookworm resulting from poor sanitation to create a very high fatality rate among the labourers. The administration noted the high incidence of hookworm in 1907:

> (It) spread considerably in some districts—Tanga, Wilhelmstal, Pangani, Mohoro and Kilwa—primarily where a large number of workers are brought together in unhygienic conditions such as plantations.[55]

On the Usambara plantations it was estimated that seventy to eighty per cent of the labour force was infected.[56]

Peasants were also recruited to build the railways. The lack of sanitation facilities and unhealthy working conditions again testify to the employers' indifference to the health of the labour force. 13 000 men were working on the Central Railway in 1913 and outbreaks of typhoid and smallpox were common. Sanitary conditions at these work-sites contributed to the general health problem as noted in this passage:

> Along the road and railway track under construction between Mombo and Moshi, and Morogoro and Mpwapwa, hookworm is spreading all the time amongst the thousands of workers and has claimed numerous victims.[57]

The First World War

Less than a decade after the wars of conquest had ended, Germany and Britain began four years of intense warfare on Tanganyikan soil. From 1914–1918 the two imperialist powers fought with great loss of life to the civilian population.

A very sizable segment of the population in East Africa was either conscripted or recruited to serve in the two armies. The British used over 350 000 Africans in the East African Carrier Corps and over ten per cent of these men perished.[58] The commander of the German forces, General von Lettow-Vorbeck, estimated that 'hundreds of thousands' of Tanganyikan carriers and porters served his troops and officers during the war.[59] The death rate among these carriers must have been equally high.

Malnutrition, disease and overwork were the main contributing factors leading to this high fatality rate. General von Lettow-Vorbeck wrote the following account in the latter part of the war about malnutrition among the African troops and carriers under his command:

> It was impossible to get the calories of nourishment necessary for a fighting man from the daily cereal ration, fixed at 600 grammes of meal.[60]

The same condition prevailed among the men serving in the East African Carrier Corps, according to Dr C.J. Wilson, a British medical officer in Kenya:

> The appalling mortality among the African porters who accompanied the fighting troops and maintained the lines of communication was a feature of the campaign outstanding in its grim tragedy. An early and unforgiveable mistake was made when it was proposed to maintain the Corps in the field on a ration of nothing but mealie meal. In spite of the most vigorous protests of those who realised the inhumanity of following such a proposal, the attempt was made.[61]

The carriers were essential for victory. In East Africa they were required to do the extremely difficult work of transporting supplies which was often done by vehicles in other theatres of the war, and the men had to do this while suffering from malnutrition:

> Undernourished porters had to move heavy equipment over a terrain that lacked roads. The porters marched at an average of 15 miles per day with an average load of forty pounds.[62]

Infectious diseases spread rapidly among the semi-starved and overworked porters. For example, here is an account of one epidemic in 1916:

> In the same month that Tabora was occupied the supply lines along which the stores reached the military forces in the west were nearly severed by an outbreak of virulent cerebro-spinal meningitis among the porters. The disease spread rapidly along the routes traversed by the caravans.[63]

At the same time these porters in the west of the colony were hit with the meningitis epidemic other porters to the east, at Handeni, were hit by an outbreak of typhoid as described in this account, written by a British doctor:

> A group of miserable African porters, horribly emaciated, watched us go past. Our own porters spoke with them and we soon heard it whispered that all the water here was bad

> and that dysentery was everywhere. All the land in the neighbourhood suggested nothing in the world but squalor and disease. On our right a long shed, on which lay 200 Africans, left by the Germans to die, was ominously labelled 'typhys', the German word for typhoid.[64]

Towards the end of the year the hospitals under British administration were filled to capacity with over ten thousand troops. There was no room for porters and carriers. Infectious diseases spread rapidly among them, reaching an extremely high death rate the following year as reported by a British medical officer:

> Over a period of twenty-four weeks in 1917, the deaths recorded were 11 484, that is an average of more than sixty-eight daily. All that one can say is that these casualties in the Carrier Corps were part of the cost of winning the war. Porter transport was absolutely essential for the maintenance of the fighting troops in the fields.[65]

Perhaps we should put the medical officer's conclusion another way: those casualties were the price the civilian population had to pay for a change of colonial exploiters.

The civilian population experienced the effects of the war in other ways. For example, the German troops lived off the land when they could by expropriating peasant crops. Here is General von Lettow-Vorbeck's account of this practice at Kondoa:

> The whole strength of our people was required for patrols and the outposts, and for collecting supplies. As far as the eye could reach, the whole country was covered by native cultivation. The principal crop, which formed the main supply of the troops—was mtema, a kind of millet, which was just ripening. Most of the natives had run away; the supplies from Dodoma had been unable to keep up with us, and so our subsistence depended almost entirely on the stuff which the foraging parties of the companies were able to bring in.[66]

Troop movements spread contagious diseases among the civilian population. Epidemics were not uncommon among the malnourished peoples; smallpox broke out in 1917 and was widespread until 1920. A final legacy of the war was the 1918–19 influenza epidemic which originated in war-torn Europe and spread rapidly to the colonial world. In Tanganyika it is estimated to have caused 50 000 to 80 000 deaths.[67]

During the war the civilian medical services were taken over by the military. Troops in the German army were vaccinated against smallpox produced by the Germans in the colony. They also produced quinine at the Amani Research Institute to be used against malaria. As a result the German forces were much better prepared to contend with malaria than were the British who were forced to send home 12 000 or 15 000 troops because of it in 1917.

For the people of Tanganyika, the First World War was in many ways a continuation of the war of conquest in a more intense form. This explains why the population decline which had been initiated with the first military encounter in 1889 did not end until after the First World War.

British colonialism: 1918–1938

The hospitals and medical facilities abandoned by the Germans during the war were taken over by the British and were used primarily for their troops from 1917–1919 when the medical services were transferred to civilian administration.

The British established a medical department with two branches. The first was the medical branch which administered curative services while the second was the sanitation branch which was responsible for preventive services. In general the work of the former branch was confined to the urban areas and emphasised the cure of the sick. The latter was responsible for the prevention of illness and was primarily confined to rural areas.

The curative role was given priority over prevention under both German and British administrations. This emphasis on the cure of the sick rather than prevention of diseases was carried to the colony from the metropolitan country. There are two reasons that the capitalist countries in Europe stressed the curative branch of medicine. First, under monopoly capitalism health care became a commodity with a substantial exchange value resulting from the length and complexity of a doctor's training. The doctor then sells his services, that is, he realises the exchange value, by serving the individual patient able to purchase the doctor's cure.[68] The second reason that cure is given priority over prevention in the capitalist system has been mentioned earlier. Poverty is the main social cause of infectious diseases, and impoverishment of the majority of the population is a product of capitalist development. The members of the medical profession have not, on the whole, challenged the system on the grounds that it is incompatible with the good health of the majority. Rather, the medical profession under capitalism has accepted the sytem and has prospered through its monopoly of healing knowledge and curative services.

Curative services in the colony operated according to the same basic principles, and their main service was to the ruling class. In the colony hospitals and doctors were introduced primarily to provide cure and care for the European population. Doctors in private practice would be many or few according to the size of the expatriate population which had the money to pay for their services. Thus, private practitioners were attracted to colonies with wealthy settler populations as in Kenya, and they stayed away from Tanganyika. The Director of Medical Services in Tanganyika noted this phenomenon in the Legislative Council in 1944: 'There is not a single British-European doctor earning his living from private practice in the whole of this Territory'.[69] He concluded his remarks by contrasting this with the fact that there were many British private practitioners in Kenya.

The preventive services in Tanganyika were of an extremely limited nature and were basically carried out to contain the spread of infectious diseases into and within the areas of European settlement. In the rural areas the sanitation branch was to spot the outbreak of infectious diseases and prevent them from reaching epidemic levels. The goal of this extremely narrow conception of preventive medicine was to contain the spread of disease in the village population, not to eliminate the social causes of infectious diseases which would involve the expense of basic improvements in village sanitation, water supply and hygiene education.

The priority given curative services is clearly reflected in the medical budgets. The sanitation branch regularly received less money from the administration than the medical branch. In 1920–1, the sanitation branch was allocated only twenty-three per cent of the departmental budget and the following year the figure dropped to twenty-one per cent, with one third of it for Dar es Salaam.[70]

The British took over the German hospital system without making any fundamental changes in it. The dual system of separate and unequal facilities remained intact. The contrast in hospital services for the European and African population of Dar es Salaam in 1920 deserves mention here. The following description was given by the Principal Medical Officer:

> We have inherited from the Germans some medical buildings which compare favourably with any in Tropical Africa. The European Hospital, Dar es Salaam, is capable of accommodating fifty beds easily . . . It has a separate maternity section, well-fitted X-ray room and photographic dark room, and room for the examination of eye cases, spacious operating theatre, outpatient department and quarters for the nursing staff and Medical Officer. It faces the Indian Ocean and receives the benefit of the sea breeze . . . . It is lighted by electricity from the main town supply. Adjoining it are the bacteriological institute, dispensary, mortuary, chapel, laundry, etc.[71]

The Principal Medical Officer then describes the Sewa Haji Hospital as follows:

> At the other end of the town near the Gerezani Creek is the Sewa Haji hospital for Indians and Natives, a curious rambling collection of buildings of which the administrative block is the outstanding feature. Its capacity is also about fifty beds, a number which is insufficient for the needs of a native town with a population estimated at twenty or twenty-five thousand, as well as for the K.A.R. Garrison, civil police, prisoners, raliway and other Government Native and Indian empolyees.[72]

The ratio of beds to population served was approximately 1 : 10 for the European Hospital and 1 : 400–500 for the Sewa Haji Hospital.

Separate and unequal facilities were not confined to the coastal cities. For example, inland in Tabora the pattern persisted. The European hospital with twenty-two beds served a total European population of 158 individuals while the African population had seventy-five beds for 18 299 persons.[73] Here the ratio of beds to population served was 1 : 7 for the European population and approximately 1 : 240 for the African population.

The racial and class structure of the colony was reflected in the colonial policy for staffing the hospitals. European doctors served at the top while Asians served below them in the capacity of 'sub-assistant surgeons' and clerks. At the bottom of the structure were Africans working as attendants, vaccinators, clerks, storekeepers and labourers.

The inequalities of this structure were further reflected in the salary scale. For example, in 1926 the following wages were received by the employees of the medical services: 115 Europeans received £51 402; 102 Asians received £20 770; and 1 881 Africans received £19 860.[74] The average European salary in that year, which was in no way exceptional, was more than double the Asian salary and forty-five times greater than the average salary of the African employee.

The salaries of the small European staff usually accounted for at least one-half of the annual budget of the medical department.[75] This vast sum stands in contrast to the small amount allocated for health services for the rural majority. In 1926 the budget showed that the European staff was to receive two and a half times more in salaries than was to be spent for medical services for the $4\frac{1}{2}$ million people in the rural areas.[76]

There was always a shortage of staff, and the colonial administration was reluctant to train Africans to fill the vacancies. Immediately after the war the medical administration bemoaned the shortage of low-level African staff but it did little to change the situation. For example, over 1 500 young Africans had gained medical experience in Tanganyika during the First World War in the African Native Medical Corps, but the Tanganyikan Government apparently made no effort to recruit them for civilian medical work.

When government did move to train African staff it was for work at the lowest levels. In 1926 it began training African subordinate staff because Europeans didn't want to work in the rural areas and African labour was cheap. Three positions were created for this new staff. They were the dispenser, district sanitary inspector and tribal dresser. The first were trained to work as hospital assistants. The second were responsible for spotting the outbreak of contagious diseases in the rural areas. The third were responsible for providing medical care for the peasants.

All the subordinate staff was underpaid, inadequately trained and overworked. The situation of the tribal dresser illustrates the point. In 1929, 247 tribal dressers treated 190 500 patients. The dressers had received only three months of first-aid training as preparation and they worked for shs. 20 per month.[77]

The indifference of the government to the health needs of the peasants is also clear from the outcome of the Kahama maternity, welfare and health investigation. The project was initiated in Kahama district in 1927 after earlier reports indicated that the majority of the children in the district were unhealthy. Governor Cameron expressed concern and proposed a large scale investigation into the question of health care for the peasants. He gave these reasons for the survey:

> Money has been provided on next year's estimates for an intensive campaign in the Kahama District in order to obtain reliable information and statistics in regard to the physical progress or otherwise of a typical section of the native population. What we want to ascertain is whether there is any truth to the repeated statement that the natives are diminishing rather than increasing in numbers . . . We want to know the diseases which occur amongst natives and their causes . . . In fine we want a very serious and comprehensive study of the life of a typical native, male and female, bringing out all the points which may be of use to us in our efforts to shape affairs in the manner which will benefit the native population.[78]

One would assume from that statement that there was a change in government policy and health care would be forthcoming. But further investigation into the course of the survey shows the assumption to be wrong. Practically as soon as the survey was begun it was stopped because of an epidemic of sleeping sickness, and the study was subsequently abandoned and never attempted again!

The plantation system established by the Germans continued to have a dominant role in the British colonial economy. Food shortages in the countryside were still a primary force causing the peasants to leave their villages to seek work on the plantations. Under British administration, however, regulations were enforced to medically screen the labour. The government adopted this measure for two reasons. First, it wanted to prevent contagious diseases being carried onto the plantation. Second, the physically fit would be the most productive labour. This policy did not result in an improved standard of health for those who passed the medical examination, nor was it even possible for many of the physically fit to stay healthy once they were on the plantation. Because of the unsanitary conditions maintained by the planters the new recruit was fortunate if he didn't contract hookworm or some communicable disease soon after his arrival. The Labour Commissioner's Report for 1925 gives an insight into the conditions of the plantations:

> The most serious defect on almost all plantations is undoubtedly the sanitary accommodations. Proper facilities for ablutions and washing of clothes seldom exist, while the latrines are usually of a most primitive type and badly kept; flies and mosquitoes abound, and the whole camp is in an objectionable condition.[79]

But it is quite clear that in the colony the employer was taking no responsibility for the health of the worker. Hookworm continued to be a major cause of death in the plantation labour force throughout the colonial period although as early as 1920 the Senior Health Officer had explained that simple sanitary improvements would eliminate hookworm from the plantation:

> The prevention of the disease presents no special difficulties . . . Estate owners and managers must be made to provide adequate latrine facilities for their labour.

But the administration did not compel the owners and managers to clean up the plantation, and, as a consequence, they remained among the most unsanitary and unhealthy work sites in the colony.

By the 1920s, capitalist exploitation of labour was most advanced in South Africa. Research was being done to determine the minimum health measures necessary for maximum profits to be gained from the African labour force. Labour policies and practices in the Rand mines were observed by colonial administrators outside South Africa who sought to emulate them.

In many ways these South African labour policies set the pace for other colonial administrations and employers to follow. For example, in 1927 the Medical Officer of Health in Tanganyika made a visit to South Africa. He judged that South African capitalists were introducing improved sanitation measures for African labour and the results were profitable. This is his observation:

> Every opportunity was afforded of seeing the medical and sanitary arrangements made for mine employees. It has been

> shown on the Rand that no expenditure is too heavy which will produce such an improvement in the conditions of the workers, as will be likely to result in increased efficiency . . . All this improvement of hygienic conditions for the native is carried out, not for philanthropic reasons, but because it is found to give a cash return for more efficient work resulting from improved health and well-being.[81]

The Medical Officer of Health returned to Tanganyika to be one of the representatives of a new point of view which argued that better sanitation and health facilities for peasants and workers would pay off handsomely for employers. This minority viewpoint became more widespread around the Second World War although it never gained general acceptance in the colony, and productive forces remained at a low level throughout the colonial era.

The health problems of the Tanganyikan people living in the urban centres between 1918 and 1938 were fairly uniform, and we have selected examples from Dar es Salaam to illustrate our general points. The major problems were associated with residential segregation, sanitation, water supply, and urban diseases.

The pattern of residential segregation which had been enforced by the Germans was continued under British administration. Town planning regulations were designed to keep the races separate. In the early 1920s there were three zones in Dar es Salaam: one restricted to Europeans, a second primarily for Asians, and the third for Africans.[82] The pattern was found in the other important towns of the colony.

The colonial authorities claimed that segregation was required because the different races practised different health standards. However, upon closer examination their claim is incorrect for the different levels of health in the urban areas were primarily a result, rather than a defensible cause, of segregation. Through segregation of the races the authorities could discriminate in the health services offered to them. In Tanga, for example, the European community of a few hundred persons was receiving three times as much for sanitation in 1922 as the African community of thousands of persons.[84] The European community received first class sanitation services while the African community received practically nothing. This type of discrimination was common and the result was a higher level of health in the European zones.

The discriminatory practice of providing adequate and inadequate sanitation facilities to the different zones is apparent in the service of waste disposal. The government built sewers in the European sector of Dar es Salaam but it neglected to build them in the African zone. People in the latter zone were obliged to rely on pit privies which were breeding places for flies and mosquitoes, which led to a higher incidence of disease.

The colonial administration also discriminated in the supply of water to the different zones. Piped water and private wells were the norm in the European zone. In the African zone there were a few wells, often grossly contaminated, and nine government standpipes to serve over twenty thousand people. It is obvious that personal hygiene is highly dependent upon an adequate supply of water, and the Europeans were the only community that had such a supply.

The major urban diseases were tuberculosis (TB), malaria, and vitamin deficiency diseases. The first was primarily a result of overcrowding due to poverty. Dwellings built to conform to the building code in the African zone were estimated to cost about £70.[85] Because of the high cost of building, most workers were obliged to rent. Overcrowding resulted from attempts to cut down on expenses and TB spread in the congested African zone.

Malaria is a disease which received more attention from colonial authorities, yet surprisingly little was done in the capital to combat it. The German administration recruited a specialist who had helped eradicate it from the Panama Canal Zone. He was of the opinion that it would be easier to eliminate from Dar es Salaam and he made a proposal to do so, but it was not carried out because of the First World War.[86]

After the war the British did not follow up on the project. In 1925, the government voiced concern that loss of labour time was enormous due to malaria in the capital. Yet the administration was more concerned with keeping down expenses, for only £2 000 was allocated for anti-malaria work that year.[87] The sums set aside for this work over the next thirty years continued to be meagre and the results were unimpressive. The inhabitants had to rely on quinine which was sold in the Post Office until the 1950s as the main preventive measures against the continued presence of the malaria-bearing mosquito.

There is very little evidence to indicate that the administration considered vitamin deficiency diseases a health problem in the capital even though malnutrition was widespread. The average income of the workers in Dar es Salaam at the beginning of the Second World War was still quite inadequate to cover his living expenses. At that time the Health Officer gave the following pertinent statistics:

> A man, wife and child are estimated to require 30/- a month to live decently in the town. An average labourer earns seventy-seven cents a day, which even working thirty one days a month yields only Shs. 23/87.[88]

Obviously it was not possible to have a nutritionally balanced diet on such a low income.

In the 1930s the worldwide capitalist depression made an impact on the health of peasants and workers in the colonies. Among the steps taken in Tanganyika which affected the labour force were wage cuts and reduction of the scant medical services. This decision to reduce health services was made against the small opposition within the ruling class which argued that it was unprofitable to have an unhealthy colonial population. In England a member of this opposition was the Professor of Parasitology at the Liverpool School of Tropical Medicine who expressed these views to British capitalists with interests in the colonies:

> My whole argument goes to show that a very large part of the potentially productive areas of the tropics is stagnant as a market, solely because of the ill-health of the people. Such an outpatient clientele is not likely to prove a remunerative one for the exchange of commodities: the wretched people must be restored to moderate health, so that they can produce their raw materials for your trade and thus obtain purchasing power for the manufactured articles which they wish to buy and you to sell.[89]

However, the argument still proved fruitless and the cutbacks began in 1930. Expenditures that year in the medical budget were £261 529. By 1936 the figure had dropped to £173 271, and the allocation did not reach the 1930 level again until 1943.[90] Yet during that thirteen year period the number of inpatients requiring health care doubled.[91] The number of doctors in the urban hospitals was reduced and vacancies in medical staff positions were not filled.

The rural areas also suffered from these cutbacks. New projects were abandoned and training schemes fell far short of their goals. Staff were not upgraded. The African subordinate staff was cut by over one-third in the rural areas even though the tribal dressers were attending more patients in the local authority dispensaries than were being seen in the urban outpatient and inpatient departments.[92]

At the same time as these drastic reductions were taking place in the medical services the production of export crops increased. It is important to observe that the only major crop which declined in production for sale during the depression was grain, and it was the workers' main source of food.[93]

Increasing malnutrition resulting from wage cutbacks in Tanganyika during the depression was part of a worldwide pattern. Workers in the metropolitan countries were suffering from an increasing number of vitamin deficiency diseases during the 1930s. In England, for example, Sir John Boyd-Orr offered compelling evidence based on his nutritional studies which indicated that workers' health had suffered a long period of decline under capitalism. Here is his conclusion: 'The nutritional value of the diet of the British working class has shown a deterioration from the eighteenth century to the present'.[94] Thus nutritional research was encouraged in England during the depression in an effort to establish minimum dietary and nutritional standards which, if followed, would reverse this trend.[95]

At the international level there was debate on the question of nutrition and the League of Nations Technical Committee on Nutrition attempted to lay down general nutritional guidelines for government and employers in 1936.[96] The dilemma created throughout the capitalist world by the depression was a difficult one to solve indeed: how could production be increased and malnutrition prevented while reducing the wages of the working class?

The British Colonial Secretary responded to the debate in Geneva by requesting a report from each colony on the state of nutrition within its borders.[97] The government in Tanganyika was to appoint a committee to advise the metropolitan government of 'the consequences which improvement in nutrition may have upon the economy of the Territory'. The committee was appointed and made its investigation. This was the conclusion of its report:

> Improvement in nutrition . . . will mean more contented labour on the plantations and in the mining industry, and

> contented labour brings the best type and an adequate supply of workers. It will reduce the enormous wastage of such labour as now occurs in days taken off on account of sickness, the search for food or lack of food to work regularly. Greater output in native and non-native industries means more exports with the resultant improvement in the economic and financial part of the Territory.[98]

In response to this report, a three-year survey was approved but not completed because the outbreak of the Second World War caused a re-evaluation of priorities.

The Second World War

During the Second World War, Tanganyika was a recruiting centre for labour and troops. But the memories of famine and death during the First World War remained in the minds of the people and they did all they could to avoid a repetition of such experiences. Government recruiters through the East African colonies had an extremely difficult time meeting their quota. In Tanganyika, evidence of resistance is found in the Provincial Commissioner's reports for 1939 and 1940:

> 1939. In a few areas (of Lake Province) notably Biharamulo District, the outbreak of war caused a genuine apprehension, understandable in view of their experiences in the last war, that the young men would be taken as carriers. The Bazinza and other tribesmen . . . disappeared in large numbers into the bush for some days.
>
> 1940. Eastern Province. The more timid tribesmen betrayed nervousness and in some cases retired to the bush.
>
> Lake Province. A number of Sukuma, particularly from the Maswa District, deserted. The majority from the Sukuma districts, excepting Mwanza, were conscripts (rather than volunteers).
>
> Southern Highlands Province. At first the call for recruits was undoubtedly most unwelcome. Men were wanted quickly and there was no time for preliminary groundwork designed to counteract memories of the carrier corps of the last war . . . .
>
> Western Province. As was to be expected conscription for the East African Military Labour Service proved too sudden an innovation for the . . . Waha of Kigoma District who took

> alarm despite all measures taken to assure them that they were not required for combatant service. The repercussions spread northwards to the Kibondo Division . . . To continue (conscription) would inevitably have resulted in a mass exodus of the people to the bush . . . whilst the most violent reaction to conscription came from the Waha, the Wafipa were not unalarmed . . . (and) many took to the bush or vanished across the border.[99]

The men who were recruited, or conscripted because of resistance, were given a stringent medical examination. Over a quarter million men were examined in Tanganyika. While a good number passed the medical examination the reasons for rejecting a large number of men provide an insight into the general state of health in the colony. The Director of Medical Services made this report in 1943:

> Figures for the percentage of rejects at medical inspection for employment show that our population is exceedingly undernourished. In the Lindi depot alone, thirty per cent of the labour examined was rejected; of those forty per cent were underweight as well as suffering from other disease; . . . In the Lake Province forty per cent of 13 912 were rejected for military or special services.[100]

Food shortages and famine caused by the war contributed to the general state of malnutrition while troop movements led to the spread of communicable diseases. The main military communication line, the Great North Road, passed through the heart of Tanganyika: Mbeya, Iringa, Dodoma and Arusha. Thousands of recruits travelled along this road where frequent outbreaks of infectious diseases in the troop camps spread to the local civilian population.

In spite of the increasing health problems the government cut back on the civilian health services by transferring doctors, medical staff and facilities to the military. Civilian nutritional studies were also curtailed in favour of nutritional studies for the military which resulted in the preparation of vitamin extracts for the soldiers. The quinine supply for Dar es Salaam was diverted to the military and there was a resurgence of malaria in the capital.

British Colonialism: 1945–61

There were no major changes in health and medical policies during the final two decades of colonial rule in Tanganyika. Throughout the postwar years the preventive health services were neglected; the sanitation services remained inadequate; staff shortages were acute; budgets were limited; the major development plan fell far short of the goal, and the nine-tenths of the population which lived in the rural areas received very little attention from the medical authorities.

Malnutrition was widespread through the final years of colonialism. In 1947 the first Nutritional Officer was appointed and a few nutritional surveys were made after that date. In the Mlalo basin of the Usambara mountains, research established that the general state of nutrition was poor.[101] In Dar es Salaam it was found that the worker with a monthly income of shs. 87 was spending 66–70 of it on nutritionally deficient food.[102] After independence the Human Nutrition Unit of the Ministry of Health and Social Welfare reported that there was 'no convincing evidence' that the level of nutrition in Tanganyika had improved under British rule.[103]

Staff shortages were a feature of medical services throughout the colonial era, but they became acute by 1949 when almost half of the forty-nine positions for Medical Officers were vacant and there were only sixty-four nurses in government service throughout the country.[104] Yet, in the face of these shortages, recruitment of Africans into the medical services remained slow. African women were not trained and employed as government nurses or midwives until 1943, when wartime conditions made it necessary. By 1949 there were only twelve women being trained in government schemes as nurses and none at all being trained as midwives that year.[105]

Tanganyikan colonial policy prevented Africans from becoming medical doctors before the Second World War. It was only in 1938 that the first two men were sent to Makerere for medical training. It was not until 1953 that Tanganyikans could be licensed as doctors in spite of the acute shortages immediately after the war.[106] There were only fourteen Tanganyikan doctors in government service in 1960.

The limited rural health services were conducted through a scattered and uncoordinated network of dispensaries after the Second World War. The claim was made by administrators that rural health services were limited because the peasants would not use them due to the 'persistence of custom and tradition'. However, the statistics of the immediate postwar period show the claim to be incorrect. Over 1·4 million new cases were treated by the rural dispensaries in 1946. The evidence is clear that the peasants needed and sought medical care, but these services were not substantially expanded after the war.

However, the government was willing to increase the mission medical services in the rural area prior to Independence. Government grants were increased from £6 000 in 1946 to an all time high of £152 000 by the end of the colonial era.[107] The reason for this policy of increasing allocations became clear in the light of our earlier evaluation of the mission medical work. On the basis of that evaluation it seems reasonable to conclude that the Colonial Government was supporting the medical role of the missions in order to increase their conservative ideological influence in the period of nationalism after the Second World War.

A twenty-year development plan was drafted by the government in 1947. The failure of this plan is apparent from a brief examination of the gap between the stated goals at the time of drafting and the actual achievements at the time of independence. It was forecast that there would be a need for 2 000 medical practitioners and 44 000 beds within twenty years. At Independence, fifteen years after the plan was drafted, there were only 400 medical practitioners and 19 000 beds.[108]

Construction of a number of small hospitals and clinics took place in the postwar period, and the Princess Margaret Hospital (Muhimbili) was built in Dar es Salaam. But this brief period of construction was coming to an end shortly before Independence.[109]

When we look back over the period of colonial rule we realise that the low priority given to medical and health services in the postwar period was not exceptional. The medical facilities were created in the colony for the small European ruling class and the minority of Africans and Asians directly in their service. To meet these health priorities the emphasis was on cure and the facilities were situated in the towns and cities. Rural medical facilities and a strong programme of preventive medicine would have benefited the other nine-tenths of the population. But under colonialism the size of the population exceeded the demand for them as producers, so the government remained relatively uninvolved in the maintenance of health facilities for the reproduction of this sector of the population. That is the main reason Tanganyika was burdened with a major problem of medical and health care when it became independent.

Notes

1 L. Berry, *Tanzania in Maps*, London, 1971, p. 159.

2 Cited by E.N. Mngola, 'Cholera' in L.C. Vogel, *et al*, *Health and Disease in Kenya*, Nairobi, 1974, p. 181.

3 *Annual Report of the Development of German East Africa 1906/7*, p. 10, hereafter cited as *GAR*.

4 A. Redmayne, 'Hehe Medicine', *Tanganyika Notes and Records* (*TNR*) 70, 1969, p. 37.

5 P.W. Kent, 'Tuberculosis' in Vogel, p. 195.

6 B. Ehrenreich and D. English, 'Witches, Midwives and Nurses', *Monthly Review*, xxv, 5, Oct. 1973.

7 See Redmayne.

8 See the section of 'Scientific Medicine' in J.D. Bernal, *Science in History*, vol. 2, London, 1969, pp. 564–5.

9 G.W. Harley, *Native African Medicine, with Special Reference to its practice in the Mabo Tribe of Liberia*, London, reprinted 1970, p. 192.

10 A.T. and G.M. Culwick, *Ubena of the Rivers*, London, 1935, pp. 394ff.

11 The Wachagga call it *gezi* or *ngezi*, while the Masai call it *sumategi*. J.M. Watt, and M.G. Breyer-Brandwijk, *The Medicinal and Poisonous Plants of Southern and East Africa*, Edinburgh, 1962, p. 786.

12 *Ibid.*

13 *Ibid.*, p. 787. The Wahaya call it *miasha* or *muzilanyama*, while the Wasambaa call it *mtele*.

14 *Ibid.*, The Wahehe call it *mfageriro*, the Wachagga *kirjasi* or *mlimangombe*, the Wapare *kidongadwa*, and Wasambaa *mshiwizo*.

15 *Ibid.*, p. 535. The Wachagga call it *mdela*, Wanyamwezi *kachenche*, Wasambaa *lufyambo*, Wasukuma *enfiambo*, Wayao *xongalso*, and Waswahili *mongaluchi*, or *mtipitipi*. In Zanzibar it is called *matscho ya tipitipi*.

16 *Ibid.*, and J.M. Dalziel, *The Useful Plants of West Tropical Africa*, London, 1937, p. 225.

17 I.H. Burkill, *A Dictionary of the Economic Products of the*

Malay Peninsula' Kuala Lumpur, 1966, p. 7.

18 Watt, p. 786.

19 Burkill.

20 Watt.

21 W.D. Raymond, 'Native Materia Medica', *TNR*, 2, Oct, 1936, p. 54.

22 For North America see V.J. Vogel, *American Indian Medicine*, University of Oklahoma Press, 1970.

23 J.D. Bernal, *The Social Function of Science*, Cambridge, 1939, p. 16.

24 See the section of 'Social Medicine', in J.D. Bernal, *Science in History*, vol. 3, London, pp. 977–9.

25 H.F. Dobyns, 'Estimating Aboriginal American Population: An Appraisal of Techniques with a new Hemispheric Estimate', *Current Anthropology*, Oct. 1966, p. 414.

26 W. Rodney, *How Europe Underdeveloped Africa*, London and Dar es Salaam, 1972, p. 106.

27 R.R. Kuczynski, *Demographic Survey of the British Colonial Empire*, vol. II, London, 1949, pp. 123, 215 and 322.

28 H. Kjekshus, 'Ecological Control and Economic Development', University of Dar es Salaam History Research Seminar Paper, 1974, unpublished, pp. 34–5.

29 Kuczynski, p. 327.

30 Kjekshus, p. 47.

31 *Ibid.*, p. 51.

32 *Ibid.*, p. 61.

33 D.P. Clyde, *History of the Medical Services of Tanganyika*, Dar es Salaam, 1962, p. 13.

34 W.D. Foster, *The Early History of Scientific Medicine in Uganda*, Nairobi, 1970, 0. 78.

35 Quoted in Kjekshus, p. 57.

36 Clyde, p. 28.

37 *GAR*, 1970/8, p. 3.

38 Survey by the Culwicks cited in Kuczynski, pp. 378–80.

39 J. Iliffe, *Agricultural Change in Modern Tanganyika*, Nairobi,

1971, p. 8.

40 Yet, during the first decade of this century the Germans were importing large quantities of rice from India to Tanganyika. The amount in 1906/7 was 11 million kg. *GAR*, 1906/7, p. 28.

41 Sir Stanley Davidson *et al*., *Human Nutrition and Dietetics*, 5th edn., 1972, pp. 54, 96, 140, 142, 150 and 162.

42 See W.R. Ackroyd, *Conquest of Deficiency Diseases*, Freedom from Hunger Campaign Basic Study, Serial No. 24, World Health, 1970, pp. 17–34.

43 Makerere University, *Preliminary Report on Nutrition in Tanganyika Territory*, 1949, p. 4, and Tanzania, Ministry of Health and Social Welfare, Human Nutrition Unit, *The History of Nutritional Activities in Tanzania*, Dar es Salaam, 1970, p. 19.

44 Quoted in J. Kreysler, 'History of Nutrition in Tanzania' in Tanzania National Scientific Research Council, *The Young Child Study, Tanzania*, Dar es Salaam, 1973, p. 13.

45 Clyde, pp. 2–4.

46 *Ibid*., pp. 9–10.

47 Foster, p. 51.

48 *Ibid.*

49 A. Beck, 'History of Medical and Health Services in Kenya (1900–50)', in Vogel *et al*., *Health and Disease in Kenya*, p. 98.

50 M. Wright, *German Missions in Tanganyika, 1891–1941*, Oxford, 1971, p. 72.

51 C.J. Hellberg, *Missions on a Colonial Frontier West of Lake Victoria: Evangelical Missions in North-West Tanganyika to 1932,* Lund, 1965, p. 177.

52 A.E.M. Anderson-Morshead, *The History of the Universities' Mission to Central Africa*, vol. 1, London, 1955, p. 246–7. For a similar practice during the same famine see S.V. Sicard, *The Lutheran Church on the Coast of Tanzania, 1887–914: with Lutheran Church on the Coast of Tanzania, 1887–914: with special reference to the Evangelical Lutheran Church in Tanzania, Synod of the Uzaramo-Uluguru*, 1970, p. 140.

53 J. Richter, *Tanganyika and its Future*, London, 1934, p. 69.

54 Beck, p. 99. For an excellent account of the Carrier Corps see D.C. Savage and J.F. Munro, 'Carrier Corps recruitment in the

British East African Protectorate, 1914–8', *Journal of African History*, vii, 2, 1966, pp. 313–42.

55 *GAR* 1907/8, p. 9.

56 *Tanganyika Medical Department Annual Report*, 1920, p. 69, hereinafter cited as *TAR*.

57 *GAR*, 1908/9, p. 11.

58 Beck, p. 94.

59 General V. Lettow-Vorbeck, *My Reminiscences of East Africa*, London, 1920, p. 24.

60 *Ibid.*, p. 177.

61 A. Beck, *A History of the British Medical Administration of East Africa, 1900–50*, Cambridge, 1970, p. 64.

62 *Ibid.*

63 Clyde, p. 63.

64 *Ibid.*, p. 68.

65 *Ibid.*, pp. 58–9.

66 Lettow-Vorbeck, pp. 138–9.

67 *TAR*, 1920, p. 80.

68 M. Segall, 'The Political Economy of Doctors' Social Practice, Consciousness and Training under Capitalism', University of Dar es Salaam, Department of Sociology Seminar Papers, 1974, unpublished.

69 Quoted in Kuczynski, p. 384.

70 African Medical and Research Foundation, *The Health Services of Tanganyika*, London, 1964, p. 3; and *TAR*, 1921, p. 74.

71 *TAR*, 1920, p. 12.

72 *Ibid.*, p. 13.

73 *Ibid.*, and *TAR*, 1921, p. 116.

74 *TAR*, 1926, pp. 138–9.

75 *TAR*, 1921, 10–11; and *TAR*, 1923, p. 11.

76 *TAR*, 1926, pp. 138–9.

77 African Medical and Research Foundation, p. 8.

78 Clyde, p. 126.

79 *TAR*, 1925, p. 33.

80 *TAR*, 1920, p. 69.

81 *TAR*, 1924, pp. 46–7.

82 *TAR*, 1924, p. 161.

83 *TAR*, 1920, p. 62.

84 *TAR*, 1922, p. 132.

85 *TAR*, 1925, p. 26.

86 *TAR*, 1927, p. 47.

87 *TAR*, 1925, p. 41.

88 Clyde, p. 135.

89 D.B. Blacklock, *An Empire Problem, the House and Village in the Tropics*, Liverpool and London, 1932, p. 15.

90 Clyde, p. 133.

91 *Ibid.*, p. 156.

92 African Medical and Research Foundation, p. 10.

93 Tanganyika, *Report of the Committee to Advise on the Supply and Influence of Native Labour in Tanganyika*, Dar es Salaam, 1938, p. 9.

94 Sir John Boyd-Orr in Horace B. Davis, 'Imperialism and Labour: an analysis of Marxian Views,' *Science and Society*, xxvi, 1962, pp. 32–3.

95 See 'Nutrition' in Bernal, vol. 3, p. 878.

96 Davidson *et al.*, p. 59.

97 See G.M. Cullwick, 'Nutrition in East Africa,' *Africa*, xiv, July 1944, pp. 401–10.

98 Tanzania, Nutrition Unit, *The History of Nutritional Activities in Tanzania*, compiled by S.A. Mohamed and J.M. McKeog, Dar es Salaam, 1970, p. 12.

99 Quoted in Kuczynski, pp. 345–6.

100 *TAR*, 1943, p. 4.

101 Tanzania, Ministry of Health and Social Welfare, p. 21.

102 Kampala, Makerere College, *Preliminary Report on Nutrition in Tanganyika*, Kampala, 1949, p. 5.

103 Tanzania, Ministry of Health and Social Welfare, p. 26.

104 African Medical and Research Foundation, p. 19.

105 *Ibid.*

106 *Ibid.*, pp. 22–3.

107 *TAR*, 1949, p. 11, and Tanganyika, Ministry of Health and Labour, *Annual Report of the Health Division*, 1961, vol. 1, 1963, p. 34.

108 African Medical and Research Foundation, p. 15.

109 *Ibid.*, p. 26.

10. The End of the Colonial Era

M.H.Y. Kaniki

The period to be covered in this chapter is relatively short, roughly from the mid-1950s to the early 1960s. The major purpose here is to examine, albeit briefly, the nature, scope and dynamics of the process of decolonisation in former Tanganyika and Zanzibar. We have to consider how Tanganyikans collectively (and where possible individually) expressed nationalism and finally overthrew colonialism. A number of questions will have to be considered in order to shed some light on the problem. Why, for instance, did the British leave Tanganyika and Zanzibar when they did? Why couldn't they leave earlier or much later? Had their departure been long-planned or was it contrary to their earlier plans? How complete was the pull-out? What was the socio-economic background of the heirs to the colonial throne? What were the long and short-term motives of different groups and individuals actively involved in the nationalist movement? And, finally, how was it that Tanganyika (and the other East African colonies) recovered her *Uhuru* through peaceful means while Zanzibar had to resort to force and carry out a bloody revolution?

Decolonisation is of fundamental significance to Tanzania, as, indeed, it is to the rest of the African continent. It enabled Tanzanian societies to recover their *Uhuru* which had been lost for seventy years. To some extent, therefore, decolonisation was a kind of revolution. It involved struggle, suffering, sacrifice and humiliation. *Uhuru* was not 'given back' to Africa as many apologists of colonialism argue or imply. They speak of the 'transfer of power' from the colonial regime to nationalist leaders as if the process was with the blessings of the colonalists.[1] This is misleading. All the evidence reveals that all former colonies, Tanzania being no exception, had to struggle for their *Uhuru*. *Uhuru* was won in Tanzania not as a result of British initiative, but indeed despite all British resistance and machinations.

This brings us to an important question: why did the colonialists, be they French or British, pull out of the colonies when they did? Certainly the pull-out had not been anticipated, even as late as the late 1940s. As one of the framers and custodians of British colonial policy has observed, until the 1940s British colonialists based their attitudes and actions on the assumption that there was indefinite time ahead.[2] The change of attitude after the mid-1950s came with increasing realisation of decreasing profitability of colonial relations. The social and economic changes which had taken place in the colonies mitigated effective and profitable exploitation of the colonies. The civil and labour unrest which plagued most colonies after the outbreak of the Second World War revealed the limitations of colonial relations in effective exploitation of the underdeveloped colonial resources, both human and material. International public opinion, too, was not in favour of political domination of some countries by others. Thus by the early 1950s it became clear that for imperialism to thrive in the colonies, formal political presence was to be withdrawn. But the colonialists would not withdraw political control before they had created conditions conducive to economic exploitation in the absence of such political control. It was in the attempt to create such conditions that the colonialists were involved in bloody struggles in Malaya, Vietnam, Aden and Kenya. To them the struggles were worthwhile, as they had to create conditions which would enable them, to use the words of Jack Woddis, to go in order to stay. The fast constitutional changes all over Africa during the 1950s were part of this process. The colonialists made every effort to surrender political power into the 'right hands', to people who would take care of their economic interests or who at least appeared to be potential representatives or agents of international capital. As Sir Andrew Cohen has observed, it was the duty of the colonial Governors, the leading flagbearers of imperialism, to control and guide this delicate process which produced heirs to the colonial throne.[3]

One more general observation should be made at this stage. The rise of nationalism was a direct product of colonial relations. By the 1950s the social and economic changes which had taken place for decades had produced a political climate in which colonialism could not thrive. The participation of many people in the production of cash crops, for instance, created all kinds of grievances which in turn led to the rise of rural discontent and radicalism. Organised workers too, who were a creation of colonialism, worked for its downfall. Education was another factor which did not serve the colonialists as they had expected. Colonial education was intended to produce people who were intelligent and able enough to implement policies from above, but subservient enough to accept perpetual political domination. Only a limited number of avenues were open to them in employment and further training. Evidently the colonial policies aimed at blocking the way for any local skills which might effectively compete with the expatriate firms which enjoyed the protection of the colonial state apparatus. Thus those members of the educated elite who made best use of the new opportunities in trade and education found their opportunities for further advancement blocked by the administrative, educational, and commercial policies of the colonial administration and the mercantile firms. At this stage the contradictions of the colonial situation became apparent. Education had shown the educated elite their rights which, they believed and argued, were not very different from those of the European minority in the colonies. It was in the struggle to win these rights that the need to destroy colonialism was realised. This was a complicated issue which presented formidable problems. It did not take long before the petty bourgeoisie discovered that their own rights could not be won without the active support of other groups of sufferers under colonialism. Accordingly, they rallied the masses behind them, articulated the grievances of their kith and kin, and led movements aimed at destroying the very system which had created them. Thus colonialism, like capitalism, produced its own grave-diggers.

The decolonisation of Tanzania is divided into two sections, the first dealing with the mainland or former Tanganyika and the second with Zanzibar. As regards the mainland, more will be said about the activities and achievements of the Tanganyika African National Union (TANU) than about other political parties. TANU was the first political party to emerge in Tanganyika and it dominated the politics of decolonisation to the end. Thus from time to time TANU and 'the nationalist movement' are used interchangeably. As for Zanzibar, the activities of all the political parties will be touched upon, but greater emphasis will be given to the Afro-Shirazi Party (ASP) and the Zanzibar Nationalist Party (ZNP).

Tanganyika

Nationalism in Tanganyika has its roots in the distant past but the nationalist movement which recovered the country's independence is an affair of the 1950s, and then the coordinator of nationalist sentiments and activities was TANU. It was at the Annual Conference of the Tanganyika African Association (TAA) held in Dar es Salaam from 7 to 10 July 1954 that the Union was born. Thus the seventeen TAA delegates became the founding members of TANU. These were:[4]

Mr J.K. Nyerere	—	Territorial President
Mr Germano H. Pasha	—	Western Province
Mr N.K. Kirilo Japhet	—	Northern Province
Mr Joseph Kimalando	—	Northern Province
Mr C.O. Milinga	—	Eastern Province
Mr A.C. Iranga	—	Lake Province
Mr L.M. Bagohe	—	Lake Province
Mr S.A. Kandoro	—	Lake Province
Mr Kisungutwa Gabara	—	Lake Province
Mr S.M. Kitwana	—	Lake Province
Mr Tewa Saidi Tewa	—	Eastern Province
Mr D.W.A. Azizi	—	Eastern Province
Mr A.K. Sykes	—	Eastern Province
Mr A.W. Sykes	—	Eastern Province
Mr G.P. Kunambi	—	Eastern Province
Mr J.P. Kassella	—	Eastern Province
Mr John Rupia	—	Eastern Province

Mr Julius Kambsrage Nyerere, a teacher at Pugu Secondary School, hitherto almost unknown to the masses of Tanganyika, was elected President and Mr John Rupia Vice-President. Born at Butiama, a village near Musoma on the shores of Lake Victoria, in 1922, Nyerere belonged to one of the smallest ethnic groups in Tanganyika, the Wazanaki, to which his father, Nyerere Buritc, was Chief. He received his primary education in Musoma, and secondary education at Tabora, a town in the heart of Tanganyika. Later he studied for two years at Makerere College, Uganda, from which he graduated with a Diploma in Education in 1945. He returned to

Tabora to teach at St Mary's Secondary School. In 1949 he entered Edinburgh University, and graduated as a Master of Arts in 1952. On his return to Tanganyika, he resumed teaching, this time at the leading Roman Catholic Secondary School, Pugu, which was one of the leading schools in the country.

Unfortunately, it is not possible at the moment to assess accurately the impact of different influences on Nyerere during these formative years. Two general observations, however, could be made in this respect. First, Nyerere had suffered the numerous humiliations and inconveniences arising from colonialism, which bound him to the rest of the Africans in Tanganyika, including all the founder members of TANU. Second, his experience as a student both in East Africa and Britain exposed him to situations which required analytical examination of colonialism. It was also during his student life that he broadened his political horizons, general outlook and organisational capacities.[5] No doubt his stay in Britain gave him confidence to face the colonial oppressors. He had mastered both their language and their political tactics. All this, however, would not change his status, that of a colonised man, who must suffer economic exploitation, racial segregation, cultural subordination and all sorts of injustice.

It was with this understanding that within a year of his election to the office of Territorial President of TAA, Nyerere recognised the inadequacy of the association as a political body to challenge and confront the colonial authorities. He set to work to draft a new constitution which would completely reorientate the association's objectives and policy. The new constitution was enthusiastically adopted in July 1954 by the association's annual conference which also renamed the association. Thus TAA formed the foundation on which TANU was built. The two organisations differed in one major respect. TANU had a narrower focus than TAA: TANU was basically a political body while TAA was semi-political and semi-cultural. TANU's first objective was categorically stated in the first constitution: to prepare the Tanganyika African for self-rule and to fight relentlessly for national freedom—*Uhuru*.

Other objectives included: to fight tribalism and any other factor which would hinder the development of unity among Africans; to abolish all sorts of segretation; to encourage and help workers to establish trade unions; and to co-operate with other organisations whose aims and objectives were not contradictory to those of TANU.

Essentially TANU was a political party or nationalist movement not an association. The Union confessed no ideology and membership was open to all Africans in Tanganyika.

The discussion conducted at the annual conference during which TANU was born shows clearly that Tanganyika had reached a high level of political consciousness, partly through the activities of TAA. It was evident right from the start that TANU intended to act as spokesman for all sufferers, and to champion the grievances and aspirations of the masses. The conference dealt with broad policy issues some of which remained unsolved twenty years later. Themes covered at the conference included the election of Legislative Council members; education for Africans in Tanganyika; tax on cotton, coffee, cattle; problems of destocking; and the position of the British Queen in Tanganyika.

As regards education for Africans, the conference resolved that the government should introduce universal compulsory primary education in order to fight illiteracy more effectively. The policy of limiting African primary education to four years only was condemned as 'a curse for the whole country' because it did not prepare the recipients to be productive members of the community.[6] They recommended that the government should fundamentally modify the 'extremely hopeless' middle school education by introducing vocation-based education. It was further resolved that Kiswahili should be promoted in elementary as well as higher schools. A special committee of four, comprising S.A. Kandoro, G.P. Kunambi, J.K. Nyerere and N.K. Japhet, was appointed to solicit funds from all over the country for the promotion of education. It was agreed that a sum of shs. 2 500 should be spent in meeting travelling expenses of the committee members. Each of the four provinces represented at the conference was expected to contribute shs. 600 by the end of August, 1954, for this purpose.

Another issue which occupied the conference was the taxation system in the rural areas, especially in Northern and Lake Provinces. The conference strongly opposed the proposed tax on coffee, arguing that coffee growers were already paying dues to their co-operative societies and unions in addition to the poll tax paid by other people. They further noted that the current cotton prices left the producers with no profit margin. The office of the President of TANU was directed to ask the government 'to stop this business at once and improve the situation'.

The conference received grievances from the cattle-producing areas of Lake Province. The delegates complained that farmers were subjected to a tax of shs. 1/50 for each head of cattle. They were also forced to reduce the number of cattle by ten per cent. To add insult to injury, the delegates argued, the price of the cattle was assessed by only one buyer, the well-known capitalist company, Tanganyika Packers.

This company fixed the prices at between shs. 30 and shs. 150 per head of cattle. If the owner of cattle disagreed with the low prices offered by Tanganyika Packers he had no alternative but to slaughter the heads of cattle brought to the market. He had to show hides to the Native Authority as evidence that he had obeyed the order to destock. This report received the sympathy of the conference, and a committee of eight, including the President, was appointed to approach the government for redress.

The last important issue discussed at the conference was the position of the Queen of the United Kingdom in Tanganyika. It was emphasised that Tanganyika was a Trust Territory and not a colony. As such the Queen of the United Kingdom should be referred to simply as 'The Queen' and not 'our Queen'. This observation, apparently originating from Nyerere, caused a sensation among the delegates. According to S.A. Kandoro, the introduction and passing of this observation proved to the TAA politicians that Nyerere was a brave and wise leader.[7] To make sure that all people in the country knew their political status, that of being under Trusteeship, the conference resolved that the government be approached to fly the Union Jack and the United Nations flag side by side.

This resolution, which implicity refused to acknowledge the Queen's sovereignty over Tanganyika, soured relations between TANU and the colonial administration right from the early days of the Union. Twining, the Governor of Tanganyika during the crucial years of TANU, was according to his sympathetic biographer, 'a man who felt very strongly about loyalty and royalty'.[8] Of all TANU's 'sins' it was the anti-Queen resolution which perhaps upset him most, and he probably neither forgave nor forgot it.[9]

The radicalism expressed at the conference raised the morale of the delegates. On their return to the province, TANU members enthusiastically publicised the Union, recruited new members and attempted in different ways to establish legitimacy for the union as a nationalist movement. The call to fight for national freedom was easily understood, thus the enthusiastic response in most parts of the country. Indeed, in some parts of the country, for example, Singida District in 1955, the enthusiasm reached proportions which made some people regard the influence of TANU as an infection.

This initial enthusiasm, however, does not mean that TANU was operating on prepared ground: one important obstacle had to be overcome right from the start. People had to be educated to trust the effectiveness of TANU tactics. According to their experience and traditions a struggle could not be effectively waged without the use of arms. It was through the use of arms that one group could conquer another group and impose its political domination. Likewise a group could only liberate itself from political domination through combat. This had been the experience of almost all societies in Tanganyika. Relations between neighbouring ethnic groups had confirmed the significance of war as an arbiter; the same concept was endorsed during the Maji-Maji rebellion war of 1905 to 1907 when Tanganyikan societies lost their *Uhuru* decisively to the Germans. Furthermore, even relations between the so-called civilised nations sealed the belief that after all political power can only be achieved through military conquest. This was clearly demonstrated during the two World Wars. During the early years, therefore, TANU had to politicise and educate the people to the effect that *Uhuru* would be regained through non-violent means.

From the start TANU waged the struggle both at home and abroad. The leadership recognised the significance of the United Nations as regards the political status of Tanganyika. They effectively exploited the influence of this organisation in bargaining for *Uhuru*. In March 1955, when TANU was not yet a year old, the movement sent its president, Mr Nyerere, to present their case to the Trusteeship council. Nyerere won the admiration of the Trusteeship Council as he expounded the hopes of his people. He explained that the major objective of TANU was to prepare the people of Tanganyika for independence. As a first step towards that goal TANU sought to see the establishment of elective principles, with the African securing a majority in all representative public bodies in accordance with the Trusteeship Agreement and Article 76 of the United Nations Charter. Nyerere also informed the council that the Africans in Tanganyika desired a categorical statement from the Trusteeship Council and the British Government that the future government of

Tanganyika would be primarily African. This kind of assurance, he argued, would destroy false hopes on the part of the non-Africans and false fears in the Africans.

On his return to Tanganyika Nyerere resigned from teaching in order to devote all his energies to the nationalist movement. In the meantime, TANU branches had been established in many districts of the country. In 1955 Nyerere carried out his first countrywide tour and listened and talked to people, giving encouragement where there was despair and dispersing different kinds of fear. The tour enabled him to assess, however roughly, the political potential of the masses and the kind of organisational problems TANU was likely to face.

Stumbling blocks

Far from what most distant observers want the world to believe, the nationalist movement in Tanganyika did not have a smooth and easy route to success. TANU faced opposition from many quarters in Tanganyika: from individuals, organised groups, established institutions, political parties and the colonial government. At times opposition arose out of ignorance, but the most effective opposition came from well-informed quarters with genuine fears of losing privileged positions in society. Probably the group which was most upset by the objectives of TANU were the flag-bearers of colonialism, who, if TANU succeeded, would be the immediate and probably the principal losers. Their reaction to the growing influence of TANU throughout the period from 1954–61 shows clearly their fear and awareness of TANU's devastating capacity.

Naturally, TANU faced opposition and hostility from the Colonial Government right from the start. As soon as it was learned that TANU had replaced TAA, the legislation governing the operation of societies was amended to create stumbling blocks for TANU. The Registrar General of Societies used various delaying tactics to frustrate the efforts of TANU members. TANU leadership, however, adopted a compromising spirit without sacrificing the fundamentals. As a result of their foresight and negotiating skill the union was at last registered on 30 October, 1954. This, however, did not mean automatic registration for TANU branches, as each branch had to apply for registration. This acted as a delaying device and, as we shall see, it gave district commissioners and district officers power to check the influence of TANU. By the end of 1954 only a few branches had been registered. They included Dar es Salaam, Tabora, Tarime, Singida and North Mara. In the following year a few more branches were registered. Among them were Rungwe, Musoma, Bagamoyo, Kisarawe, Ukerewe, Kilosa, Kilwa, Iramba and Lindi.

All these branches were registered despite colonial opposition and all sorts of colonial machinations. District Commissioners in Singida and Musoma were especially vicious. They used the colonial political machine to intimidate, detain and even imprison TANU leaders. They used chiefs to harass TANU members and sympathisers. To their great surprise, however, their hostility towards TANU acted as a catalyst and gave the Union increasing solidarity in the struggle to rid the country of political domination and racial humiliation.

Closing TANU branches and banning TANU activities were other effective methods employed by the Colonial Government to check the spread of TANU. This tactic was first employed in Sukumaland where rural radicalism and TAA activities had given the colonial regime appreciable headaches. In October, 1954, the Mwanza branch was banned. Subsequently the government declined to register the Shinyanga, Geita, Malamapaka, Nassa and Nera branches. These steps were taken, it was alleged, for two reasons: first because the TANU leadership in the region was in the wrong hands; and second because TANU pronouncements had been subversive. It was not until October 1958 when TANU pressure had become almost irresistible, that the government allowed TANU branches to operate in Sukumaland.

A number of other branches had similar experiences. Among them were Dodoma, Iringa, and Kondoa-Irangi. In Tanga province alone four branches, Lushoto, Korogwe, Pangani and Handeni, were mercilessly victimised. The experiences of these branches was quite dramatic. The Lushoto branch was banned in August 1956 and was not registered until August 1959, and this after a protracted struggle by the TANU leadership at national and provincial levels. The Korogwe branch was banned in April 1957 and was not registered until July 1959. Both branches were in Usambara District ruled by Chief Kimweri Mputa Magogo. It would appear that TANU's difficulties in Korogwe and Lushoto arose from two factors. First, TANU leadership in Lushoto included members of an anti-Magogo and anti-chieftancy faction, so TANU appeared to strengthen the enemies of the chief, and to be the potential destroyer of the chiefs as a privileged group under colonial rule. Second, Tanga province was an important base for the settler-dominated United Tanganyika Party (UTP) established early in 1956 to oppose TANU. By banning TANU activities in most districts in the province the government was in effect attempting to create a monopoly for UTP. But things did not work according to plan.

TANU did not die in Tanga Province. Not even in Usambara, where the union was banned longest. It operated underground; people held TANU cards in secret; members were recruited at night or during the day in the shambas. The existence of TANU during the period it was banned is borne out by the fact that when the union was allowed to operate in 1959 it had thousands of members.

The United Tanganyika Party (*UTP*)

In the meantime, early in 1956, the government made a significant advance in its effort to arrest the growth and spread of the nationalist movement. Through the initiative of Governor Twining[10] the unofficial members in the Legislative Council who had been nominated by the Governor formed the 'multi-racial' United Tanganyika Party. Membership was open for people of all races, unlike TANU where non-Africans were not eligible for membership. But it became evident within a short time that the openness of UTP was nothing more than a propaganda device. In practice, the party was intended to be an instrument of European political domination in Tanganyika. African members and to some extent Asian members too, were essentially used to cover the real intentions of the European oligarchy; Africans were by no means intended to be among the principal beneficiaries of UTP activities. UTP found its most ardent members among the white settlers of Tanganyika who wanted to control the political machinery of the country. The President, Mr Ivor Bayldon, a rich pyrethrum and coffee farmer near Mbeya, was favoured by Twining.

TANU and UTP differed on one fundamental point—the future position of different racial groups in Tanganyika. TANU's stand was clear right from the start. People of different races should have equal rights as citizens, but since Africans formed the vast majority of the population, political power after the end of colonisation would inevitably be in the hands of the Africans.

According to this line of thinking, any constitutional changes should be aimed at progressively increasing African representation in the legislative and decision-making bodies of the country. Clearly this strategy was not in the interests of the non-Africans, and it did not take them long to react accordingly. UTP was founded to guarantee non-Africans, especially Europeans, a special space in the politics of Tanganyika. UTP turned out to be the institutionalised defender and promoter of the parity system whereby the legislative bodies in the country comprised equal numbers from each of the three racial groups—African, Asian and European. Though the non-Africans formed a tiny minority, the weight of their colour was supposed to balance the numerical weight of the Africans. On this point TANU and UTP were diametrically opposed, and TANU leaders exploited this point, since it made African UTP members appear to be the stooges of the colonial regime, enemies of *Uhuru* and betrayers of the African cause. By the closing years of the 1950s, an African UTP member appeared in the eyes of many to be a traitor, and one of the nastiest associations one could be linked with was UTP.

The mobilisation of international sympathy

In November 1956 TANU sent their President to argue their case at the United Nations for the second time. On 20 December 1956, Nyerere addressed the 579th meeting of the Fourth Committee of the United Nations General Assembly. He disclosed to the committee that there were in Tanganyika approximately 8 000 000 Africans, 70 000 Asians and 25 000 Europeans. Among other things, he called on the Tanganyika Government to declare that 'our country will be developed as a democratic state. Since ninety-eight per cent of the population are indigenous Africans, this will naturally be primarily an African state.'[11] TANU was making an assault on the government and the representatives of economic imperialism in Tanganyika. As Nyerere came to recall when addressing the Trusteeship Council in July 1961, 'the innocuous statement which I made to the fourth committee and a subsequent one which I made upon my return to Tanganyika, got me into some trouble with the authorities.'[12]

Nyerere returned to Dar es Salaam on 21 January 1957. A big crowd of jubilant TANU members and sympathisers met him at the airport, and a long procession of singers, dancers, etc., escorted him to his home in Magomeni, one of the popular African residential areas in Dar es Salaam. The reception Nyerere received was on the one hand a clear indication of TANU's popularity and strength and, on the other hand, an indication of the people's acceptance of Nyerere as their leader to the promised land of *Uhuru*.

Nyerere's speech at the United Nations infuriated and perturbed the Colonial Government. Within three months of his return in April 1957, the Tanganyika Government published a well-argued twenty-five page pamphlet as a reply to and commentary on Nyerere's speech.[13] The pamphlet, it was argued, was issued to demonstrate the 'serious misrepresentations'[14] contained in Nyerere's speech, which emphasised the unnecessary general backwardness of Tanganyika, and according to the Colonial Government was directed to two main ends: 'the self-glorification of Mr Nyerere and the denigration of all that has been done for the people of Tanganyika, within the space of a single generation, by the Administering Authority in general and by the unselfish efforts of many hundreds of individuals, both officials and non-officials in particular'.[15]

As regards Nyerere's claim to speak 'on behalf of my people', the government simply rejected the legitimacy of TANU. They argued that it would have been more accurate for Nyerere to speak of 'my organisation', which comprised only one out of eighty inhabitants of Tanganyika, rather than of 'my people'. The government emphatically, but erroneously, rejected the leader of TANU as a representative and spokesman of the vast majority of Tanganyikans. 'What is certain is that Mr Nyerere has no right to speak for the vast majority of the people of Tanganyika. They will continue, if they are not misled, to prefer the path of quiet progress and peaceful co-operation'.[16] This observation is a good testimony of the short-sightedness and obstinacy of colonial regimes. But instead of reducing the potency of TANU these obviously malicious gestures by the government increased Nyerere's popularity and intensified TANU's solidarity. Thus government anti-TANU propaganda was self-defeating.

Another issue discussed by Nyerere at the United Nations was the existence and operations of UTP. He openly pointed out the fact that UTP aimed at 'the domination of the Africans by the Europeans with the help of the Asians and the Africans'.[17] On this sensitive issue the Colonial Government could not hide its political aspirations and interest in promoting European domination in Tanganyika through constitutional devices. The official pronouncement will speak more emphastically here:

> Jealousy has presumably inspired this slur on an association which at least seems to be making an attempt to build itself into a genuine political party rather than a racial cabal. Its widely distributed manifesto repudiates domination by any race and Mr Nyerere's accusation is a good example of a well-worn technique of falsely accusing an opponent of aims or views which one in fact holds oneself.[18]

The Colonial Government did not limit its anti-TANU campaign to the towns, it mobilised political forces at the grassroots to spread a hostile attitude towards TANU. In May 1957, a month after the publication of the pamphlet attacking Nyerere's speech to the United Nations, the government called the first ever convention of representatives of Chiefs in Tanganyika. Altogether sixty-two chiefs from all provinces met an Mzumbe, near Morogoro, from 14 to 16 May. The exact purpose of the convention is not quite clear, but the timing and the issues discussed suggest that the colonial regime was taking advantage of its monopoly of institutionalised political power to fight any nationalist sentiments. In his opening speech on Tuesday, 14 May, Governor Twining attempted to drive a wedge between the traditional rulers and the nationalist movement. He emphasised the significance of chiefs as the custodians of tribal values which formed the real heart of tribal life. Without mentioning TANU by name, he accused the union of propagating alien political ideas which paid no respect to traditional rulers and traditional values. The Governor further accused TANU of propagating colour prejudice and racial segregation among the people.[19]

Evidently Twining's speech was intended to mislead the chiefs, and he met with some success. When TANU sent its president Nyerere to the United Nations for the third time (in June 1957), the Colonial Government despatched one European official, Mr Fletcher-Cook, as special envoy, and Chief Thomas Marealle, then Paramount Chief of the Wachagga, to dilute or oppose Nyerere's impact at the United Nations. Accordingly, Marealle addressed the Trusteeship Council on 17 June 1957. Using the very tactics applied by Twining at Mzumbe, he avoided a direct attack on TANU, but his main arguments contradicted TANU's aspirations and immediate objectives.

On the following day Nyerere addressed the Trusteeship Council and 'congratulated' Marealle on his speech. Then Nyerere expressed his disappointment with the Tanganyika Government's failure to declare that Tanganyika was essentially an African country. The President of TANU also criticised the government's uncompromising attitude regarding TANU's demand to increase African representation in the Legislative Council to fifty per cent. He further proposed tripartite electoral system through which members of the Legislative Council would be elected in 1958. According to this system every voter would have to vote for three candidates, an African, a European and an Asian. This meant each constituency would have three members. Nyerere also took this opportunity to expose the unholy alliance between the Tanganyika Government, UTP and the European-owned press in Tanganyika. He further questioned the democratic value of the proposed general elections in 1958 if the government continued to support and aid UPT, an opponent of TANU. To sum up, Nyerere asked for four concessions: a target date for Tanganyika's Independence; intermediate dates for constitutional reforms leading to Independence; universal suffrage in the election to take place in 1958, and the lifting of restrictions on TANU and the ban on him to make public speeches.

In order to arrest the expansion of TANU and to make its leader politically impotent, Governor Twining nonimated Nyerere a member of the Legislative Council in July 1957. Nyerere accepted the nomination, presumably with mixed feelings. Within less than half a year, however, after attending only two meetings, 'he had tasted the cup of bitterness'[20] and decided to quit the council. In his letter of resignation to Governor Twining, the President of TANU explained at length why he had to quit. The main factor was the uncompromising spirit of the government regarding TANU's demands. On 16 December 1957, Nyerere used the party bulletin, *Sauti ya TANU* No. 18, to explain his stand and the decision he had taken. His concluding remarks, which boosted his image as a nationalist leader, are worth quoting at some length:

> I have given everything that it was in my power to give, and what I have given has been rejected. I came to the council expecting a little of the spirit of give and take. That spirit is not there. I would feel that I am cheating the people and

> cheating my own organisation if I remained on the council, receiving allowances and attending sundowners as an Honourable Member, giving the impression that I was still of some service on that council, when in fact I know that I am useless. I had, therefore, no alternative but to tender my resignation, and to ask that my resignation take effect from Friday, 14 December 1957, the day my last compromises were rejected by Government.[21]

In the meantime, TANU had taken root in many districts, and in some districts it was flourishing. By the middle of 1957 membership stood at between 150 000 and 200 000. The party was also widening its scope of operations and aspirations. The political growth of the party was clearly demonstrated at the Annual Conference held at Tabora from 21 to 25 January 1958. In many ways, this was one of the most important party conferences[22]. It was attended by 152 members from all provinces, who discussed almost every aspect of life in the country. Indeed the confidence and militancy shown at the conference shows clearly that TANU was now entering maturity. preparing to share political power with the Colonial Government. As regards education, the conference directed the Executive Committee of the party to ensure the introduction of free primary education lasting six years, the expansion of secondary education on a multi-racial basis, government recognition of TANU schools, and the establishment of an institution of higher learning in Tanganyika. The institution for higher learning would be established with funds raised by TANU[23]. The conference further directed the Executive Committee to establish a special committee to deal with educational affairs.

The most important, and probably the most delicate, issue discussed during the annual conference in January 1958 was TANU's stand regarding the proposed general elections to be held in 1958 and 1959. The controversial point was the racial parity. Delegates engaged in a heated debate which almost divided the party. Some members advocated boycotting the elections which appeared to be little more than a mockery. Others, including the President of the party, stood for co-operation with the government. They argued that boycotting the election would automatically give TANU's opponents and enemies a monopoly of the legislature. On the other hand, TANU's participation would provide the party with an opportunity to fight for the nationalist cause from within. This viewpoint was adopted by the majority, and delegates left Tabora with enthusiasm to prepare for the general elections.

A number of radical resolutions were passed at the conference. In one of them TANU members pledged to adopt a non-co-operation policy if the Tanganyika Government refused to grant the country internal responsible government in 1959. The conference authorised the President of TANU to explain this resolution to the public. Nyerere took the platform at the Police Grounds, Tabora, and with great oratorical skill, dramatised the evils and disgrace of political domination by foreigners. At the height of his speech he wept, igniting mass hysteria among the crowd who joined him in shedding tears. This symbolic gesture acted as an important morale-booster among Africans all over the country.

But this great success could not heal all the wounds inflicted on some members during the Conference. One prominent member, Mr Zuberi Mtemvu, and a few followers felt Nyerere's policy towards non-Africans in Tanganyika was unnecessarily moderate. Consequently, shortly after the conference Mtemvu decided to quite TANU and formed his own organisation, the African National Congress (ANC). ANC's policy was 'Africa for Africans', but this motto did not appeal to Africans as Mtemvu had expected, most likely because of TANU's strength and popularity at this time, and the new organisation really never took off. Mtemvu was the only ANC candidate for the Legislative Council in 1958, and in 1960 only he and another candidate contested the elections. At the end of 1960 the ANC had only nine 'organised branches' as against TANU's 498.[24] But this new organisation made some impact in some parts of the country, especially in Tanga Province and the Lake Victoria area.[25]

Factors favouring the Nationalist movement

It is convenient at this juncture to examine, albeit briefly, the major factors which facilitated the growth of the nationalist movement. These factors included the existence of TAA, effective leadership, use of Kiswahili and the co-operation and sympathy of several organisations in Tanganyika. TAA contributed to the growth and spread of TANU in a number of ways. TANU inherited a territorial base which the Association had developed for more than two decades. Thus from the start TANU operated as a nationalist movement fighting for the *Uhuru* of the whole of Tanganyika,[26] and representing all the inhabitants regardless of race, creed or ethnic origins. Furthermore, TANU inherited from TAA a relatively high degree of political consciousness and radicalism in the rural areas. Rural discontent in Sukumaland, Ulurguru Mountains, Usambara, Meru, Kilimanjaro and elsewhere had found expression through the TAA[27]. The alienation of land on the slopes of Mount Meru, for instance, created political fears and suspicion in many parts of the country where African political leaders had a following. Thus the Wameru came to be regarded merely as a single example of the many categories of sufferers under colonial rule. The name of Kirilo Japheth came to be connected not merely with the Meru land case, but also with the wider struggle against European domination in Tanganyika.

But we must strike a note of caution here. We know relatively little about rural discontent and radicalism in colonial Tanganyika. Even the useful contributions by Cliffe,[28] Saul[29] and Maguire[30] have left a substantial gap. More research at the grassroots is required to identify the potency and local dynamics of rural radicalism. It is not satisfactory, for instance, to regard the rural population as an amorphous and undifferentiated mass with harmonious interests. The category of rural population commonly referred to as peasants were (and remain) of different economic statures. For example the cash incomes of the Chagga and Bahaya coffee farmers and Sukuma cotton farmers were much more than those of Nyiramba millet farmers and Makonde cassava farmers. Even among those relatively better-off groups, there were inequalities the exact extent of which we do not known. It would be useful to map extensively the relationship between economic prosperity and the level of political involvement in the nationalist movement.

Another asset TANU inherited from TAA was effective leadership. In many districts TANU did not start from scratch in developing leadership. The TAA politicians became the first promoters and guardians of TANU. People like Joseph Kimalando and Kirilo Japheth in Northern Province, and Paul Bomani in Lake Province used the legitimacy of TAA to establish and consolidate legitimacy for TANU. Then, unlike the leadership in nationalist movements in many parts of Africa, TANU leaders avoided squabbles which could divide the party. Indeed until well after Independence the party united solidly under the wise leadership of Nyerere. This does not mean that the nationalist movement was free from all divisive forces; far from that. As noted above, there were disagreements and conflict, but this is, in fact, the essence of politics. The ANC was a clear manifestation of division in the movement, but it did not present a really serious threat.

Kiswahili, as a *lingua franca* of Tanganyika, played a substantial role in uniting the activities of the nationalist movement. The language is understood almost everywhere in the country, and in most cases TANU leaders, especially those at provincial and national level, addressed public meetings in Kiswahili. Most leaders were (and are) fluent in the language and, therefore, there was direct and undiluted communication between the leaders and the masses. Nyerere combined a good command of Kiswahili and a remarkable ability to dramatise issues for effective communication. The ability to communicate in Kiswahili made TANU leaders easily acceptable as leaders of the whole of Tanganyika rather than of this or that ethnic group.

Support from and sympathy of other organised groups strengthened the bargaining power of TANU. The party's constitution encouraged co-operation between TANU and other organisations whose objectives and policies were not contradictory to those of the nationalist movement. During the early years TANU sought basically to co-operate with other organisations, but as the movement gathered greater momentum and strength it tended to control the other organisations. The relationship between TANU and the Tanganyika Federation of Labour (TFL) and between TANU and the co-operative movement, are particularly interesting. It did not take long before organised wage labour discovered that TANU was the overall 'spokesman' of the oppressed masses, including the workers.

TANU, on the other hand, was not late to realise the significance of organised labour in the struggle against colonialism. The movements remained separate, but there was co-operation and mutual sympathy. During 1957 and 1958 TANU and TFL moved close to each other. At the Annual Conference of TANU held at Tabora in January 1958, Mr Rashidi Kawawa, General Secretary of TFL, was elected a member of the Executive Committee of TANU, and later during the year he became a TANU candidate for the legislative. Thus organised labour gave the nationalist movement the badly-needed skilled manpower. The only organisation which contributed more in this respect was the co-operative movement, from where the nationalist movement recruited three members of the first cabinet.[31]

TANU not only used organisations created by others but also created its own. By 1956 a Youth League of the party and a women's section had been established. These organisations popularised the nationalist movement all over the country, and played an important role in mobilising the masses to support TANU. Both the TANU Youth League (TYL) and the women's section (which became *Umoja wa Wanawaka wa Tanganyika* (UWT) in 1962) gave warmth and colour to TANU public meetings and demonstrations. Through their melodious songs and chants, they condemned colonialism and praised TANU, apparently the only organisation with the capacity to end colonial exploitation. By the closing years of the 1950s the women's section of TANU, under the dynamic leadership of Titi Mohamed, was one of the most effective instruments of the party.

External influences also facilitated the growth and expansion of TANU. First, there was a sympathetic response from the United Nations which boosted the morale of Nyerere and other TANU leaders. The leaders of the nationalist movement knew that ultimate say regarding the future of Tanganyika, a Trust Territory, was to come from the United Nations, and not from Britain, a mere caretaker. But the caretaker was not a shadow, it was a reality. Its attitude towards the colonial peoples had to be changed in order to give political independence to its dependencies. Fortunately for Tanganyika, the British are sensitive to public opinion,[32] and the leadership of the nationalist movement exploited this sensitivity at the United Nations.

The other external factor which facilitated the decolonisation of Tanganyika was successful decolonisation elsewhere in Africa and Asia. The independence of Ghana in March 1957 was especially significant: it boosted the morale of black Tanganyikans and gave TANU leaders a feeling of 'it can be done'. By the second half of 1957 it was felt that what Kwame Nkrumah and his colleagues had done for the Gold Coast, Nyerere and his colleagues could do for Tanganyika.

Contrary to what is commonly believed, the rise of the ANC strengthened TANU in two ways. First, it acted as a catalyst in the promotion of party solidarity. TANU members and leaders had to deepen their commitment to the party and to intensity their propaganda in the face of outside competition and attack. Second, the policy of the ANC, which openly refused non-Africans equality in the future independent state, scared Europeans and Indians much more than TANU had done. After the rise of the ANC the unholy alliance against TANU lost some of its potency. The *Tanganyika Standard* drastically changed its attitude towards TANU, which was now regarded as a party of moderates, while the ANC was presented as a party of extremists.[33] These developments partly account for whatever little co-operation the colonial administration offered TANU from the second half of 1958. It would appear that from this time the colonial administration saw TANU as 'the safe hands' to which political power should be surrendered. Indeed Turnbull's attitude towards TANU and Nyerere seems to have been a deliberate effort to isolate extremists and ensure that TANU, and not ANC, inherited the political kingdom.

It would appear that the only serious threat to the unity of TANU came from the All Muslim National Union of Tanganyika (AMNUT). In 1959 they petitioned the Colonial Government to delay the independence of Tanganyika until the educational gap between Christians and Muslims had been narrowed. The fears expressed by this organisation arose from the fact that most of the Africans holding high positions in the party and government then were Christians. This group included Nyerere himself. The fears expressed here were to a large extent genuine. Christians had preferential entry into education, a commodity which had been heavily under the control of Christian missionaries. The fact that this commodity gave people different skills and increased their productive capacity and earning power suggests that by the 1950s social differentiation could be identified along religious lines. The Muslims saw the Christians collectively as aspiring heirs to the colonial throne, as the potential elite likely to control and dominate the resources of Tanganyika after the departure of the British. To some extent, therefore, the fears of AMNUT arose out of the then existing inequalities between Muslims and Christians as groups. Ironically, however, the demand of AMNUT was addressed to the very authorities which were responsible for the unsatisfactory state of affairs. To expect the Colonial Government to correct the situation was to miss the point.

Leaders of the nationalist movement had to fight the divisive pressure from AMNUT with extensive propaganda, educative exposition and lobbying.[34] They faced the challenge with determination and an uncompromising spirit, thereby preventing the development of a precedent which could have crippled the nationalist movement. In the end Muslim leaders in Tanganyika, probably in response to TANU's repeated call for unity, denounced the Jemand of ANMUT. In a letter to the Chairman of the Post Elections Committee, dated 10 August 1959 and signed by one Yakubu S. Mtungumwa, forty-three Sheikhs dissociated themselves from AMNUT's demand and condemned the organisation as representing only a handful of self-seeking people.[35] This ended the threat from religious sentiments. No other factor, not even ethnicity, was allowed to shatter the solidarity of the nationalist movement. No splinter group ever took root as a political party.

One thing should be stressed in considering the role of leadership in the decolonisation of Tanganyika. As elsewhere in Africa, the leaders did not create the contradictions of the colonial situation, they did not create grievances of different groups of people. All they did was to identify themselves with the masses and to give direction, focus and colour to the numerous grievances arising from colonial contradictions.

It is probably convenient at this point to say a few words about the relationship between the nationalist movement in Tanganyika and similar movements in Africa. Right from the start TANU adopted a pan-Africanist outlook. The party actively co-operated with other nationalist movements in Africa, especially those in Zanzibar (Afro-Shirazi Party), Central and southern Africa. TANU believed (and still does) that the political independence of Tanganyika would be incomplete as long as other parts of the continent continued languishing under colonial oppression. It was out of this conviction that the party actively supported and aided the liberation movements in Central and southern Africa.

The militancy shown at the Tabora Conference in January 1958 perturbed the colonial administration which saw TANU and Nyerere as their number one enemy. It appeared to the Colonial Government that the best way to contain the militancy of the nationalist movement was to put Nyerere out of circulation. On 9 July 1958, about three weeks after the departure of Governor Twining, Nyerere, the president of TANU appeared before a Dar es

Salaam Resident Magistrate charged with libel against two District Commissioners and the use of defamatory statements against colonial administrators. Nyerere had boldly reacted against colonial machinations to arrest the influence of the nationalist movement. These were the exact words which exposed the District Commissioners and then caused a sensation in Tanganyika: 'These same officials would have people committing perjury in court in order to vilify TANU. These same people who intimidate and punish innocence, cajole and reward crookery, have the temerity to invoke law and order'.[36]

During the trial Messrs M.N. Rattansey and K.L. Jhaveri of the Asian Association and Mr D.N. Pritt, QC, appeared for the accused. On 12 August 1958, the Resident Magistrate delivered his judgement. Nyerere was convicted on two charges of criminal libel and was fined shs. 3 000, (£150) or six months' imprisonment in default of payment. TANU paid the fine, apparently with contributions from members and sympathisers, and saved their leader from going to jail, which had become an important school from which many politicians in colonial Africa and Asia had graduated. The decision to pay the fine was apparently reached to make sure Nyerere stood in the first general election to be held within a month or so. The government had not expected the apparently poor workers and peasants of Tanganyika to foot the fine so easily. Nyerere's case increased his popularity and gave the party even greater solidarity and a feeling of achievement. TANU's popularity in the country was demonstrated during the first general election.

The election was held in two stages, it was claimed 'for administrative reasons'. The first stage was in September 1958 with elections in five provinces: Tanga, Southern Highlands, Eastern, Northern and Western. The second stage covering the remaining provinces was in February 1959. The elections were based on the parity system. Only TANU and TANU-supported candidates won. All the UTP candidates, including the Chairman, lost miserably. Nyerere was elected for the Eastern Province. The TANU-supported non-African candidates included Mr D.N. Bryceson and Mr Amir Jamal. It is probably worth noting that the African National Congress made very little impact indeed. Even its leader, Mr Zuberi M.M. Mtemvu, who fought the election in Tanga Province, polled only fifty-three votes during September, 1958, thereby losing his shs. 500 (£25) deposit.

The general election in 1958–9 demonstrated the weakness of opposition to TANU and the strength of the nationalist movement. The elections also set an important precedent. In subsequent elections no opposition to TANU really made an impact on the country's policy.

Thus by March 1959, at the completion of the general election, there were altogether thirty non-official members in the legislature, with Nyerere as their leader and D.N. Bryceson as his deputy. Within a matter of months, and with the approval of TANU, five of the elected members had crossed the floor of the house to become the first Tanganyikan non-officials in history to hold ministerial portfolios. These TANU ministers, as the five members came to be known, were Solomon N. Eliufoo, Abdallah S. Fundikira, Dereck N. Bryceson, C. George Kahama and Amir H. Jamal. The last-named has remained a member of the Cabinet to this day.

It is interesting to note that the leader of the group, J.K. Nyerere, had not accepted a ministry. His main task was to organise and strengthen the party in and out of the legislature.

In August 1960, Tanganyika went to the polls in the second general election. The results once again demonstrated the nation's confidence in TANU. TANU won seventy out of the seventy-one seats! No opposition party won a seat. The only seat which TANU lost was won by an independent candidate, Mr H.E. Sarwatt, in the Mbulu constituency. But even in this case, the opposition was not directed against TANU as a party it was against the official TANU candidate. Mr Saewatt was himself an active TANU member, This composition of the legislature remained the same until 1965 when one-party democracy was legalised in Tanzania. Following this great victory, early in September 1960, Tanganyika attained Responsible Government with an elected majority in the legislature Nyerere became the first Chief Minister. Four more influencial TANU men—Paul Bomani, Rashidi M. Kawawa, Oscar S. Kambona and Asanterabi N. Swai—joined the Council of Ministers. By this time it had become evident that TANU would lead Tanganyika to independence within a short time.

Then Tanganyika, under the leadership of TANU, made fast constitutional advancement. In March 1961 a constitutional conference was held in Dar es Salaam, instead of the traditional venue, London. The results of the conference were probably more encouraging than TANU and all Tanganyikans had ever expected.

On 1 May 1961 Tanganyika attained internal self-government, and Nyerere became the first Prime Minister, heading a cabinet of twelve.

The big and long-awaited day came on 9 December 1961, when the Union Jack was finally lowered. It was a day of great jubilation all over the country, with the word *Uhuru* conveying its real meaning to the masses of Tanganyika. In his Independence Message Nyerere emphasised the significance of this political independence without giving a false picture of the realities of life. 'We are celebrating a victory. Yet it is essential that we remember even on that day that what we have won is the right to work for ourselves, the right to design and build our own future'.[37]

The Prime Minister also took the opportunity to emphasise TANU's belief in human equality and dignity.

> We have agreed that our nation shall be a nation of free and equal citizens each person having an equal right and opportunity to develop himself, and contribute to the maximum of his capabilities to the development of our society. We have said that neither race nor tribe, nor religion nor cleverness, nor anything else, could take away from a man his own right as an equal member of society. This is what we have now to put into practice.[38]

Zanzibar

The politics of decolonisation in Zanzibar were more complicated than in Tanganyika. A number of factors contributed to this: firstly, the history of the islands produced a population divided both racially and socially. Arabs, both rich and poor, educated and illiterate, regarded Africans as descendants of slaves, as people who had to be excluded from certain positions and who had to accept Arab leadership in all walks of life, including the politics of decolonisation. To worsen the situation, this arrogant attitude was reciprocated in many Africans in the form of an inferiority complex.

Secondly, Arabs, especially in Zanzibar Island, owned most of the fertile arable land where clove and coconut plantations were established. Most of the Africans living on such land were squatters whose security depended wholly on the goodwill of the Arab landlords. This relationship, though to some extent symbiotic, also reinforced the superior/inferior relationship between the Arab and the African. The relationship, moreover, carried with it latent seeds of discontent and violence. But the discontent could not come to the surface as long as the equilibrium of attitudes remained undisturbed. With the rise of nationalism and party politics, however, this equilibrium was upset and African/Arab relations were, to a considerable extent, polarised along the lines of the 'haves' and the 'have nots'. Strictly speaking, therefore, there were two nationalisms in Zanzibar: Arab nationalism and African nationalism. Both were basically determined to see the end of colonial rule and the departure of the British. Where the two racial groups disagreed fundamentally was on the question of heirs to the colonial throne. Each group vehemently claimed the sole right to control public affairs and monopolise political power after Independence. To the Africans, who formed the vast majority of the population, the departure of the British could not suffice; it could not give them the dignity and respect they had lost to Arabs and Europeans. The essence of their nationalism was to take over political power and control the affairs of the islands. This was exactly what the Arabs were determined to resist to the very bitter end.

Thirdly, the British protected, nurtured and respected the Arab elite as the natural and legitimate rulers of Zanzibar society. Consequently false hopes and uncontrolled arrogance developed among the Arab community. Although the Arab elite advocated self-determination, majority rule and British withdrawal, they saw themselves and behaved as the natural spokesmen and leaders of all Zanzibaris. Like the leaders of UTP in Tanganyika, and probably to a greater extent in this case, they received assistance from the Colonial Government in education, political manoeuvre, and civil service employment.

The main ethnic groups of Zanzibar

Four main population groups could be identified in Zanzibar and Pemba throughout the colonial period: Africans, Arabs, Asians and Europeans. As the table below shows, in the late 1940s as was the case during most of the twentieth century, Africans formed the vast majority of the population.

The African group in Table 10·1 comprised the three ethnic groups of the islands and the mainland African population. The figures given in the 1948 census are as follows: Hadimu, 41 750; Tumbatu, 46 000; Pemba, 59 750; mainland African, 51 000.

Table 10.1 DISTRIBUTION OF POPULATION BY ETHNIC GROUPS, 1948

	ZANZIBAR ISLAND		PEMBA ISLAND		TOTAL	
RACE	NO.	PER CENT	NO.	PER CENT	NO.	PER CENT
African	118 652	79.3	81 208	70.9	199 860	75.7
Arab	13 977	9.3	30 583	26.7	44 560	16.9
Asian	13 907	8.8	2 104	1.8	15 211	5.8
Comorian	2 764	1.8	503	0.4	3 267	1.1
Goan	598	0.4	83	—	681	0.3
European	256	0.2	40	—	296	0.1
Other	221	0.2	66	—	287	0.1
Total	149 575	100.0	114 587	100.0	264 162	100.0

Source: M.F. Lofchie, *Zanzibar: Background to Revolution*, Princeton, 1965, p. 71.

Two important points are worthing noting at this juncture. First, Arabs were a small minority, less than one-fifth of the total population of the Islands and fewer than the mainland Africans. However, in Pemba, the number of Arabs exceeded the mainland Africans.

Second, the word 'African' is quite inclusive and hides many differences. The African population falls into four major groups. The Hadimu form the main indigenous population of Zanzibar island. They are essentially descendants of pre-sultanate immigrants from the mainland. They mostly live in the eastern, southern and south-eastern parts of the island, and their main centres of concentration include Kizimkazi, Kwacha, Unguja and Bwejuu. The Hadimu were colonised by Omani, Arabs under Seyyid Said. Hadimu is an Arabic word meaning 'slaves', a nickname given to the indigenous African population by the Arab settlers.[39] The Tumbatu are of African and Arab descent. Unlike the Hadimu, they were not conquered by the Omani Arabs, but were forced to accept Arab overlordship shortly after the middle of the nineteenth century.[40] The Pemba are the indigenous inhabitants of Pemba Island. Some of them, like some Tambatu, have some Arab blood. Unlike the Hadimu, the Pemba were not conquered by the Omani immigrants. Tradition has it that the Pemba accepted Arab settlers on a friendly basis. This belief explains in part the relatively friendly attitude of Pemba Africans towards Arabs[41].

Among all the three ethnic groups of the islands were people who claimed a greater degree of Persian blood, and who referred to themselves as 'Shirazi'. The term 'Shirazi' was preferred in an effort to dissociate those concerned from Africanness which, in Zanzibar especially, had been connected with slavery, degradation and exploitation for generations. In a society where it was so difficult for Africans to climb the social ladder, there was every temptation for people to use the label 'Shirazi' as a status symbol, and as a passport to higher places. Thus the concept of a Shirazi or mixed Afro-Persian ancestry has come to embrace all the three main indigenous ethnic groups of the island. By the 1940s the original notion of a Shirazi community, which 'referred especially to those segments of the original population which claimed a particularly high admixture of Persian descent', had lost its meaning, and was 'widely used simply to distinguish all indigenous Africans in terms of descent and length of residence, from the relatively recent mainland arrivals'.[42]

The mainland African population of Zanzibar came from a variety of mainland ethnic groups, but particularly numerous were the Nyasa, Nyamwezi and Yao. Two main groups comprise the mainland African community: decendants of African slaves taken to Zanzibar to work the clove and coconut plantations, and modern voluntary migrant labourers. For many years there had been a social gap between Mainlanders and Shirazis, the latter looking down upon the former. It is quite likely that in addition to the issue of slavery, differing kinds of occupation and residence helped to perpetuate the sense of social distance between the two communities. The mainlanders were predominantly employed in the towns, either in domestic service or in manual work as labourers; those engaged in agriculture were in mose cases squatters on land to which they had no permanent right. Shirazis, on the other hand, were a more rural community, and were predominantly fishermen and farmers on privately-owned or community-held labd.[43]

Distance between the Mainlanders and Shirazis is responsible for one of the most striking features of Zanzibar nationalism—the failure to create an all-African nationalist movement. Despite their numerical strength, the Shirazis could not give leadership or direction to the rest of the African community. In fact lack of Shirazi solidarity contributed substantially to the stalemate during the general election in 1961. The Arabs took advantage of the disunity among Africans and isolated the Mainlanders. 'By portraying the Mainlanders as an unwanted intruder in a land where Shirazis and Arabs had always lived together in peace, the ZNP was able to employ the Shirazis' sense of separateness as a means of gaining thier political support'.[44]

Table 10.2 POPULATION OF ZANZIBAR AND PEMBA IN 1948.

	ZANZIBAR		PEMBA		PROTECTORATE	
COMMUNITY	NO.	PER CENT	NO.	PER CENT	NO.	PER CENT
Shirazi	81,150	61.2	67,330	60.2	148 480	60.8
African	37 502	28.3	13 878	12.4	51 380	21.0
Arab	13 977	10.5	130 583	27.4	44 560	18.2
Total	132 629	100.0	111 791	100.0	244 420	100.0

Source: Lofchie, p. 250

The Asians were numerically next to the Arabs. Many Asian families had established themselves in Zanzibar by the beginning of the twentieth century, but Asians played a negligible direct role in the politics of Zanzibar during the colonial period. They were satisfied to engage their energies in trade and commerce as long as the regime in power created conditions conducive for the exploitation of the islands' resources, both material and human.

The Europeans, mainly British, were a tiny minority mostly engaged in administration. Their main role in the politics of decolonisation was to nuture, protect and advise the group they had chosen to become heirs to the colonial throne. Part of the outcome of this policy has been well summarised by Lofchie:

> Thus, the Arab regime, which previous to the arrival of Great Britain had consisted of little more than the Sultan and a limited circle of personal officers and agents, grew into a sizeable bureaucratic structure composed of trained and skilled Arab

Background to party politics

Before the rise of political parties, political activity in Zanzibar was organised along and expressed through ethnic associations. Arabs, Mainlanders, Shirazis and Asians (Indians) each had a semi-cultural and semi-political association. The Arab Association was originally formed by the rich and influential Arabs to fight for compensation for Arab ex-slave owners affected by the abolition of slavery. With time, however, the association widened its scope to protect the general privileged position of the Arab Community. During the 1950s, when Britain was widening political participation in her colonies, leaders of the Arab Association, Mr Amour Zahor and Sheikh Ali Muhsin being at the forefront, recognised the need to organise along broader lines if they were to capture political power into their hands.

The African Association was formed in 1934. Most of its supporters were Mainlanders, and it was associated with TAA till the late 1940s. During the mid-1950s the Association was prepared to accept Rankines's constitutional recommendations which would eventually lead to majority rule. This step revoked Arab nationalism. Fearing the possibility of eventual defeat by the weight of numbers, the Arabs demanded 'independence now'. The Africans, knowing very well that 'independence now' meant nothing more than a call for complete Arab hegemony, opposed the demand and called for a delay of independence until such a time as a substantial number of Africans could effectively participate in the management of public affairs. Many African nationalists, ignorant of the peculiarities of Zanzibar situation, found it difficult to understand the rationale of the Africans' demand.[46] How, they agreed, could true Africans oppose the call for 'independence now'?

The Shirazi Association was formed in Pemba in 1939, but later spread its activities to the rest of the protectorate. The motivation behind its formation was to safeguard the interests of the indigenous African population. The association was divided on its policy towards the Mainlanders. While Hadimu Shirazis advocated co-operation with mainland Africans, the Pemba and Tumbatu Shirazis advocated a policy of isolation and dissociation.

Party politics and the failure of nationalism

Party politics in Zanzibar, as in the rest of East Africa, came rather late compared, say, to most of West Africa[47]. As elsewhere in colonial Africa, the fundamental aim of the political parties was to capture political power from the colonial administration. Significantly many policies, strategies and prejudices of the associations were carried over to the era of party politics.

The Zanzibar Nationalist Party

One of the most influential organised sources of opposition to colonial rule in Zanzibar was the Zanzibar Nationalist Party. The most striking feature of this party is probably the fact that, unlike most political parties in colonial Africa, it originated from a backward rural area where systematic articulation of political issues was a rare phenomenon. The origin of ZNP goes back to the middle of 1955, at the climax of the constitutional conflict between the colonial administration and the Arab Association[48] when a group of peasants in the village of Kiembe Samaki (Fish Corner) formed a political party which they called the Nationalist Party of the Subjects of the Sultan of Zanzibar (NPSS). The party advocated multi-racialism and the creation of an independent state to be headed by the Sultan. It did not take long before the Arab elite discovered the potential usefulness of NPSS in advancing Arab interests in the Protectorate. By December 1955, informal contacts between NPSS and ZNP had been established, with Sheikh Ali Muhsin, then principal leader of Arab Nationalism, as chief negotiator.[49]

Shortly after NPSS had established legitimacy Arabs began to join openly. Ali Muhsin and Amour Zahor were its first Arab members. They campaigned to win more members from their and other communities, and within a short while changed the party's name to the Zanzibar Nationalist Party. The capture was over; the next task was to change the party 'from a rural peasant league into an Arab-dominated urban nationalist movement'[50]

The capture of the NPSS gave the Arab elite a nucleus of Africans with which to justify their widely publicised multiracial policy. And right from the beginning the ZNP portrayed a nationalistic image. Membership was open to all racial groups, and shortly before the election of July 1957, the party called for 'freedom now'. All these gestures, however, should not be allowed to obscure the true intentions of the Arab elite. The ZNP was open to all as long as leadership came from the Arabs to guarantee the perpetuation of Arab domination in Zanzibar. The Africans were recruited not to share the political kingdom with the Arabs as equals, but to act as a catalyst which would hasten Arab success without affecting the power structure. Many Africans, especially Shirazis, failed to see things in this perspective, consequently they could not question the wisdom and apparent goodwill of the leaders of public opinion for generations. This tendency is not surprising. Though the Africans as a group were exploited and degraded, one factor—Islam—bound most of them to the Arabs. qanibar had great religious homogeneity which tended to weaken the intensity of social antagonism. In short the position of Arabs in Zanzibar made it difficult for many Africans to reject the offer of Arab leadership. 'As the founders and bearers of the faith, the owners of the soil and the rulers of the land, their position embodied and defined the aspirations of all Zanzibar society'.[51] But many Africans, Mainlanders and Shirazis alike, rejected and denounced Arab leadership of the nationalist movement. They decided to fight colonialism in their own way; to abolish both British and Arab domination.

The Afro-Shirazi Party

Disunity between Shirazis and Mainlanders continued in the era of political parties. Early in February 1957, apparently in response to the formation of the ZNP and the scheduled election in July 1957, leaders of the African and the Shirazi Associations met to discuss the possibility of forming a joint political party which would compete with the ZNP. The Hadimu Shirazi leaders, Sheikh Thabit Kombo (a former railway engineer) and Ameri Tajo (a Quranic school-teacher), came out in favour of unity. Many Shirazis, however, especially in Pemba, opposed the merger[52]. The two Associations in Zanzibar Island agreed to form the Afro-Shirazi Union (ASU) and to co-operate in the forthcoming election campaign, but there was no agreement regarding a merger of the two associations. Sheikh Abeid Amani Karume, President of the African Association, was elected President, and Sheikh Thabit Kombo, then secretary of the Shirazi Association in Zanzibar, took the office of General Secretary.

In July 1957, the people of Zanzibar Protectorate went to the polls for the first-time. The election demonstrated the political potential of the ASU. The Union won three out of the six contested seats in the Legislative Council. Two seats (for Pemba constituencies) were won by the Pemba Shirazi independents supported by the Pemba Shirazi Association. The sixth seat was won by an Indian independent who stood in the Indian commercial centre of Stone Town. Significantly, the ZNP won no seat. After the election the ASU effected a complete merger and renamed itself the Afro-Shirazi Party (ASP). The two Shirazi independents in the Legislative Council combined forces with the ASP but retained the separate identity of the Pemba Shirazi Union.

The defeat of the ZNP has one element worth amplifying here. In both constituencies where ZNP and ASU candidates opposed each other directly, the ZNP candidates suffered a disastrous defeat. In the Ng'ambo constituency Abeid Amani Karume defeated Ali Muhsin Barawani by 3 328 votes to 918. In Zanzibar South Ameri Tajo defeated Amour Zahor Said by 5 380 votes to 1 679[53].

The results of the election had two contradictory effects on the politics of Zanzibar. On the one hand, they acted as a morale-booster to the supporters of Afro-Shirazi unity, but, on the other hand, they cautioned the Arab elite on the devastating capacity of the deprived classes if the ballot box was to be used without rigging. Indeed, the experience gained from the 1957 election influenced the nature and intensity of party struggle during subsequent elections.

After the 1957 election both the ZNP and the ASP became determined to mobilise public opnion and lead Zanzibar to independence. By 1958 political awakening had come to affect all walks of life among the African population. Intense political rivalry between the two parties became the order of the day[54] and continued until 1963. A striking feature of Zanzibar politics during this period was the polarisation of racial relations. Neither the ZNP nor the ASP showed willingness, let alone ability, to create an atmosphere which would assure both Africans and Arabs of 'a place at home' after the departure of the British. Party rivalry between 1958 and 1963 clearly revealed the contradictions of the colonial situation in Zanzibar. While one racial group was determined to defend its privileged position at any cost, the other group was equally determined to end foreign domination once and for all.

The Zanzibar and Pemba People's Party

Towards the middle of 1959 a misunderstanding between the top leadership of the ASP on the one hand and the Pemba Shirazi members of the legislature and Mr Tajo on the other reached a peak. Tajo was expelled from the ASP. The two Shirazi members from Pemba, Mohamed Shamte and Ali Sharif, resigned from the party in protest. Towards the end of the year the three men formed the Zanzibar and Pemba People's Party (ZPPP). The party was open to members of all races, but it was especially meant for Shirazis who wanted to avoid Arab domination in the ZNP and African control in the ASP. Within a short while the ZPPP received the full support of the Pemba Shirazi Association, which had refused to be absorbed into the ASP. Soon afterwards the Association merged with the ZPPP. Thus the ZPPP inherited a mass base and an organisational network from the Pemba Shirazi Association.

The period between the formation of the ZPPP and December 1963 was one of cut-throat political rivalry and racial bitterness. Political campaigns, especially from June 1961, were accompanied by instances of violence between the supporters of rival parties. Party conflict was easily transformed into racial conflict. Lofchie has cogently summarised the background to this state of affairs.

> The roots of the trouble lay in the very nature of Zanzibar politics, particularly in the fact that party membership is either based or regarded as being based on racial divisions with the result that for Zanzibaris party conflict is barely distinguishable from racial conflict. In 1961, two bitter election campaigns within a six-month period fraught with anxieties about the possible enormity of the consequences of victory or defeat produced an atmosphere bordering on hysteria.[55]

Between January 1961 and July 1963, three general elections were held. In all the elections the ASP won the largest number of votes, but without a clear majority.

Table 10.3 ELECTION RESULTS, 1961 AND 1963

ELECTIONS	ASP			ZNP			ZPPP		
	VOTES	% OF TOTAL	NO. OF SEATS	VOTES	% OF TOTAL	NO. OF SEATS	VOTES	% OF TOTAL	NO. OF SEATS
Jan. 1961	36 698	40.2	10	32 724	35.8	9	19 451	17.0	3
June 1961	45 172	49.9	10	31 724	35.0	10	12 411	13.7	3
July 1963	87 085	54.3	13	47 950	20.8	12	25 609	15.9	6

Source: J. Mosare, 'Background to the Revolution in Zanzibar' in Kimambo and A.J. Temu (eds), *A History of Tanzania*, Nairobi, 1969, p. 235.

After the election of January 1961 the two major parties sought the co-operation of the ZPPP for a coalition. Here the political instability of the ZPPP was demonstrated. One of its members joined the ASP and the other two joined the ZNP. The split gave each of the major parties eleven seats in the Legislative Council, thereby causing a stalemate. One more constituency was added in Pemba to avoid another tie in subsequent elections. Then the people of the Protectorate were called to another election in June of the same year. This time the ANP and the ZPPP fought as a partnership and formed a coalition government.

The results of the two elections in 1961 disillusioned the ASP. It became clear to them that unless the whole electoral procedure was revised, their chances of leading Zanzibar to independence were extremely narrow. Significantly, the leaders of the ASP knew that the heart of their problems was the alliance between the Arab elite and the British Colonial Government, an alliance which manifested one of the major characteristics of the political economy of colonialism. The agony they experienced was loudly expressed by Sheikh A.A. Karume, president of ASP, in May 1962:

> We say that the British Government has always been unjust to the African people of these islands and has done us the greatest wrong. When the British Government took over the responsibility of protecting these islands, it had in mind the intention of protecting only a small section of the minority immigrant element . . . The British Government has made these elements arrogant, conceited and selfish . . .
>
> We therefore now clearly state that no government will be acceptable to the majority of the people unless that government is predominantly African in character. If there is any one who imagines that when the British leave these islands they will hand over power to the immigrant element who total a mere 42 000 out of a population of 300 000, let that person or persons forget it . . . We thus openly declare that what has happened in South Africa and the Sudan we shall never allow to happen in these islands . . . The majority must rule; that is democracy[56].

Shortly before the July 1963 election a conflict in the ZNP reached a peak and led to a split of the party. The defectors, led by Abdul Rahman Mohammed Babu, who was still then General Secretary of the ZNP, formed their own party, *Umma* (the Masses). The cause of the split was apparently long-standing ideological differences at the top, especially between Muhsin and Babu. The former had a religious and conservative outlook, seeing Islam as the chief binding force among ZNP members. Babu, on the other hand, had adopted a more progressive line, subscribing to socialist ideas. But the issue which triggered off the split was a disagreement over electoral strategy and the party's sincerity in its efforts to achieve a multi-racial society. Babu was especially opposed to the party's policy of running candidates in constituencies where ethnic sentiments would favour them[57].

The defection of Babu was a serious blow to the minority dominated ZNP. Babu had been the chief strategist of the party, and he had contributed substantially to its success in the 1961 elections. The new party attracted 'the entire range' of anti-government elements. Indeed 'Umma's real significance lay in providing a centre through which Babu and his close personal associates built a unified political movement out of the myriad groups opposed to ZNP'[58].

The polls were given a last chance in July 1963 to decide the fate or destiny of the majority. This was the last election before Independence. The *Umma* party did not contest the election, but a poll of over ninety-nine per cent was 'concrete evidence of ubiquitous concern over the outcome'[59]. The results were, however, even more discouraging than ever before. As Table 10.3 shows, the ASP won more votes than the other parties combined, yet they won only thirteen seats out of a total of thirty-one. The ballot box had failed to hand over political power to the majority. On 10 December 1963, the ZNP-ZPPP coalition, with eighteen seats in the Legislature, led Zanzibar to Independence with Mohammed Shamte, the Pemba Shirazi, as Prime Minister and Ali Muhsin as Minister of Internal Affairs. But to most Africans this was Arab Independence; true Independence was yet to come. Clearly, the results of the July 1963 election were a clear manifestation of the failure of nationalism in Zanzibar. Nationalism which gives political power to an unacceptable minority is essentially sterile and politically explosive.

It is convenient at this point to explain how in three successive elections the ASP got a disproportionately low number of seats in the Legislature. The main factor was the size of the constituencies. Many ASP strongholds were twice or more the size of ZNP strongholds. The most revealing example was the division of constituencies in the January 1961 elections. Stone Town, a ZNP stronghold which was already a small constituency, was divided into two, Stone Town South and Stone Town North, with respectively 1 080 and 1 395 electors. This step meant that the Colonial Government was deliberately increasing the number of seats which ZNP was certain to win. The gravity of this measure and the shamelessness of those who implemented it are clearly revealed by a comparison between the Stone Town constituencies and two ASP strongholds, Chaani and Mkokotoni. The former had 5 537 electors and the latter 5 446. Had both of these constituencies been reduced to the size of Stone Town South, each would have five constituencies in which the ASP would almost certainly win. Thus, basing our argument on the sizes of these constituencies, the ASP was robbed of eight seats from these two constituencies alone. During the July 1963 election this maneouvre was slightly modified, but the carving of constituencies was still the main weapon with which the ASP was finally deprived of the right to lead the country to Independence.

The Revolution

After the July 1963 election the ASP was left in no doubt that constitutional means could not win political power for the majority. Their disenchantment is not difficult to understand. The Colonial Government had condemned violent means like those used by *Mau Mau* in Kenya. From the early 1950s the founders of the party believed and followed political propaganda praising the significance of constitutional devices in the establishment of democratic institutions. To their surprise, however, in July 1963 they discovered that they had, in fact, been participating in a political process which merely consolidated the position of their opponents and oppressors. The only alternative, it appeared, was to depart from constitutionalism and resort to violence. Accordingly, the Afro-Shirazi Party in collaboration with the *Umma* Party carried out a bloody revolution on 12 January 1964. Within a day or so the ZNP–ZPPP coalition government was overthrown. The ex-Ministers were imprisoned, but the Sultan, Jamshid bin Abdalla, fled to Britain, where he lives on British charity to this day.

It is not possible at this stage to assess with precision the part played by different groups and individuals in the revolution. Okello's book,[60] which should not be regarded as authentic, is of little use. The recent three-volume history of the ASP represents an official viewpoint which should be balanced by an uninvolved trained historian. Certainly further research is required on this important topic of Tanzania's recent past.

Despite the ignorance surrounding us, however, it is possible to make a number of general observations. First the Zanzibar revolution took place after the failure of peaceful and universally accepted means. Second, the revolution took place, not when the oppressor was strongest and most oppressive, but, on the contrary, when the oppressor was most vulnerable. The Afro-Shirazi/*Umma* alliance could not contemplate overthrowing the British colonial government. They had to wait until the departure of the British. Nor was the ZNP–ZPPP coalition government given time to consolidate itself militarily. It can therefore be argued that the Zanzibar revolution was a manifestation of violence of hope rather than violence of despair. The probability of success pushed anti-governments into action.

Third, though by January 1964 the oppressor was weak and not all that effective in implementing oppressive and suppressive measures, the suffering of the ASP and the majority of the African population was at its peak. There was little physical suffering, but psychological suffering, which is more important in this respect, was intense. This state of affairs was worsened by the constitutional developments elsewhere in Africa, especially among Zanzibar's neighbours. Tanganyika recovered her independence in 1961, Uganda in October 1962, and Kenya in December the following year.

Conclusion

This chapter has examined the last stages of the struggle against colonialism in Tanzania. To a large extent the nationalist sentiments gathered strength from contradictions arising from the colonial situation. The nationalist leaders did not create the situation. All they did was to co-ordinate and direct mass discontent and anti-colonial activity. For the mainland independence came earlier than all those involved had imagined, say, in the early 1950s. Three points need to be made in these concluding comments. First, the nationalist movement was run and engineered in the name of *Uhuru* and 'the people' to such an extent that it hid the motives of different groups and individuals. True enough, 'the people' wanted *Uhuru*, but *Uhuru* for what? And who were 'the people'? It is necessary to analyse the nationalist movements and identify different groups and their motives. It is certain, for instance, that the major motives of the leaders were different from those of the masses. All struggled for *Uhuru*, but ultimately *Uhuru* meant different things for different people. A critical examination of the nationalist movements in former Tanganyika and Zanzibar shows clearly that the nationalist leaders saw themselves as the principal beneficiaries of decolonisation. To a large extent the masses were recruited because the elite could not conquer the political kingdom alone. Indeed, this was the situation in the rest of Africa.

Second, the nationalist movements lacked ideology. The leaders insisted on seeking first the political kingdom which, they argued, would bring everything else. Clearly the movements fought the chief agents of capitalism, but not the system itself. The masses were mobilised not to be liberated from the fetters of capitalism, but to be more effectively exposed to exploitation. The petty bourgeoisie were out not to end social inequality, but to change the chief participants and principal beneficiaries. Mwalimu Nyerere has recently called our attention to this fact, and it is worth quoting him at length:

> Yet in Tanzania the great mass campaigns of the 1950s and early 1960s were for independence. We campaigned against colonialism, against foreign domination. We did not campaign against capitalism or for socialism . . . It was fatally easy to identify the things that you were fighting against as people of this other race—the Europeans . . . Almost throughout Africa, therefore, the first and most vocal demand of the people after independence was for Africanisation . . . they simply demanded the replacement of white and brown faces by black ones . . . many leaders of the independence struggle themselves saw things in these terms. They were not against capitalism; they simply wanted its fruits, and saw independence as the means to that end. Indeed, many of the most active fighters in the independence movement were motivated—consciously or unconsciously—by the belief that only with independence could they attain that ideal of individual wealth which their education or their experience in the modern sector had established as a worthwhile goal.[61]

Even the Zanzibar revolution was not based on any ideological commitment. The ASP leaders abhored the glaring inequalities in Zanzibar mainly because they appeared along racial lines. Even the ideology of the *Umma* party does not appear to have influenced the ASP top leadership before the revolution. It would appear that the many steps taken to reduce inequality since 1964 were dictated by circumstances rather than by prior ideological commitment. After the revolution leaders could not just go back to the pre-revolution period. Furthermore, the revolution was itself a school. Leaders had to develop and adopt a new political outlook if they were to survive. Thus there was no need of the equivalent of the Arusha Declaration in Zanzibar.

Significantly, even the custodians of international capital identified the nationalist leaders with forces of imperialism. During Tanganyika's Independence most of the expatriate firms and banks in the country congratulated the country and her leaders, and hoped for good relations with the government for many years to come.[62] They did not see the country's independence as a threat to their interests. Evidently the management of the Standard Bank and the National and Grindlays Bank (both incorporated in the United Kingdom) could not then imagine Nyerere, a man they regarded as a well-educated gentleman, always operating according to the rules of the game, nationalising their banks unilaterally.[63]

Lastly, the departure of the colonists was not as real as it appeared at the time of Independence. True enough, the Union Jack was lowered and national flags were hoisted, but neither Tanganyika nor Zanzibar was anywhere near economic independence. The economic forces of imperialism were as powerful as ever, and they continued to control and exploit the resources of these dependencies. This by no means implies that political independence was meaningless. Far from it! All it means is that political independence by itself was not enough. Economic and social decolonisation had to be carried out to make Independence a complete reality. Indeed the significance of political independence cannot be overemphasised. It gave the two countries the right to design their own policies; to choose their own priorities, friends and enemies; and to determine their own fate. In revolutionary terms the winning of independence should be seen as a first revolution in the process of liberation. With political power in their hands, the people of Tanganyika and Zanzibar could carry on the second revolution—the social revolution—which would liberate the masses from all oppression and exploitation. Indeed it was their control of the state apparatus which enabled the two countries to unite in April 1964. Likewise, the policy of Socialism and Self Reliance adopted in 1967 to check and eradicate exploitation of all kinds, could not be dreamed of without the control of political power. The political kingdom was won more than a decade ago. It remains to be seen how and to what extent 'all the other things' will be added.

Notes

1 D.E. Apter, *Ghana in Transition*, New York, 1966.

2 Sir A. Cohen, *British Policy in Changing Africa*, London, 1959, p. 29.

3 *Ibid.*, p. 37, gives the tactics used by colonial Governors.

4 See *Minutes of the First Conference of TANU*, p. 1.

5 For example his views on race problems in 'The Race Problem in East Africa', J.K. Nyerere, *Freedom and Unity*, Dar es Salaam, 1966, pp. 23–9.

6 *Minutes of the First Conference*, p. 3.

7 S.A. Kandoro, *Mwito wa Uhuru*, Dar es Salaam, 1961, p. 73.

8 D. Bates, *A Gust of Plumes*, London, 1972, p. 254.

9 *Ibid.*

10 I am grateful to Mr Alistair Ross for this information.

11 G. Dunheved, *Julius Nyerere: a biography*, Dar es Salaam, 1961, p. 6.

12 *Ibid.*, p. 7.

13 See *Some Comments on Mr Nyerere's Speech at the Fourth Committee of the United Nations*, Dar es Salaam, Government of Tanganyika, 1957.

14 *Ibid.*, p. 5.

15 *Ibid.*

16 *ibid.*, p. 6.

17 *ibid.*, p. 6.

18 *Ibid.*

19 *First Convention of Representative Chiefs of Tanganyika, 14th–16th May, 1957*, Dar es Salaam, Government Printer, 1957, p. 2.

20 Dunheved, p. 7.

21 Nyerere, *Freedom and Unity*, pp. 51–2.

22 Most of the information on the Tabora Conference comes from Kandoro, pp. 111–37, which is known to be authentic.

23 In 1960 over a year before Independence, TANU gave their headquarters building along Lumumba Street to the Ministry of Education to accommodate the first University College in the country. This step was taken to push the allegedly poor Colonial Government to provide higher education to more Africans. The building acted as a core of the University College until July 1964 when the College moved to the new campus at The Hill. TANU did not take back their building, which now houses the Institute of Adult Education.

24 G.A. Maguire, *Toward 'Uhuru' in Tanzania*, Cambridge, 1969, pp. 339.

25 For the East Lake area see *ibid.*, 338–52; for West Lake see Goran Hyden, *Political Development in Rural Tanzania*, Nairobi, 1969, pp. 42, 131.

26 A.J. Temu, ' The Rise and Triumph of Nationalism', in I.N. Kimambo and A.J. Temu, (eds.), *A History of Tanzania*, Nairobi, 1969, p. 195.

27 *Ibid.*, p. 197–208. Fo a detailed account of rural discontent in Sukumaland see Magquire, pp. 112–59 and *passim*.

28 L. Cliffe, 'Nationalism and the Reaction to Agricultural change in Tanganyika during the Colonial Period', *Taamuli*, Dar es Salaam, vol. 1, July 1970.

29 J.S. Saul, 'On African Populism', in G. Ionescu and E. Gellner, (eds.), *Populism*, London, 1968, pp. 122–50.

30 Maguire.

31 See, for example, Bomani's speech in Mwanza, 'Mwafrika', Dar es Salaam, 3 October 1959.

Mr Paul Bomani, first Minister for Agriculture and Co-operatives had been General Manager of the Victoria Federation of Co-operative Unions Ltd, 1955–60; Mr C. George Kahama, the first Minister for Home Affairs, was formerly General Manager of the Bukoba Native Co-operative Union; and Mr A. Nsilo Swai, first Minister for Commerce and Industries, was formerly General Manager of the Meru Co-operative Union.

32 South West Africa under the racist regime of South Africa had the same status, but things have been quite different.

33 The *Tanganyika Standard*, 29 January 1958, 18 February 1958.

34 See, for example, P. Bomani's speech in Mwanzi, 'Mwafrika', Dar es Salaam, 3 October 1959.

35 Kandoro, pp. 184–5.

36 *Sauti ya TANU*, No. 29, 27 May 1958.

37 Nyerere, p. 138.

38 *Ibid.*, p. 139.

39 M.F. Lofchie, *Zanzibar: Background to Revolution*, Princeton, 1965, p. 38.

40 Sir J. Gray, *History of Zanzibar from the Middle Ages*, London, 1962, pp. 169–70.

41 The more even distribution of fertile soil enabled relatively many indigenous Africans to establish coconut and clove plantations. This development also reduced the possibility of class conflict and class struggle between Arabs and Africans in Pemba.

42 Lofchie, p. 82.

43 *Ibid.*, p. 38.

44 *Ibid.*, p. 156.

45 *Ibid.*, p. 63.

46 J. Mosare, 'Background to the Revolution in Zanzibar', in Kimambo and Temu, p. 228.

47 In Ghana and Nigeria modern political parties were formed during the 1940s.

48 Arabs were boycotting the Legislative Council because of constitutional proposals which appeared to guarantee an eventual African majority in the legislature.

49 Lofchie, p. 151.

50 *Ibid.*, p. 153.

51 *Ibid.*, p. 76.

52 *Ibid.*, pp. 169–72. Pemba Shirazi leaders did not even attend the negotiations.

53 *Ibid.*, p. 176.

54 See M. Lofchie, 'Party Conflict in Zanzibar', *The Journal of Modern African Studies,* i, 2, June 1963, pp. 185–207.

55 *Ibid.,* pp. 206–7.

56 *Africa Kwetu*, 17 May 1962, cited in Mosare, pp. 233–4.

57 Lofchie, *Zanzibar*, *Background to Revolution*, p. 258–9.

58 *Ibid.*, p. 260.

59 *Ibid.*, p. 219.

60 J. Okello, *Revolution in Zanzibar*, Nairobi, 1967.

61 J.K. Nyerere, *Freedom and Socialism*, Dar es Salaam, 1972, p. 27.

62 See *Tanganyika Standard,* Ltd, *TANU Souvenir,* Dar es Salaam, 1961, *passim.*

63 *Ibid.*, pp. 30, 46. The banks were nationalised in February 1967, soon after the Arusha Declaration.

Index